A SERIES BY MIKE FLANAGAN

MIDNIGHT MASS

AN INTREPID PICTURES PRODUCTION

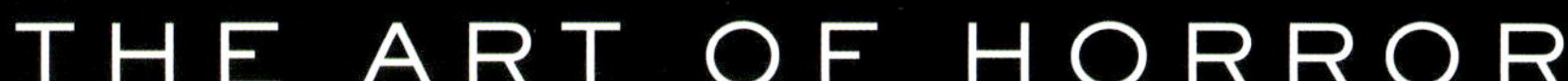

THE ART OF HORROR

MIDNIGHT MASS

THE ART OF HORROR

ISBN: 9781789097771
Limited Edition ISBN: 9781789099423

Published by Titan Books
A division of Titan Publishing Group Ltd.
144 Southwark St.
London
SE1 0UP

First edition: October 2021
2 4 6 8 10 9 7 5 3 1

Cover illustration by Jhona Almeida.

DID YOU ENJOY THIS BOOK?
We love to hear from our readers. Please e-mail us at: readerfeedback@titanemail.com or write to Reader Feedback at the above address.

To receive advance information, news, competitions, and exclusive offers online, please sign up for the Titan newsletter on our website:
www.titanbooks.com

A CIP catalogue record for this title is available from the British Library.

Printed and bound in China.

A SERIES BY MIKE FLANAGAN

MIDNIGHT MASS

AN INTREPID PICTURES PRODUCTION

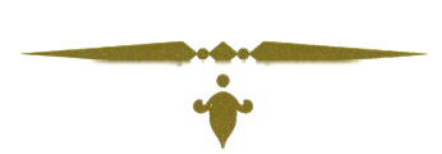

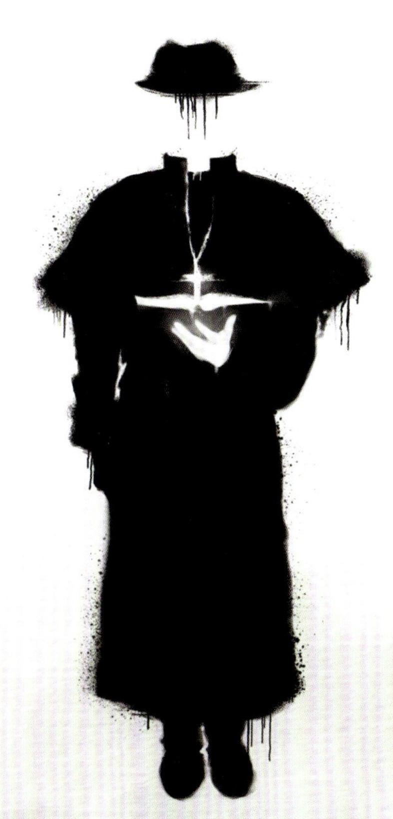

THE ART OF HORROR

WRITTEN BY ABBIE BERNSTEIN

TITAN BOOKS

CONTENTS

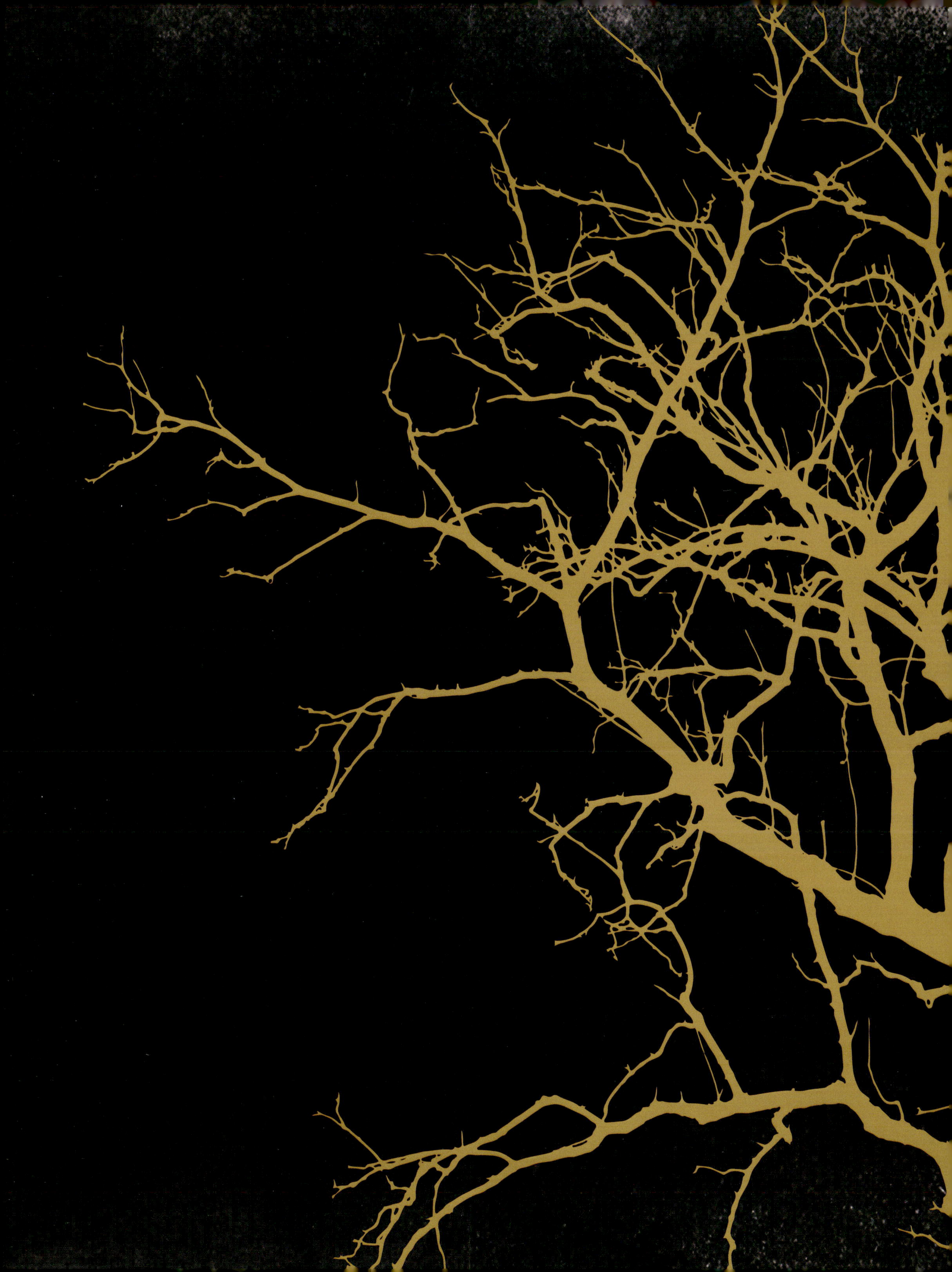

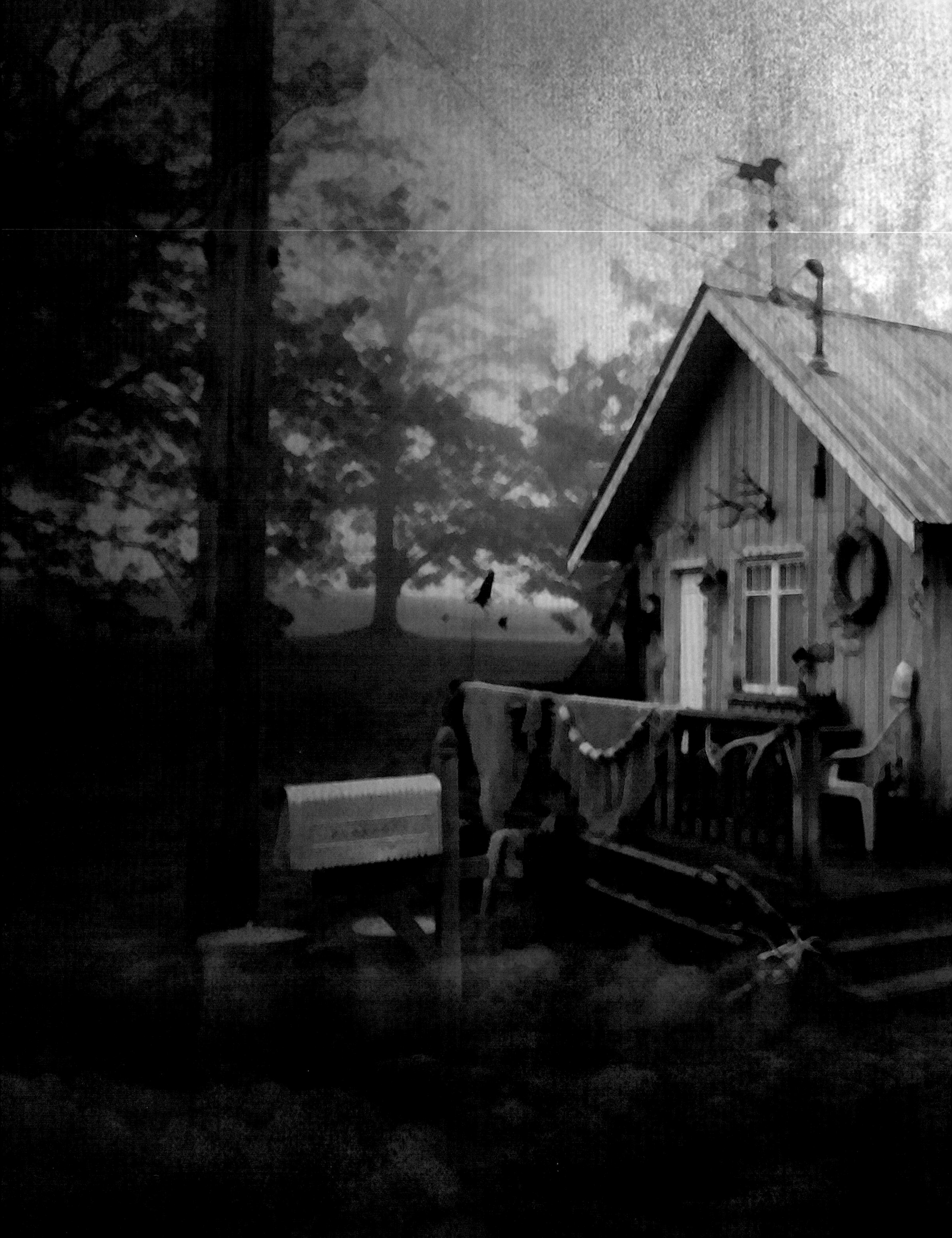

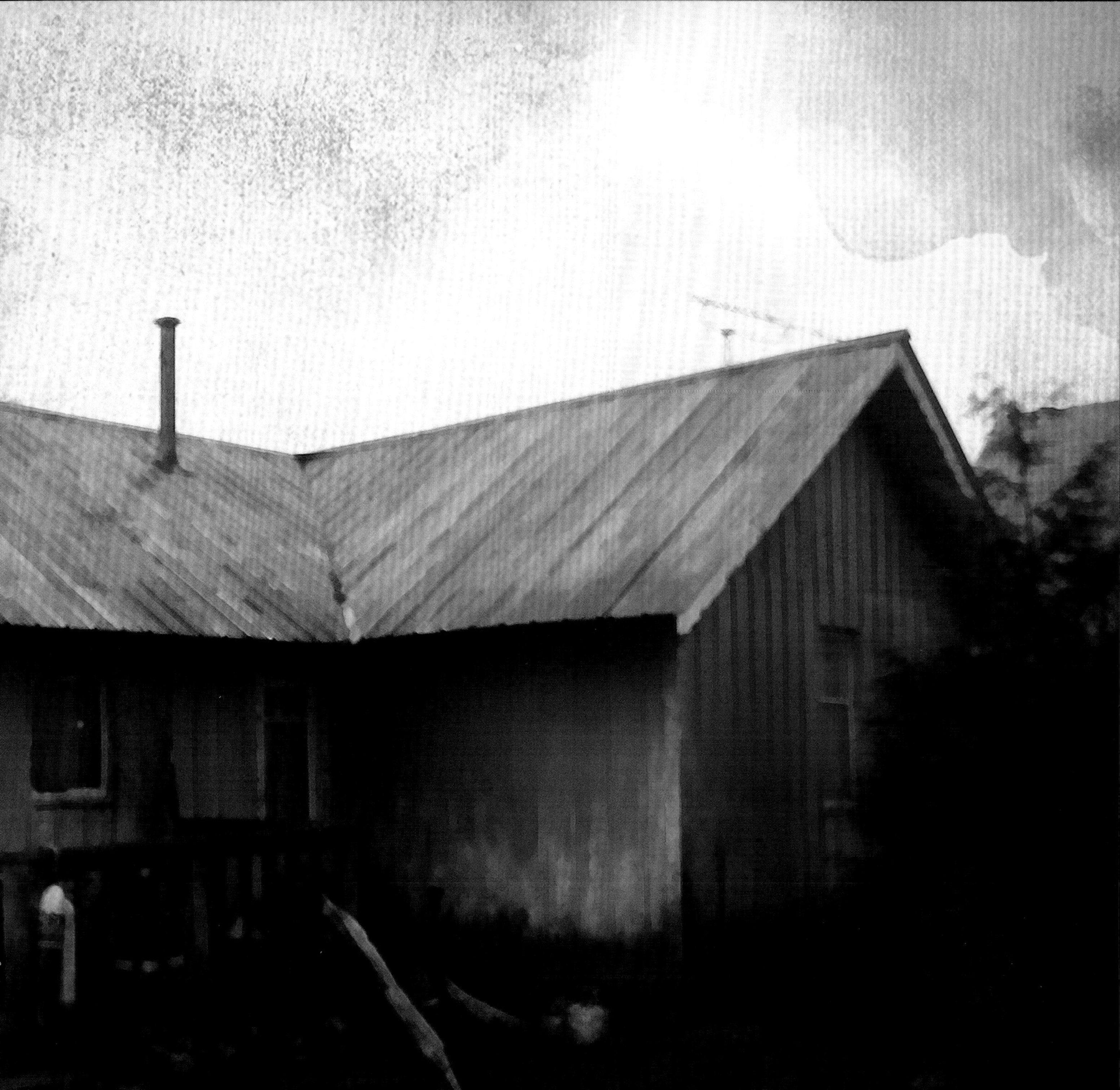

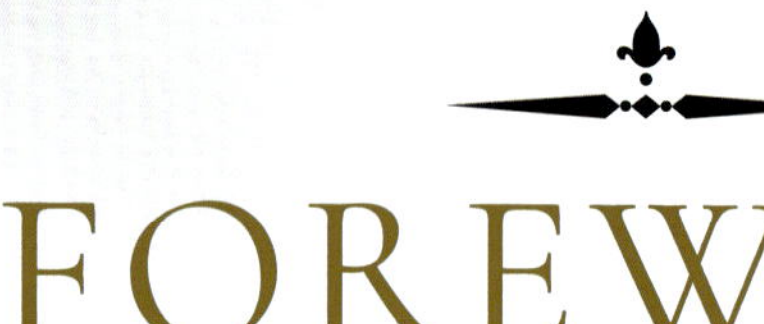

FOREWORD

BY MIKE FLANAGAN

I don't remember the first time I imagined the doomed residents of Crockett Island, but I took my first stab at a *Midnight Mass* novel in early 2010. I recently found an attempted feature script from May 2012 and a more advanced screenplay from 2013. Knowing it was too big to be a movie, Trevor Macy, Jeff Howard and I took it out as a television pitch in 2014. We had maps of Tangier, Virginia (the primary inspiration for Crockett) and concept images of a pale, bald vampire who evoked Klaus Kinski in Werner Herzog's *Nosferatu the Vampyre* (still my favorite vampire film). One by one, each of those networks passed.

In fact, when we pitched *Midnight Mass* at Netflix, the young executive who sat across the table was Blair Fetter. He didn't buy *Midnight Mass* that day, but a few years later I'd sit across from him again with another television pitch called *The Haunting of Hill House*. Netflix would buy that show, and it would change my life forever.

In 2015, I began filming a little indie feature called *Hush*. We needed to come up with a book for Kate Siegel's character to have written. I wanted it to be *Midnight Mass*. Why not, I figured: this might be as close as that story would ever get to being made.

In October 2016, we filmed *Gerald's Game*. In Stephen King's novel, there is a shelf above the protagonist's head as she lays handcuffed to her bed, and on that shelf is, among other things, a book. I knew immediately I wanted that book to be *Midnight Mass*. A crew member asked me, after we shot that scene, what *Midnight Mass* was. I smiled and said it was the best thing I never made.

2019: *The Haunting of Hill House* was a surprise hit. I was now partnered with Trevor Macy at Intrepid as we sat across from Blair Fetter once again, now with Laura Delahaye, at Netflix. The first priority would be *The Haunting of Bly Manor*, but Blair and Laura championed *Midnight Mass* to Peter Friedlander and Cindy Holland, and Netflix greenlit *Midnight Mass*.

Bly Manor and *Midnight Mass*' writers' rooms ran concurrently. I'd spend my mornings at *Bly* and my afternoons at *Mass*. We began filming Bly in Vancouver in the fall of 2019, but on weekends I'd scout *Mass* locations, refine the scripts, and gear up for the looming production. The plan was that *Bly* would wrap in February 2020, and we'd roll right into *Midnight Mass* that March without missing a beat.

"THERE HAS NEVER BEEN A PROJECT MORE PERSONAL TO ME."

MIKE FLANAGAN

It became clear very fast that we'd have to build Crockett. Every structure, every road, every streetlight. We took over a huge portion of Garry Point Park in Richmond, building our houses on the shoreline. The rest of our exteriors were built on a farm in Langley, an hour away from Bridge Studios, which housed our interior sets. Steve Arnold, our Production Designer, worked tirelessly to create a living, breathing island community out of nothing. And walking around his creation, I realized how immersive and unique this show could be.

And then the world shut down.

RIGHT/ An Easter Egg mailbox homage to the *Midnight Mass* creator.

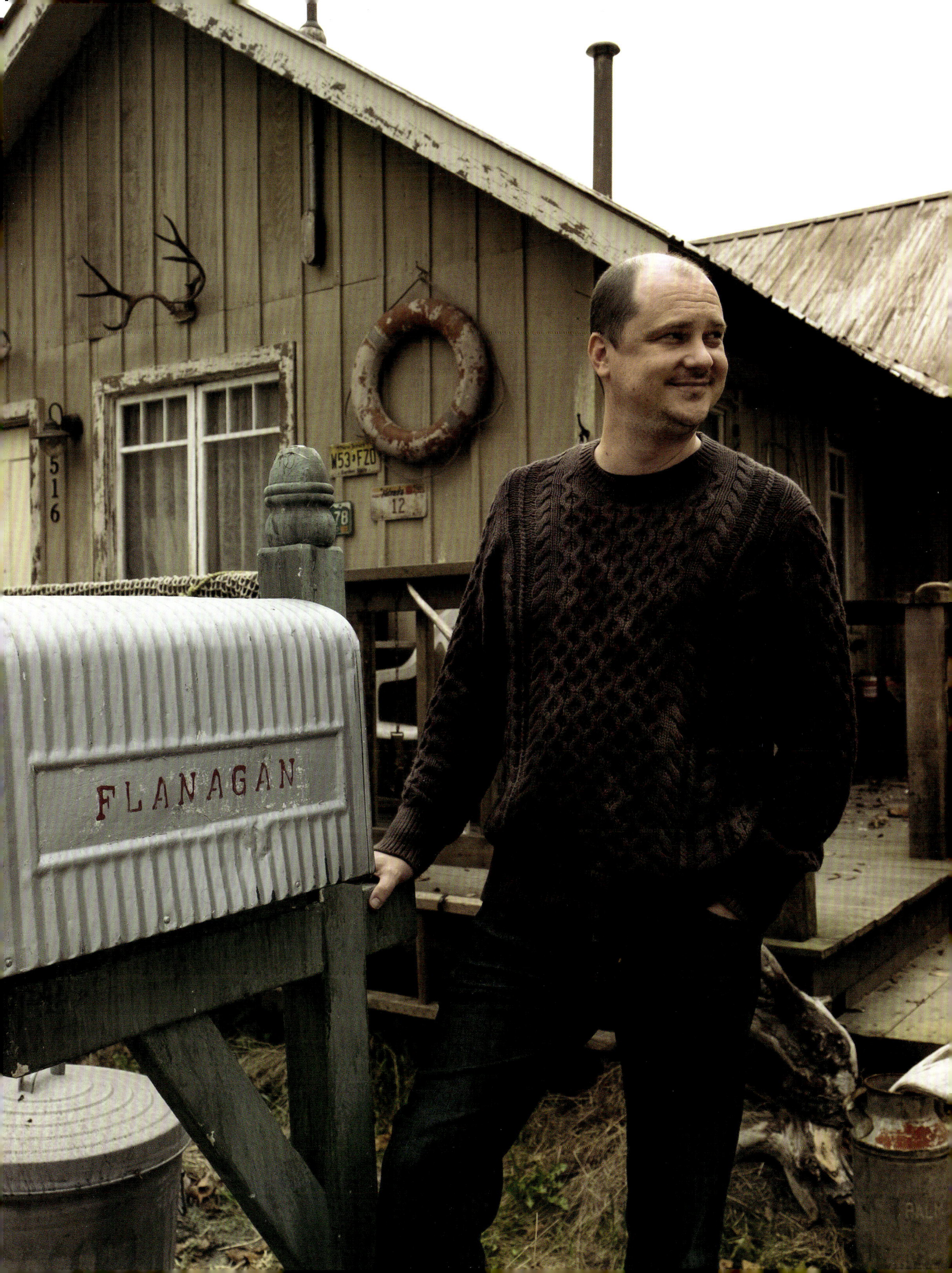
516
FLANAGAN

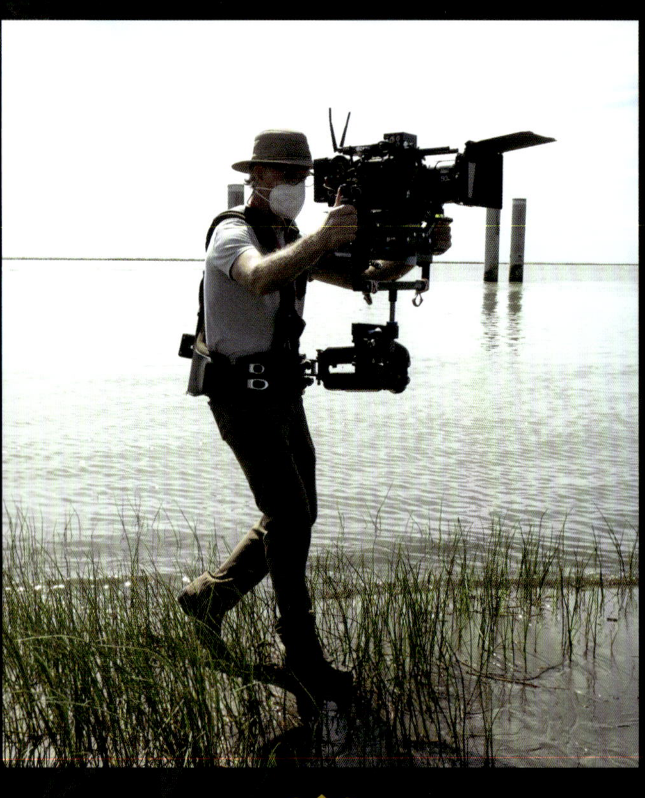

We were just a few days away from shooting when COVID-19 shut down Canada. I remember looking out the window of the plane as I flew home to Los Angeles. From the air, I could see Garry Point Park and our buildings along the edge of the water. I was leaving it behind, and I had no idea when – or if – we'd ever pick it back up.

For months, we waited. And finally, in early June, the call came in that *Midnight Mass* would essentially be the first Netflix show to go back up in this new COVID reality.

Our sets were still standing but weathered by months in the elements. Months of exposure, weather, and overgrowth that only made them better. We started shooting on August 17, 2020. We were the test case; we were the canary in the coal mine for Netflix. We held our breath, terrified every day of shutting down… and it was the best production experience of my life.

This book is a testament to the amazing work of a lot of artists. *Midnight Mass* required world-building, and these pages detail the way in which that world was built, as told by the people who built it. I am indebted to all of them. This show was a living, breathing work of art, and I was privileged to be able to walk, live, and exist within it for as long as I did.

THIS PAGE/ (TOP) James Reid filming with a Steadicam. (BOTTOM) Camera-slating Episode 1, Scene 23, in which Riley and Hassan meet.

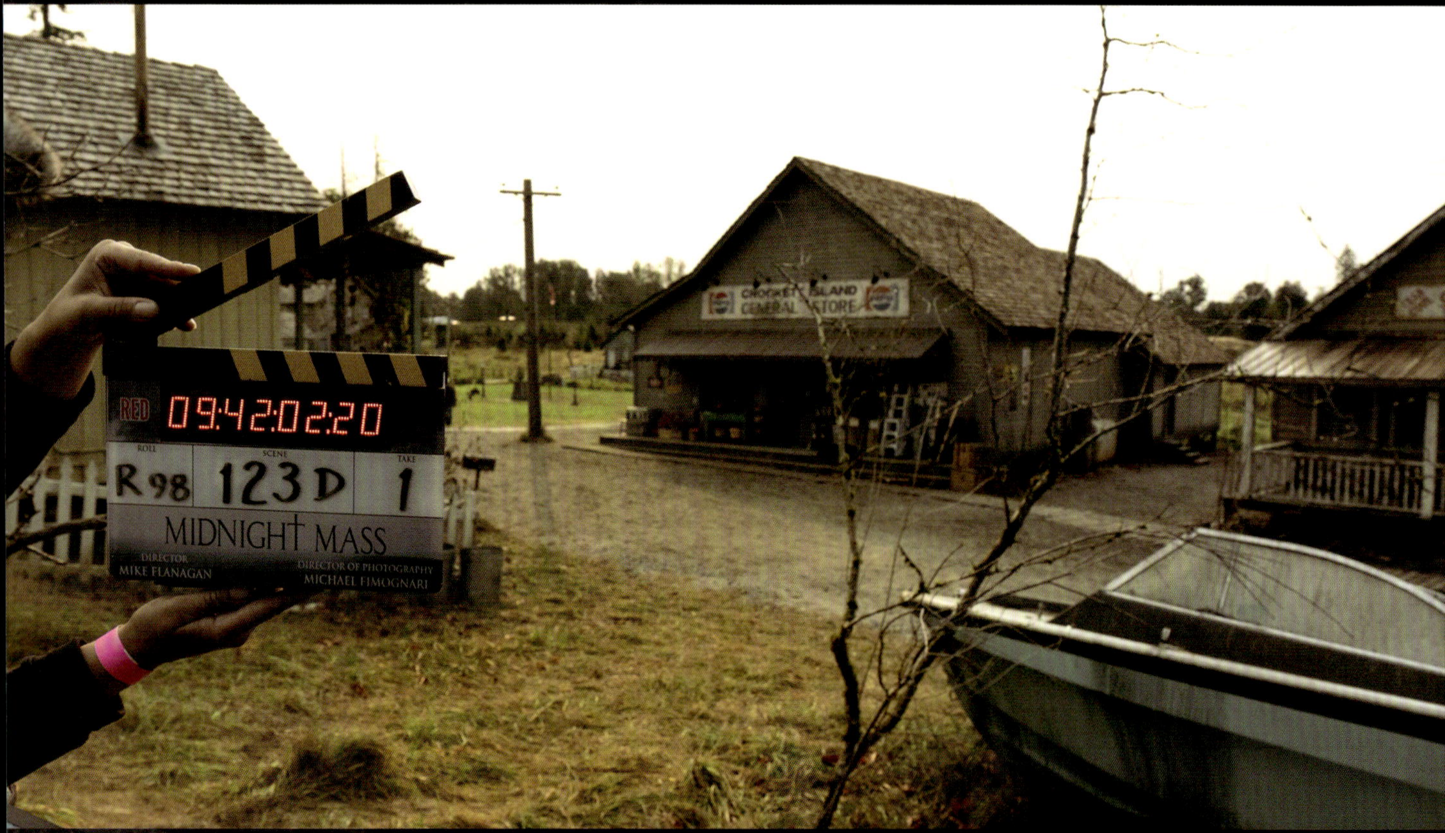

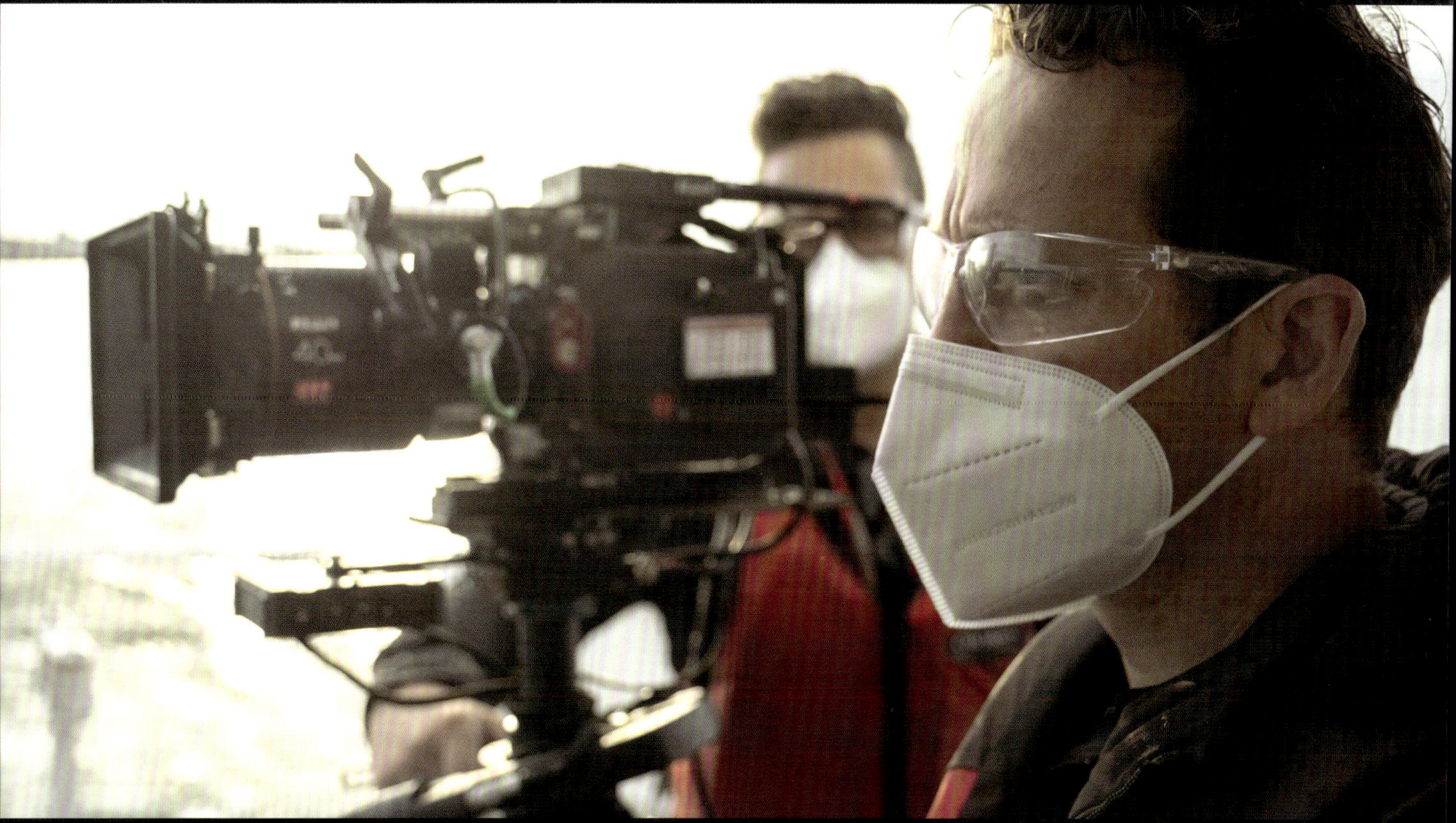

TOP/ Ryan Purcell, camera operator, in the foreground; and Aaron Haesler, first assistant camera, in the background.

I'm grateful to Laura Delahaye, Blair Fetter, Peter Friedlander and Cindy Holland for championing the project, and I'm grateful to Blair for passing on it those years ago when it honestly wasn't ready. I'm grateful to my wife Kate Siegel, who built my heaven on Earth. To my entire cast, which remains the best ensemble I've ever worked with. To my cinematographer Michael Fimognari, whom I consider my brother. To my actual brother James Flanagan, who poured as much of his self into these scripts as I did. And to my partner Trevor Macy, who was steadfast in what was probably the most challenging producing experience of his career.

Religion, I believe, is one of the ways we attempt to answer the two Great Questions that ache within us all: "*how shall we live*," and "*what happens when we die*." I don't know the answer to the second question, but *Midnight Mass* has, over the years, helped me at least begin to answer the first. I hope this artifact enhances your experience of *Midnight Mass*, and I wish you all love, luck, and forgiveness on your journeys beyond.

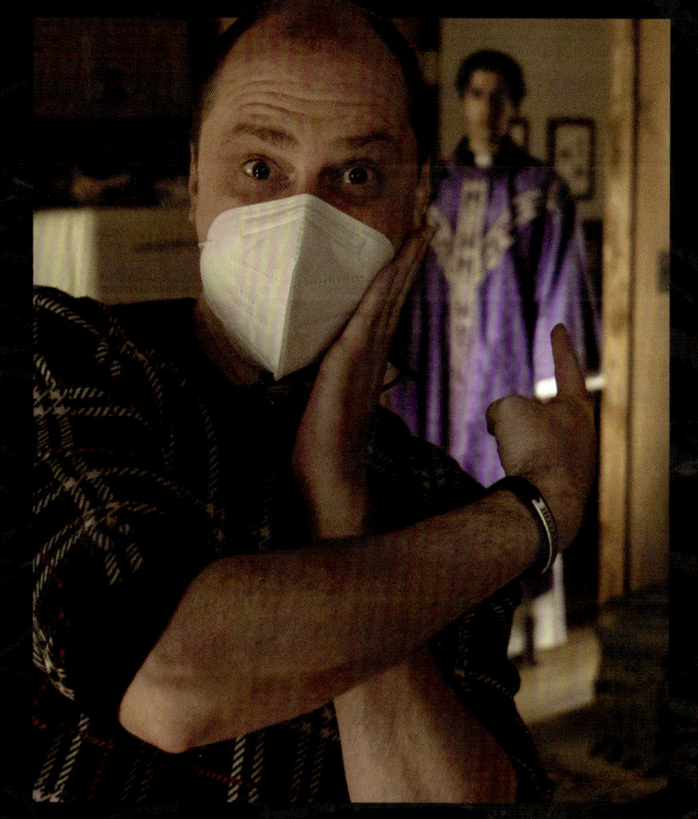

RIGHT/ Mike Flanagan is impressed by Hamish Linklater's purple vestments.

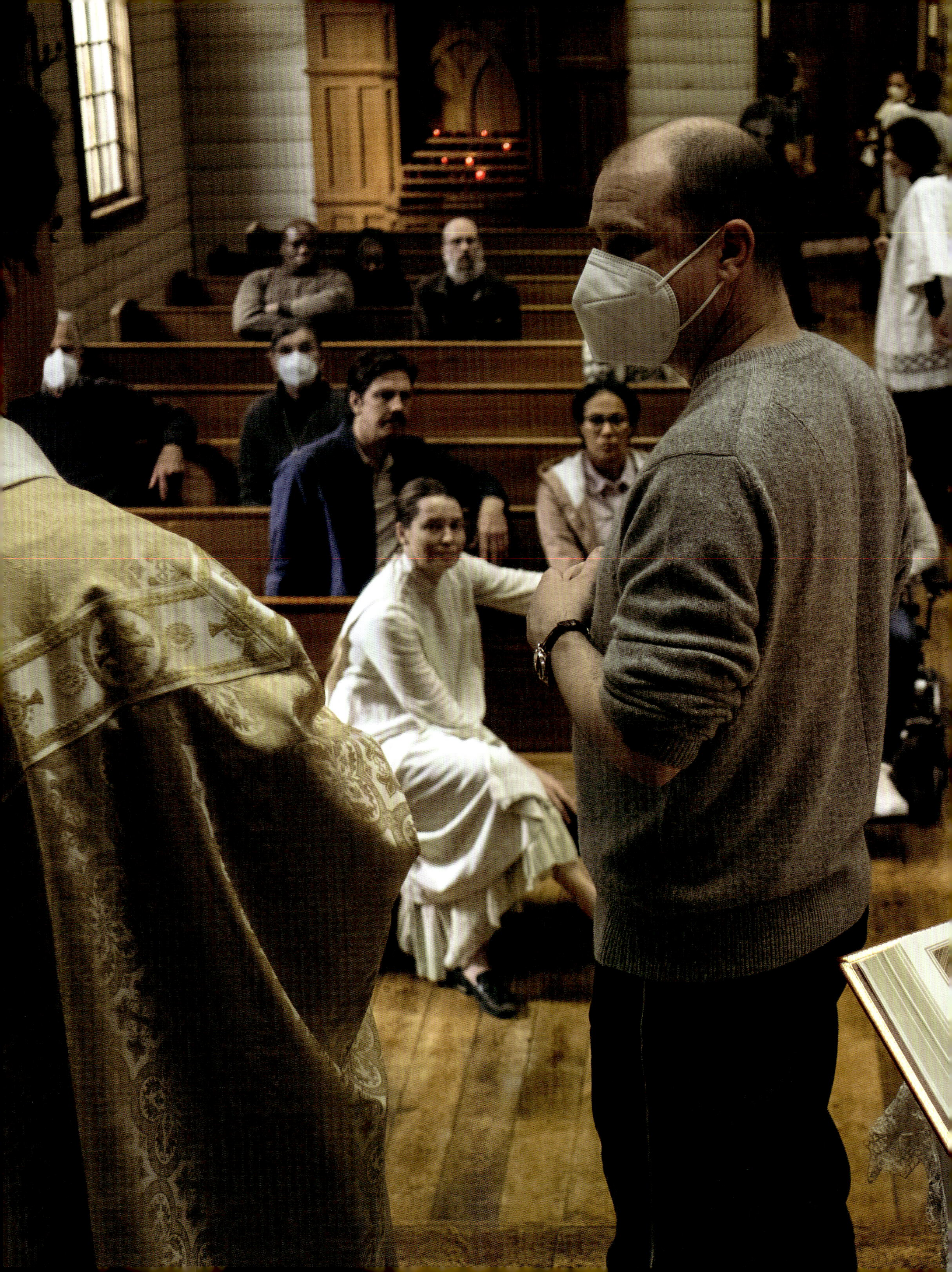

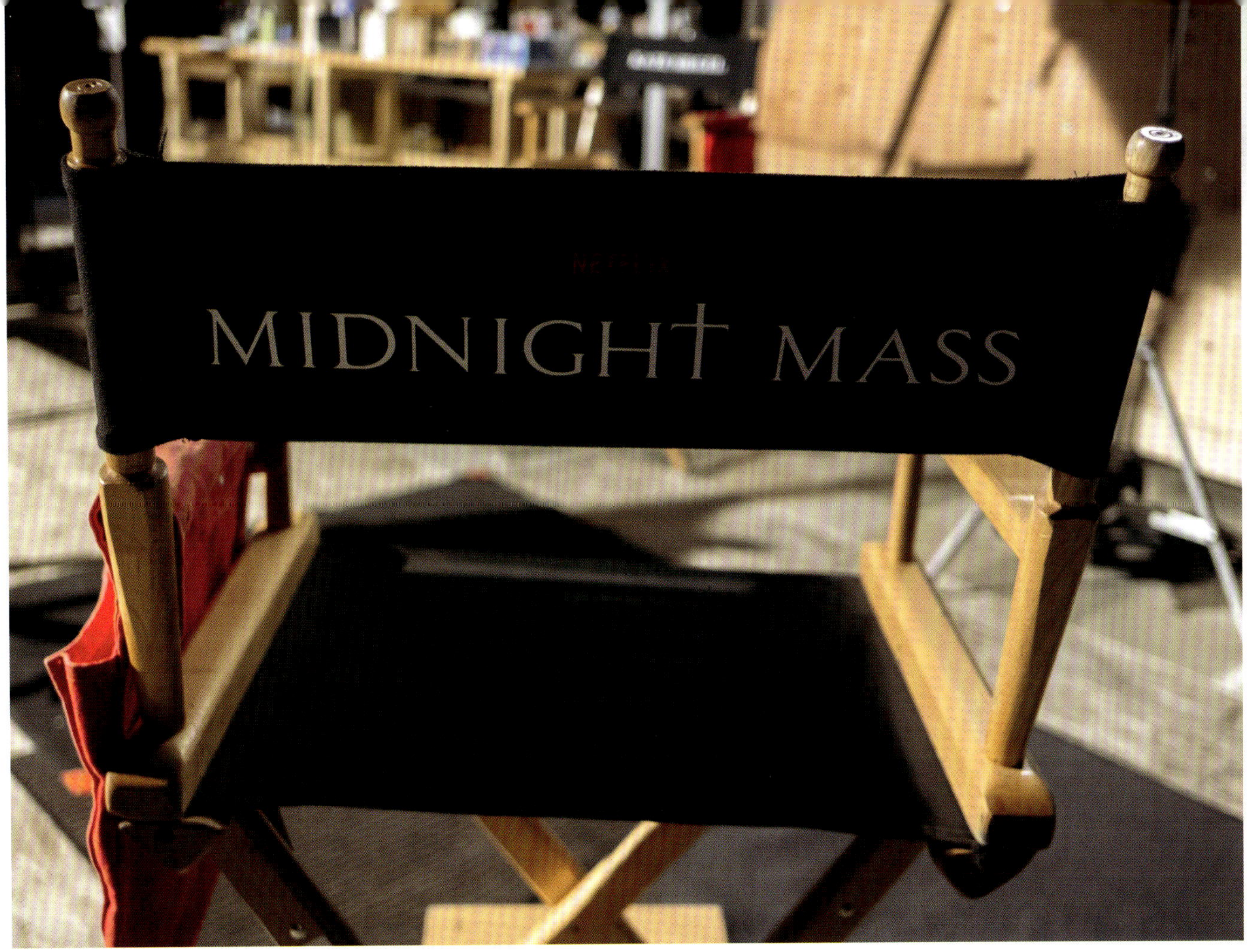

THIS PAGE/ (TOP) A director's chair sits empty while cameras roll. (BOTTOM LEFT) Fimognari, Macy and Flanagan consult the digital plan.

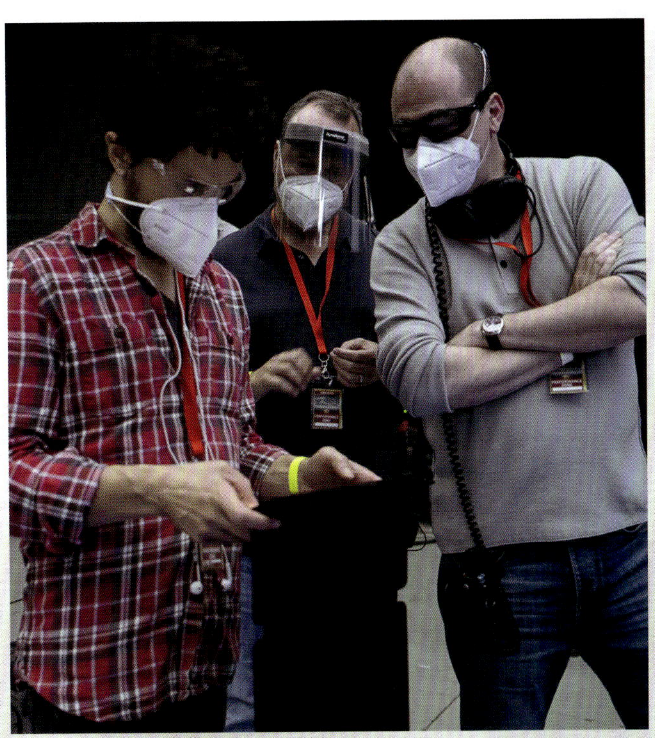

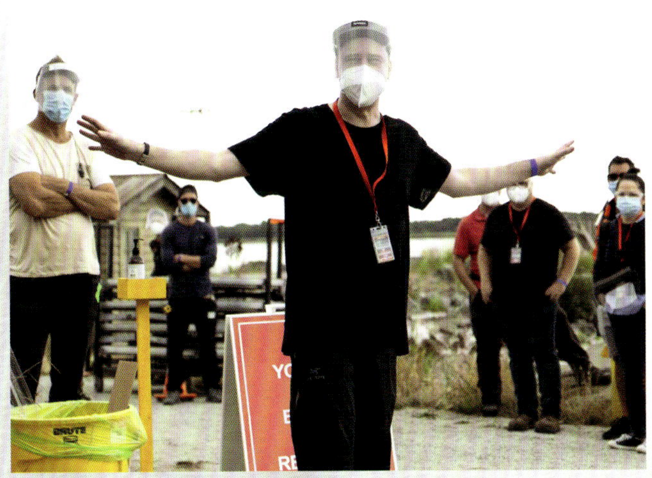

TOP/ Mike Flanagan, ensuring social distancing.

And if you happen to think on those two Great Questions, do let me know if you figure them out. I suspect I'll never know the answers, not really. As far as I can tell, though, the second question only matters in how it affects the first.

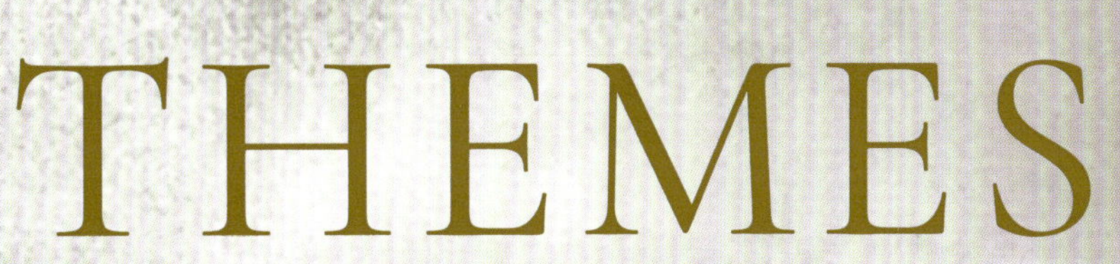

THEMES

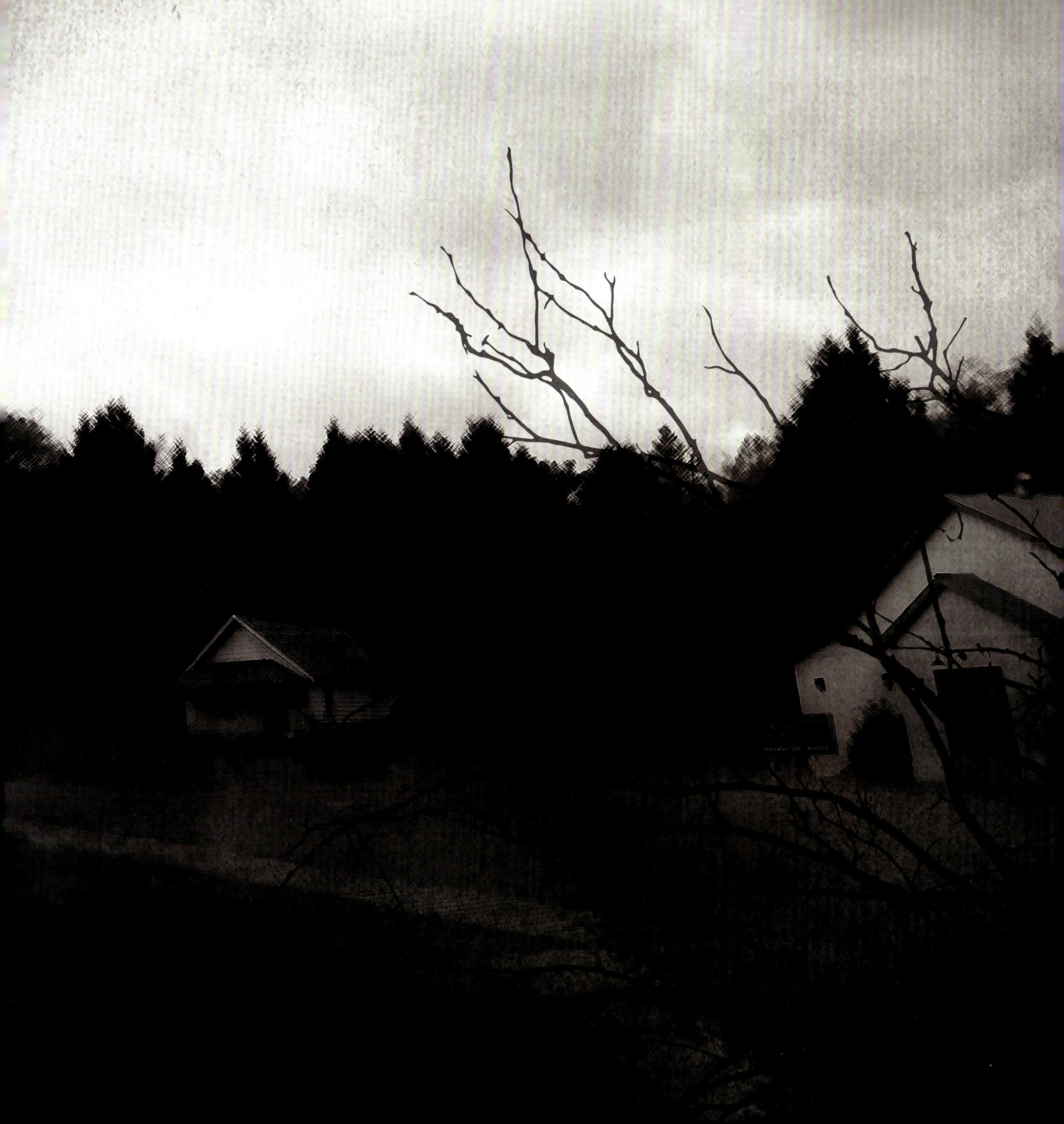

THEMES

PHILOSOPHY MEETS RELIGION

Mike Flanagan, who created *Midnight Mass* and directed all seven episodes of the miniseries, began making films on VHS in childhood. After graduating college, he worked as a film editor and cinematographer while writing screenplays. In 2011, Mike Flanagan made his first horror film: *Absentia*.

After this, Flanagan joined forces with executive producer Trevor Macy. Macy explains he saw *Absentia*, and then he and Flanagan "had a terrible pitch meeting. Mike floated a few ideas, I didn't like them. Then he said, 'I have this movie about a mirror that's like a portable Overlook Hotel.' And we both said at the same time, 'But it shouldn't be found footage.' And so, we got [*Oculus*, 2013] done. I was producing other things. But when he directed, I produced. The experience was so positive that we decided we were going to work together, and then we became partners in [Macy's already-established company] Intrepid Pictures. The reason Mike and I work so well together is we both love character-forward but genre-oriented things. I love scary things, especially if you can use genre as a lens to understand the human condition."

The duo's output includes the features *Before I Wake* (2016), *Ouija: Origin of Evil* (2016), and the adaptation of Stephen King's novel, *Doctor Sleep* (2019). Flanagan and Macy started their association with Netflix, which produces *Midnight Mass*, with the association of King's adaptation of *Gerald's Game* (2017). Flanagan and Macy went on to produce two miniseries. Netflix is also the distributor of the two miniseries: *The Haunting of Hill House* (2018) and *The Haunting of Bly Manor* (2020).

BOTTOM/ Trevor Macy and Mike Flanagan working on the epic Midnight Mass scene in the church.

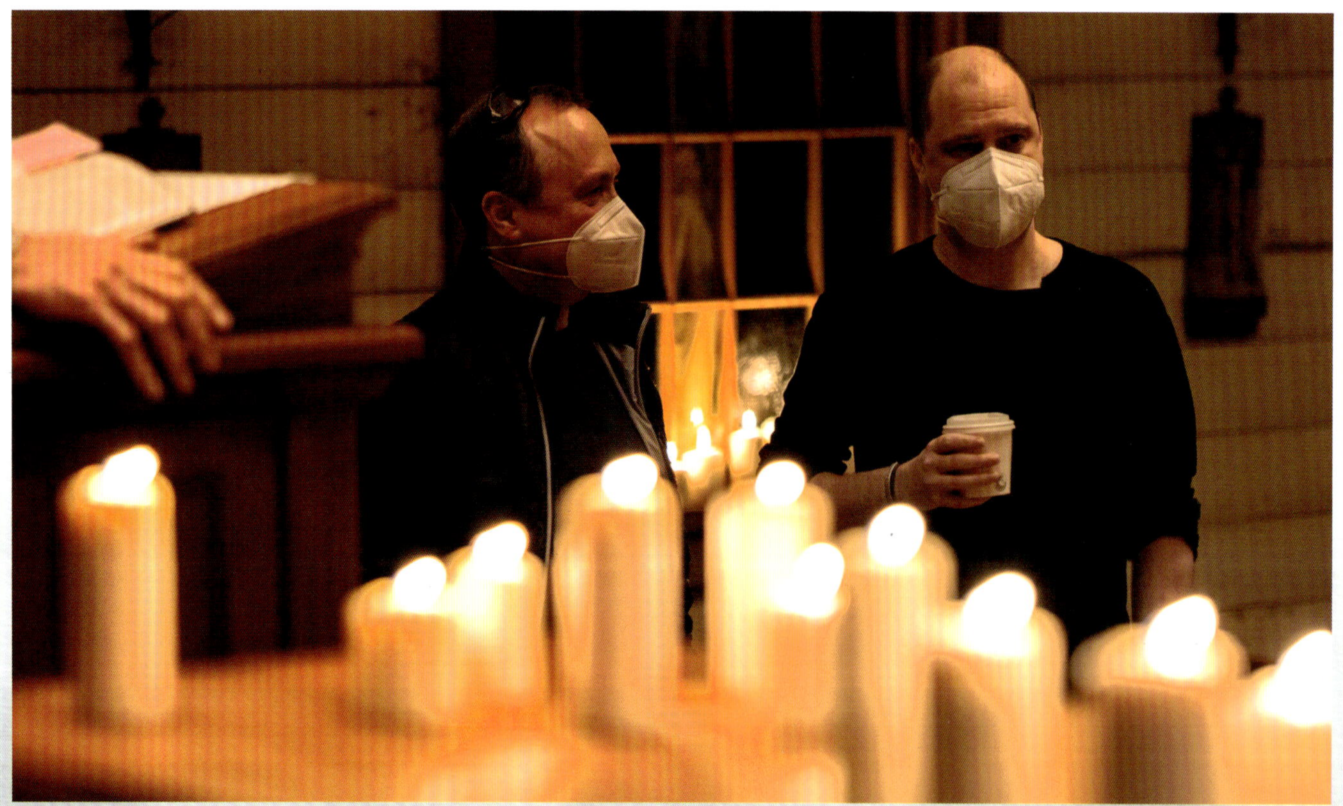

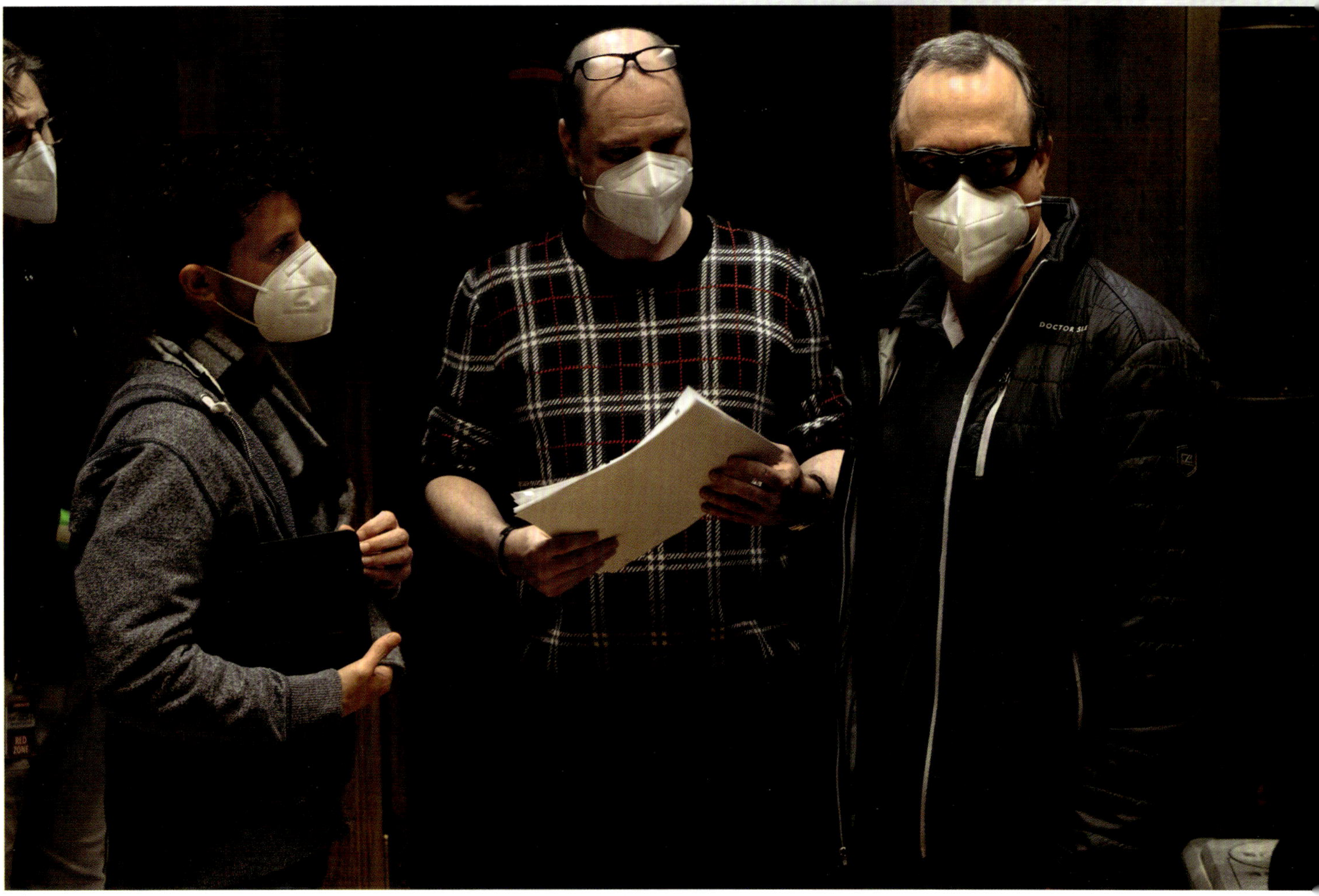

THIS PAGE/ Fimognari, Flanagan and Macy wear PPE, that includes mandatory face masks at all times, and face shields when cast were present.

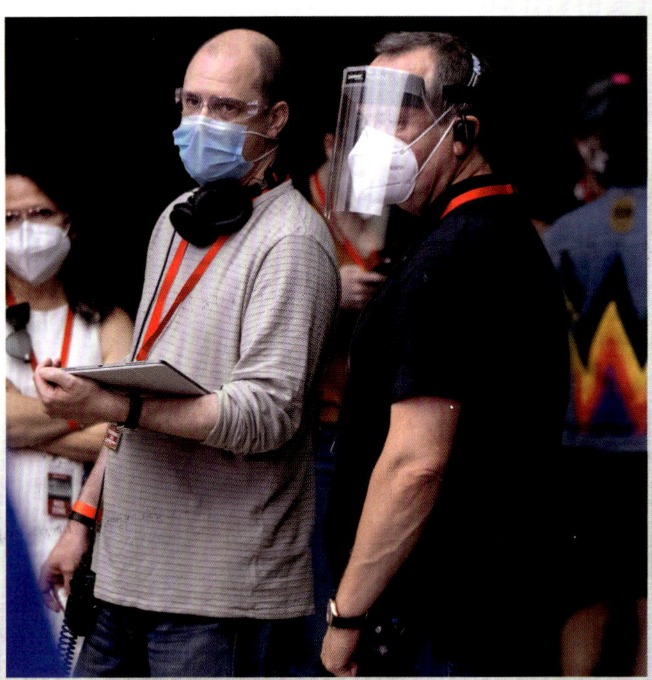

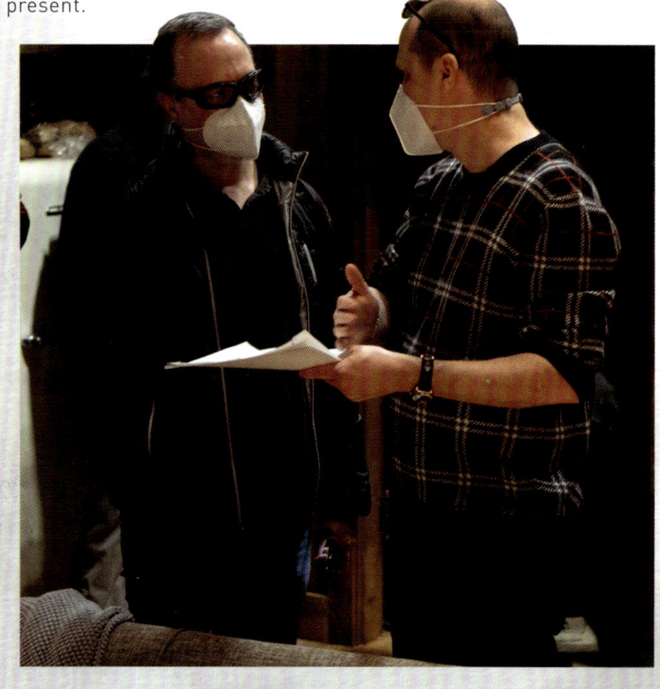

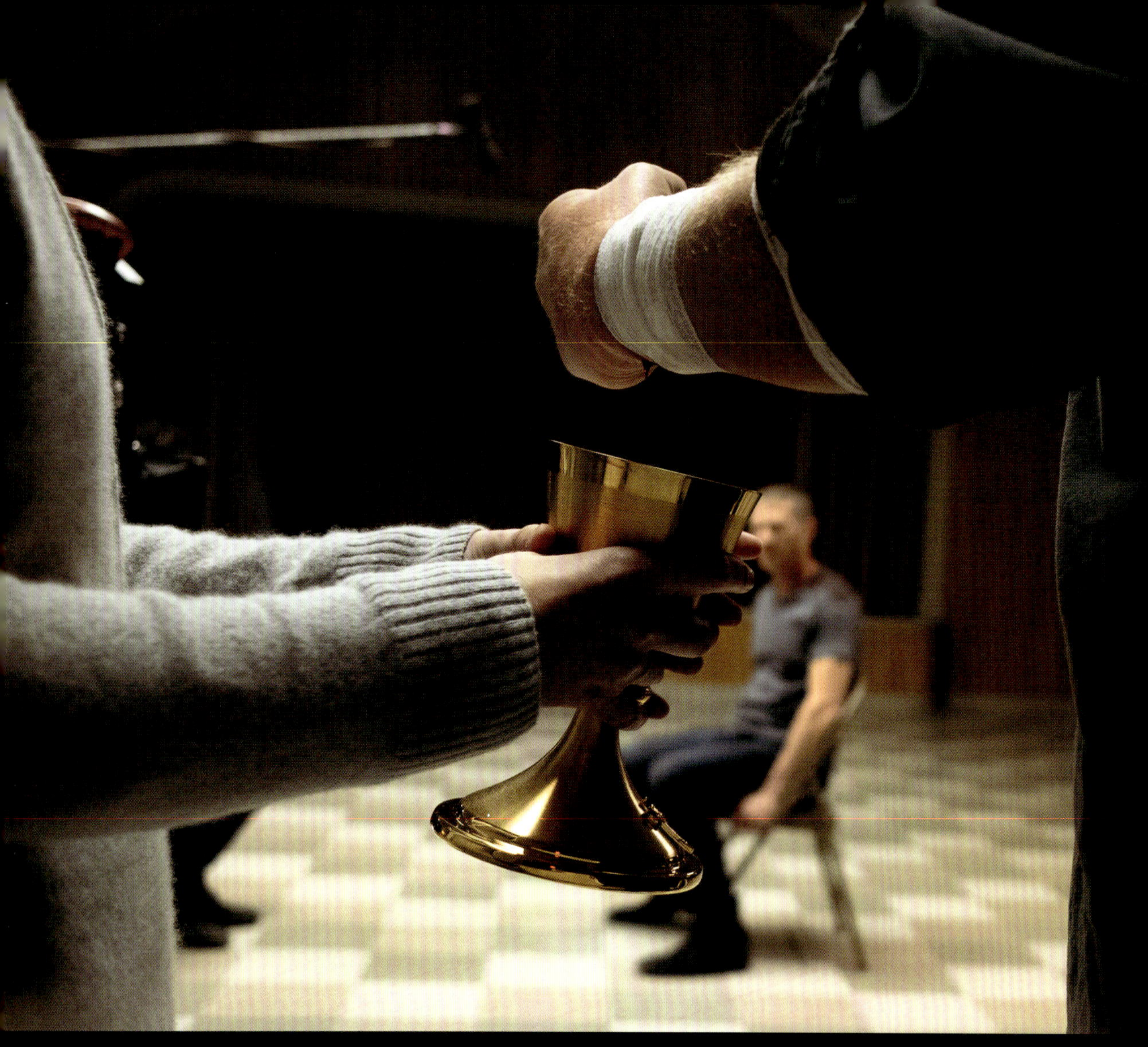

TOP/ Riley, at the rec center, doesn't realize what's about to happen.

The word "vampire" is never spoken in *Midnight Mass*, even though it is at the heart of the miniseries. Flanagan first noticed what he sees as a confluence between New Testament liturgy and vampirism "probably late in college, as I began to investigate religion. I grew up as a Catholic, I was an altar boy, on the 'Riley path'. The tagline from *Interview With the Vampire* – 'Drink from me and live forever' – is only slightly different than what I was used to hearing in church. The step from the eternal life through the body and blood of Jesus into vampirism is not a wide step, I think," Flanagan laughs. "The parallels are clear."

Actress Kate Siegel, who is married to Flanagan, observes, "As Mike was writing it, he would start dinner table conversations about how often there are references in the Bible to the drinking of the blood, rising from the dead."

The Riley character subscribes to a philosophy which is, explained briefly, that we are individuals while alive, and in death, go back to being part of the One. Flanagan encountered this concept "in a number of different places, Buddhism, for sure. I first remember seeing that idea when I was studying world religion in college. That sent me on several years of trying to examine as many faiths as I could. That had me emerge essentially as an atheist. I resonated with that idea of the collective consciousness, the theory of the One. I find it to be the closest to where our understanding of physics and science and some kind of spirituality intersect."

Midnight Mass affords Flanagan an opportunity to explore this, which is not always the case with commercial horror stories. "This project was always something very special, because it gave me a chance to dive into different perspectives and theories about what happens when we die, which I believe – as Riley and Erin both articulate in ways I'm very pleased with – is the engine driving spirituality and religion. The answer that we come to at the end of the series is the closest that I can get to articulating what I believe."

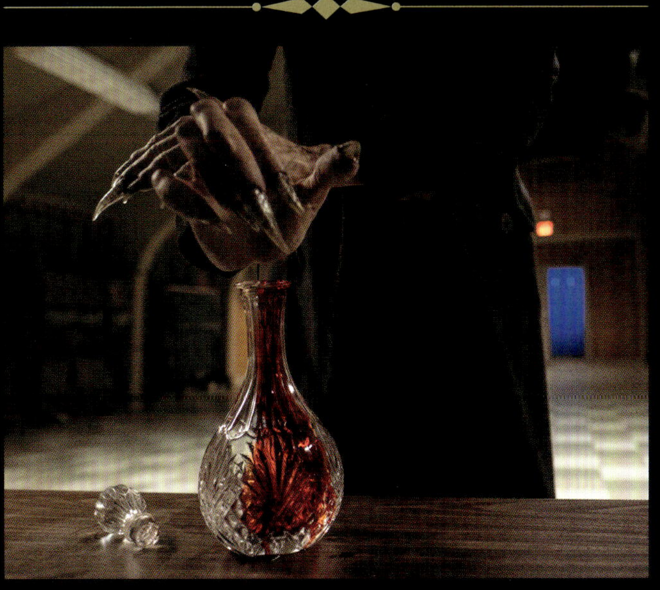

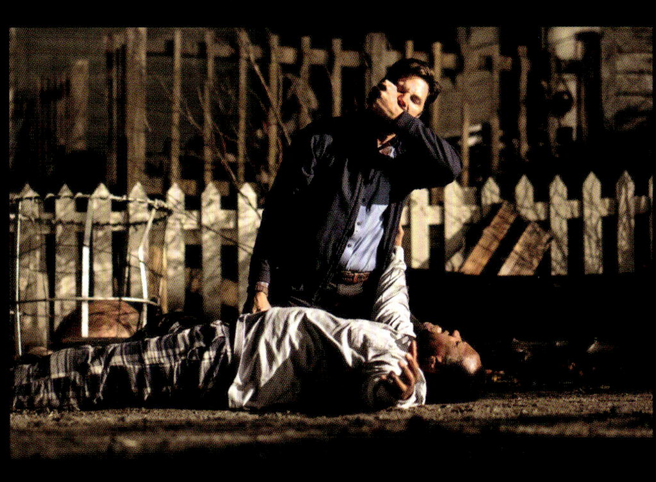

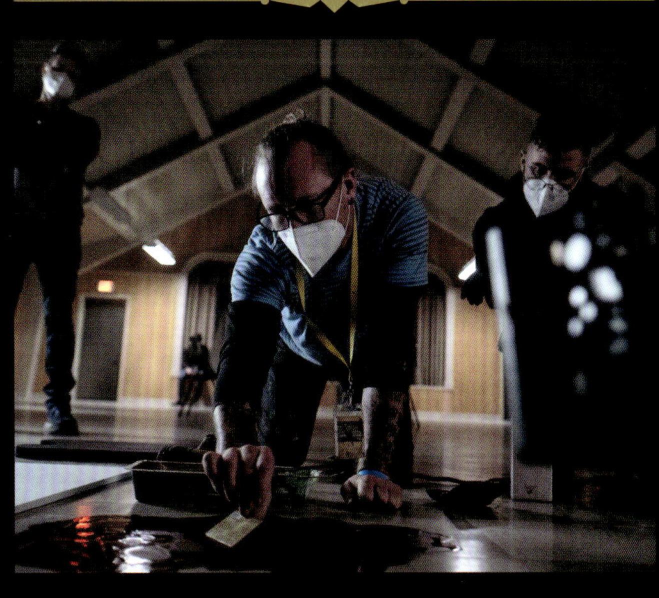

Flanagan adds he's not endorsing a specific belief system. "I think any religion can be weaponized against its own believers. Any faith can be seized upon and distorted by people who know how to do it. That's something we wanted to explore."

However, Flanagan adds, "It was important for me not to take a hardline position. When I was writing this, this was me trying to play both sides of the chessboard. The thing that I would come back to, time and time again, was vampirism – which is a genre mechanism – and religion would be second to human nature. A number of members of the congregation who have been transformed into vampires actively choose not to kill anyone. Vampirism is just an excuse for some to behave as their personalities and natures allow them to. Whereas others, even converted to this new vampiric faith, hold onto who they are, and to their values."

In writing *Midnight Mass*, Flanagan says he based many of the characters on individuals from his life. "I think we always do that when writing, but this one in particular. The characters had come together long before I knew who could play them, which is unusual for me. I love to work with the same actors again and again. But [the characters of] Riley, Erin, Father Paul, and Bev Keane all predated my association with the actors who play them."

With Riley, Flanagan relates, "A good amount of that was about subverting expectations for the protagonist. If we start someone on the tail end of an objectively heinous and problematic act" – Riley's killing of Tara-Beth in a drunk-driving accident – "when you're talking about a story that's ultimately a quest for redemption, that's a wonderful place to start."

Flanagan finds Riley's circumstances terrifying. "Coming up with things that scare me is difficult to do. I'm desensitized to the trappings of the horror genre. [But] I could have been exactly where Riley is sitting in that first scene, handcuffed on a curb, because I drove drunk. That strikes close to my heart. The only difference between myself and someone who's been through something that incredibly tragic is chance. That scares me to death, and is a marvelous place to try to explore some of the bigger themes I identify with. Most religions [promote] forgiveness and redemption, which I don't think you require a religion to have, but that's part of the fun challenge here.

THIS PAGE/ (TOP) The Angel fills a decanter with his blood. (MIDDLE) Vampirism runs amock on Crockett. (BOTTOM) Jonas Fairley, on-set painter, getting that blood splatter just so.

"Here's a crime that I could argue is incredibly difficult to forgive. How do I, as the writer, try to find a way to forgive and redeem [Riley]? How can I, as a filmmaker, paint a picture of forgiveness that can resonate with people, whether they need to aim that forgiveness at themselves, or at someone else? With Riley and his family, those questions of what do you do when you've hit a level of sin and tragedy that the normal platitudes aren't going to cut it for? You can't go to confession and wash away something that is truly life-changing. Who would I be in Riley's shoes? What would it have been like for me, as an atheist, if that belief system, or lack of a belief system, was put to a test like that? What would I need to believe? And why is it, as well, that so many recovery programs are intrinsically linked to religion? Which is a really interesting way for Riley to find his way into this dynamic with Father Paul – that you can swear all you want about where your faith is or isn't, but you go to AA, and you are going to be confronted with the Higher Power argument immediately. Does it mean you're incapable of recovery if you don't subscribe to it? AA says no, but these are the uncomfortable questions, the ones that resonated with me the most."

Flanagan and Macy had previously tackled a combination of vampire-like beings and alcoholism in *Doctor Sleep*, but, Macy observes, neither that nor *Midnight Mass* takes a conventional approach. "It's different riffs. For *Midnight Mass*, the question is, what's the version of vampire mythology that allows us to comment best on religion, society, the human condition? The transformational quality of it informed the way that the characters and the mythology developed, especially with respect to alcoholism. AA is a wonderful lens to look at human weakness, and human strength, for that matter."

The otherwise Christian community on Crockett Island has a Muslim sheriff, Hassan, whose son Ali becomes drawn to the church, unaware of the source of its "miracles." Flanagan says, "That led to some of the larger conversations I wanted to include, one of my favorites being the PTA meeting that Hassan has, not because he's angry that his son would look at a Bible, but because it was distributed at a public school. Those are important parts of the conversation that happens all over the world about how to properly separate church and state."

Is the hate-filled Bev Keane based on anyone Flanagan knows? Flanagan laughs. "I don't know how I could've held someone like that in my life for very long. It was clear very early that the monster of the story wouldn't be this supernatural thing that we dug out of the ground, although it would do its part. The monster was the thought process that let people like Bev continue to propagate more people like Bev. I keep turning on the news, and seeing 'Bev' is now a congresswoman. I'm more scared of Bev than I am of the vampire that's going to tear my throat out, because, unfortunately, I think she's the most realistic character in the show. Bev's attitude is the most vampiric element in the story, born out of people believing that they're inherently better or more deserving than other people, whether it's a difference of faith, or race, or class. It's not limited to church. It's able to create food out of nothing, because you can take any number of random circumstances, and Bev can make it fit her narrative. That, again, is the true horror for me."

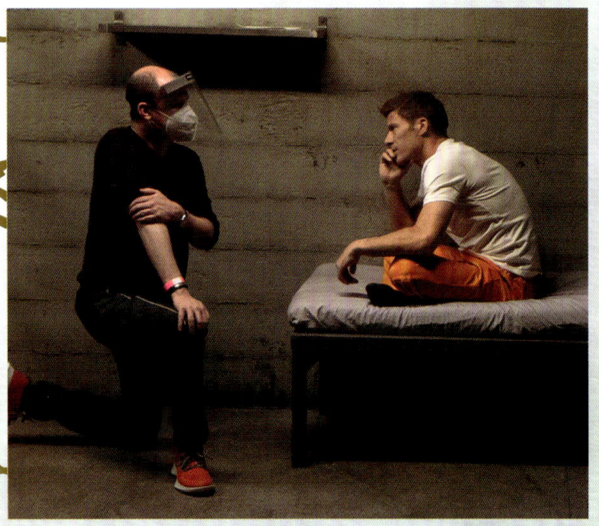

TOP/ Flanagan directs Gilford in the mainland prison set.

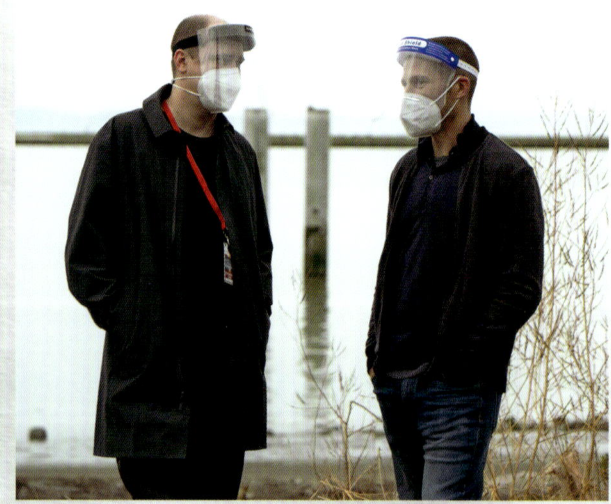

TOP/ Flanagan and Gilford working on the beach.

Flanagan relates that the secret love between Mildred and Monsignor Pruitt, aka Father Paul, which produced their daughter Sarah, "is a riff on a storyline in one of my favorite films, John Sayles's *Lone Star*. I learn more about long-form storytelling every time I watch that film. There are all these [moments] throughout that hint at the actual relationship between Chris Cooper and Elizabeth Peña's characters. Sarah saying, 'The old priest, when I was a kid, used to stare at me,' that's almost a direct lift from *Lone Star*. This was an opportunity to pay homage to that."

For all Father Paul's devotion to the priesthood, Flanagan says, "This secret that led to Sarah's existence is an ordinary love story between a man and a woman, who, for a variety of reasons, could never prioritize each other over the other obligations in their lives. I enjoyed that I didn't have to end Father Paul and Mildred as this fire-and-brimstone mouthpiece for fanaticism. Instead, it could end with two parents looking down at their child, who they've now outlived, which is some of the most devastating and relatable human tragedy there is. Some of my favorite stuff is when he puts away the collar and, in doing so, completely forfeits his role in the story as the antagonist, and to think of all the things that could have been, if they'd just made different choices – choices people make are what the show's about."

Although every character who drinks the Angel's blood and resurrects ultimately bursts into flame in the sunlight, Flanagan chooses to keep this off-camera. "[Incendiary] effects can be distracting. And I felt like by the time someone immolates, their story is over. When Riley does it, it's not about Riley bursting into flame, it's about Erin seeing, and what that means she's going to have to decide, which way she's going to row. And I loved so many of these characters so much, I didn't want to watch them burn. I'd rather see Father Paul and Mildred's silhouette in a kiss and just start to feel them breaking apart, or see Ed and Annie holding onto each other as the light hits their faces, see just a few frames of that singeing. Because I don't want the audience to watch these people die. There's an element to horror that [can become] about forcing people to spectate the death of characters. Sometimes, that's the only thing a movie has going for it, and believe me, I'm not attempting to knock it. I love *Friday the 13th*, and grew up loving it. But this was never about that. It was more important that we learned everything we needed to learn, and then these people weren't really ours anymore, and it was time to look away."

Midnight Mass's intersecting themes appeal as well to cast and crew, although different people respond to different aspects of the material.

Cinematographer Michael Fimognari says his work was entirely informed by the narrative. "In a story that is about light as an element that has the properties of taking life, the darkness, and how we perceive light, has bearing [on the narrative]."

In terms of music themes, composer Taylor Stewart of the Newton Brothers says these are not character-specific, but are more about "cultivating the town, and how the people are affected."

Costume designer Terry Anderson states, "I love how Mike's writing weaves a moral compass."

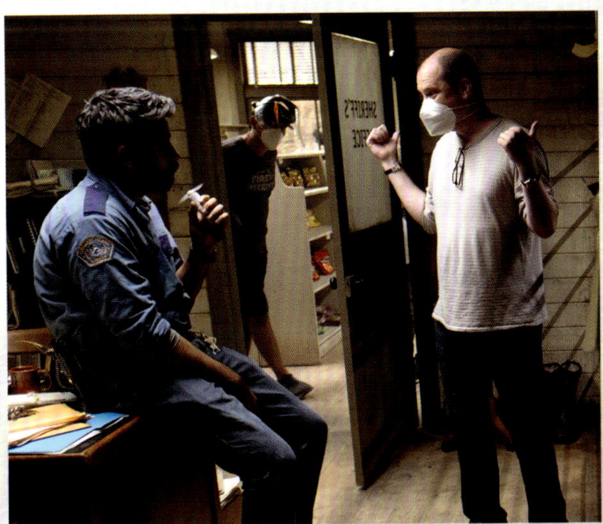

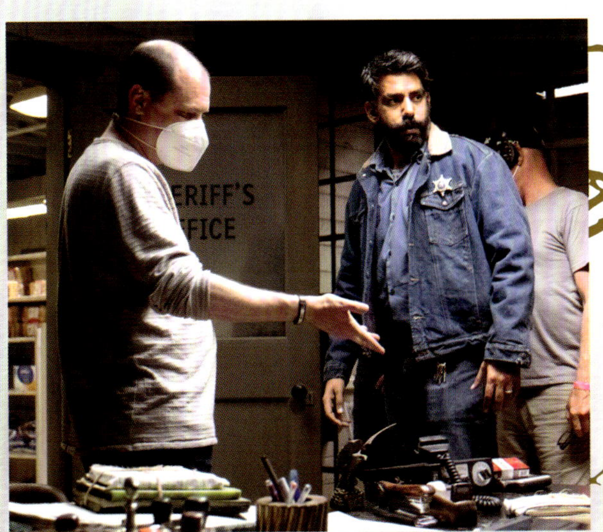

TOP/ Flanagan directs Kohli inside the sheriff's office.

Actor Michael Trucco remembers, early on, "I said, 'Mike, how has nobody ever done this?' I was raised Catholic. When you hear, over and over, 'This is My blood, drink from it, and you will have everlasting life,' that's ingrained in your brain. But when you take them out of context, 'Drink My blood, and you will have eternal life,' that's the exact [narrative of] vampires. In horror films, Catholicism and vampirism are diametrically opposed. They use Catholicism to combat vampirism. To marry the two into the same lore – it blew my mind."

Actress Annabeth Gish thinks, "It's a brilliant representation of what organized religion can become, metaphorically. I've always loved community, I've loved hymns, I've loved sacred gatherings, but I don't like shame, and judgment. I think organized religion can be the root of people's suffering."

Actor Zach Gilford says, "The scripts are amazing. It's this drama about this small town of people, who all care about each other, but we just happen to mix in vampires," he laughs. "It syncs up with a lot of my personal views, but it's such a weird show, and that's what I love about it."

Actor Hamish Linklater feels "It's a perfectly, gorgeously executed piece. It also happens to be about, what do vampirism and Communion have in common? I'd be working on it, and I'd be like, 'Gosh, this is really naughty'."

Actor Rahul Kohli was "fascinated with the story, and I liked the idea that there could be a little bit of controversy."

Actress Crystal Balint relates, "When I read the script, I thought, 'Oh, wow. We're really going there.' What I found most compelling, and also most frightening is, Mike hasn't had to do a lot of stretching to make this story work. Which isn't to say I believe that there's rampant vampirism in Catholicism," she laughs. "But I don't think you can make provocative art without pissing some people off."

Actress Annarah Cymone says, "I'm not a religious person, but religion for [Cymone's character] Leeza is something beautiful, that brings her so much strength, but it can also be used dangerously. I think the show does a good job of showing both sides of the coin."

Actress Kristin Lehman says she is likewise not religious, "but I talked to friends who self-identify as Catholic, and they were fascinated. They couldn't believe it had taken this long to explore the notion of Communion and vampirism. Mike put both in a really beautiful lens, and then a very stark lens."

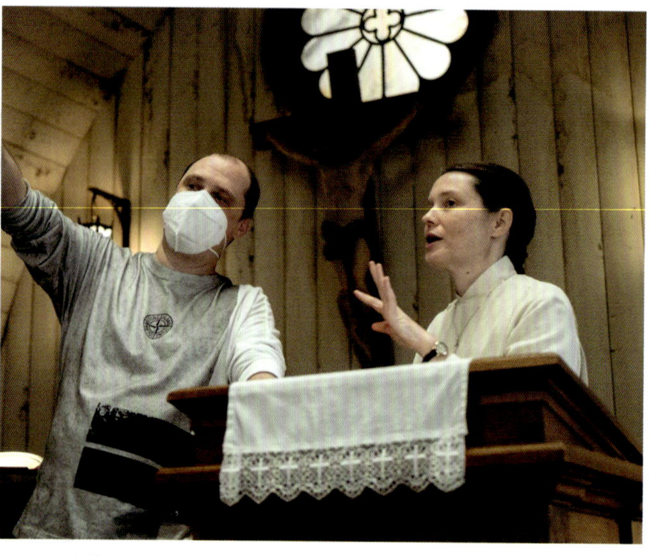

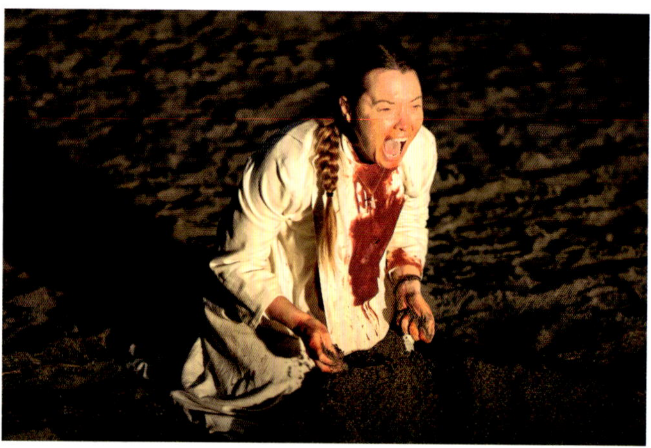

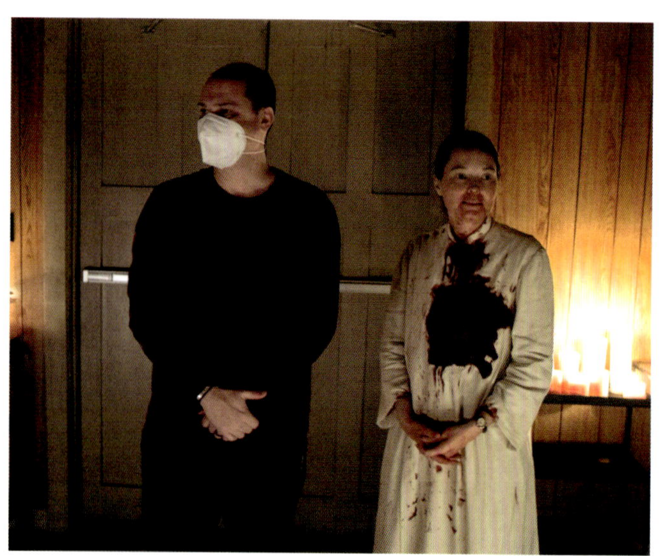

THIS PAGE/ Samantha Sloyan as Bev: confident at the pulpit, panicking on the beach, serene in blood.

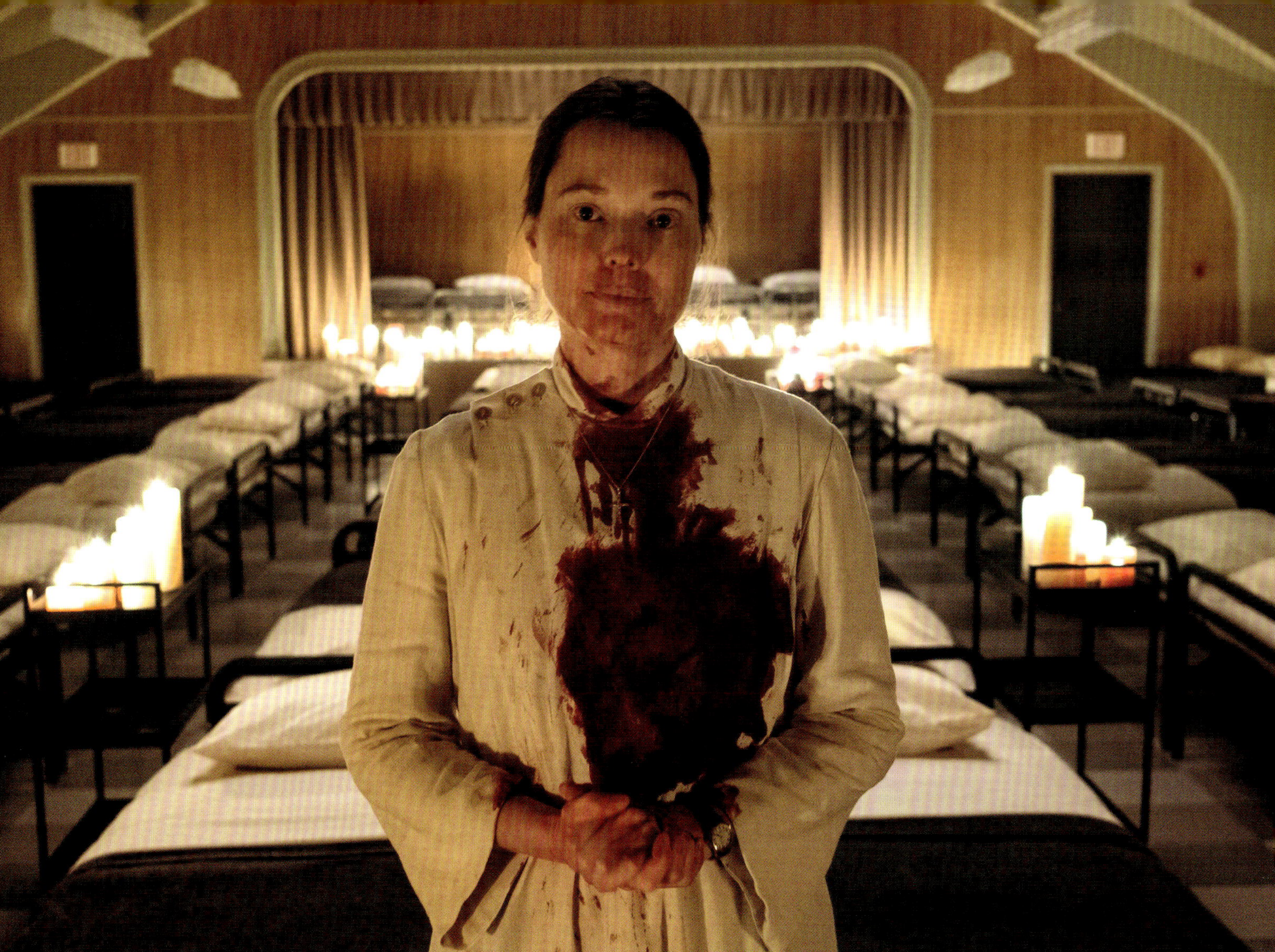

TOP/ Sloyan on Bev: "I remember a friend saying to me that mean people live the longest."

For actor Henry Thomas, "It's refreshing to see a new twist on the genre of vampires. [Also], what Mike is saying is timely, when mob rule is dominating everything."

Composer Andy Grush of the Newton Brothers says, "What's so wonderful is that it evolves through ordinary, everyday people, [and] ends up in such a unique place."

"Also," says on-set makeup FX department head, Tony "Ozzy" Alvarez, "When you finally see the Angel, I think people are going to be blown away."

Actor Louis Moffat sums it up: "What's there not to want?"

While Midnight Mass was designed to be a closed-ended miniseries, the Angel is not conclusively dead at the finale. So, could there be a Season 2? "It's not impossible," Flanagan says. "I didn't need to know if the Angel had died, because if the Angel represents fanaticism, that's never going to die. It was important to end the Crockett Island story appropriately, with the assumption that we'd never pick it back up. If that changes down the line, that's fine."

What intrigues Flanagan about horror? "I think horror exists as a genre because it's where we take our first shared emotions. We all learn how to be scared before we learn almost anything else. Horror lets us examine our fears in a safe space. I view the horror genre as opportunities for controlled bursts of courage. If you make it through a scary scene, or a scary chapter, or a scary movie, you're training yourself to be brave, in short bursts. It's like doing ten pushups, but for courage. The genre, when used properly, can make us all wiser and braver if we approach it right. If you watched a Friday the 13th movie, like I did as a kid, and lifted your hands to cover your eyes, and then a little while later, you watched the same movie and didn't do that, you've changed a little in between. I love the genre for that."

In Macy's view, horror "allows you to take a step back, and look at [fears] as if they're not your own. Fear, like laughter, is universal. And what we're afraid of tells us who we are. That's the lens genre – all genres, by the way, science fiction and fantasy, too – provides."

Flanagan actually wasn't a horror fan at first. "As a kid growing up, I was scared of everything," he laughs. "I was afraid to watch horror. I'd watch behind my hands, and have nightmares. I found books to be even scarier than movies, because they activated the imagination. But that helped me get braver. And then, before I knew it, horror was my preferred genre."

What scares Flanagan most "is always evolving, but my answer to that changed drastically when I had kids, because so many of my fears are wrapped in what could happen to my children. I'm terrified of what people can do to people. It's why I'm more afraid of Bev than I am of vampires. I'm terrified of the inevitable, potential loneliness of death. The end of *Midnight Mass* is the closest I can come to some comfort, and even that involves a type of oblivion. I'm scared of being alone. I'm incredibly scared of my kids feeling that way. I didn't know what it meant to be really scared until I watched my infant children run a fever."

Flanagan felt the horror genre helped there, too. "I can maybe understand [that real-life fear] better, and maybe fear it less, if I can transfer it to something outside of me. Some of that existential fear is in this show. There will be pieces of that in everything that I do to some extent, which is why, for all of the horror, I try to pull up at the end, to try to have some hope infused into it. Because the other thing I'm acutely aware of is that, someday, I'm going to be gone, and these [creations] are records I'm leaving behind that my kids can interrogate and use to get to know me a little. I try to keep something that will tell my kids, "Here's a moment that just says, 'Here's some forgiveness, here's some hope, it's going to be okay'."

It's a lot easier to invite viewers to explore fears metaphorically, Flanagan says. "I don't think many people would want to talk [on film] about kids with fevers, or existential panic about the afterlife. But a lot of people might like to watch a spin on *Salem's Lot* with vampires in the church. As long as I can do both, as long as I can make something fun, and we can watch a well-acted, well-constructed show that is suspenseful, and mysterious, and exciting, and thrilling, and scary, we can do that, but also maybe throw a couple glances at something more important. There might be people out there who want to talk about that, too. This project is the most overtly personal in that respect. This is hiding my personal fears a lot less. The metaphor is there, and it's still a show, but there's a lot more that's very naked."

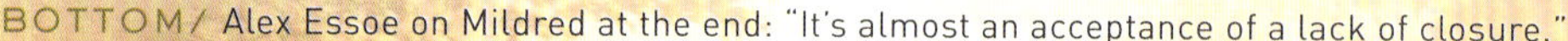

BOTTOM/ Alex Essoe on Mildred at the end: "It's almost an acceptance of a lack of closure."

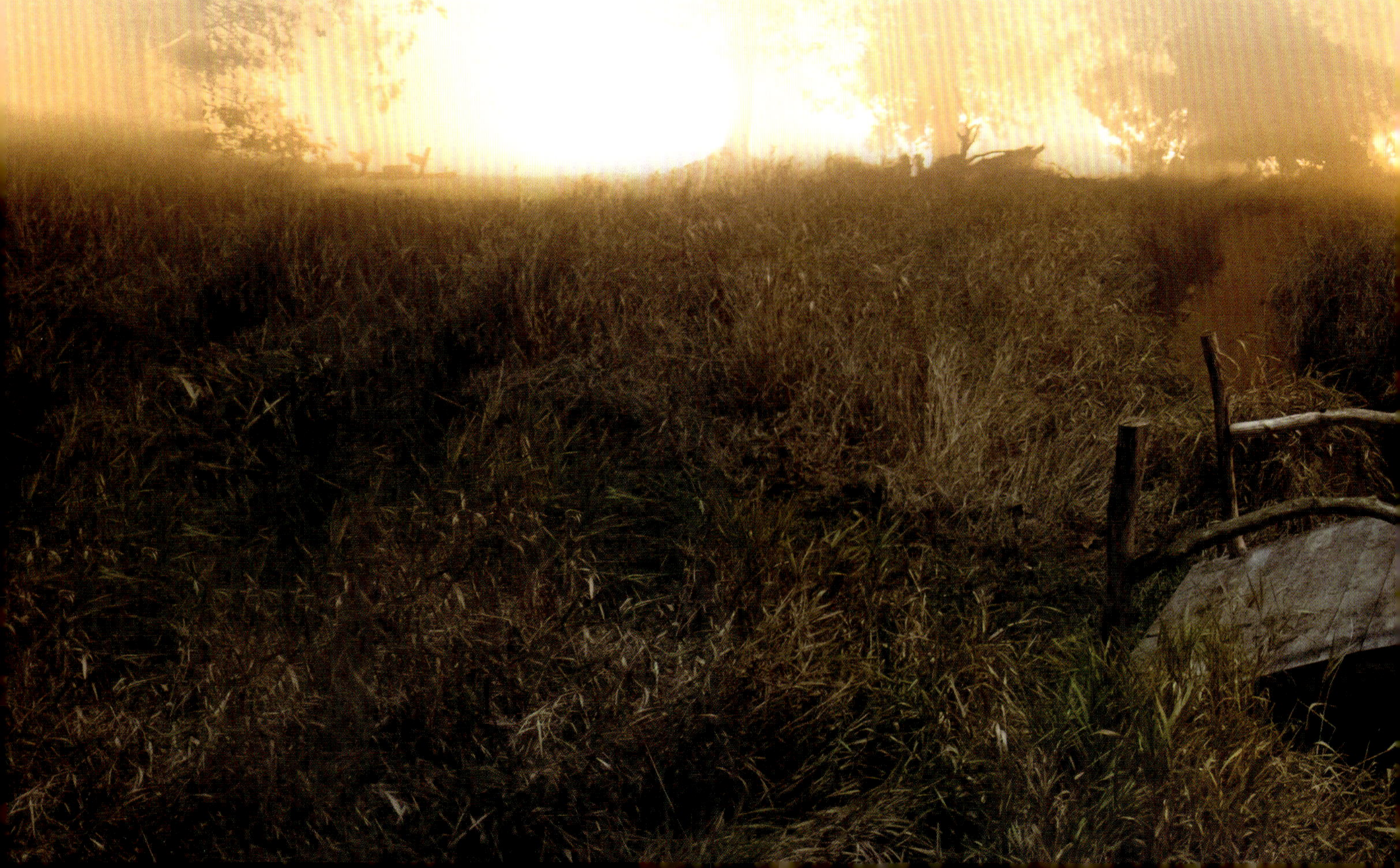

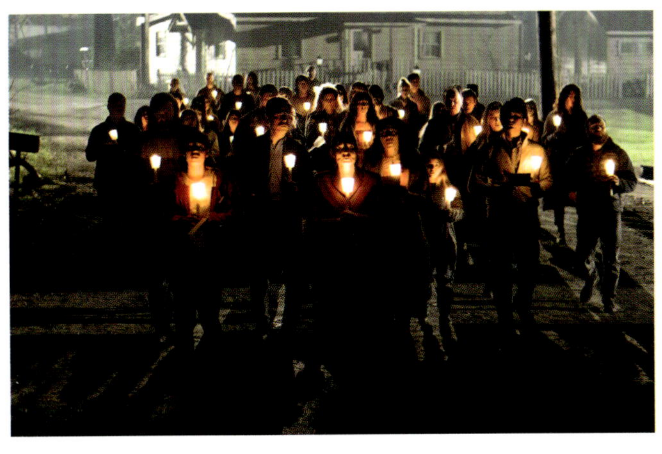

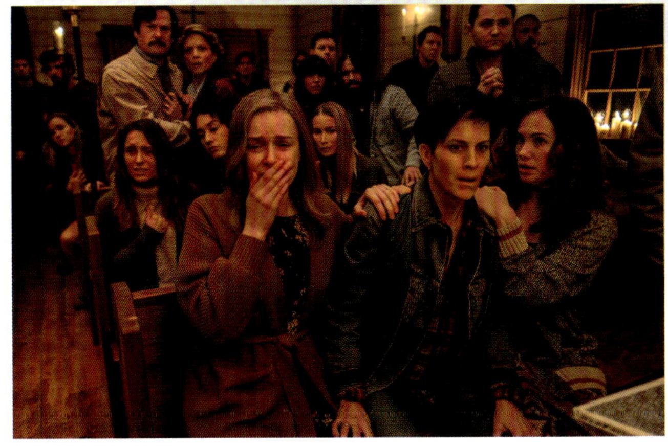

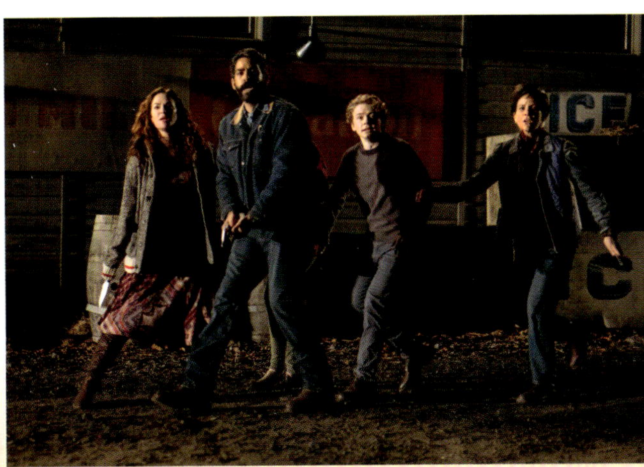

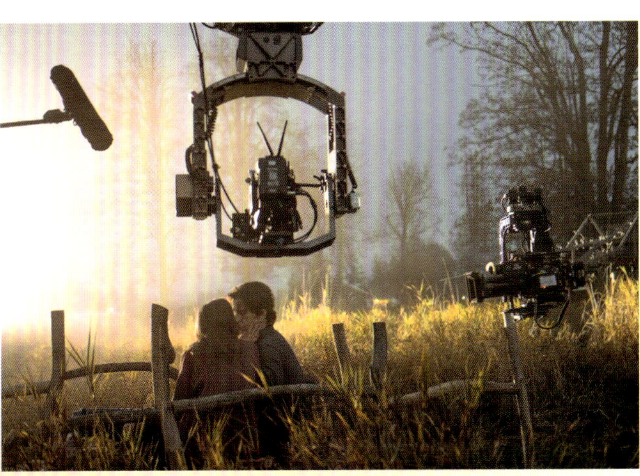

TOP/ The procession through town to the Midnight Mass, and reaction to what follows.

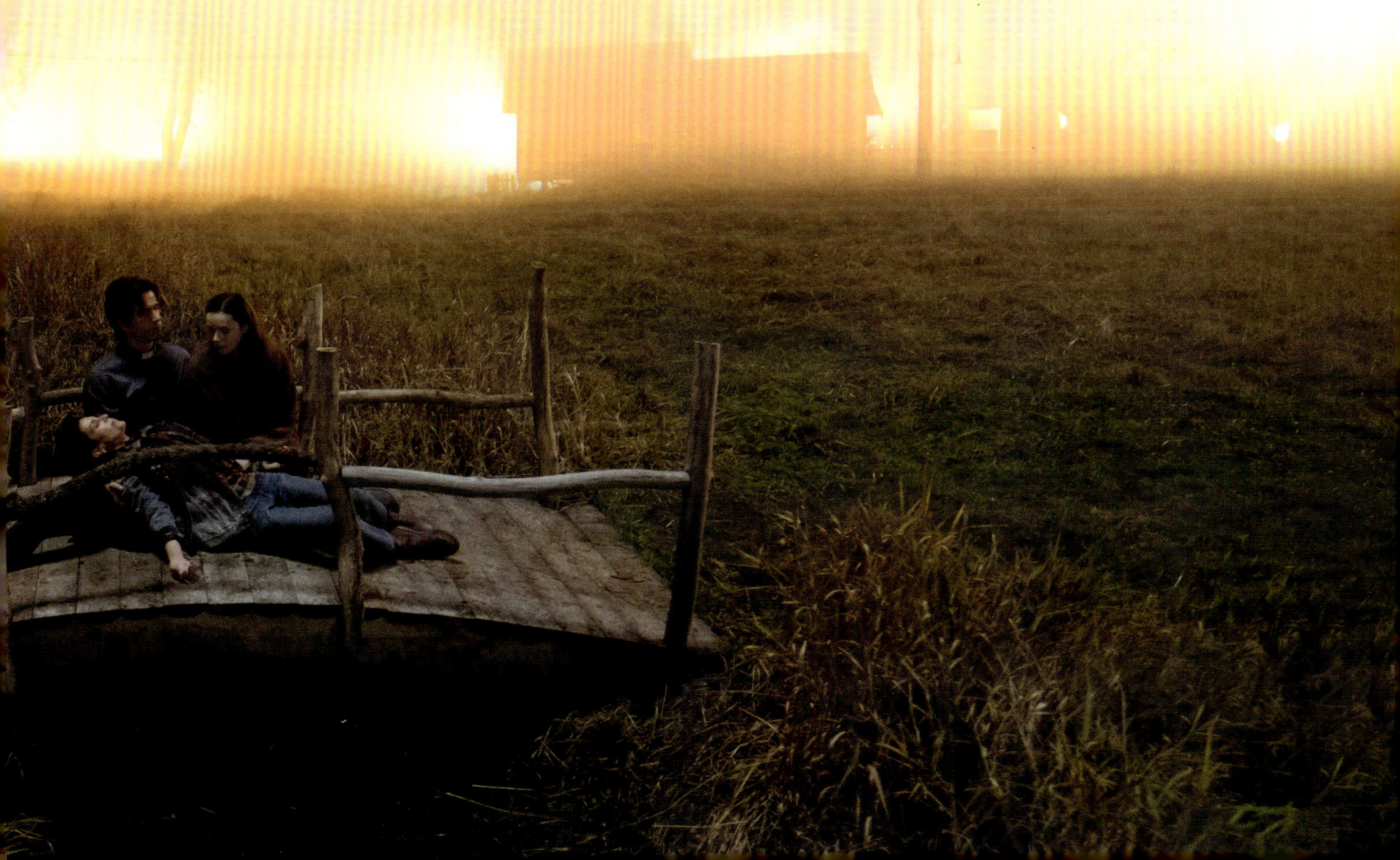

CINEMATOGRAPHY

CREATING DARKNESS

Michael Fimognari was cinematographer on Flanagan and Macy's *Oculus*, and subsequently has worked on all Flanagan/Macy projects since *Before I Wake*. Fimognari also directed two Netflix features, *To All the Boys: P.S. I Still Love You* and *To All the Boys: Always and Forever*; the latter co-starred Flanagan regular, Henry Thomas.

Fimognari says Flanagan and Macy bring him in early, "so I can weigh in on aesthetics and production logistics, whether something works for camera and lighting. Mike and I will go through the script, page by page, and build the shot list."

Their discussions extend to elements like sets that need to be built with removable ceilings, to accommodate equipment for overhead shots. Fimognari elaborates, "Mike will describe, in creative terms, why we're doing it, where we are in the scene. I will put that into very rough sketches that we can share with the team of what Mike wants the room to be, and where the actors are going to go. The art department will take that, and the production designer and the art directors will create a version of their wishes, and there's a back and forth that goes on until we reach an agreement."

Midnight Mass, Fimognari observes, is a departure from some of his previous work with Flanagan. "It's a more lived-in camera style, a more naturalistic lighting approach. With *Haunting of Hill House*, there's almost a Gothic fairytale quality. But with *Midnight Mass*, we wanted something that felt honest in its camera and its lighting. With location work, we worked hard to choose days that had the right lighting conditions, and positioned scenes according to where the sun would be, so that we didn't have to overthink it from a lighting perspective."

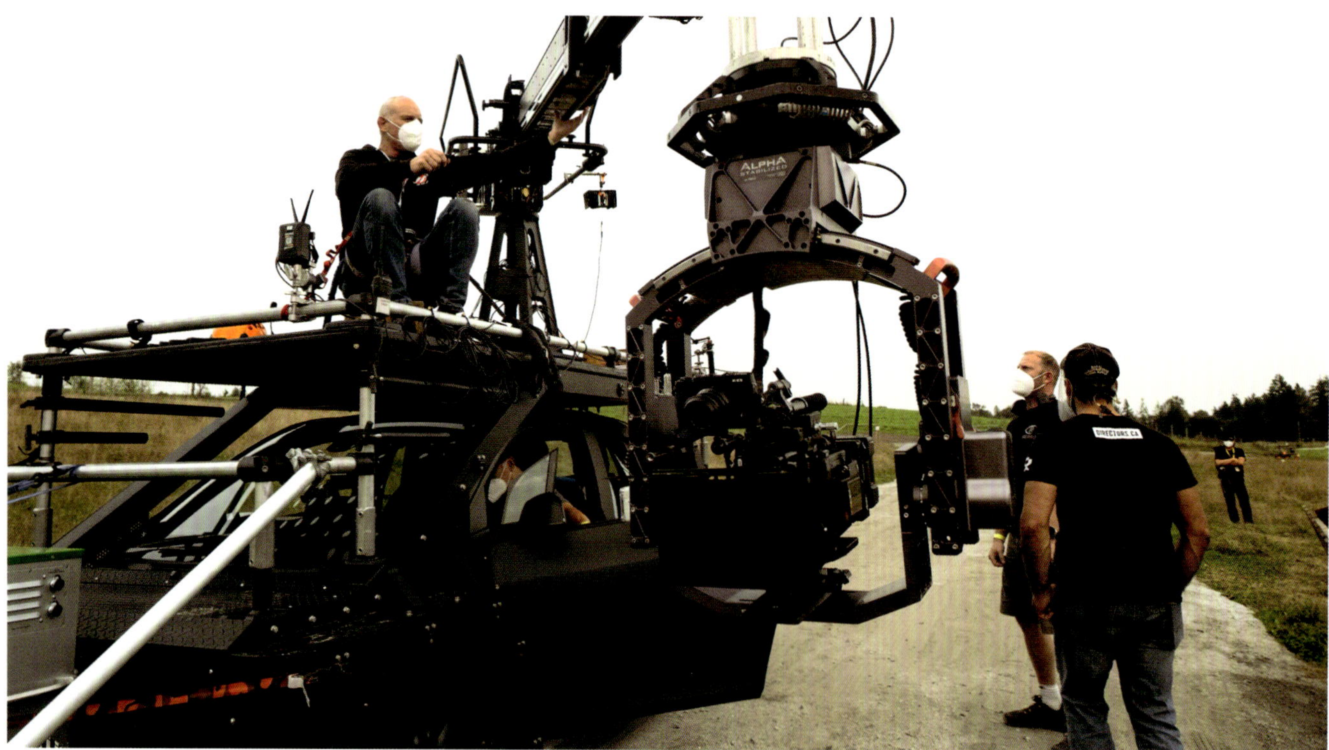

TOP/ Jack Cruikshank, dolly grip, operates a truck-mounted mobile camera rig for a road sequence.

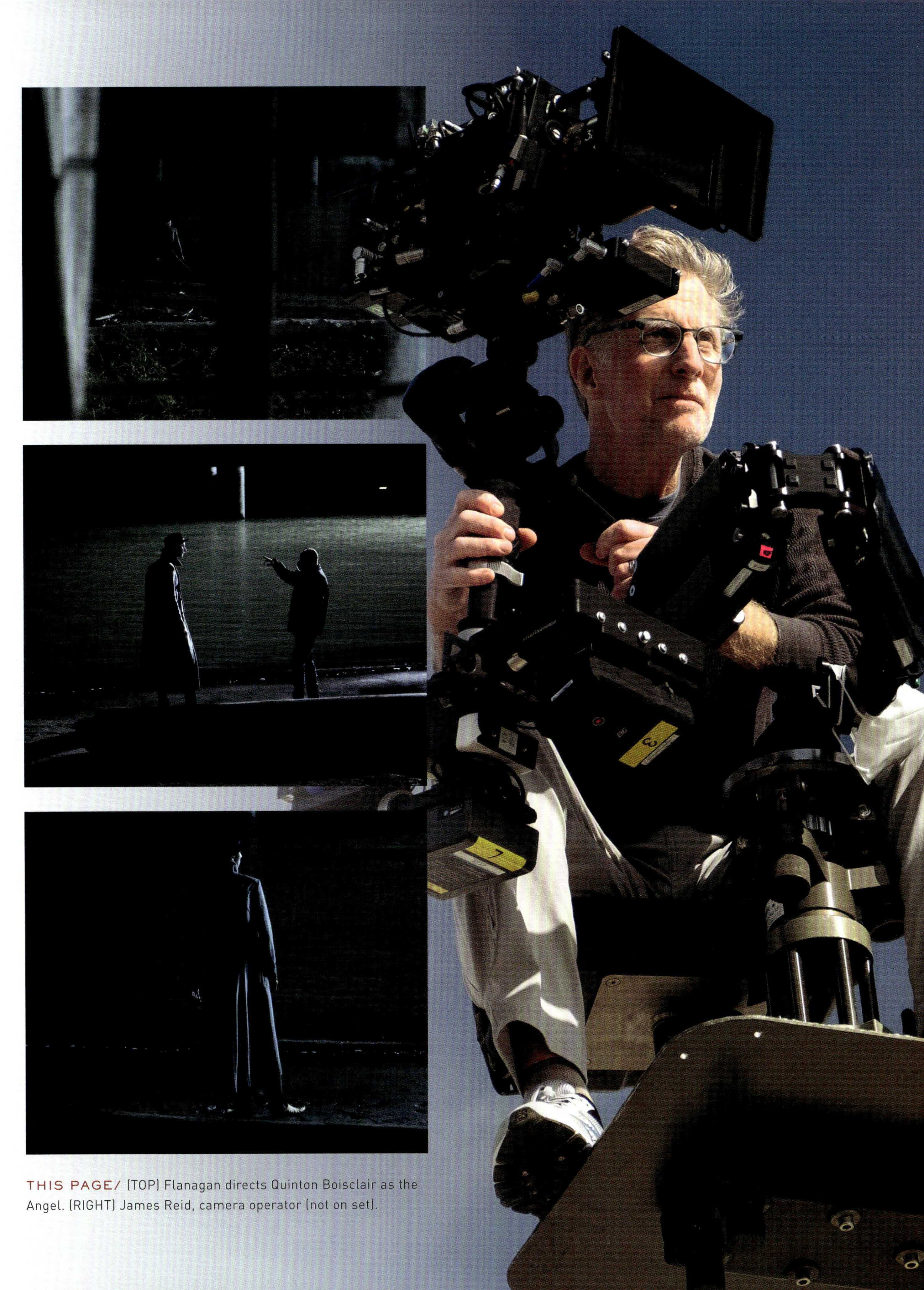

THIS PAGE/ (TOP) Flanagan directs Quinton Boisclair as the Angel. (RIGHT) James Reid, camera operator (not on set).

Flanagan says, "Fimmy and I introduced a handheld aesthetic, which is not something we've done much in our past work. We started in this docudrama, shoulder-mounted, immediate vibe that made us feel like we weren't trying to paint with light. We wanted it to feel very real. But as the supernatural elements ramped up, our cameras steadied. The handheld aesthetic started to drain away. The look of the show was an extension of the soul of the show. It needed to go through the process that the characters went through."

Fimognari relates that he and Flanagan always converse about, "What does our darkness look like? In *The Haunting of Hill House*, the darkness is a kind of liquid night, where the lights are off for story purposes, but you can still see. We can walk around the house at night when the lights are off, because we can see the shapes of the objects. But for *Midnight Mass*, we wanted something that was a little less understood, where our black levels went very black."

These aspects can always be altered in post-production with color timing (aka color correction), but with Fimognari's work, "It's mostly on-set execution. I'll always give it a little more exposure to be able to control it [in post], but it's the set contrast that gets built in. There are [night] scenes where you can see stretches of land, or a street. For that not to look like a spotlight was shining, or not to feel like a streetlight was on somewhere, we needed to have an enormous amount of light far away that would then wash the town evenly. But it's still mysterious, and sinister."

For the beach, Fimognari notes, "We wanted a softer look overall, but that changed, depending on the content of the scene. The storm clouds are dense and thick and cold. And then the storm comes in, and that same beach turns into strong lightning. The next morning, when they come out to discover the state of the beach," now covered in dead cats, "the light's harsh. It's bright, clear, sunny."

BOTTOM/ St. Patrick's Church is full for the Midnight Mass scene in Episode 6.

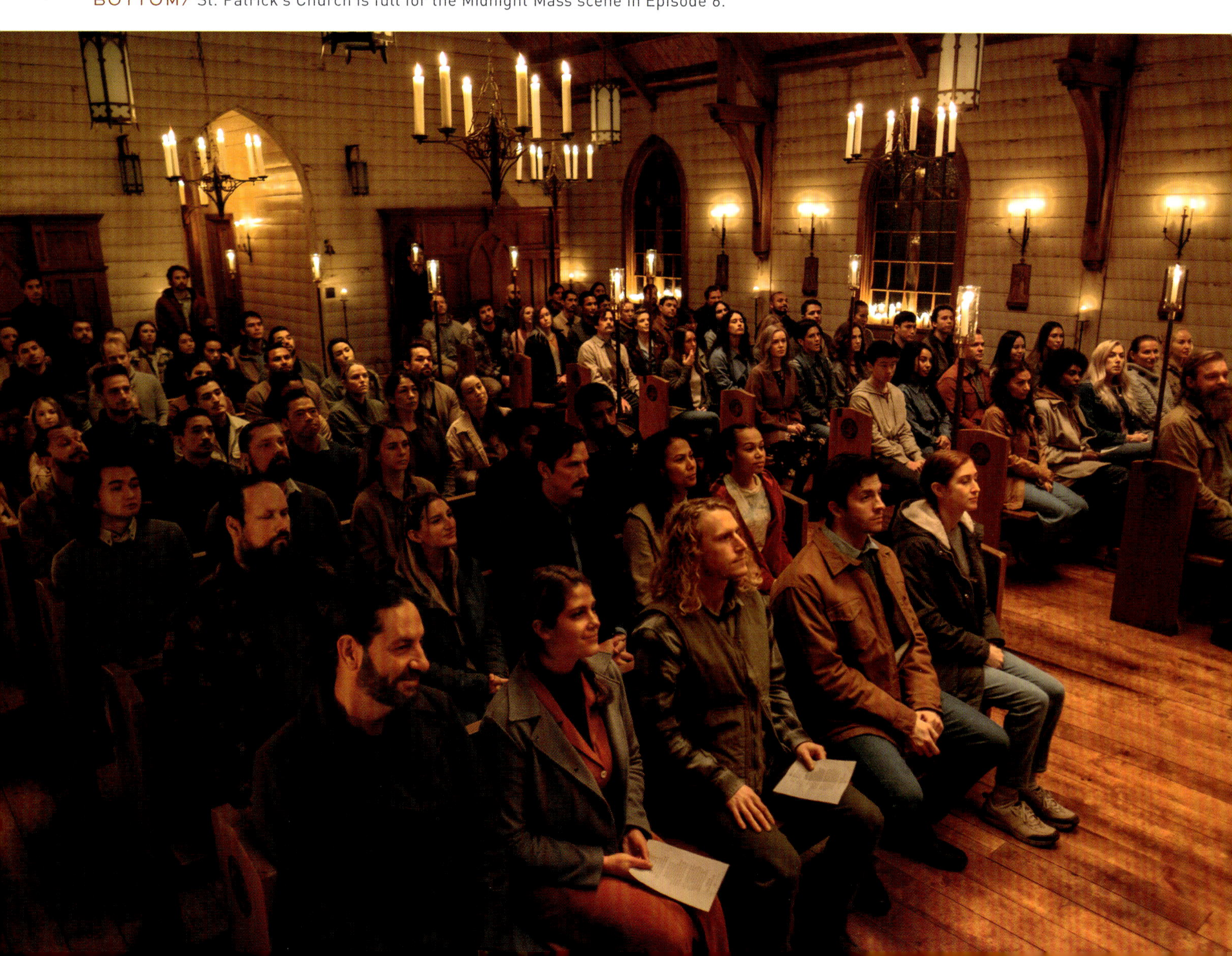

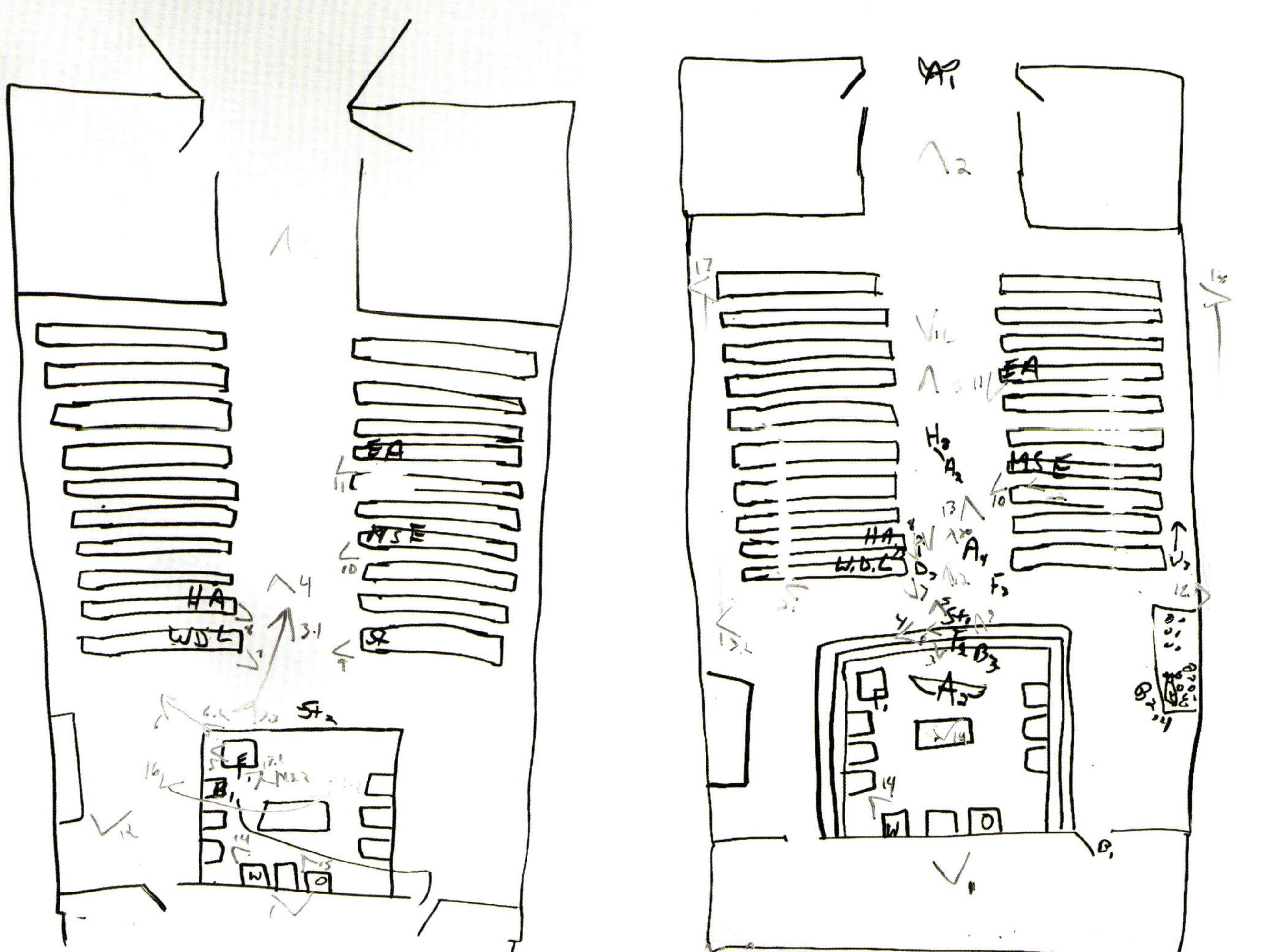

TOP/ Mike Flanagan's sketches indicate camera positions and movements, and where the actors would stand.

Fimognari adds, "Mike and I always address our lens package according to the aesthetic we choose. [For *Midnight Mass*], we went with an unfiltered anamorphic lens set, which meant that the detail, especially in the center of the lens, is very sharp."

The Angel had to be shot carefully, Fimognari observes. "Special effects makeup did a fantastic job. The trick with the Angel was about not revealing too much. Sometimes, the Angel would be where there were lights, so we would have focus in the foreground, and we would see the form of the Angel moving soft in the background, so you couldn't really resolve it with your eyes. Or, if he was in focus, it was about putting him in a silhouette, or controlling an edge light that gave you a sense of a shape, but not detail."

The monologue sequences are planned with the same exactitude as everything else, Fimognari relates. "Mike knows from the time we start whether he wants something to only exist as a single shot. Because he is able to say that early on, I'm able to get into a ballpark of what lens I'm going to need, how much physical space it's going to take to do that move, whether it's a dolly, whether it's a telescoping crane, whether the crane is going to be too loud, because the dialogue is at a whisper. I can factor that into the set build as well. I'm able to say, 'This wall's got to go, and we need another thirty feet on the outside of the set wall, because this is going to be a four-minute monologue, and we've got to do it on a fifty-foot techno crane.' Fortunately, we were able to work with some of our usual team from productions past, and they're really good."

To comply with COVID-19 protocols and have crew members avoid close proximity with each other, Fimognari explains, "We had an app that I was managing on my tablet that showed the shots, the position of the camera, and the order we were doing it." Any changes would automatically be sent to everyone's phones. "So, everybody knew what we were doing, and what was coming up next."

MIDNIGHT MASS SCENE

THIS SPREAD/ The 25-minute titular Midnight Mass in Episode 6 was the most ambitious sequence the team took on. Mike Flanagan says, "We spent more than a week filming it, it had more than 100 unique camera setups and is the most elaborate sequence I've ever done in my career – 100 extras, 40 stunt performers, blood, gunshots, creature effects, and pretty much the entire ensemble."

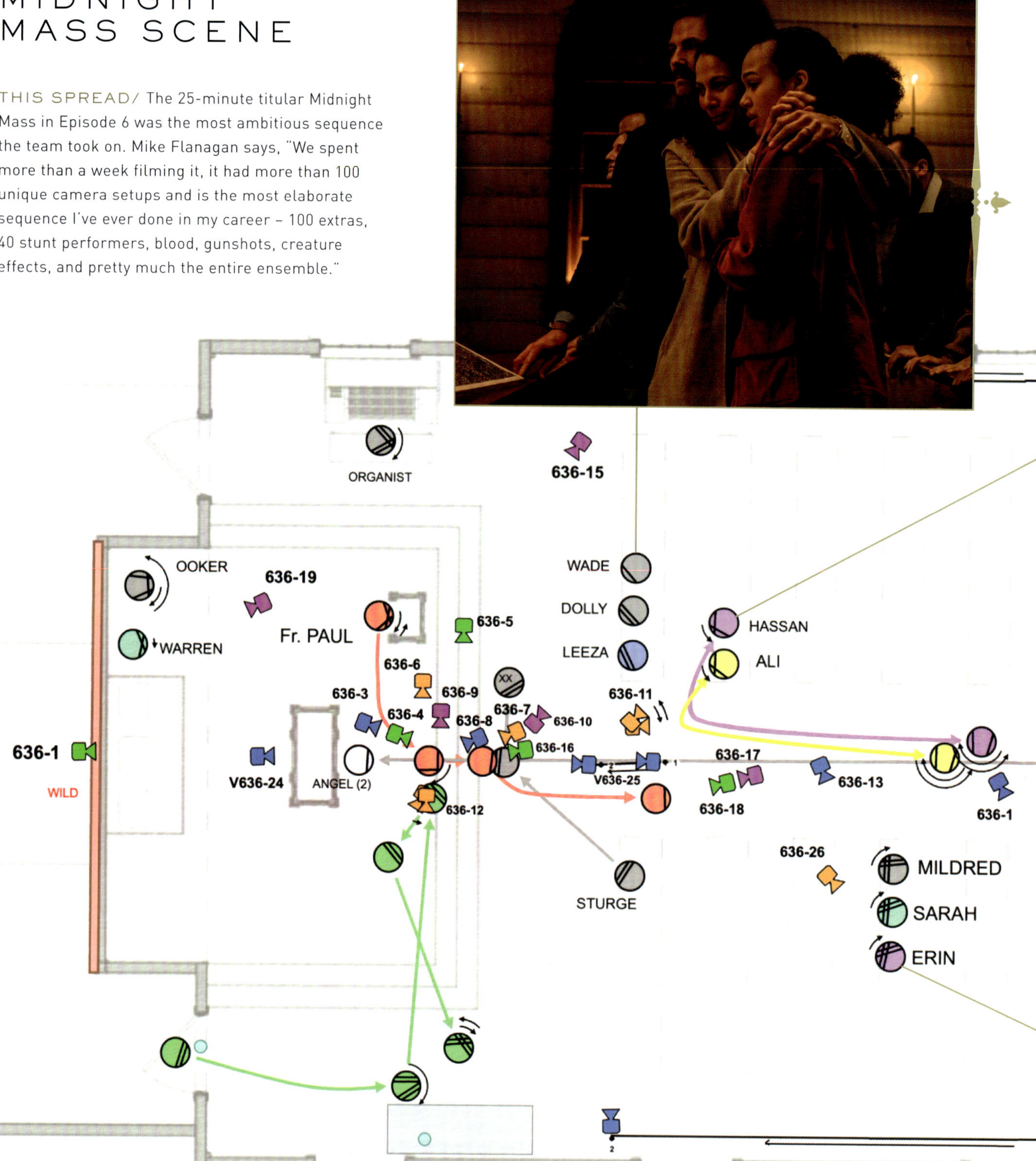

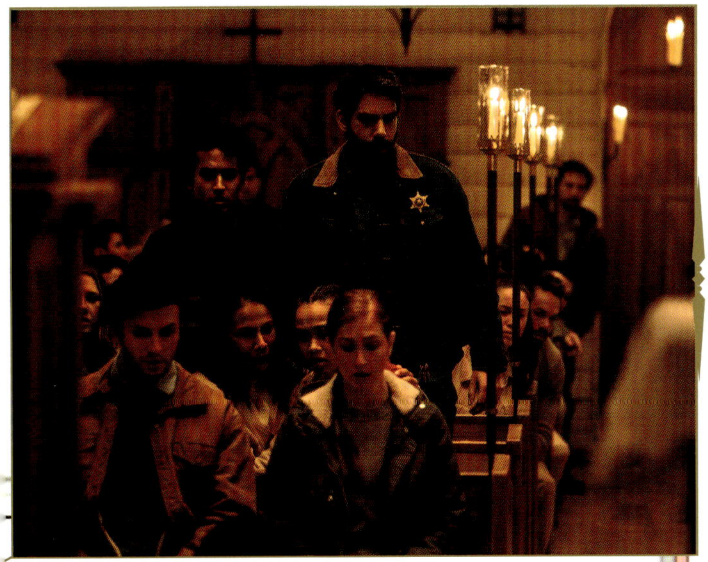

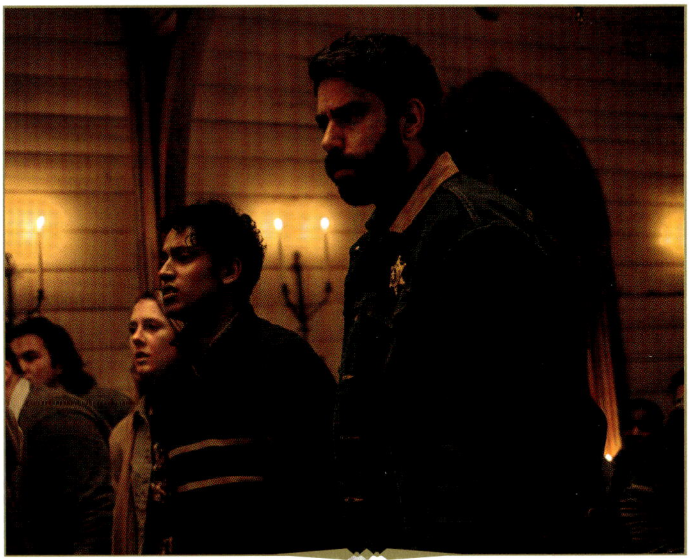

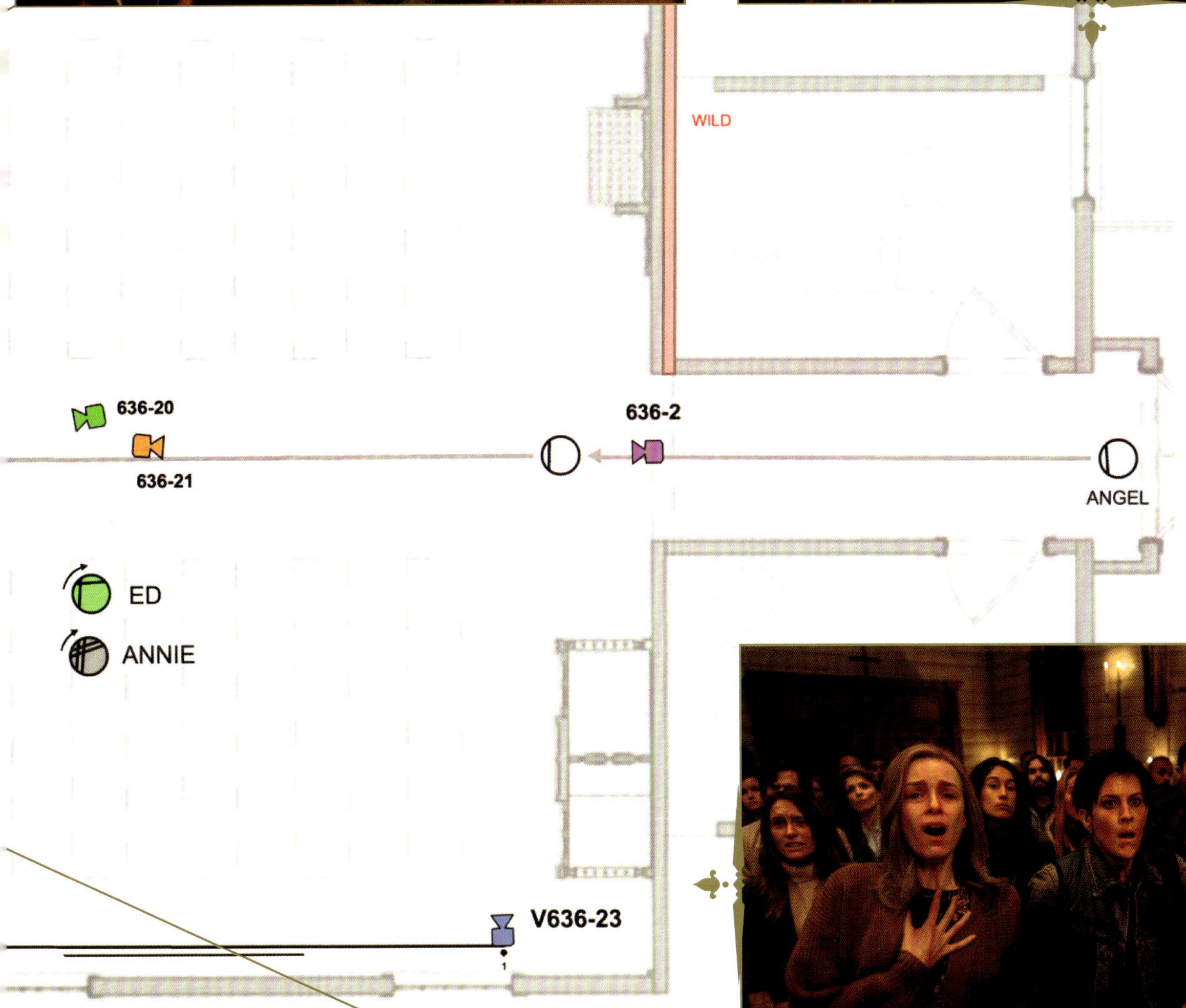

WILD

636-20

636-21

636-2

ANGEL

ED

ANNIE

V636-23

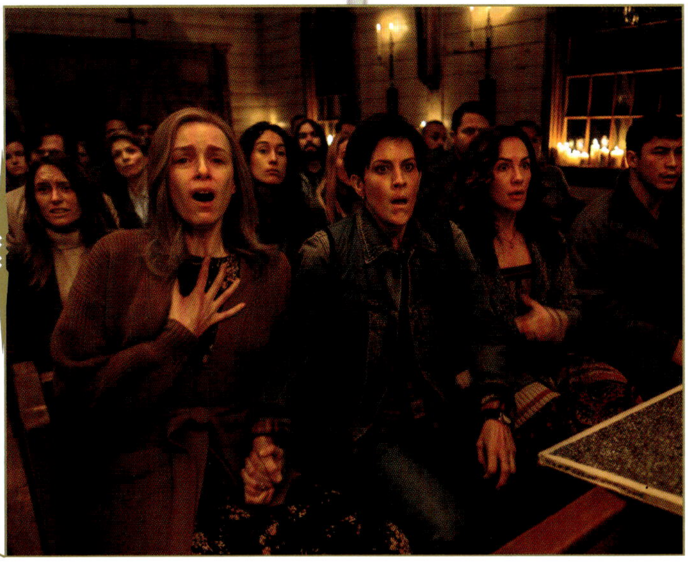

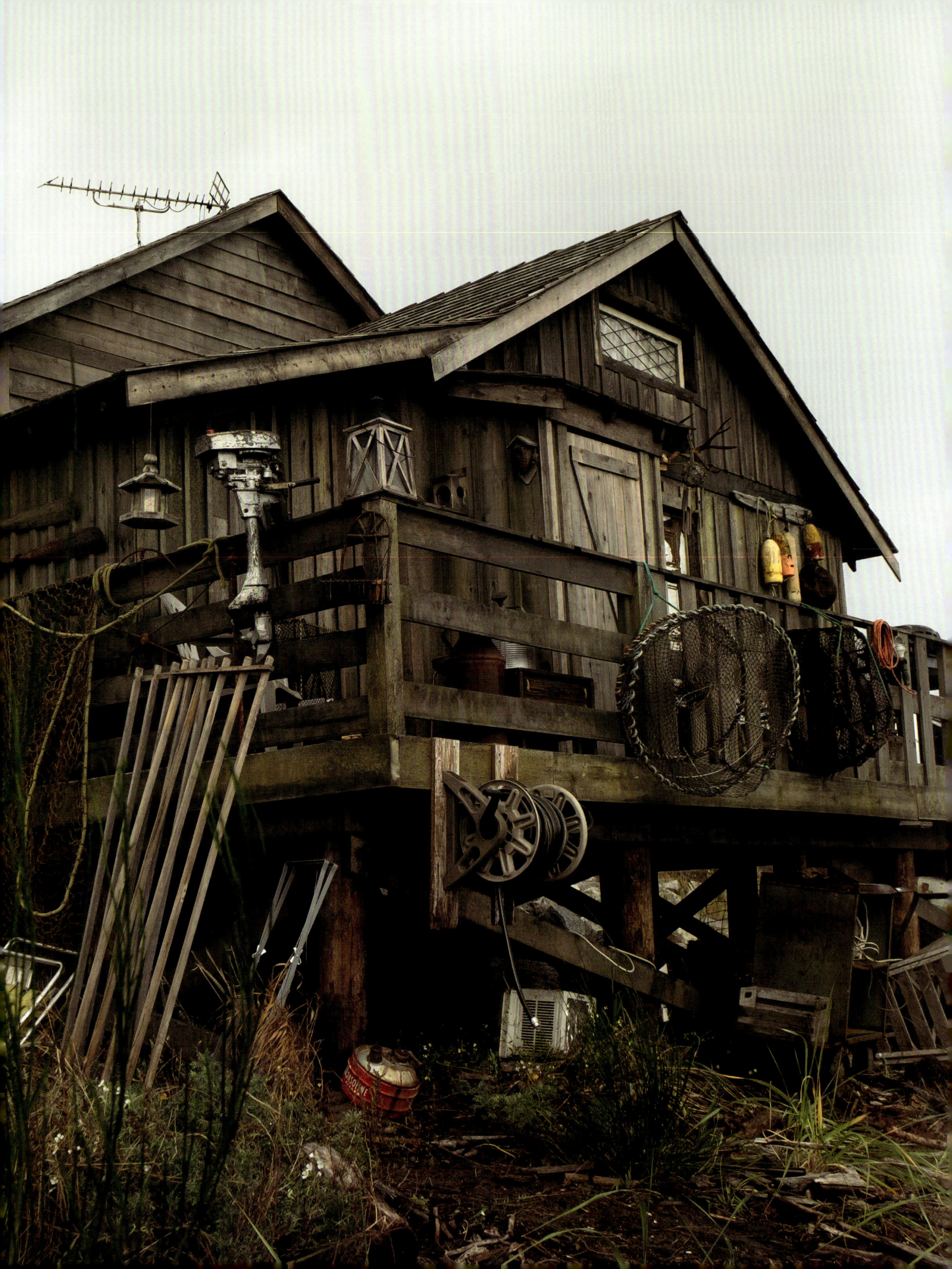

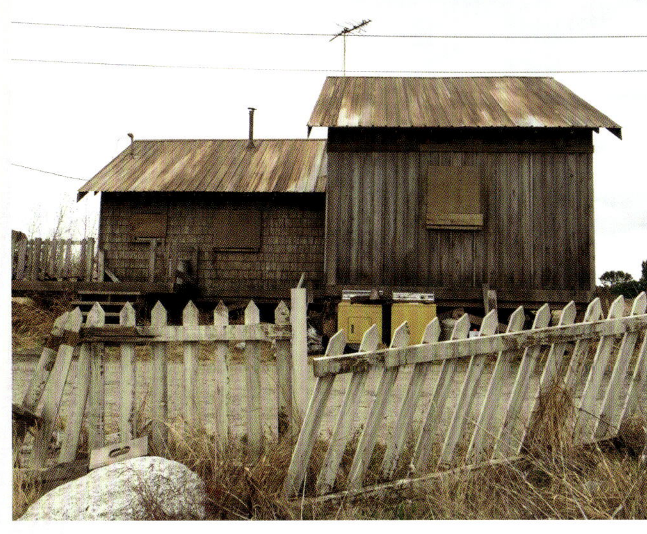

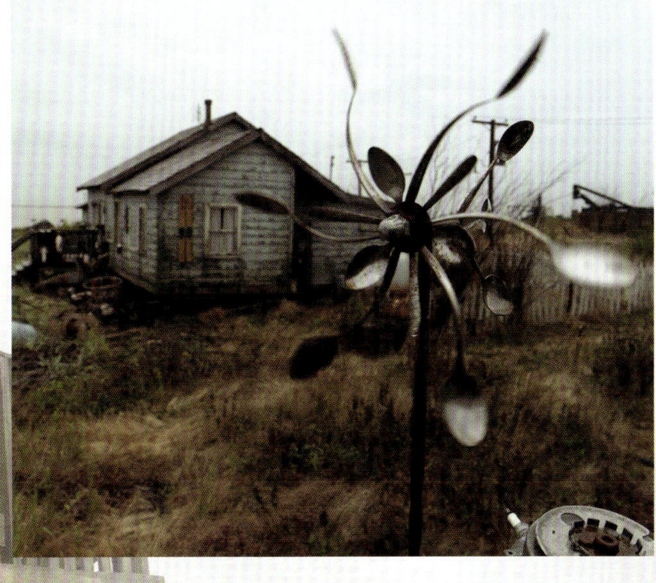

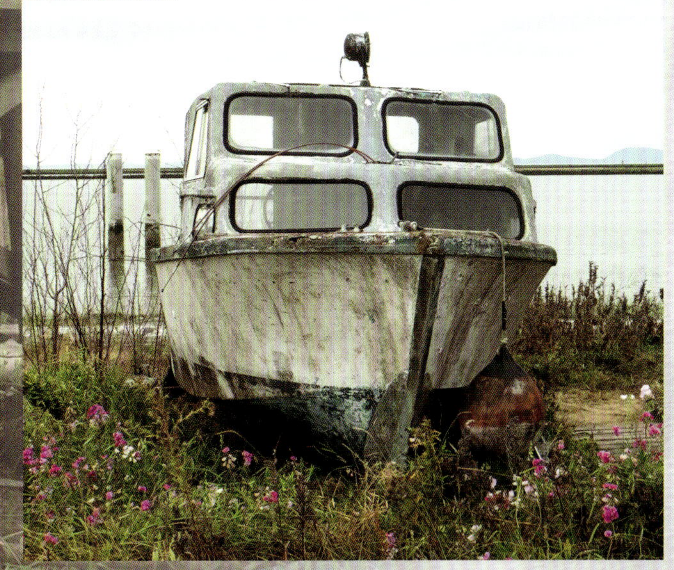

COLORS

SUBDUED PALETTE

Color, and lack thereof, plays an important role in all aspects of *Midnight Mass*.

Arnold points out that the islanders don't paint their houses. "Everything needed to be very sun-bleached and aged. I tried to keep the palette very subdued and controlled, so that it's got this washed-out quality. There are some blues and greens, but they're all very muted. We tried to not have any red, unless it was blood."

Anderson says he likewise controlled the wardrobe palette. "I tried to make costumes very tactile, so that you could feel the realness of the clothes. There's no black and no white." He cites, as an example, Monsignor Pruitt's coat, which is worn by the Angel, who we only see at night. One is actually black, but the other multiples "are a certain heather gray, which, when you take away so much of the light, it's black on camera, but there are highlights. If I'm looking at the image, I can see he's in the grey coat, but somebody else that doesn't know what they're looking at assumes that it's a black coat with light on it."

Fimognari says the island's deterioration affects the lighting. "The windows are grimy. The way that the fixtures give off light is a little bit yellow. There's very little cellphone light, or industrial light. You're mostly dealing with natural daylight that's coming through clouds, or an incandescent bulb in a household lamp."

For the climactic church sequences, Fimognari relates, "We didn't want the candlelight or the fire to feel too warm, so we took away the reds and the yellows, and left it as more of a white flame. It's still got some yellow to it, but not the kind of coziness that we associate with fire."

THIS SPREAD/ The houses indicate the subdued hues of *Midnight Mass*, evident in scenery, décor and costumes.

Flanagan observes that colors desaturate over the course of *Midnight Mass*, "so when we got to the end, and it was all about fire, it would have this divine flame that felt like the Book of Revelations. As the perspective of a lot of townspeople became more fundamental, the show became more black and white. Our shadows completely drop off into inky blackness. You'll always find a bedrock of color, but you'll feel as though all of the complexity of the color spectrum has been sapped out of it. It's rather beautiful to look at, but by the time we're in the church in Episode 6, the entire color palette of the show has become this glowing white, with this warm candlelight on the wall. Skin tone and the wood of the pews are harder to differentiate, and then it's punctuated by the blood. You have this white, red, and gold. We feel that high-contrast polarization that we're playing with thematically. That aesthetic becomes this rigid contrast, to reflect the spiritual state of our characters, that's finally interrupted by the brilliance and full color spectrum of the sunrise in Episode 7, where we take that black and white world, and suddenly paint it with every color that we can imagine."

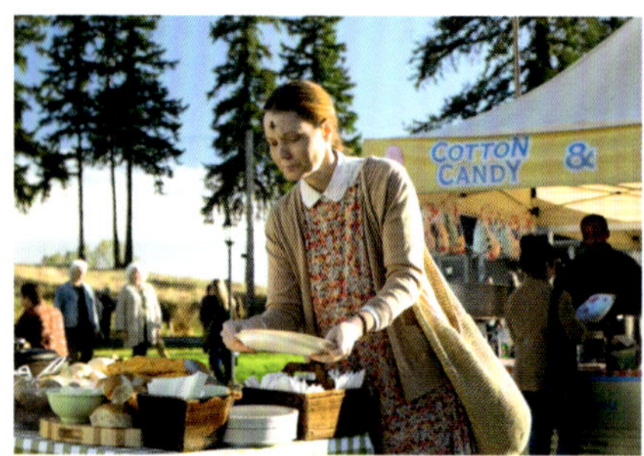

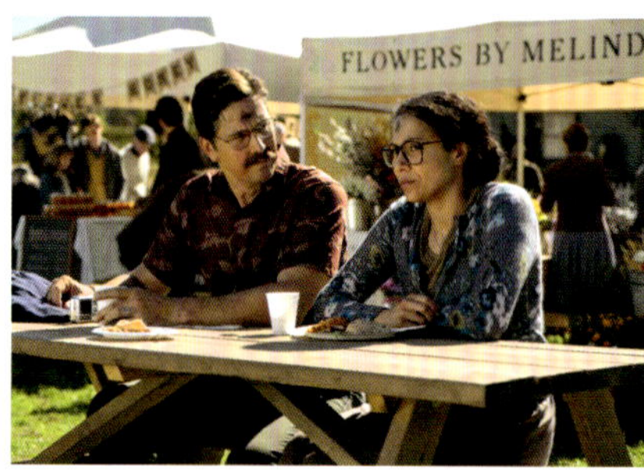

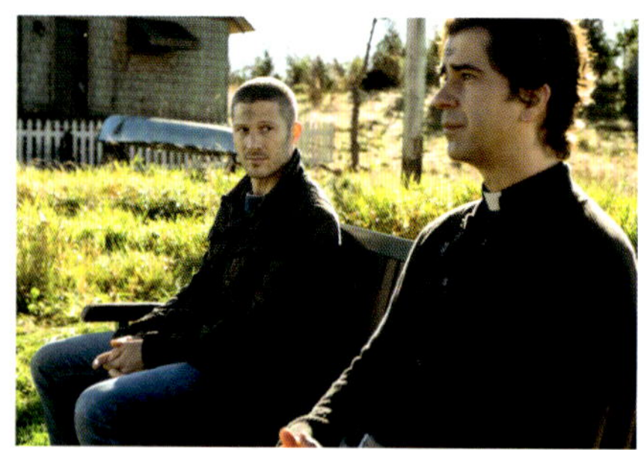

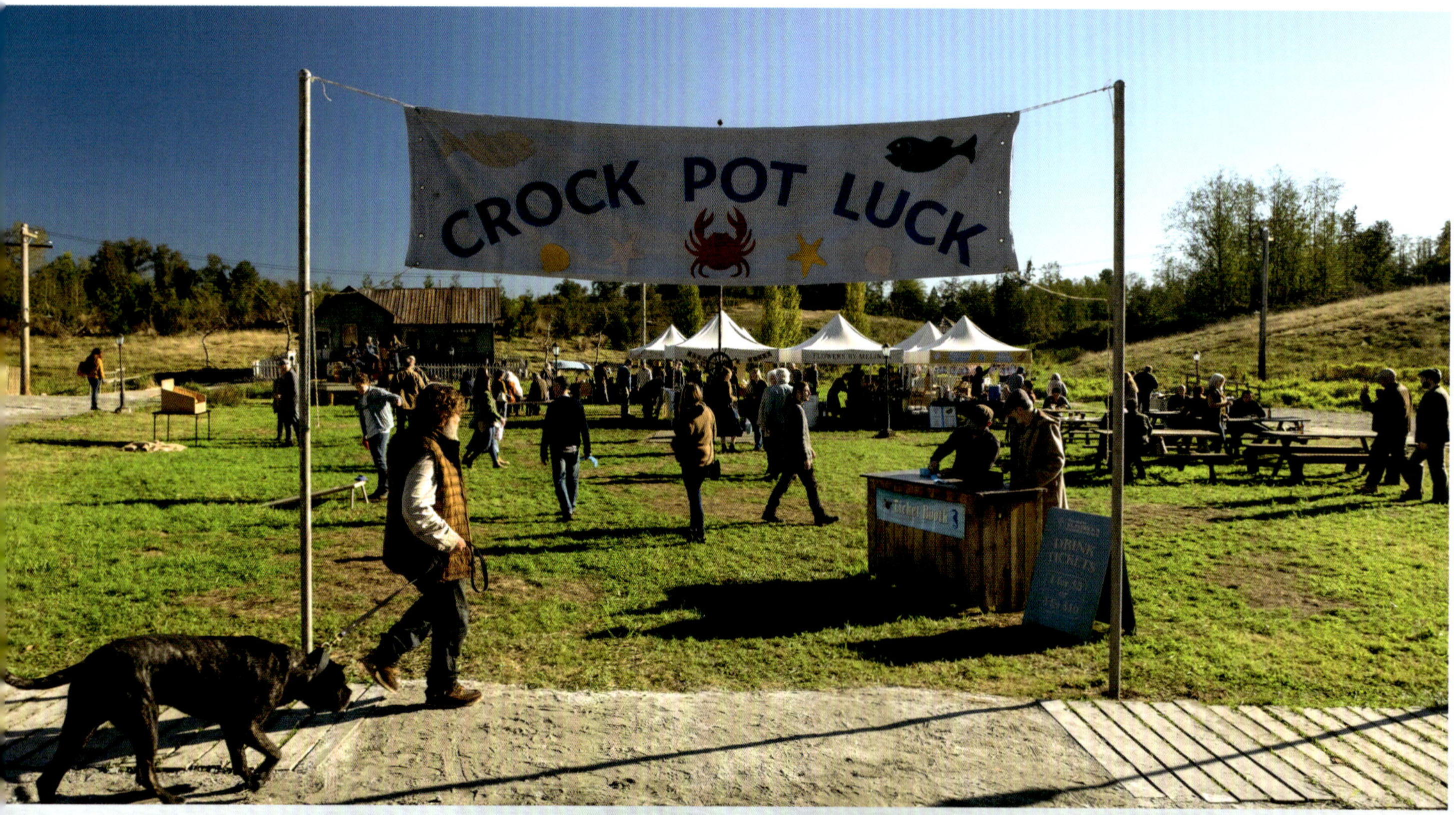

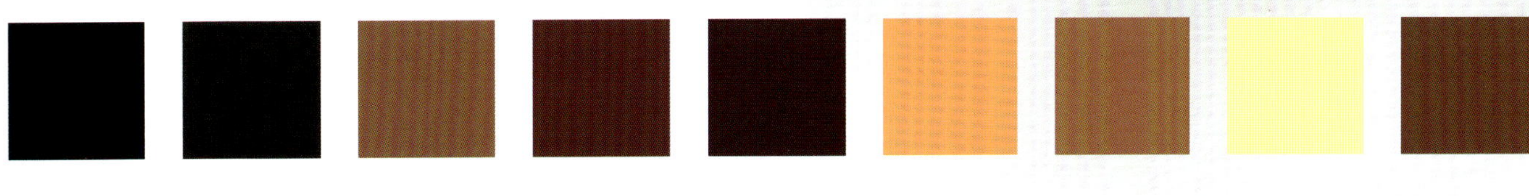

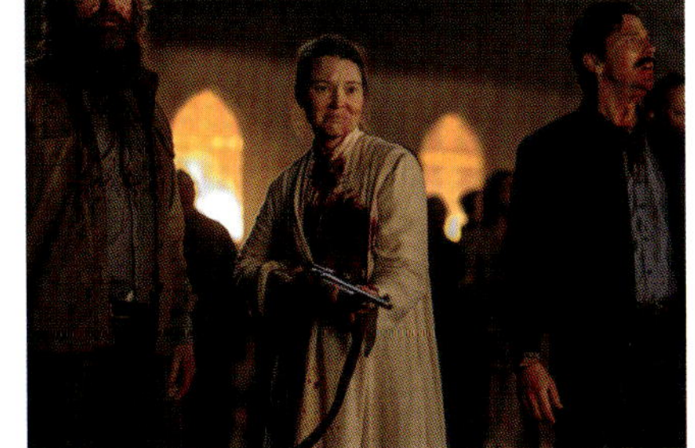

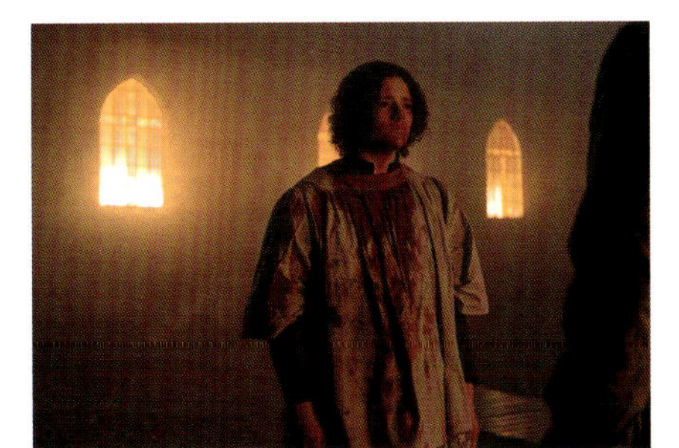

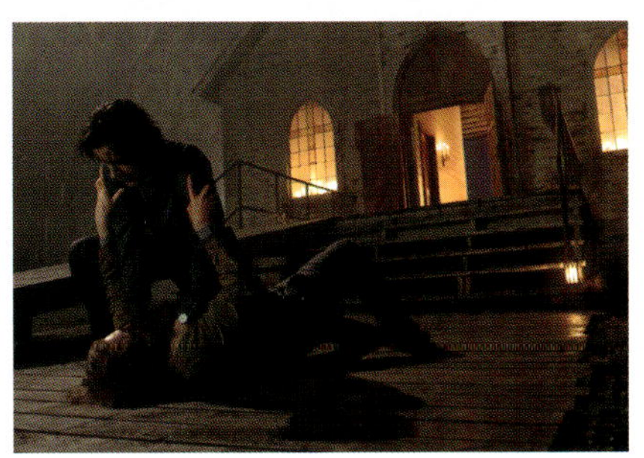

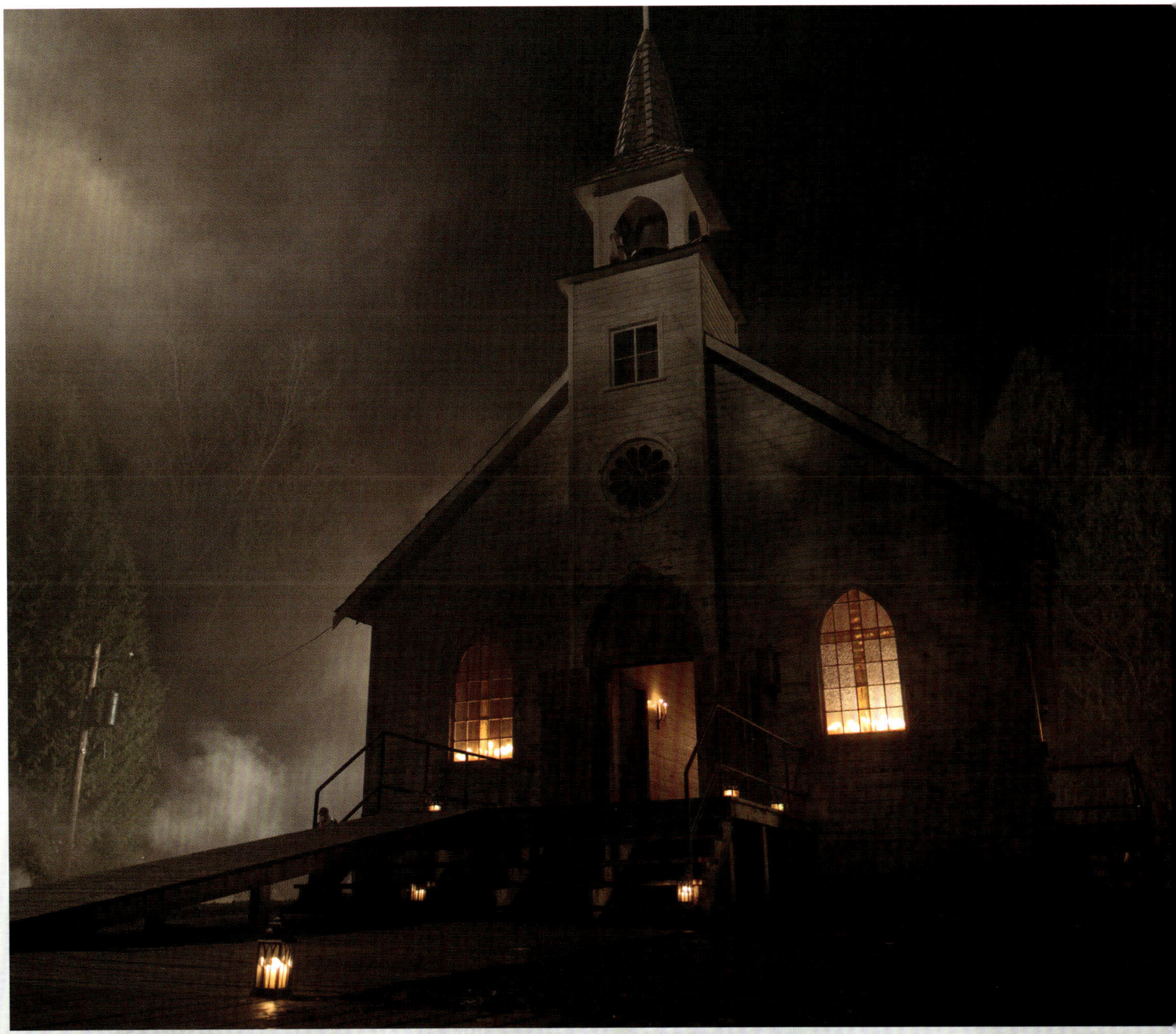

PRE-PRODUCTION

MAKING THE MIRACLE

Crockett is, Flanagan explains, "based on a real island called Tangier, Virginia. It seemed like a perfect tiny slice of America where we could explore this battle between faith and fanaticism."

However, the series wound up being set off the Pacific Northwest coast, and wasn't shot on an island. It was easier, physically and financially, Macy observes, to make parts of the British Columbia mainland look like an island. "When you're building a world, you can be judicious about what you show, and create the illusion that you're wherever you'd like. Mike and I are big believers that there are creative solutions to financial problems."

Flanagan agrees. "There are changes that come once you get into the realities of production. I try to be as specific as I can in the writing, but [cinematographer] Mike Fimognari and I did our shot list once we knew what the locations would allow."

Sets for Crockett Island were constructed outside Vancouver. "We were able to build the main part of the town on this wonderful farm in Langley," says Macy. "The coastal part we did in Steveston."

Production designer Steven Arnold's team constructed all of Crockett. Arnold relates, "We put in the roads, telephone poles, wires, drainage system, all the structures." Arnold draws his designs, interior and exterior, with pencil and paper. He then gives these to the set designers, "and they do the drafting for construction work, which is computer-drawn."

All designs incorporate room for production equipment, as well as on-camera illumination that's a plausible source for Fimognari's actual lighting. "I always design lighting into sets," Arnold explains, "a floor lamp, or an end table lamp."

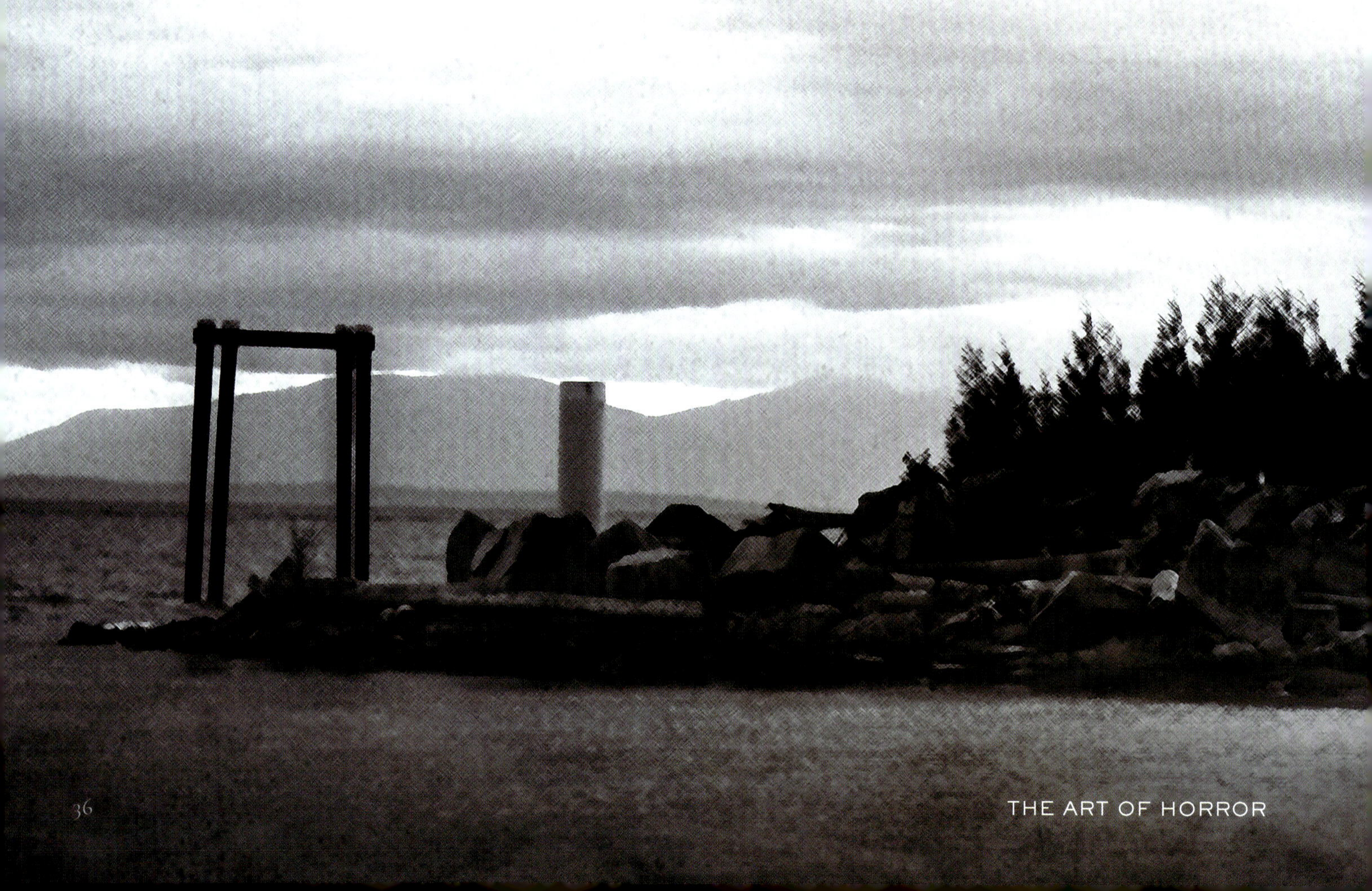

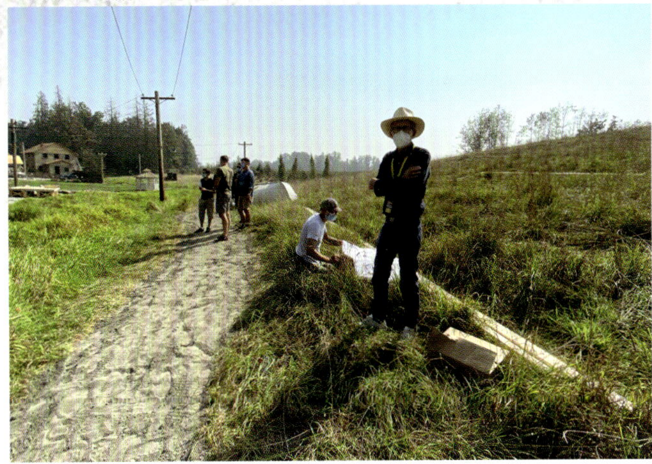

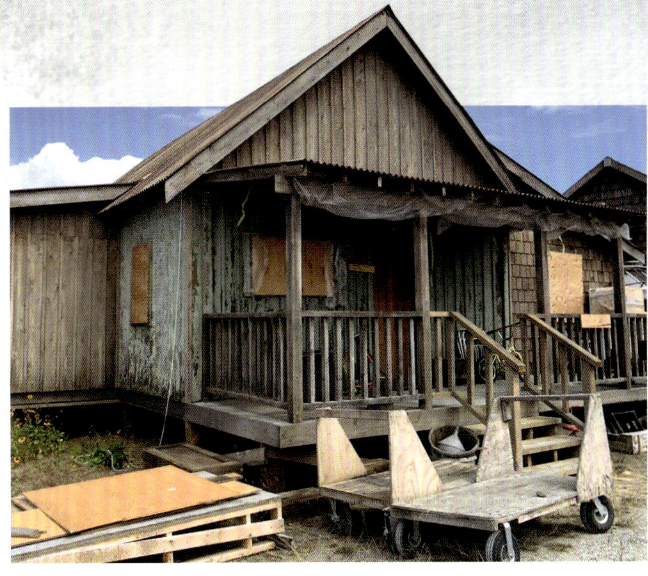

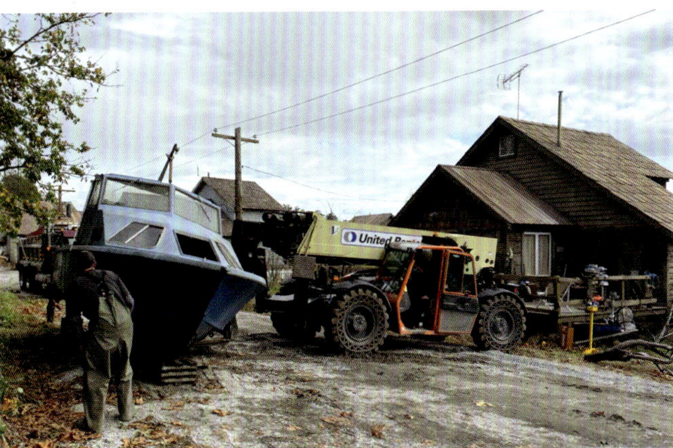

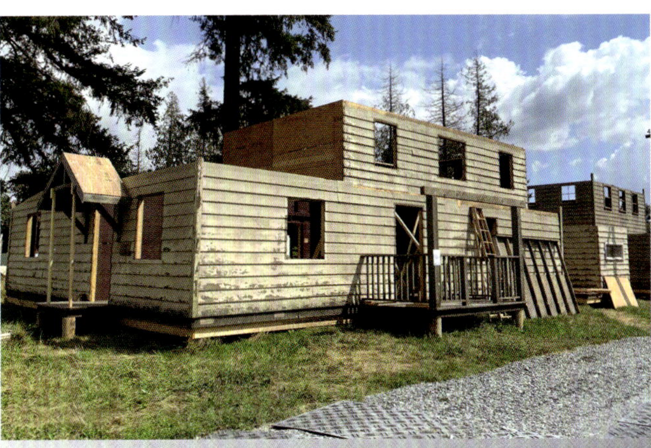

TOP/ (clockwise from TOP LEFT) Steve Arnold and the production team dresses a Crockett dirt road; An old Crockett house under construction; Another building under construction; Islanders have out-of-commission boats by their homes.

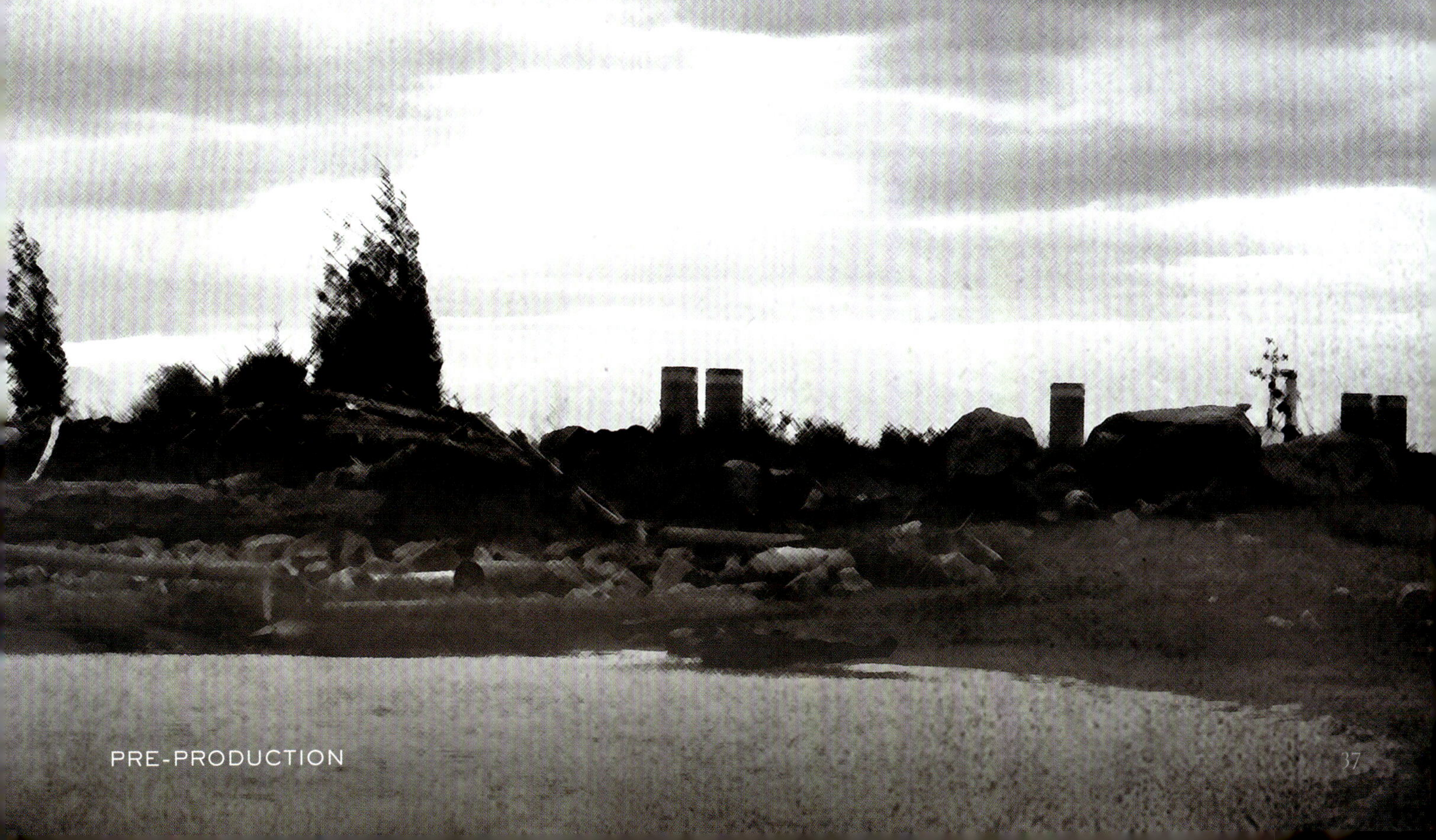

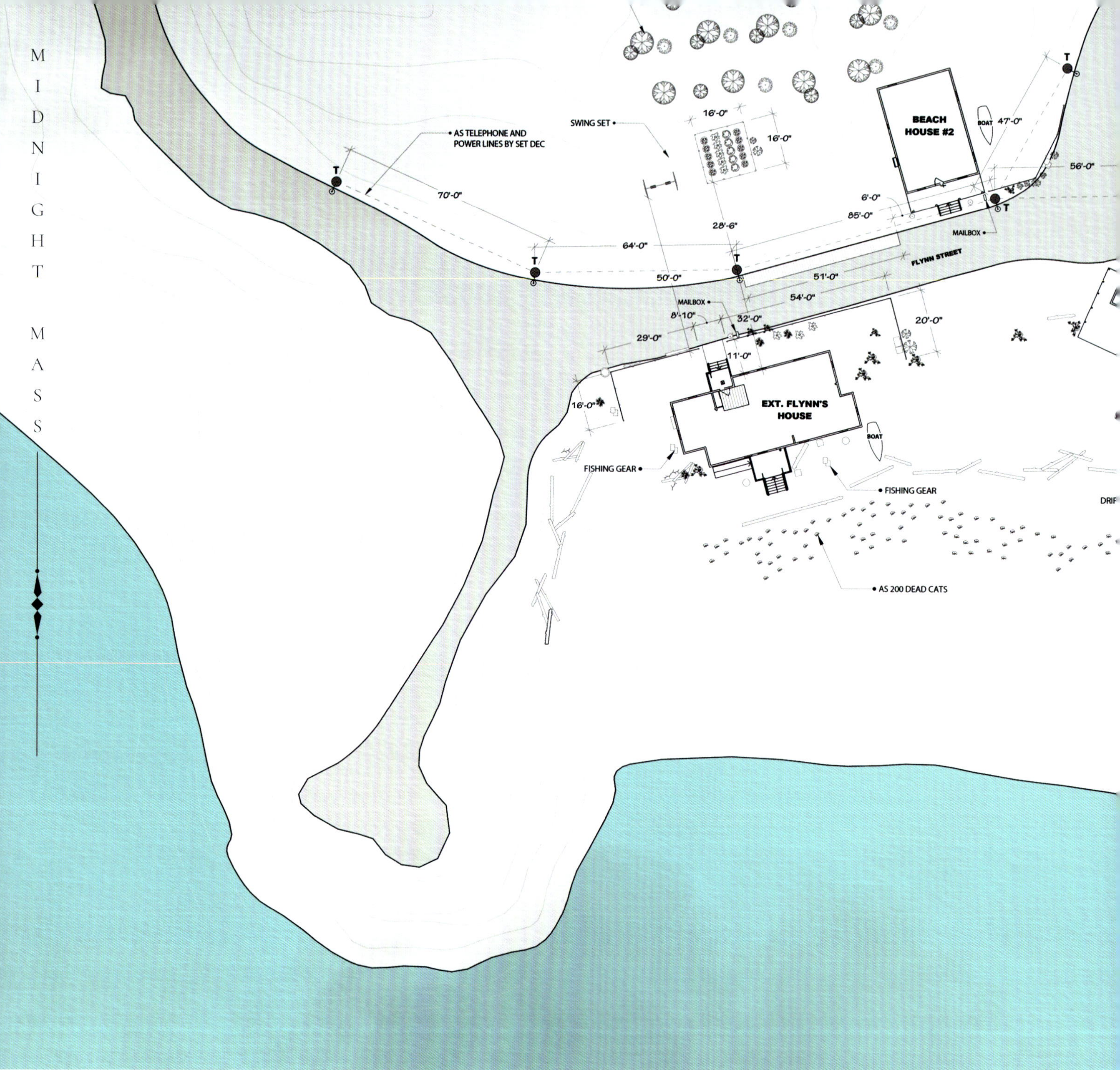

"WE BUILT EIGHT HOUSES ON THE BEACH AT THIS LOCATION. SO, WE'VE GOT ERIN'S HOUSE, WE'VE GOT FLYNN'S HOUSE, AND THEN WE HAVE MISCELLANEOUS OTHER TOWNSPEOPLE."

STEVE ARNOLD

TOP/ Production map of Anderline Farm sets, with size measurements.

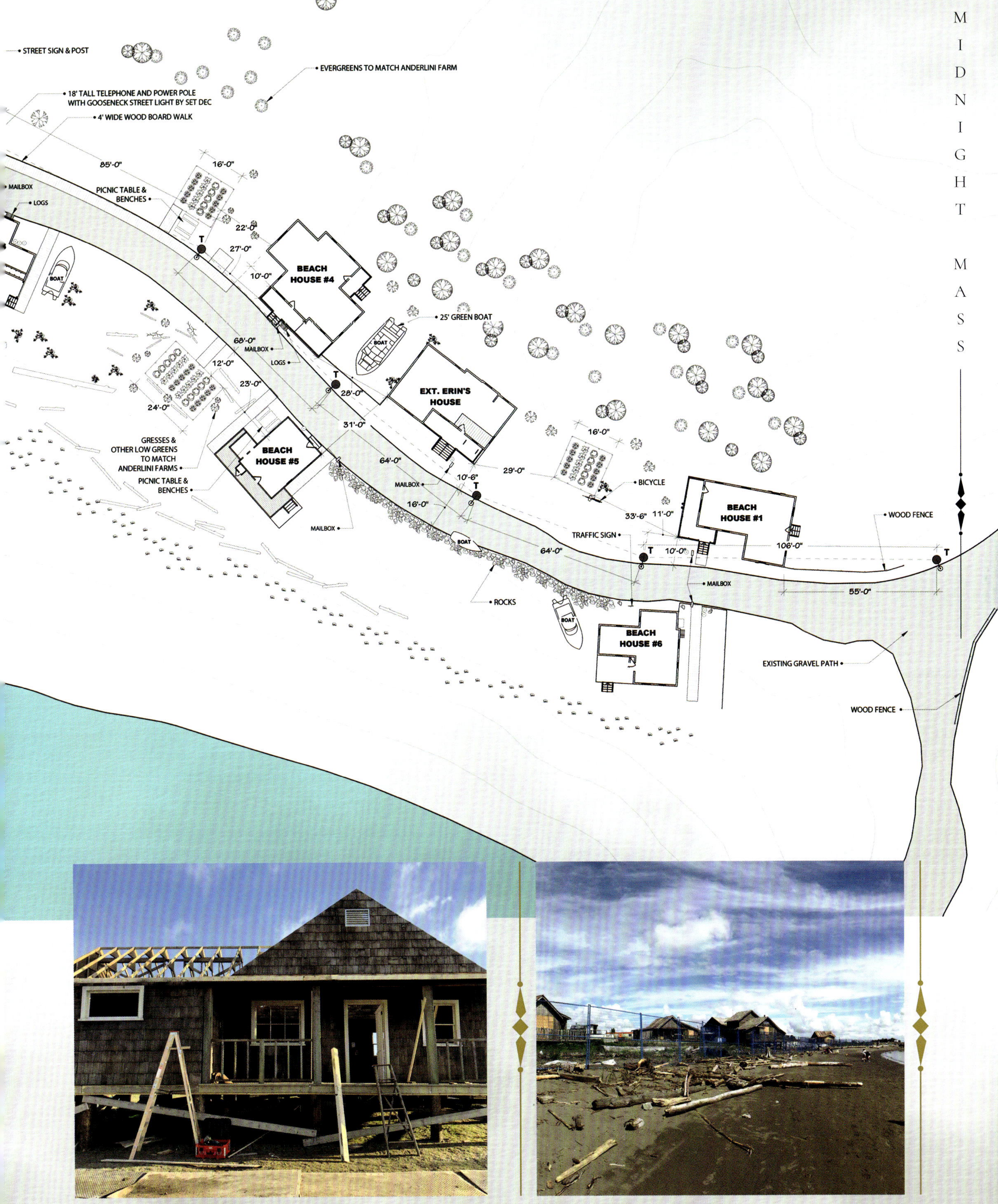
STREET SIGN & POST
EVERGREENS TO MATCH ANDERLINI FARM
18' TALL TELEPHONE AND POWER POLE WITH GOOSENECK STREET LIGHT BY SET DEC
4' WIDE WOOD BOARD WALK
85'-0"
16'-0"
MAILBOX
LOGS
PICNIC TABLE & BENCHES
22'-0"
27'-0"
10'-0"
BEACH HOUSE #4
BOAT
25' GREEN BOAT
68'-0"
MAILBOX
LOGS
12'-0"
23'-0"
24'-0"
28'-0"
EXT. ERIN'S HOUSE
31'-0"
GRESSES & OTHER LOW GREENS TO MATCH ANDERLINI FARMS
PICNIC TABLE & BENCHES
BEACH HOUSE #5
64'-0"
MAILBOX
10'-6"
29'-0"
16'-0"
16'-0"
BICYCLE
MAILBOX
BOAT
33'-6"
11'-0"
BEACH HOUSE #1
WOOD FENCE
TRAFFIC SIGN
64'-0"
10'-0"
106'-0"
MAILBOX
55'-0"
ROCKS
BOAT
BEACH HOUSE #6
EXISTING GRAVEL PATH
WOOD FENCE
T

Costume designer Terry Anderson previously worked with Flanagan and Macy on *Doctor Sleep*. His philosophy is, "I don't want to pull you out of the story, and have a costume moment. There is a modesty to this island, where a word like 'fancy' almost has a derogatory meaning. 'Why are you dressed up?' It's a lot of cotton, a lot of wool, a lot of canvas and wool raincoats."

"It's also a lot of clothing the audience never sees," adds Anderson. "Because it ended up being so cold, and we shot at night, we had silks, long underwear, heavy wool socks and other kinds of socks. Sometimes people would wear two layers of tights and shirts underneath their costumes to keep them warm. We'd also have small heating pads and hot water bottles. There is a lot that goes into just getting an actor to the set and getting them back from the set."

Those who drink the Angel's blood regain their youth. Flanagan decided to age up the actors at the beginning, then gradually return them to their normal look. Not a fan of digital de-aging, Flanagan also opted for practical appliances.

Macy hired Justin Raleigh and Fractured FX to do the special

THIS PAGE/ (TOP) A SPFX makeup artist working on part of the Angel's wing. (BOTTOM LEFT) Riley reacts to being attacked. (BOTTOM RIGHT) A SPFX makeup artist working on a dog sculpture.

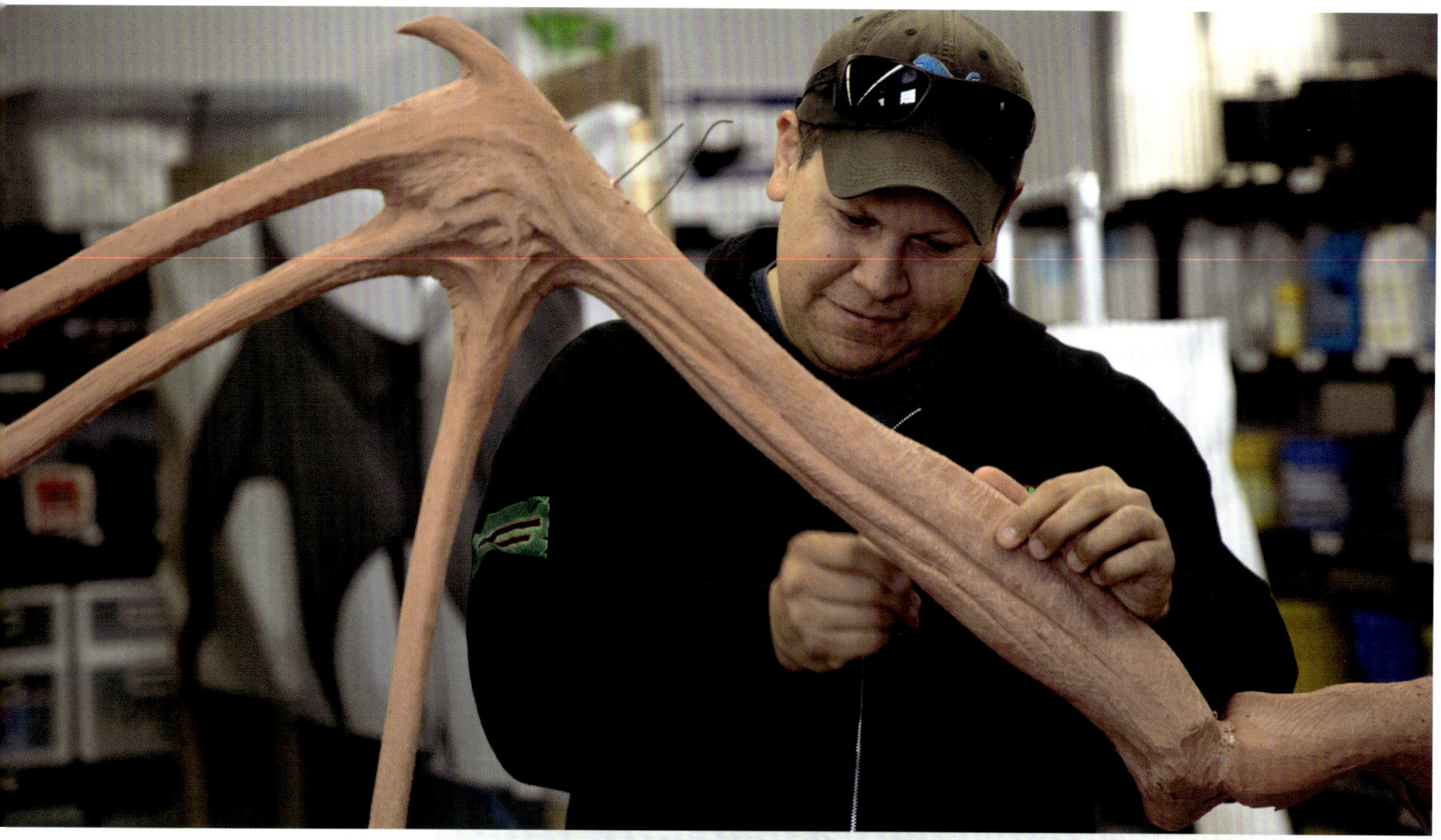

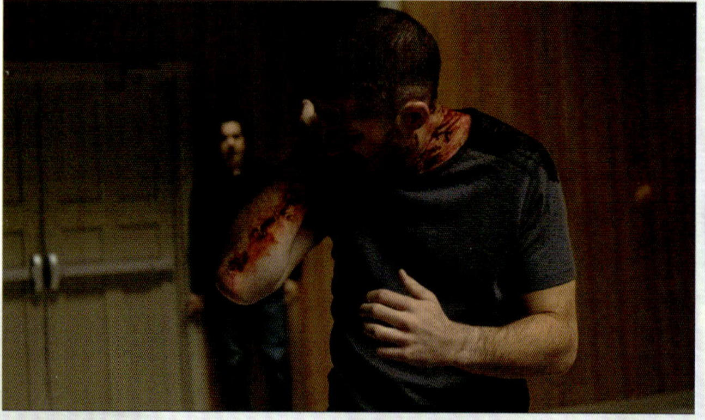

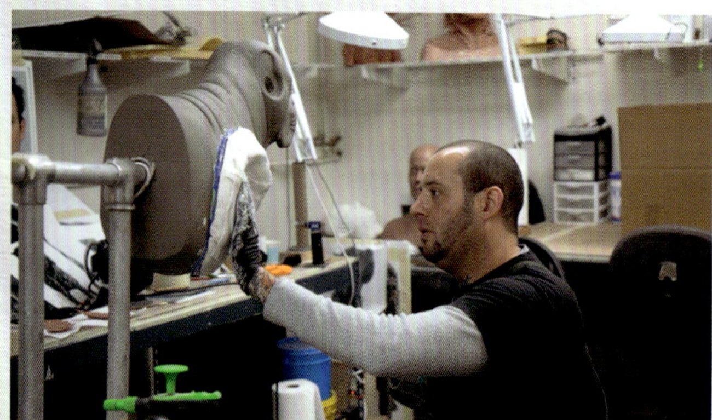

effects makeup, having previously worked with them on the film *Eli*. Raleigh says he began design work early, "because of the amount of hyper-realistic prosthetics."

COVID-19 restrictions meant that Raleigh couldn't be in Vancouver during production, so he designed at Fractured FX's Los Angeles base and brought in Tony "Ozzy" Alvarez as on-set makeup FX department head. Alvarez's team included Kelsey Berk, Harlow MacFarlane and Felix Fox.

Midnight Mass was block-shot, meaning that all sequences on a specific set are shot before moving on to the next set, a challenge when actors must be aged and de-aged. Alvarez reports, "We had multiple meetings about, 'Guys, we physically can't do this day, because we can't go from a Stage 3, which might be an hour-and-a-half makeup for both actors, another half-hour cleanup, and then put back on another [makeup] stage."

Alvarez explains, "Stage 1 is the actors' normal look. Stage 2 is stretch and stipple [stretching the skin, stippling on latex, having it dry, and powdering it to create a wrinkly texture]. Stage 3 is prosthetics."

THIS PAGE/ (TOP) Boisclair having the Angel wings attached, with help from the puppeteers. (BOTTOM LEFT) SPFX makeup artist Kelsey Berk touching up Boisclair's Angel makeup. (BOTTOM RIGHT) Alex Essoe having her "aged" makeup applied.

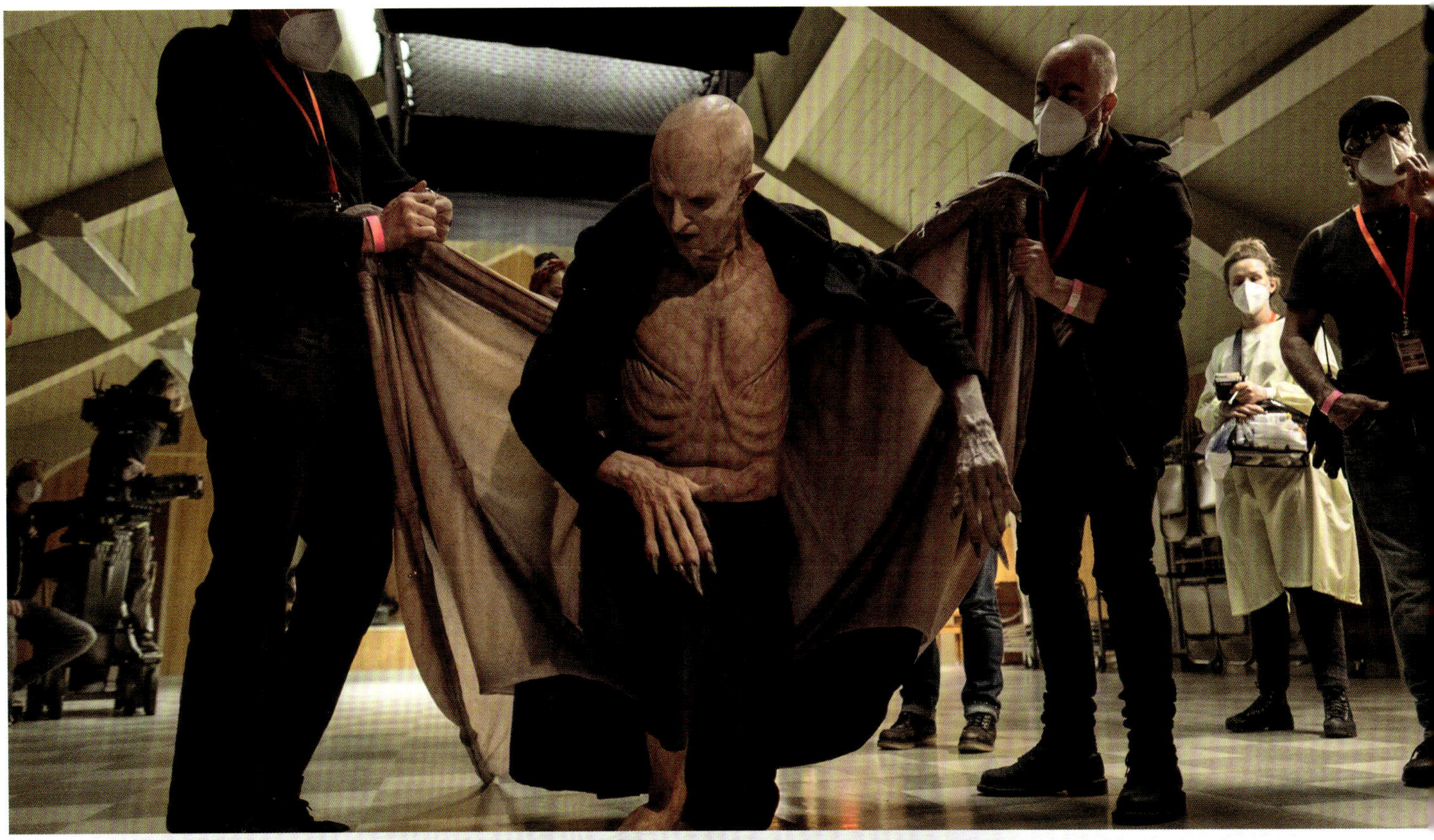

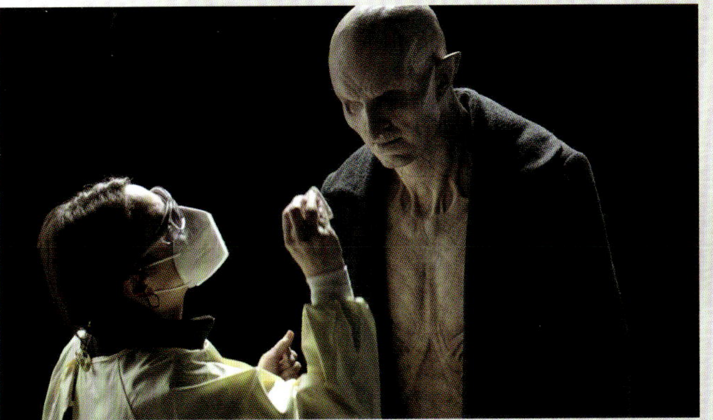

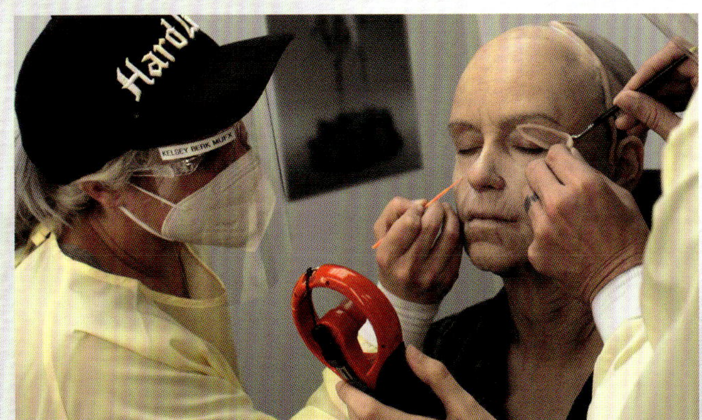

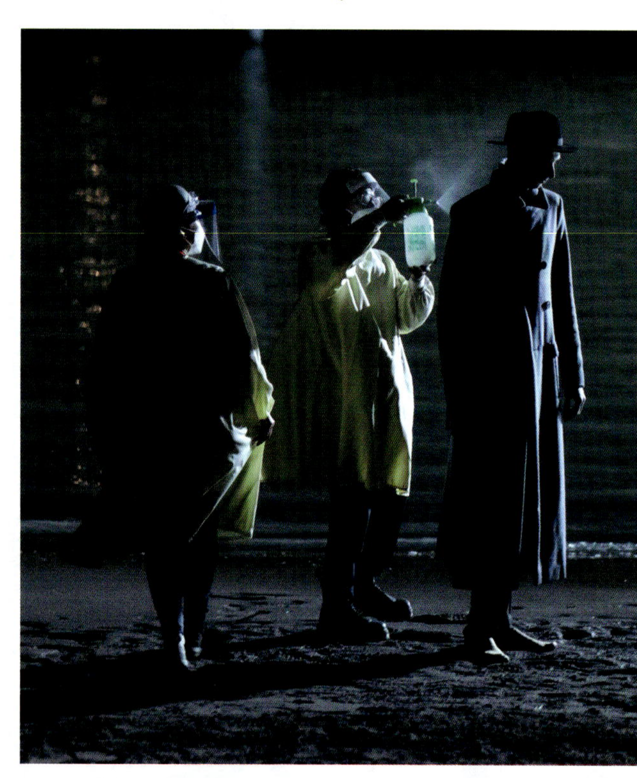

The Newton Brothers, Andy Grush and Taylor Stewart, have composed for many Flanagan and/or Macy projects, often beginning discussions with Flanagan before scripts are even completed. With *Midnight Mass*, Flanagan had selected hymns to go with particular scenes. If a hymn couldn't be used due to rights issues, Flanagan, the composers, and music supervisors Justine von Winterfeldt and Toko Nagata found alternatives.

Grush says, "The instrumentation so far is all organ and an a cappella choir. In church, we have everyone singing naturally. There are scenes where an a cappella choir sings traditional hymns with four parts."

Stewart says he stayed in the Los Angeles studio while Grush was on set. "They needed one person to perform as organist and lead the choir, and also be there to help Mike. So, I helped prepare stuff from here."

Macy relates, "We were meant to go straight from *The Haunting of Bly Manor*, which wrapped February 24, 2020, to *Midnight Mass*, which was scheduled to start [shooting] March 16, 2020. Then Netflix pushed pause on all of their North America productions on Friday, March 13."

THIS PAGE/ (TOP) Final touches being applied to the Angel's apparel. (BOTTOM) Robert Longstreet removes PPE before a take.

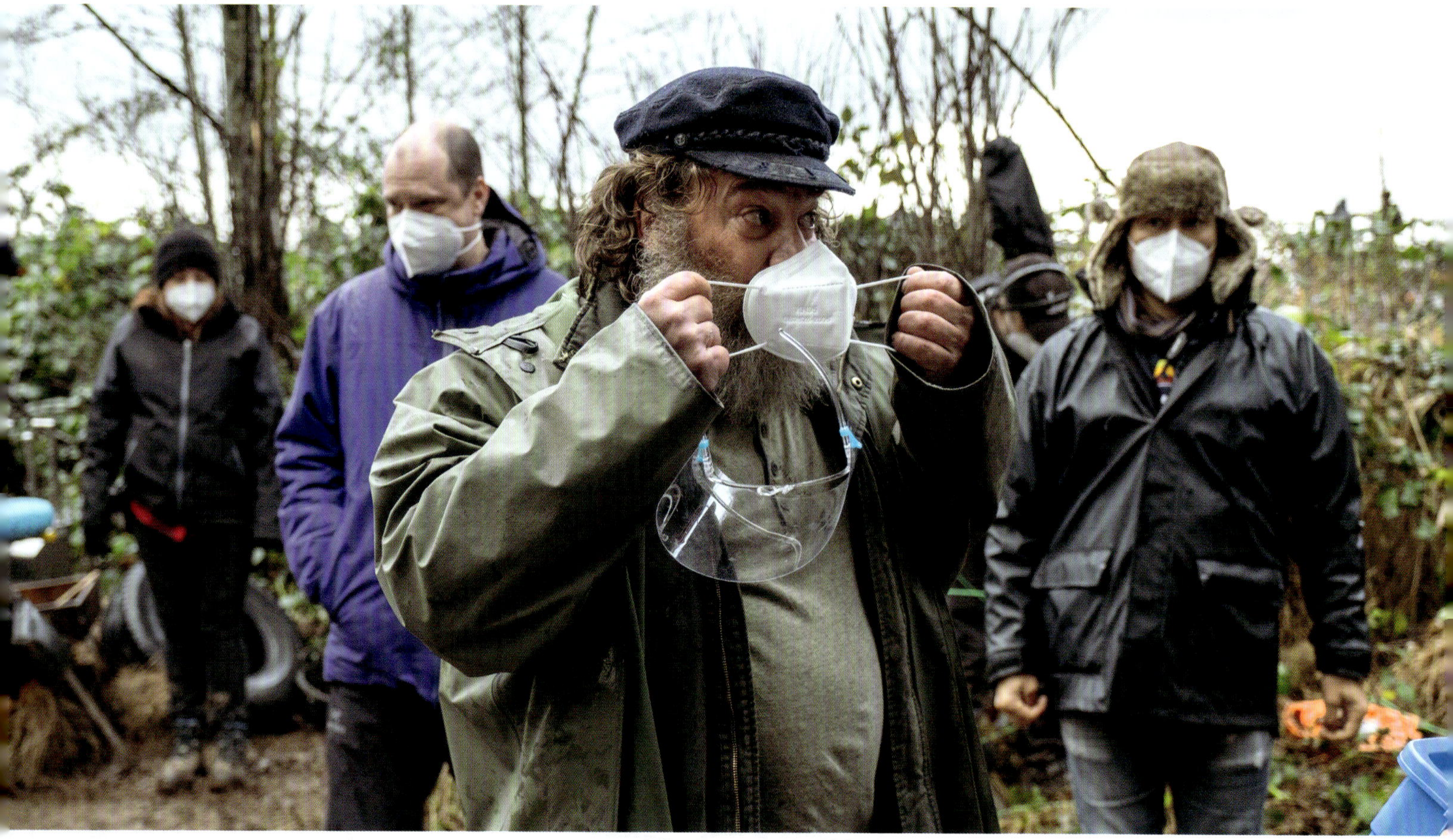

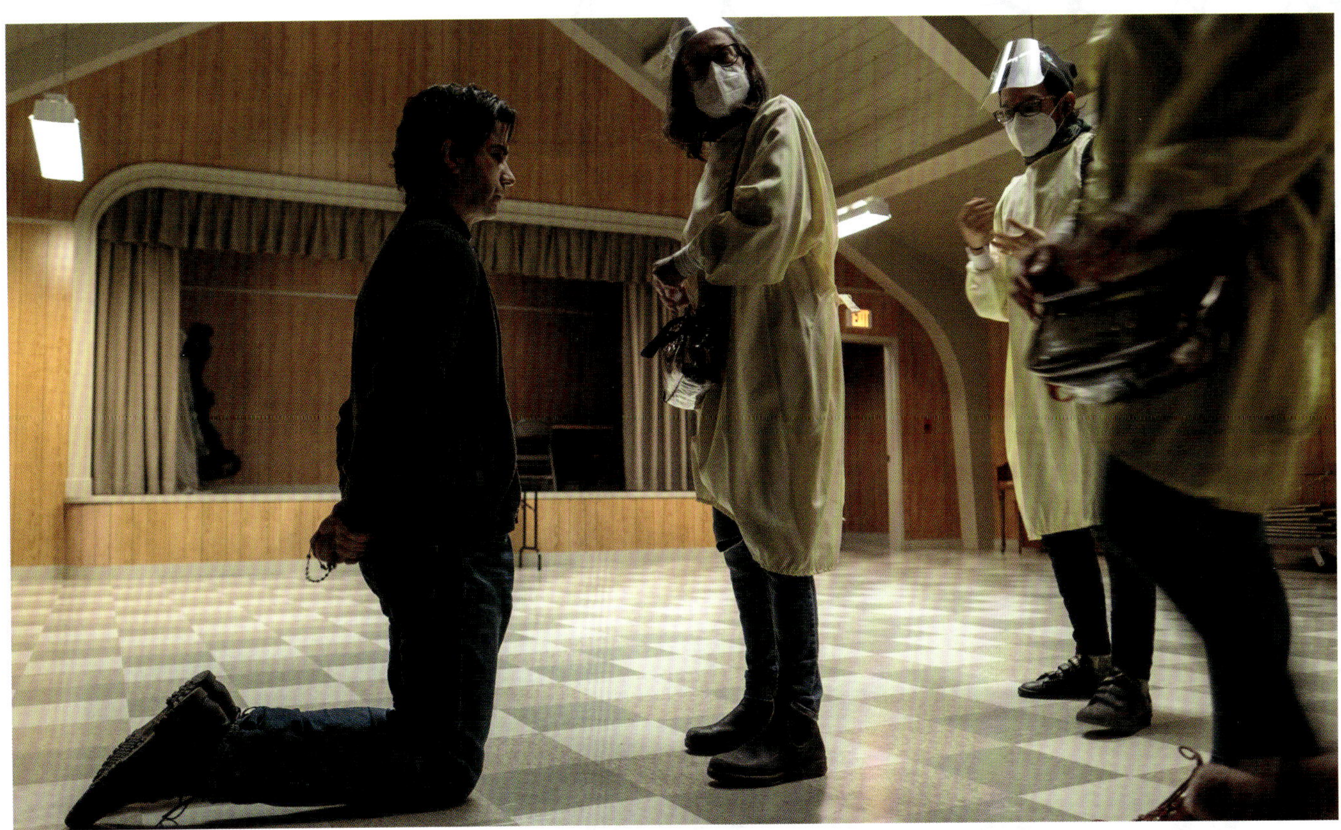

TOP/ Hamish Linklater kneels on the rec center set and Krista Young, head makeup artist, examines.

"COVID-19 hit like a freight train," says Flanagan. "We left our sets standing on the beach. I flew out [of Vancouver to Los Angeles], looked out the window of the plane, and I could see our little town from the air, just abandoned."

There was an upside to the pause, Macy relates. "The exteriors that our wonderful art department built had time to grow up. The flora grew around the houses of the town. The running joke was that we had half a million dollars of free greens work [on-set gardening]. Our friends in Vancouver and Langley were kind enough to let us leave the things up, which wasn't a given."

COVID-19 also inspired story changes, says Flanagan, who wrote in an oil spill to explain why the island was so depopulated. "We wanted to limit how many scenes required extras, so we made the change to say that only roughly a hundred souls were left on Crockett, which also added this layer of sadness, that this community had been through a disaster."

Beyond that, Flanagan says, COVID-19 meant, "We had to be incredibly precise and prepared. I think I've never had as phenomenal a crew as I had on this show. We had amazing problem-solvers."

COVID-19 Compliance departments were created for all film and TV productions. On *Midnight Mass*, this was run by Jenna Irvine, previously an assistant director. It was new territory for everyone concerned. Dr. Adam Lund and his team, plus a health and safety supervisor, provided medical expertise, and Irvine made sure safety protocols were rigorously followed.

Everyone was on a testing schedule, Irvine explains. "Anybody in the performance zone was tested weekly. The cast were tested twice-weekly." Everyone entering the set had to go through a check-in process, including digital temperature-taking. "If for any reason somebody said they were symptomatic, they were isolated, and then put in touch with our Health and Safety supervisor."

Other protocols, Irvine continues, included "wearing all of your PPE gear, all the time. If you were going to be in a red zone, near the cast, you'd wear a KN-95 mask and a face shield. We had a twenty-four-hour action clean team sanitizing everything. Morgan Beggs, our first assistant director, was excellent about keeping everybody safe."

One other difference COVID-19 caused, says Flanagan, "was that the cast didn't interact with the crew very much. We just looked like eyeballs over masks to them."

Finally, says Macy, "We started shooting August 17, had eighty-three days uninterrupted, so that was good."

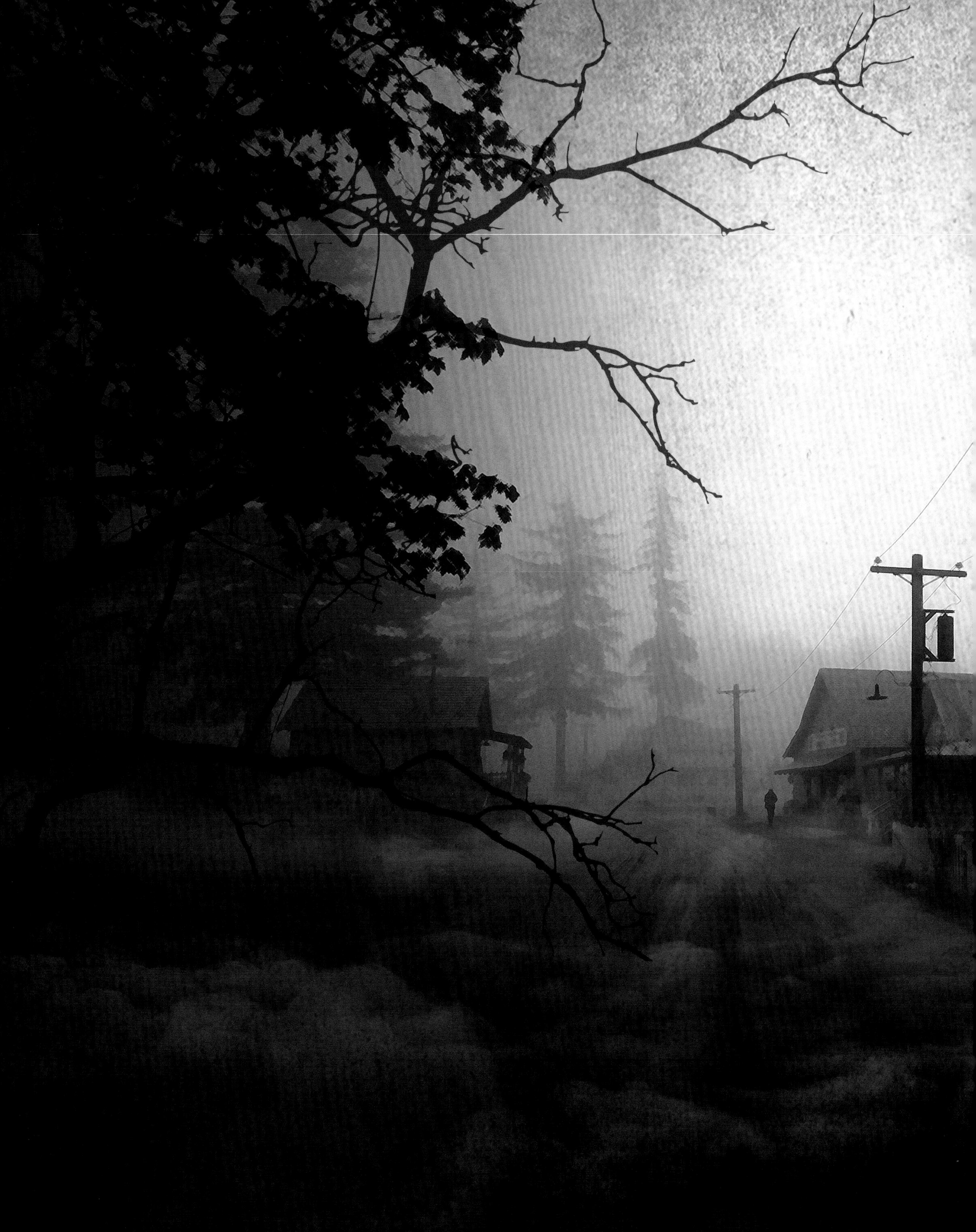

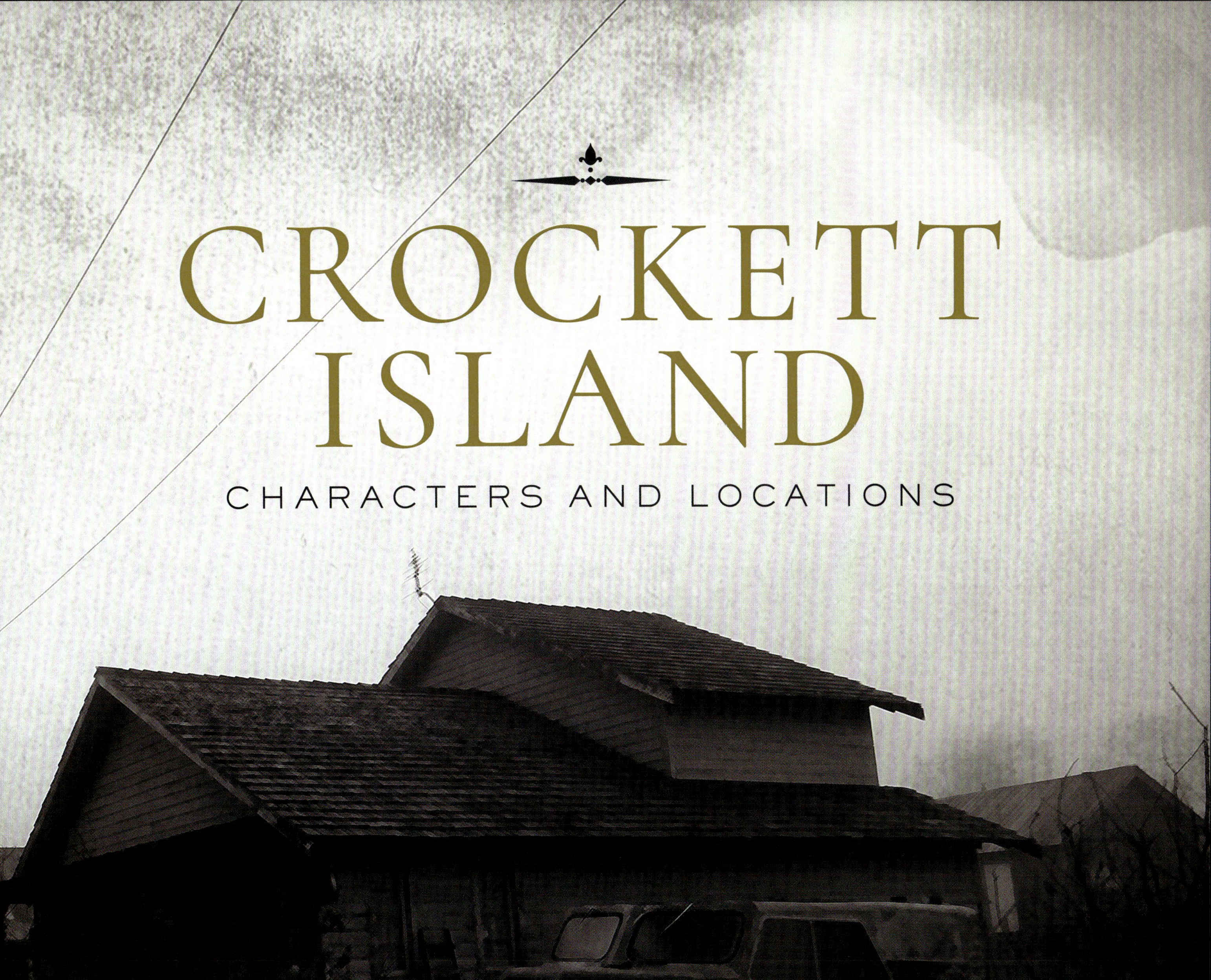
CROCKETT
ISLAND
CHARACTERS AND LOCATIONS

CROCKETT ISLAND

A QUIET LITTLE TOWN

Flanagan says, "I was blown away by what the art department accomplished in designing Crockett. I did not expect it to be so lived-in and authentic. The first time I walked through the town, which took a while, it was a large piece of land, with all of these buildings. I would look in the mailboxes, sit on the porches. The amount of detail and love that Steve Arnold and his team put into it, it was a very real place."

"Flanagan and Trevor built this whole world," says Annabeth Gish. "It wasn't just a set. Yes, we had interiors and we had exteriors and we had stages, but we had this real location out in Langley where we would go, and it was like a real freaking town. The art direction, the production design, the attention to detail, the sense of place was so palpable."

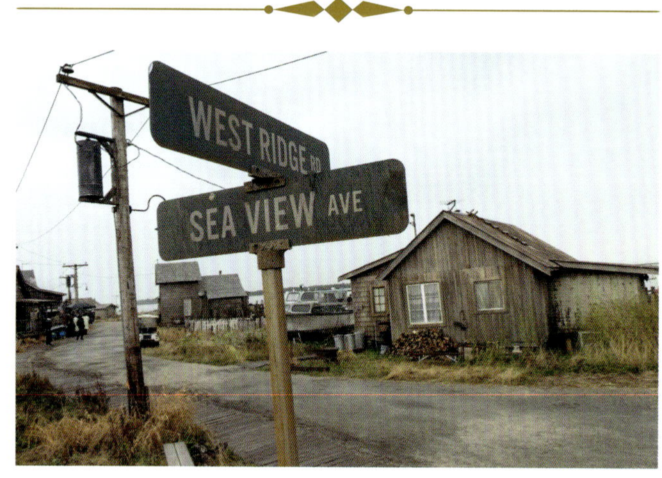

BOTTOM/ Pre-viz concept art of the streets of Crockett.

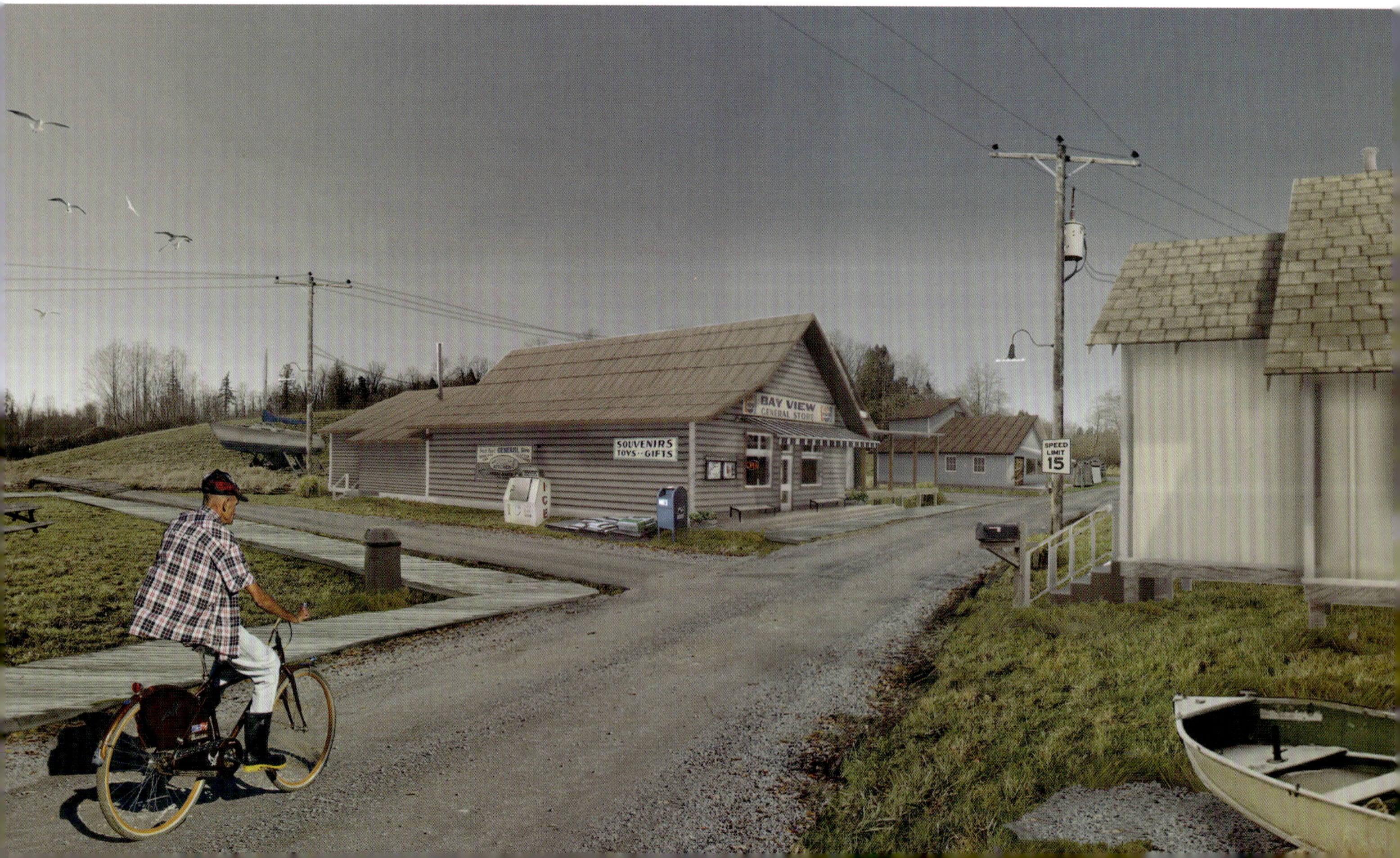

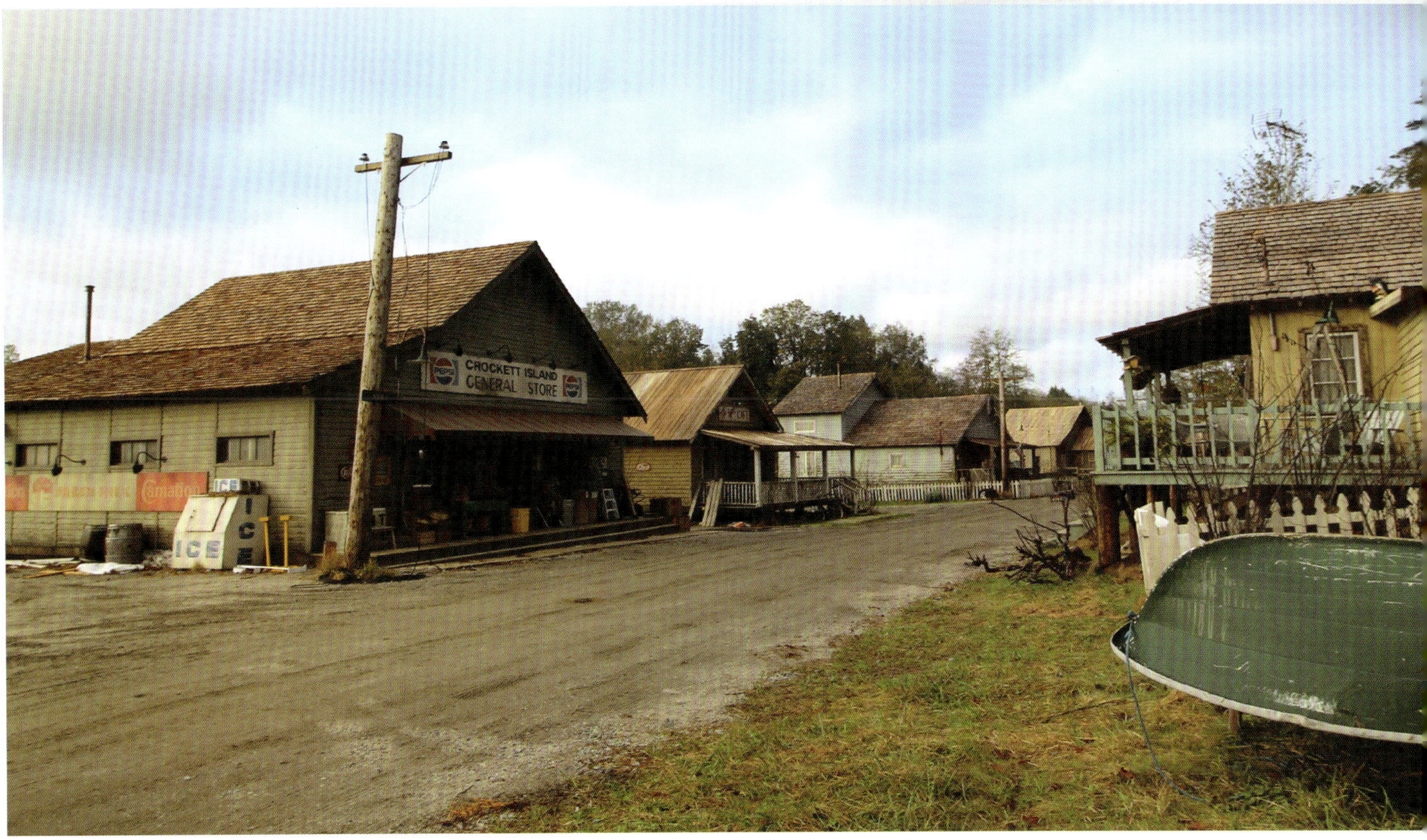

TOP/ This shot of the finished set of Crockett is almost an exact replica of the pre-viz concept art.

Despite its small population, Crockett Island is also designed as wheelchair-friendly. "Everywhere Leeza had to be, you had external ramps," says Arnold.

Crockett has a marsh called the Uppards. "It was part of the park at Steveston," Arnold relates. "It's overgrown, people have built little campfires, it was a little more remote. We used several areas of beach near there, for them getting in the rowboat, or the canoe."

Some of the rowboat and canoe scenes were shot in a soundstage, against a blue screen. Arnold explains this was because they needed a CGI sunrise. "Shooting that on location would be too hard to do in real time."

In the soundstage, little trenches of water were placed on either side of the raised boat, so that the oars would have resistance. Zach Gilford recalls, "There's a grip laying on the floor, every so often tapping the dish of water, so there's a ripple effect, for the lighting, and I'm just pretending to row."

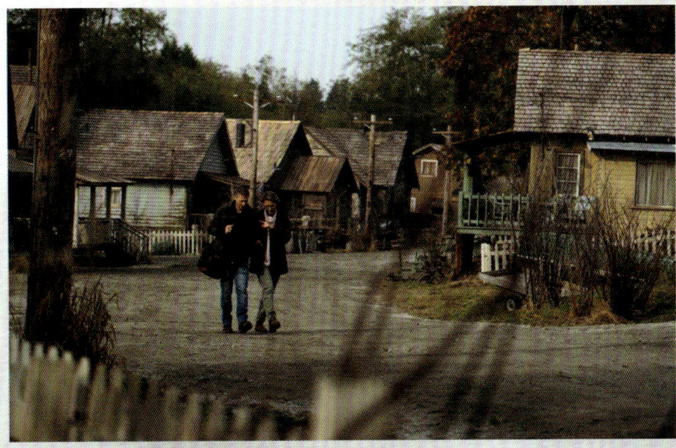

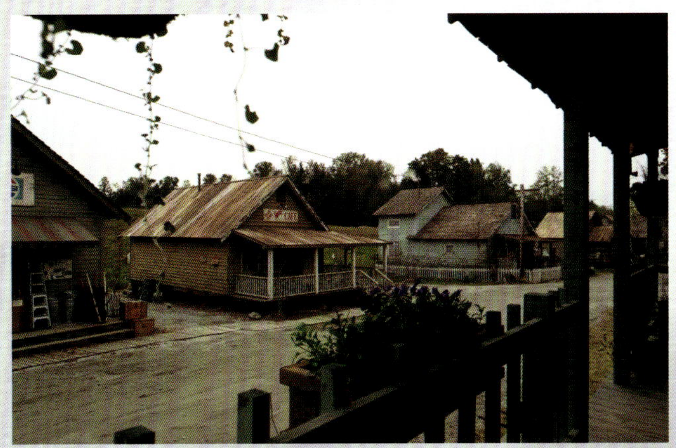

Igby Rigney laughs, "The canoe definitely gave me the most trouble. On the stage, it was perfectly fine. We did little wires to simulate the tension of rowing. Later, when we were on location in Steveston, it was really late at night, we boarded the canoe, and I tried to hop in, but the bottom of the canoe got stuck on the sediment beneath the water, and my momentum propelled me forward, and I whacked my head."

There are bridges throughout the island, but Arnold says they built a special one for the final scene with Father Paul, Mildred, and Sarah. "This one had a slight arch to it, and it was wooden, made of branches."

Flanagan recalls, "When Samantha Sloyan and Matt Biedel are perched over Kristin Lehman, drinking her blood, and they look up to find that Erin's house is engulfed in flames, that night there was a horrible windstorm. The wind was so violent that it was knocking over equipment, our COVID-19 face shields were flying up into the air to just disappear into the darkness. We pulled up one of the eighteen-wheel equipment trucks and parked it laterally in front of the actors to block the wind. We had the house burning, and embers were blowing, and Sam was sitting there in this wind, giving a speech about Revelation and the end of the world. I'd never felt that kind of energy on set before, where it didn't feel like a scene."

BOTTOM/ Crockett being built.

BOTTOM/ The finished set of Crockett.

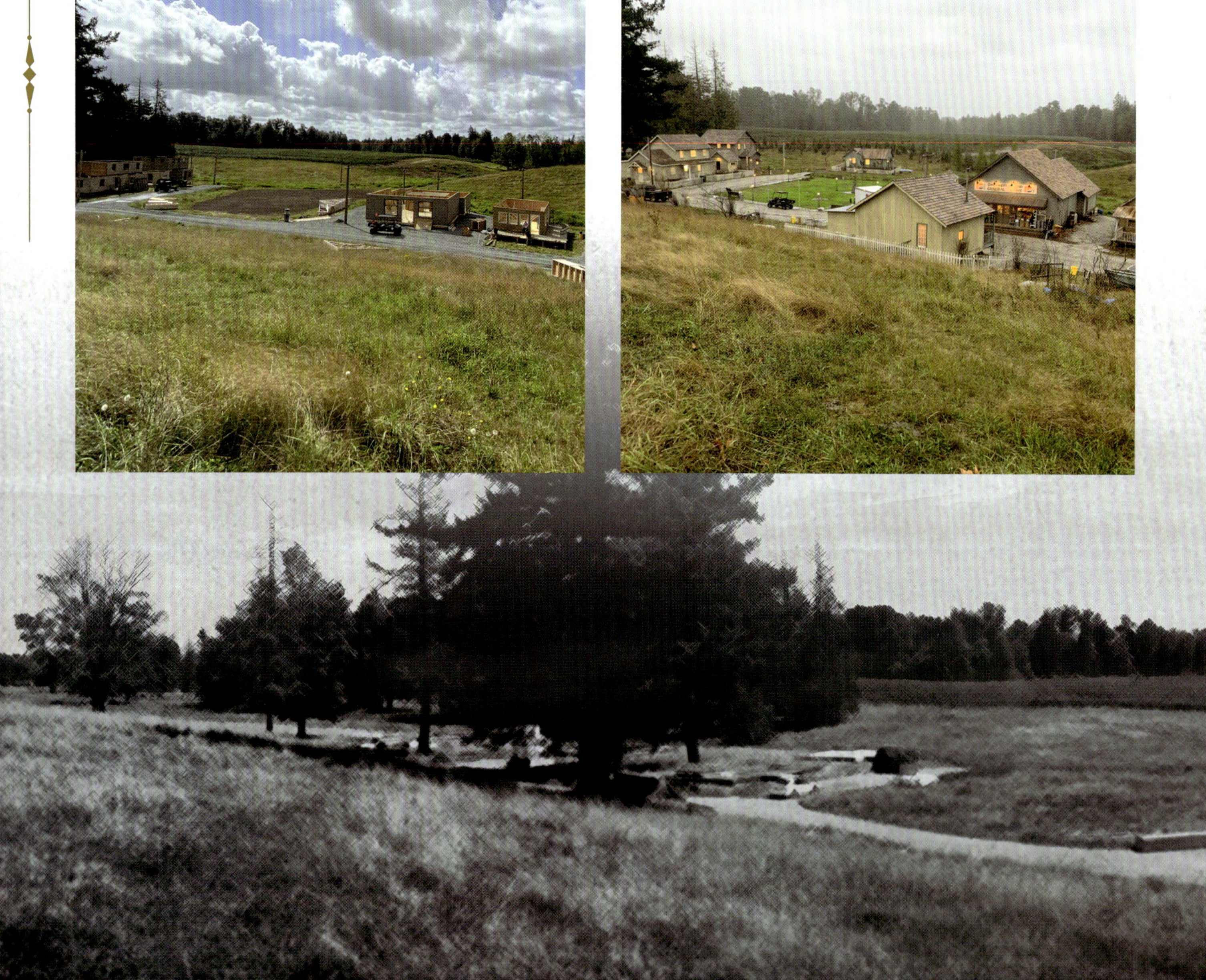

BEACH HOUSES

Arnold says he found inspiration for the Crockett beach houses in Finn Slough, near Vancouver. "It's a little waterway. I did a lot of research on that. There are ten to twelve shacks, or shanties, made up of found bits and pieces, windows from other structures, all kinds of salvaged things that people have gathered together. We took a bunch of pictures. It's a very patchwork hodgepodge of things. I liked the feel of that. [Crockett] is supposed to be very bleak, very remote, desolate, downtrodden, blue collar. We wanted it to have some history to it, some age to it. Finn Slough had been around for probably fifty, maybe seventy-five years. You couldn't tell how old it was, but it wasn't new."

Production was given permission to build structures on the beach, which, Arnold notes, "is a pretty rare thing." They had to be careful with endangered plants and wildlife. "We had to petition to [be allowed] to remove a lot of the driftwood and beach logs. There was eelgrass, which is an endangered plant that is underwater at high tide, but when the tide is out, it's exposed."

Because it was a beach, "We couldn't dig, we couldn't put any poles in, so everything had to be done from the top down. We had these very large, concrete lock blocks. We were allowed to drop those, and then we cabled down the buildings to those, so they didn't blow away, because we did have a lot of wind and weather there."

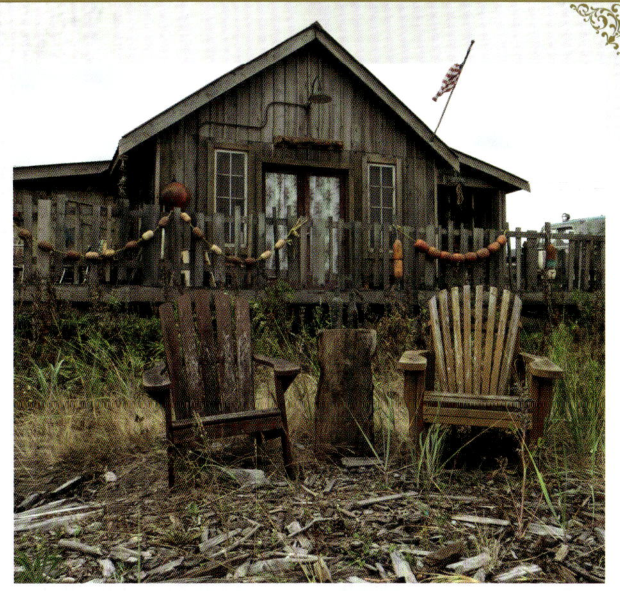

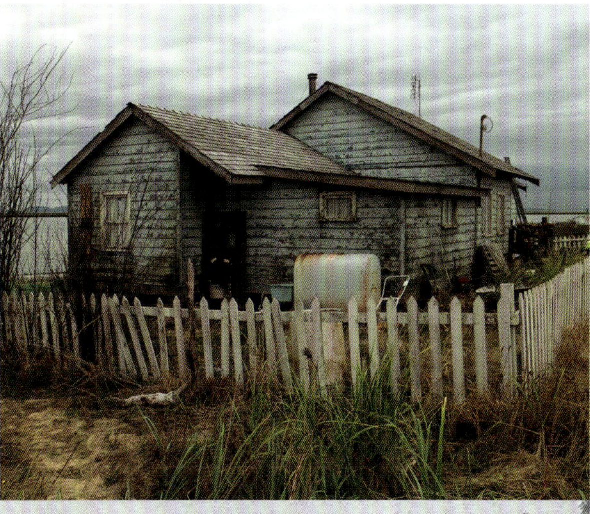

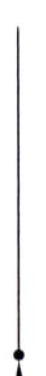

THE MYSTERY BEGINS

ANATOMY OF A SCENE

The first sign that something is seriously wrong on Crockett Island is a beach full of dead cats, drained by the Angel and washed up by the storm. No actual dead cats are involved. Instead, these are custom-made by Justin Raleigh's Fractured FX team.

Raleigh explains that the closeup "hero" cats were sculpted in detail, with "a small aluminum armature inside to give weight and proper anatomical function of the joints. We did the skin in foam rubber. The interior has a beanbag-type material, so on its side, it compresses, it has some gravity. The heads had a fiberglass core, with teeth, a palate, and tongue, and separate eyes."

The background cats were only sculpted on whichever side faced the camera. Raleigh says that these "were basically latex and polyurethane foam."

Fur was purchased from taxidermy shops that cater to the film industry. The cats were then "pelted, flocked, hand-punched, and painted." For the orange cat, "We started with a beige base fur, and then all of the orange and the pattern is hand-airbrushed."

On set, makeup FX department head Tony "Ozzy" Alvarez says he and his team "pulled out fur, cut into [the neck] and used different materials to make it look like a wound, paint it, and add blood."

What is the intended emotional impact? Macy laughs. "You're talking to the most squeamish person at Intrepid about killing animals. Nobody likes to see cats or dogs killed, but the cats drive the mystery. So, I'd like to think we did it as was necessary and effective."

BOTTOM/ Note throat wound. Alvarez: "Mike wanted bite marks on the cats."

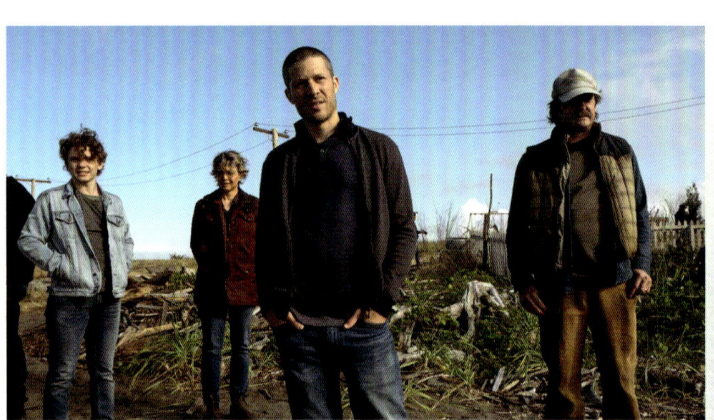

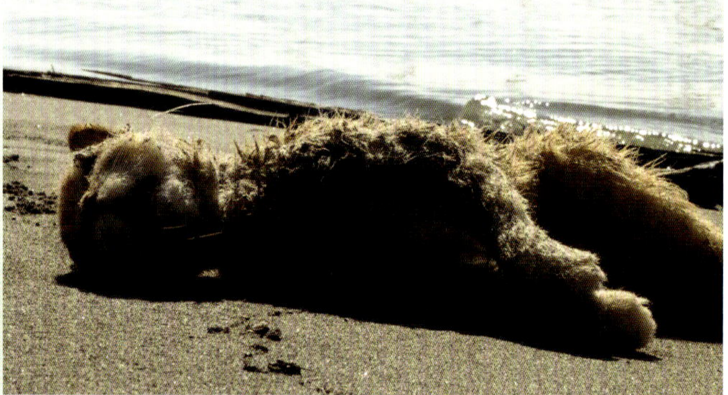

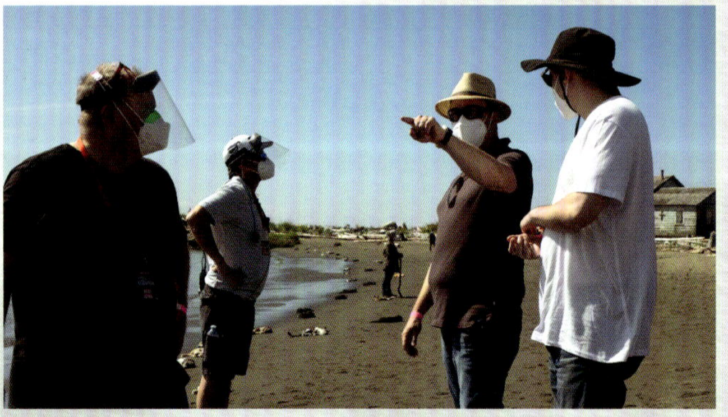

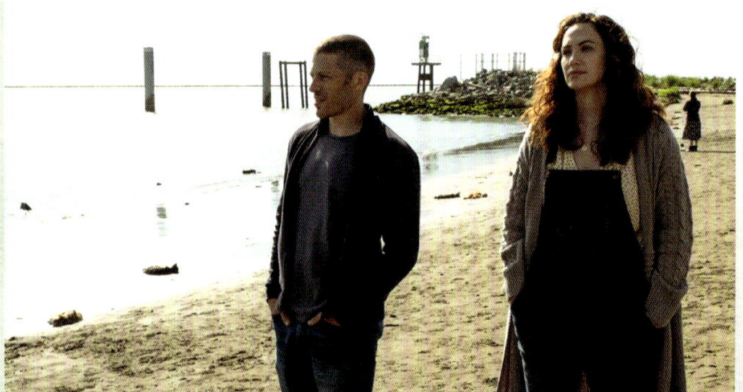

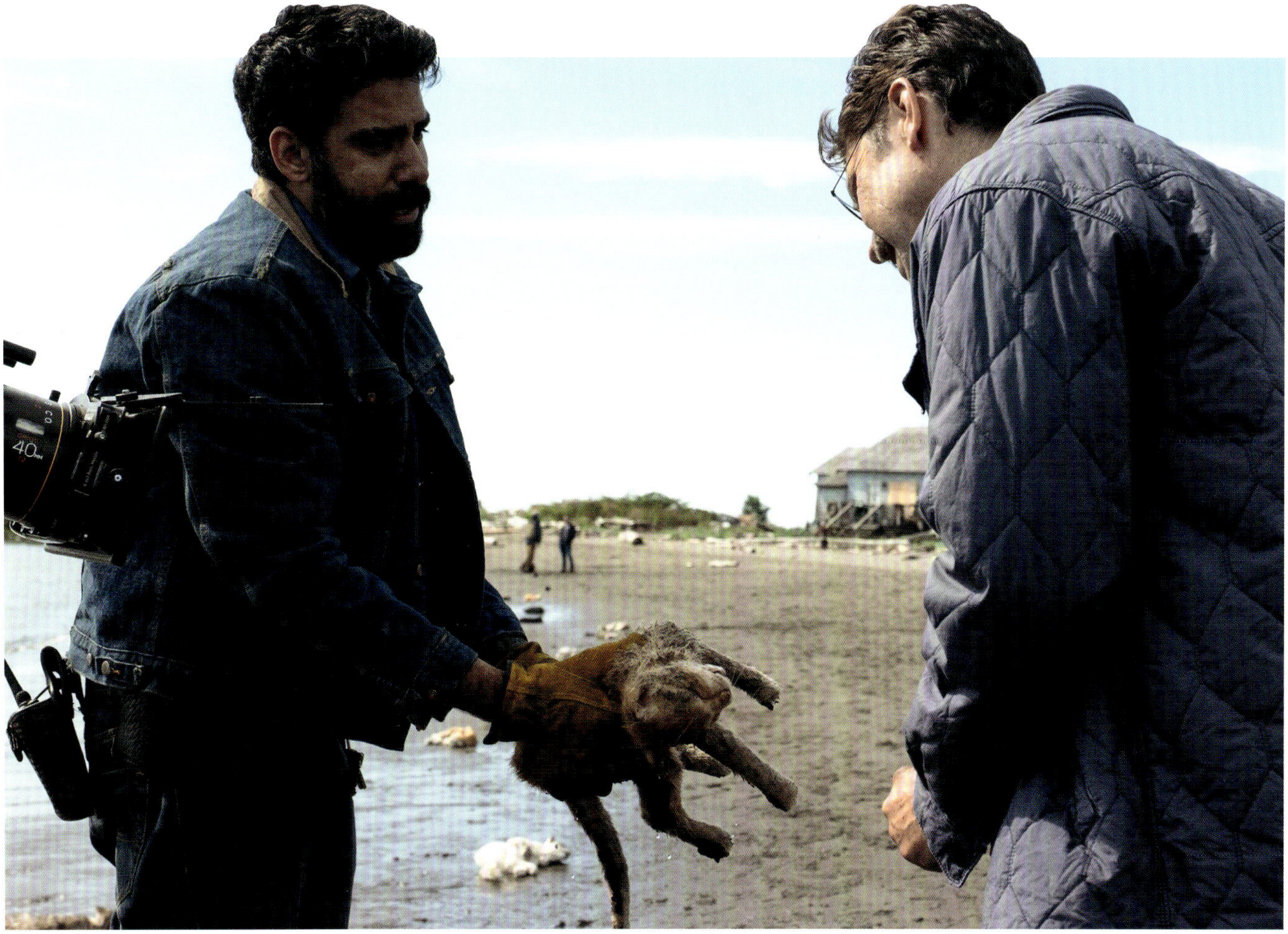

TOP/ Rahul Kohli holds a "hero" cat, with Michael Trucco.

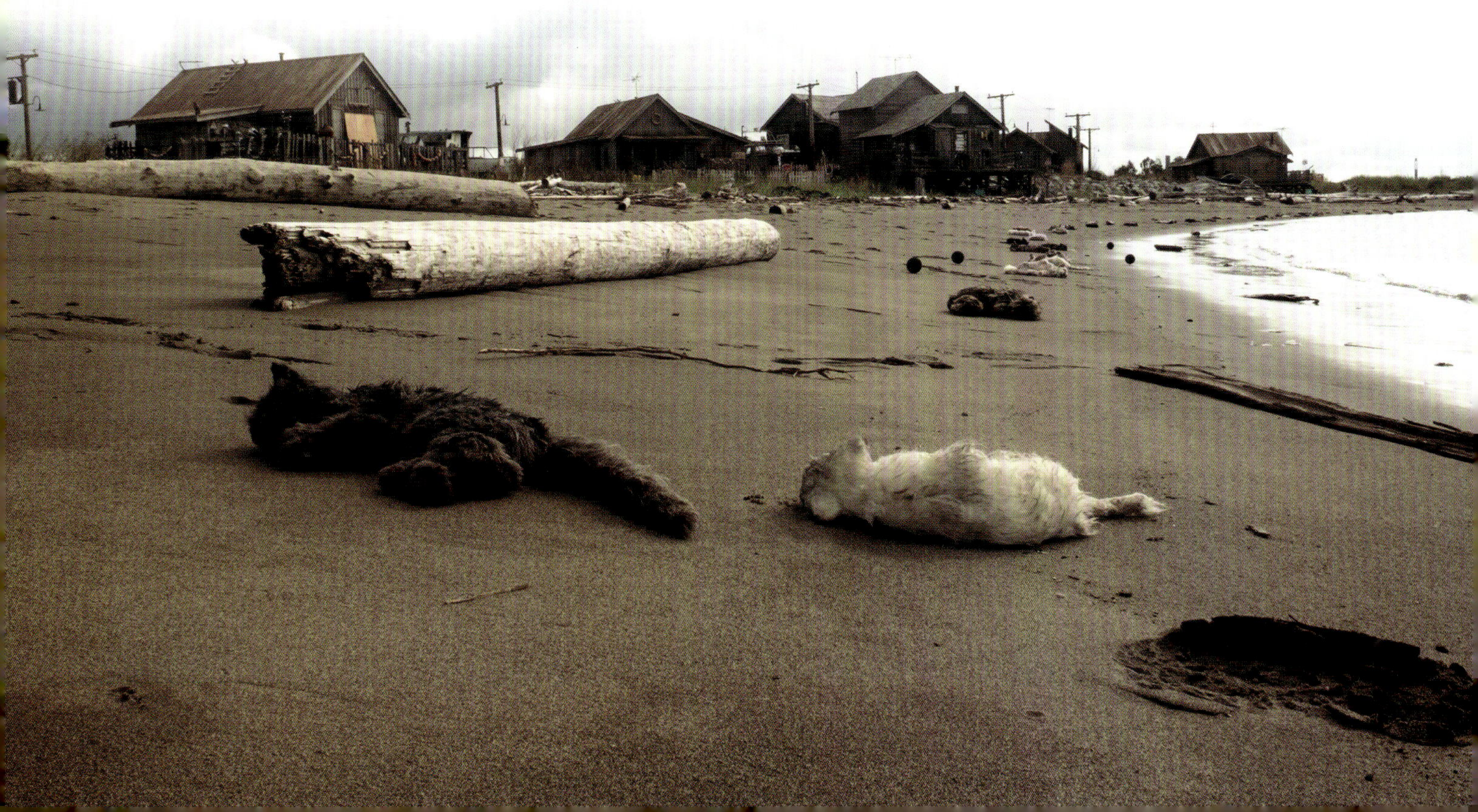

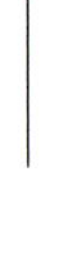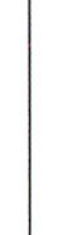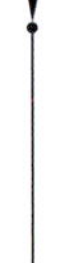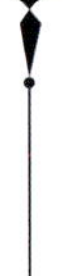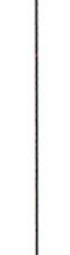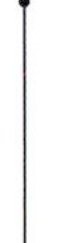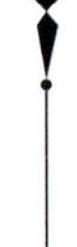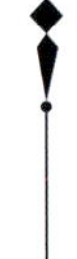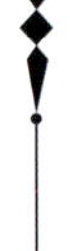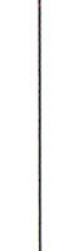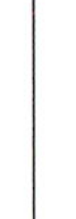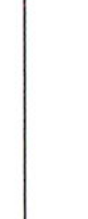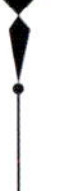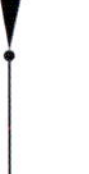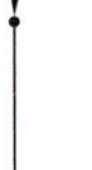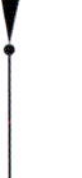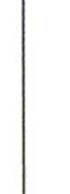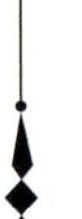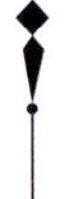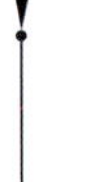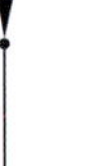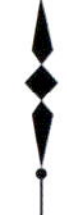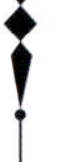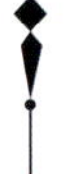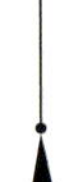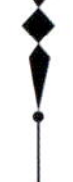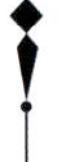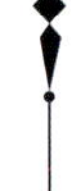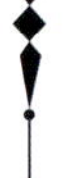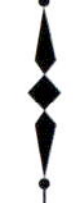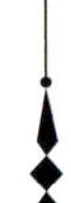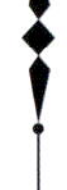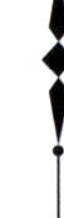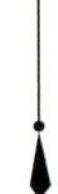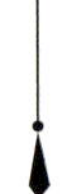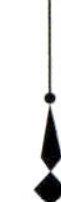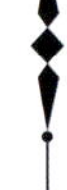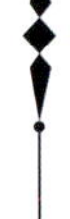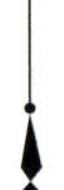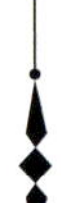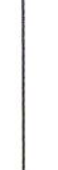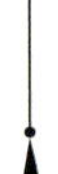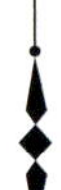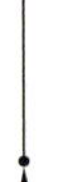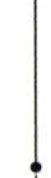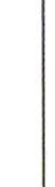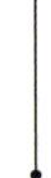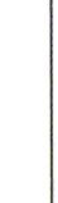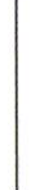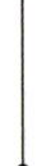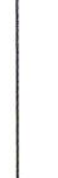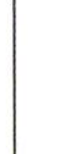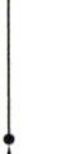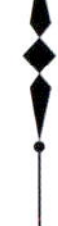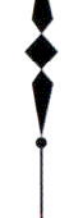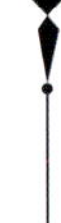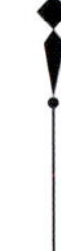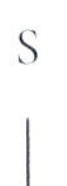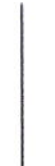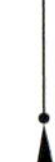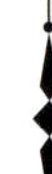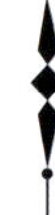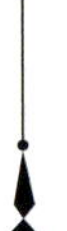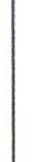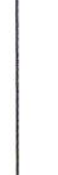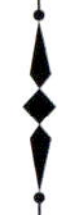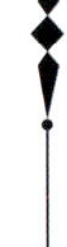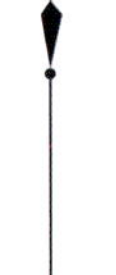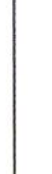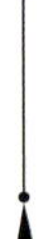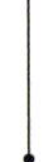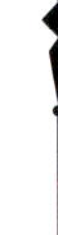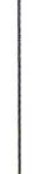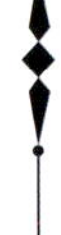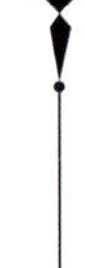

FLYNN HOUSE

SHELTER AND STRIFE ZONE

For the Flynn family home, production designer Steven Arnold says, "The father is a fisherman, and the boys help out, so I tried to make it a little more related to the blue-collar world of working on a boat, so a lot of the elements there are conducive. It's finished in wood planks on the inside, as opposed to plaster walls."

Arnold adds that the home feels masculine. "We gave Annie a nice little kitchen area, but because it's three males to one female, I felt like it needed to have more of the stamp of a male space."

Everything in the home is designed by Arnold's team, even the kitchen's floor tiles. "In Riley's room," Arnold relates, "we designed and made the wallpaper. The elements in that wallpaper are all transportation, ships and planes and boats, meant to give

BOTTOM/ Riley's bedroom, preserved from his teen years.

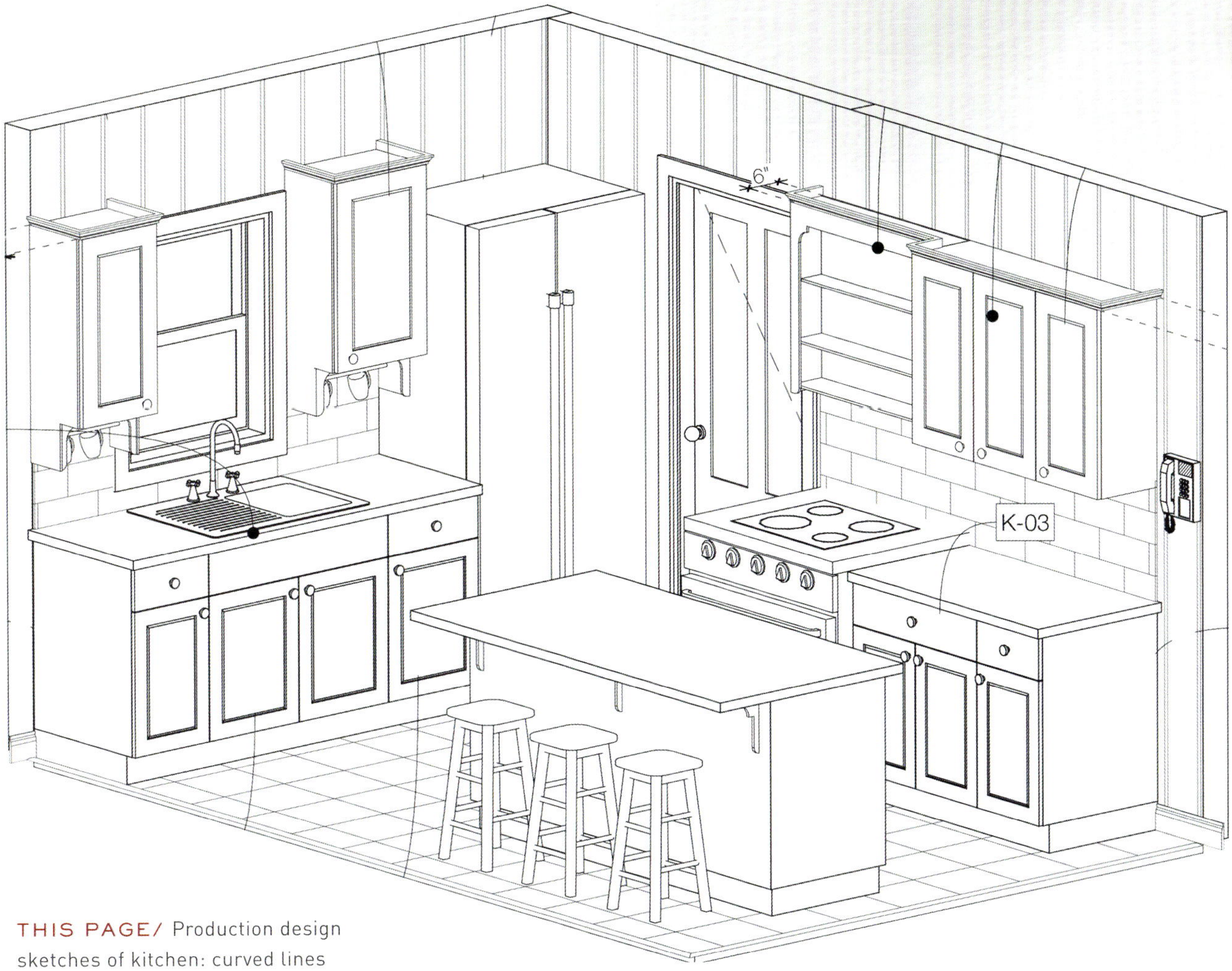

THIS PAGE/ Production design sketches of kitchen: curved lines indicate elements that move.

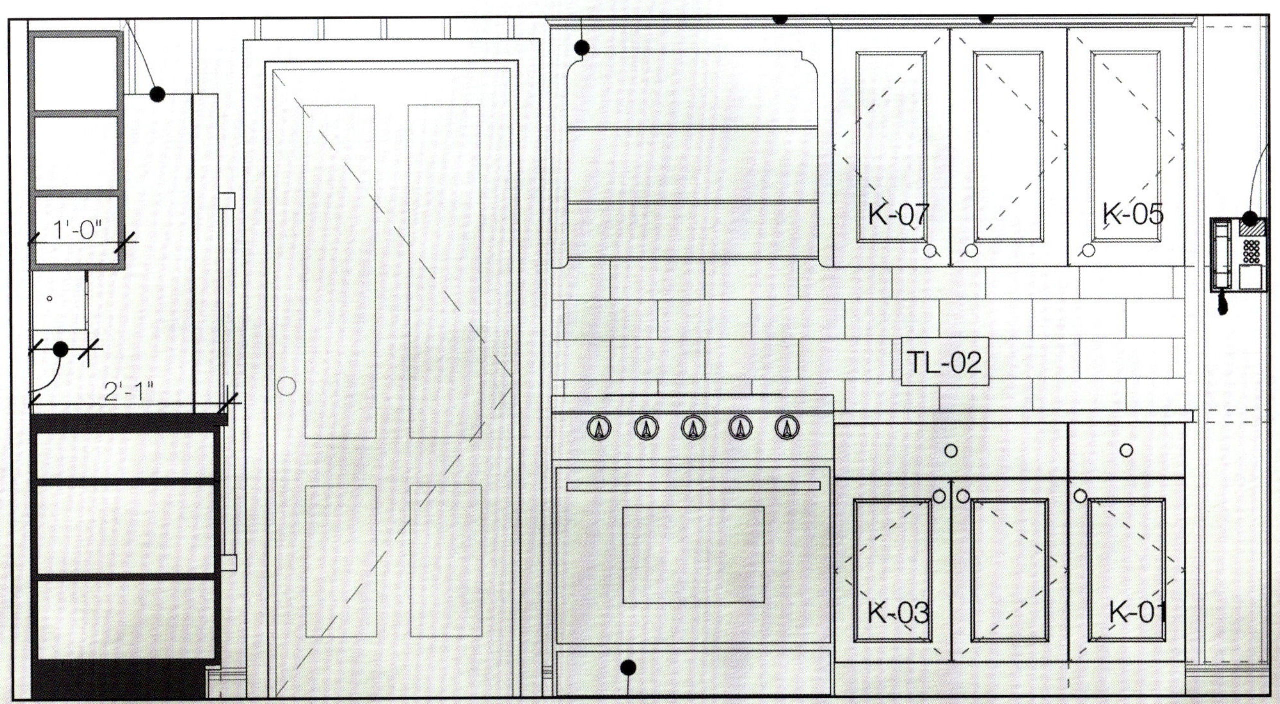

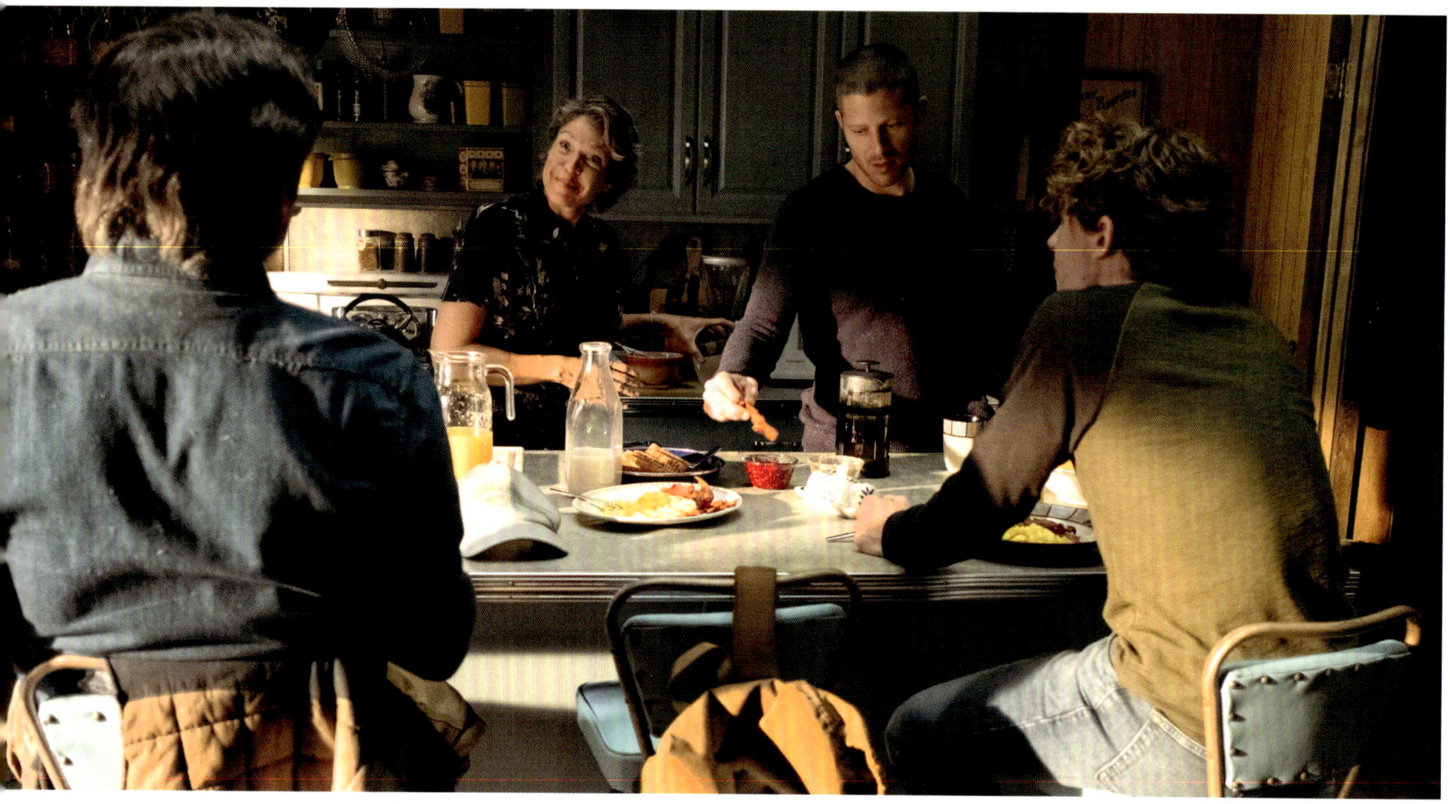

TOP/ Ed, Annie, Riley, and Warren at breakfast.

the impression that he is yearning to leave the island and go somewhere else, initially, as a child."

There are also posters of '90s sci-fi and horror entertainment. Some of these are Flanagan's passions from the period, and some are his suggestions for Riley's interests.

"With my room," Gilford opines, "it was cool to see, they were very specific about the books they had on set, or the posters that were on my wall. They all rang true. They didn't seem generic. This is what a seventeen-year-old would have put on his wall ten years ago."

Thomas was amused by real-life photos he'd supplied to the production that were digitally altered and framed to be Flynn family pictures. "You're doing a scene, and hitting a mark, and you're waiting, and looking around the room a bit, and you see yourself in a photo with someone else that you were never in, and then you forget your line," he laughs.

The set was designed to appear lighter or darker, depending

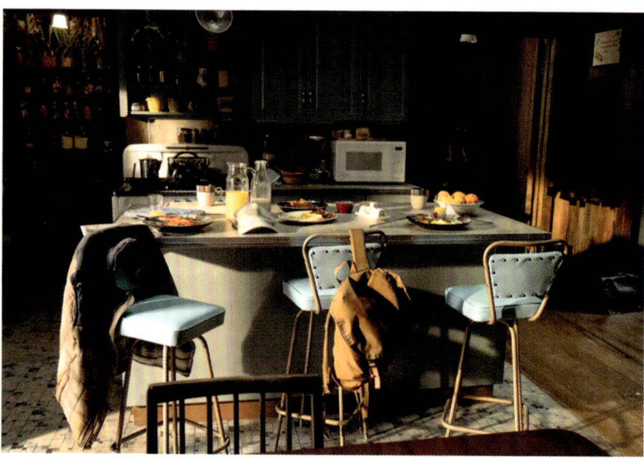

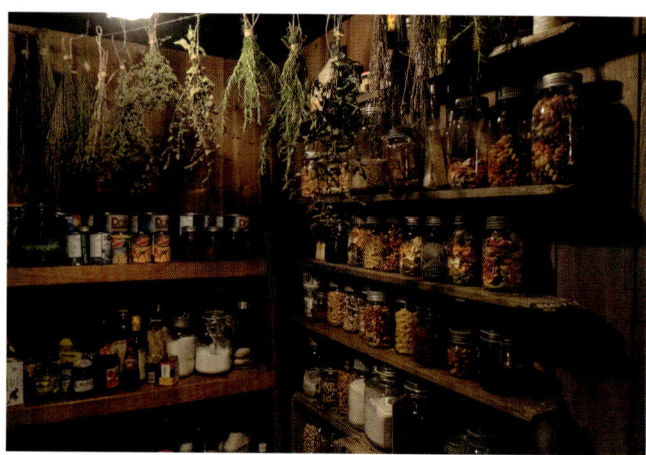

TOP/ The cabinet with the glass jars is Rigney's favorite set.

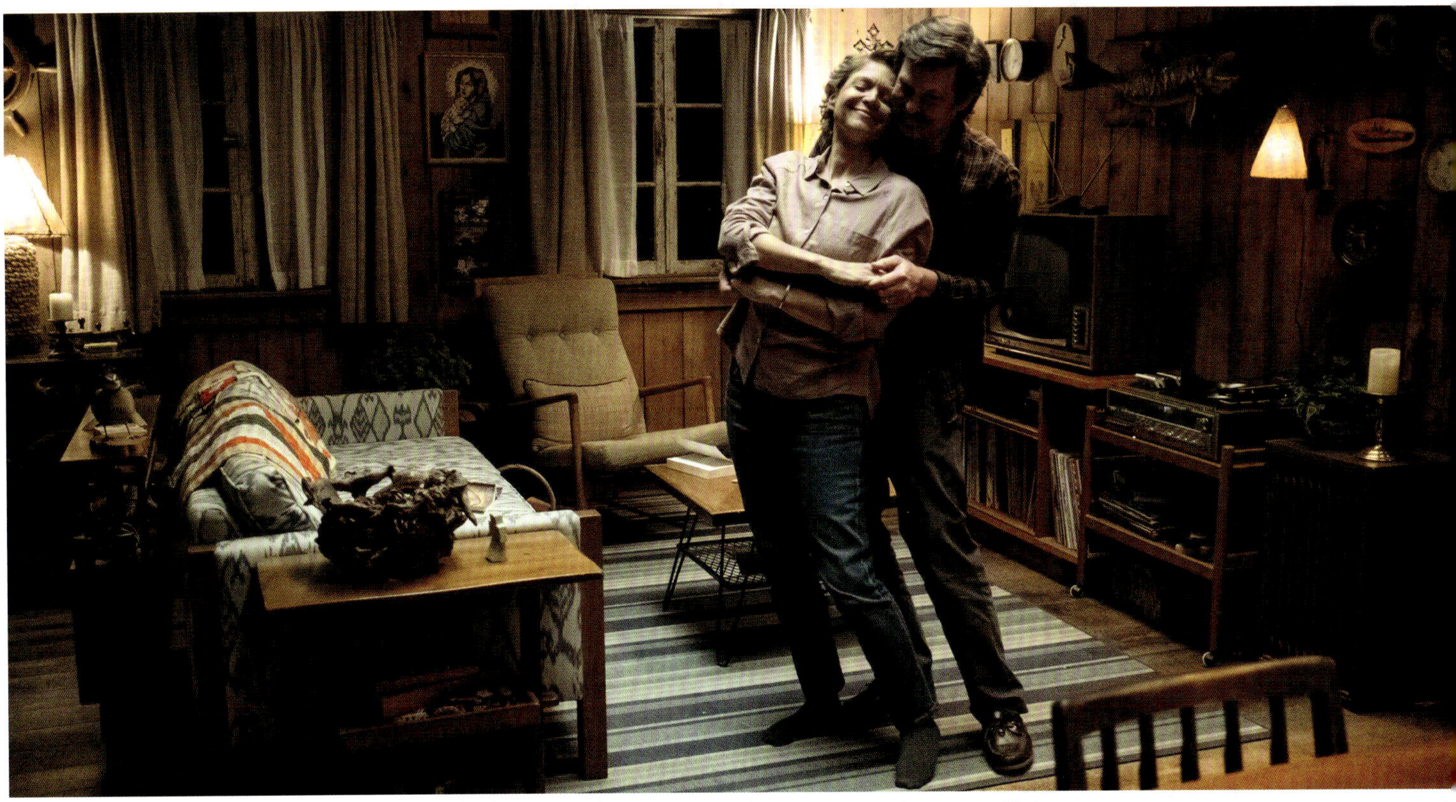

TOP/ Romance returns with youth for Annie and Ed.

on how it was lit for the mood of a given scene, without having to make physical changes. "It was actually quite dark in there," Arnold says, "without a lot of light, but when you are turning on everything, it brightens up quite a bit."

Fimognari says, "The Flynn house felt like a boat that's getting battered by the sea, and the salt air is wearing it down, inside and out. I like that that space was hard to penetrate with light, that they had built something that could survive the big storms, but that meant that it wasn't open. And so, there's a heaviness, a darkness to it."

Rigney says he especially loved "the cabinet with all the glass jars. It was very pretty and homey." He adds that his favorite scene is in the Flynn house. "It's a stupid little scene, but I came up with it on the spot. I'm walking out the door, and I grab an orange, and I throw it over the rafters. I just thought it was so cool that I threw the orange over the rafters. I have no idea why."

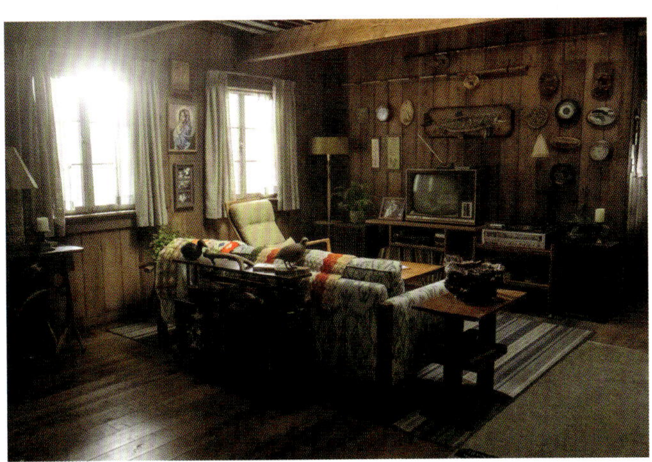

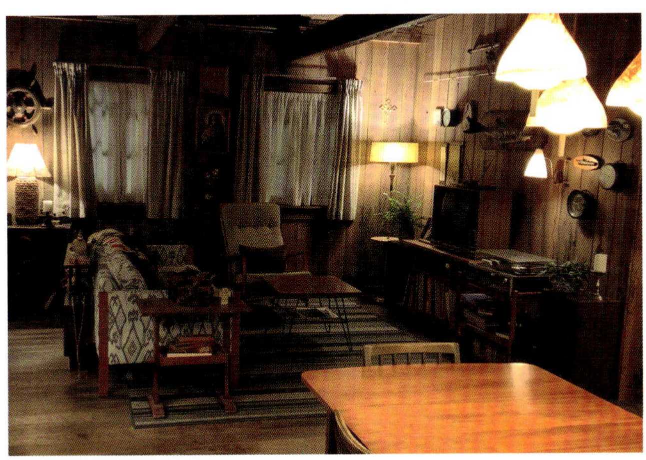

TOP/ Gilford: "Everything [the art department] made looked so real."

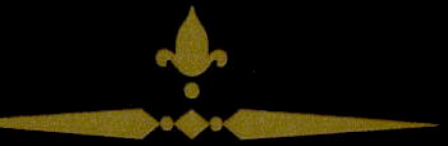

RILEY FLYNN

ZACH GILFORD

Flanagan says that, for *Midnight Mass*, "My way into the story was always through Riley. I'm three years sober. Riley is four years sober [when he returns to Crockett]. That relationship to the effects of addiction has been something that I've been wrestling with in my work for a long time. So, I poured a lot of autobiographical elements onto Riley."

Zach Gilford, who plays Riley, says he was already a huge fan of Flanagan and really wanted the role. "Riley killed someone, but I think in his core, he's a very good person. He says, 'I don't even deserve to be here. This poor girl is dead because of me, and I get to walk around?' That eats at his soul."

Gilford did a "chemistry read" opposite Siegel. Gilford already knew Siegel was cast as Erin, but didn't realize, until she told him, that she and Flanagan are married, with two children. "You are like, 'Not only do I need to look like I have chemistry with this person, but she's got the inside track to the director'," Gilford laughs.

In terms of Riley and Erin, Gilford adds, "I think their connection always was, they were the two people who knew there's a world bigger than this island out there. There are so many deep things that they have in common, there's true love there."

Although Riley only brought a duffel bag of clothes with him, they're from Chicago. This means, says Anderson, "Nothing is too dressy, but always with a little edge over the other people in town."

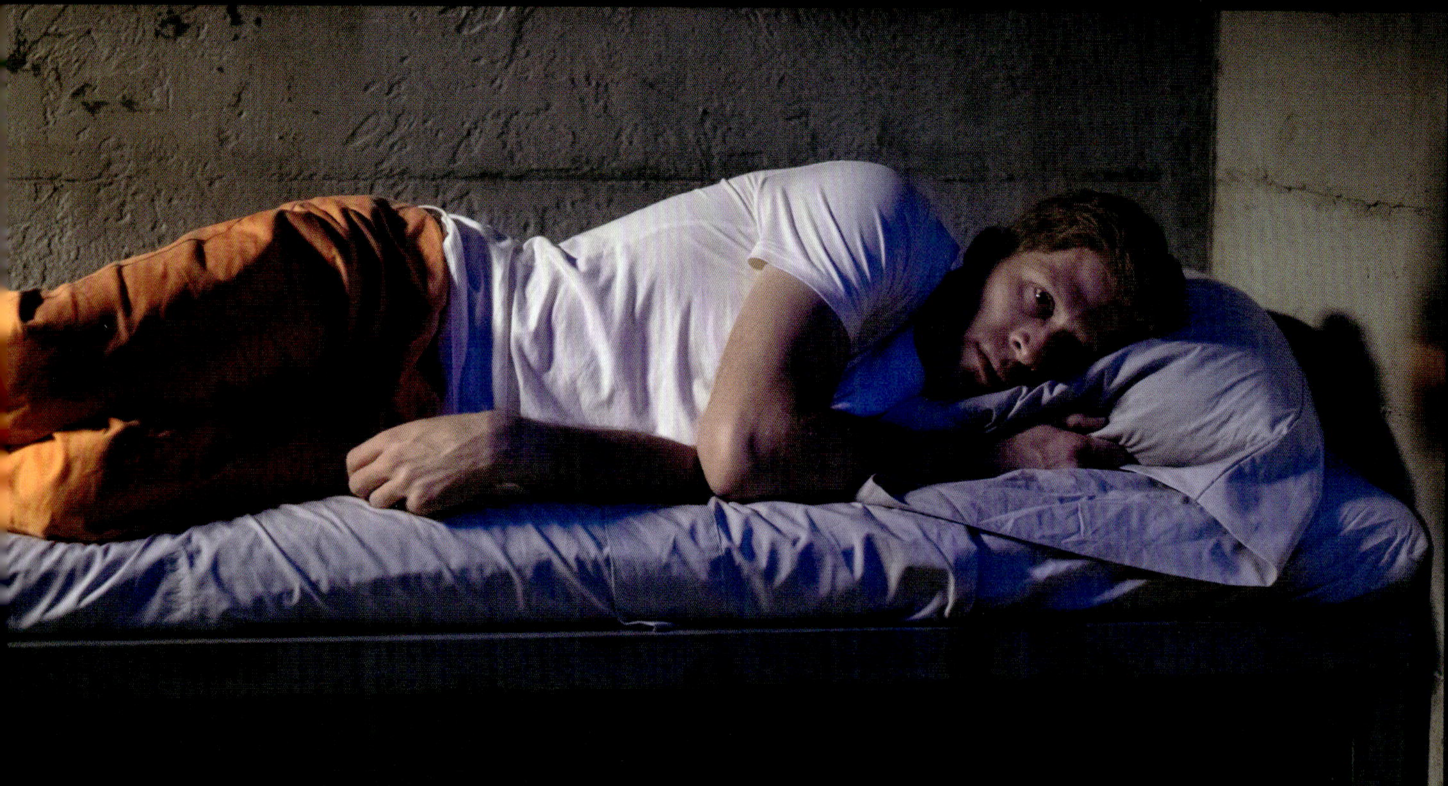

TOP/ Riley reacts to seeing Tara-Beth in his prison cell.

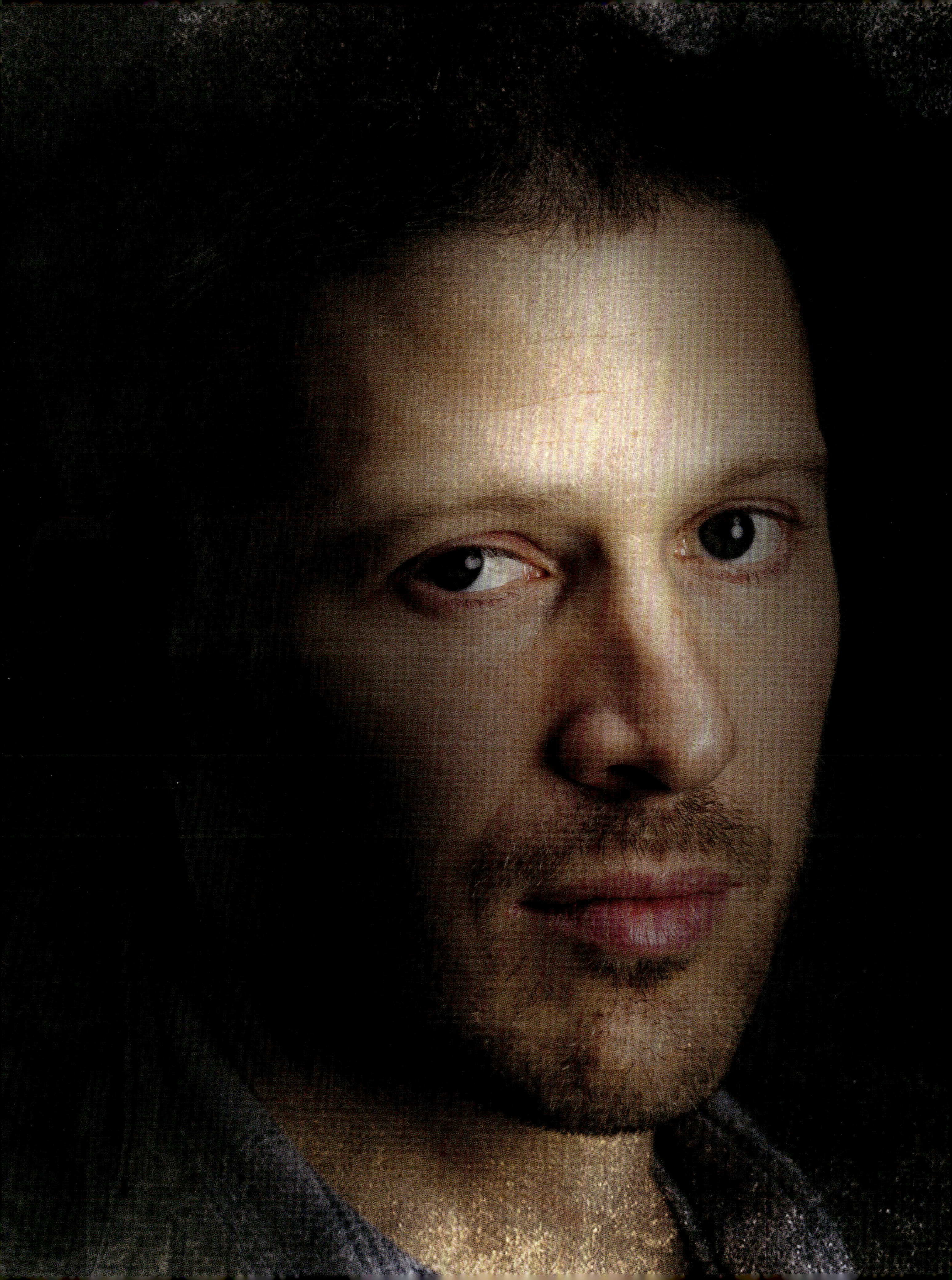

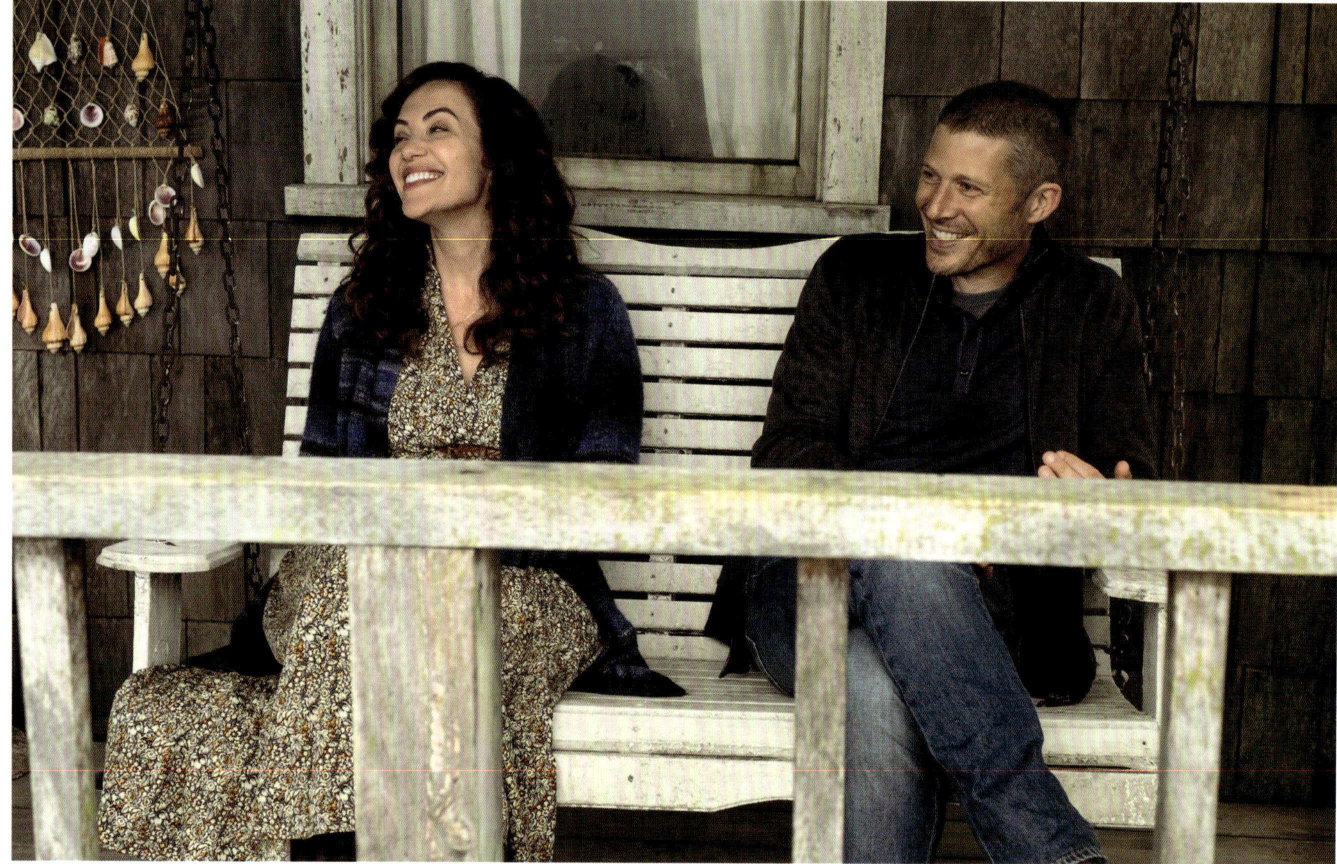

"I BELIEVE THAT IF AN INDIVIDUAL FEELS THAT WAY, IT'S NOT SOMETHING THAT LEAVES THEM EASILY, IT'S ALWAYS AT THE FOREFRONT OF THEIR MIND."

ZACH GILFORD

Gilford says that Riley's feelings about his father are "complex. [Ed] explains why he's mad at me, and then wraps up with, you wouldn't have done any of this if you had a good father. He feels like he failed as a father. That's one of my favorite scenes I've ever gotten to do, on anything. We did a take, and the focus puller said, 'Wow, that's a good scene.' And then it was all these dudes on the boat, saying, 'Man, I wish I could have had that conversation with my dad'."

As for Riley's mother, Gilford opines, "It hurts a little that she still loves him deeply."

Gilford had a terrific time working with Thomas and Lehman. "Between scenes, they'd jokingly stay in character, and have this schtick where they would talk about the randomest stuff, but be so raunchy, and so wrong. They're two of the funniest people I've ever met."

For Flanagan, the family drama was crucial. "If I can't answer the question, 'If I eliminate all the horror, what's the thing I hold onto?' I shouldn't make that movie. In this case, you could cut the vampires out of it entirely, I'd want to know what happened to the Flynn family. And it was some of my favorite work, to see from Henry and Igby and Kristin and Zach. I would have been thrilled to do a whole show about them without the vampires, but I'm also glad I got to do the vampire thing," he laughs.

How does Riley feel about Father Paul? "Father Paul earns his trust," Gilford replies. "[In real life], I have no problem with religion. At its heart, all of it is beautiful. It's when people

TOP/ Riley and Erin have a light-hearted talk on Erin's porch bench.

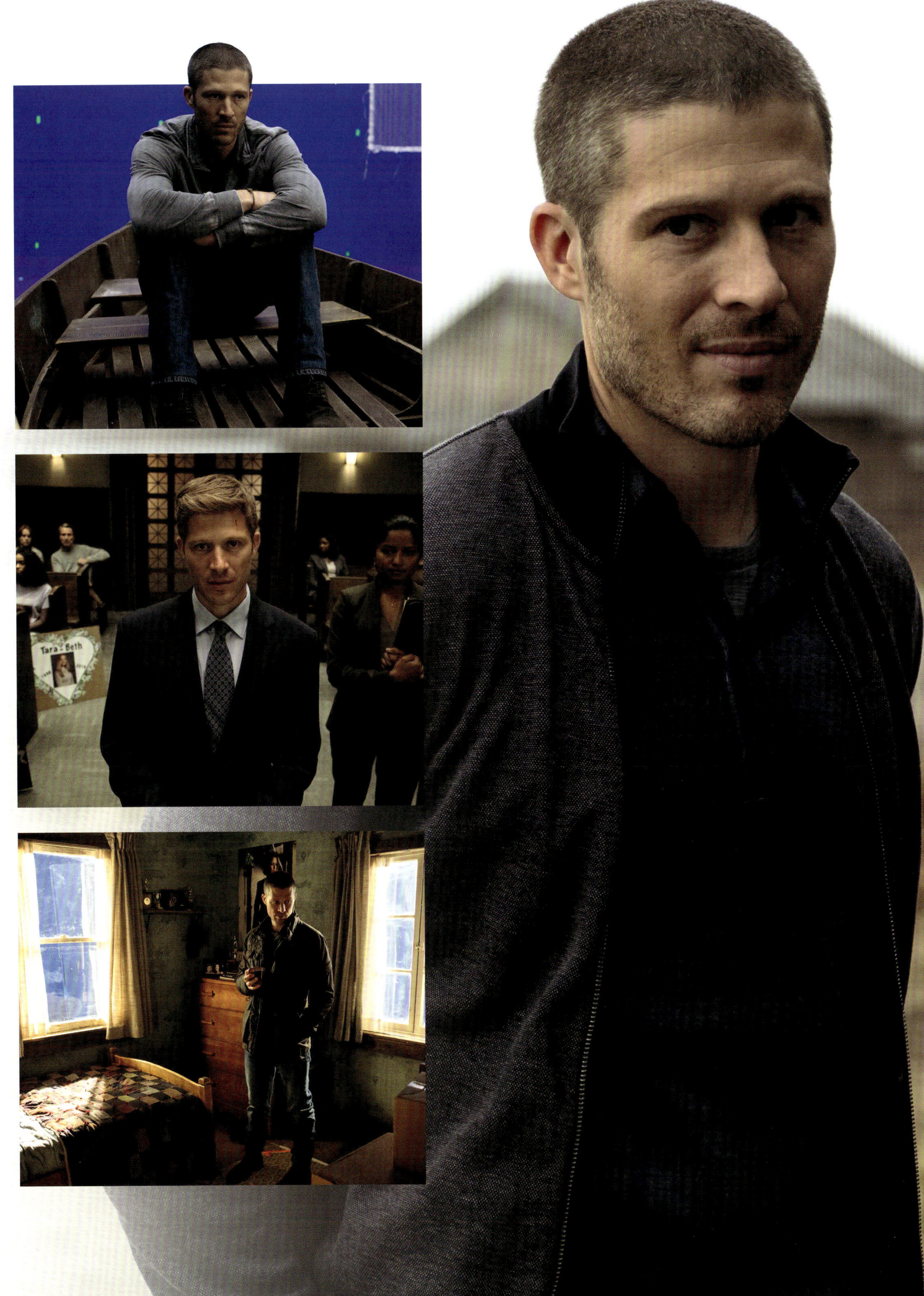
Tara
Beth

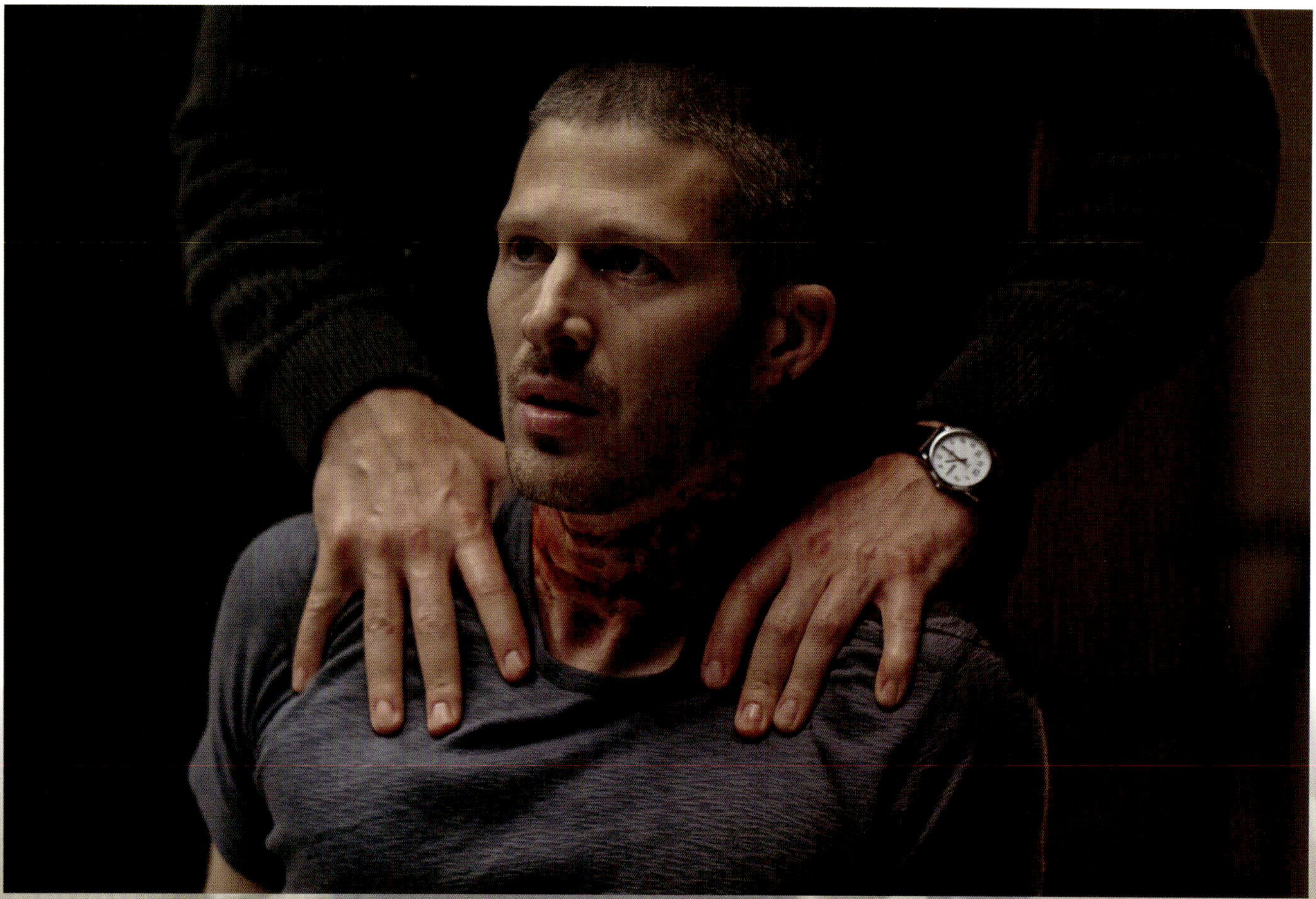

BOTTOM/ The Angel attacks Riley in the rec center.

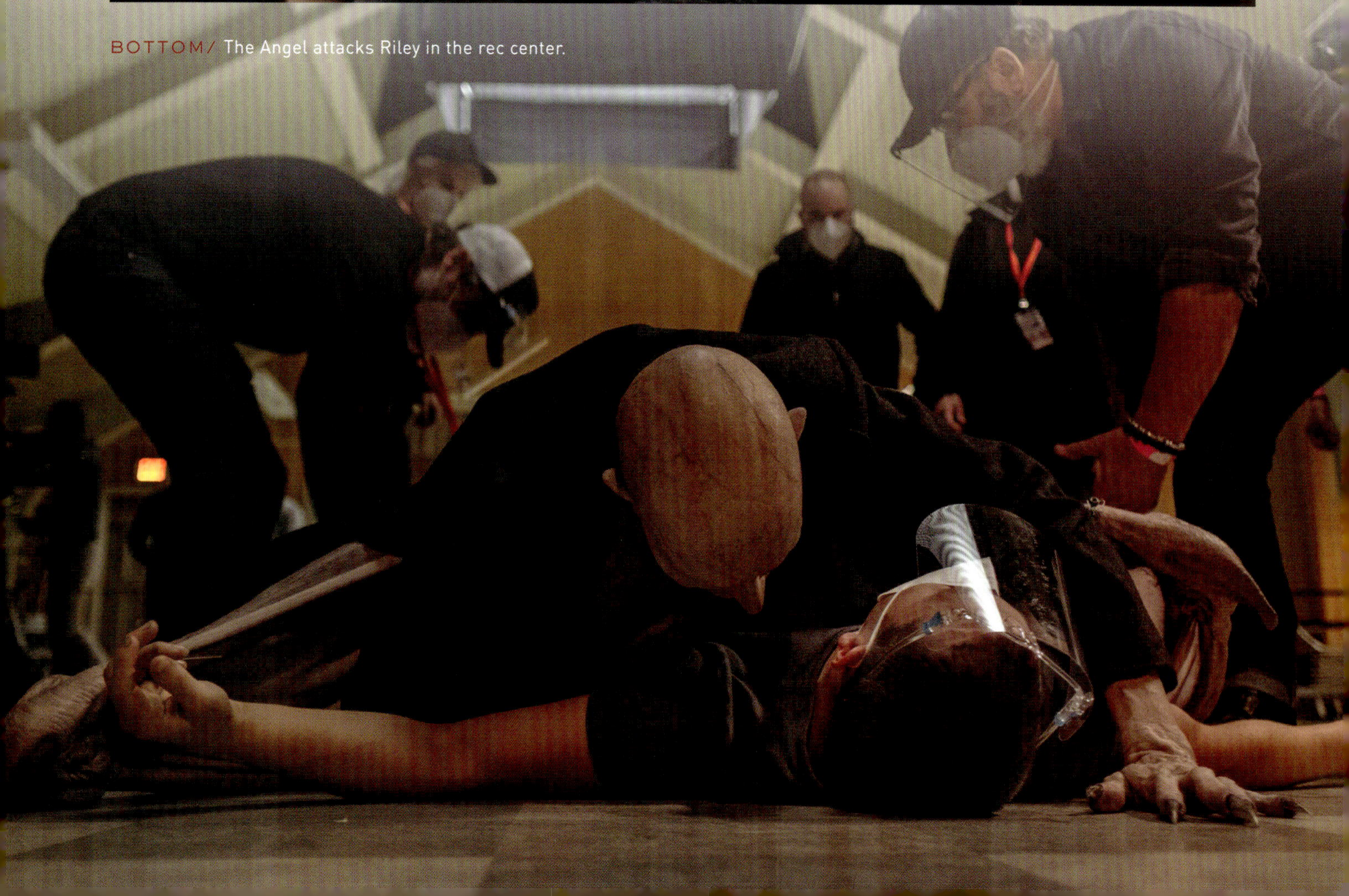

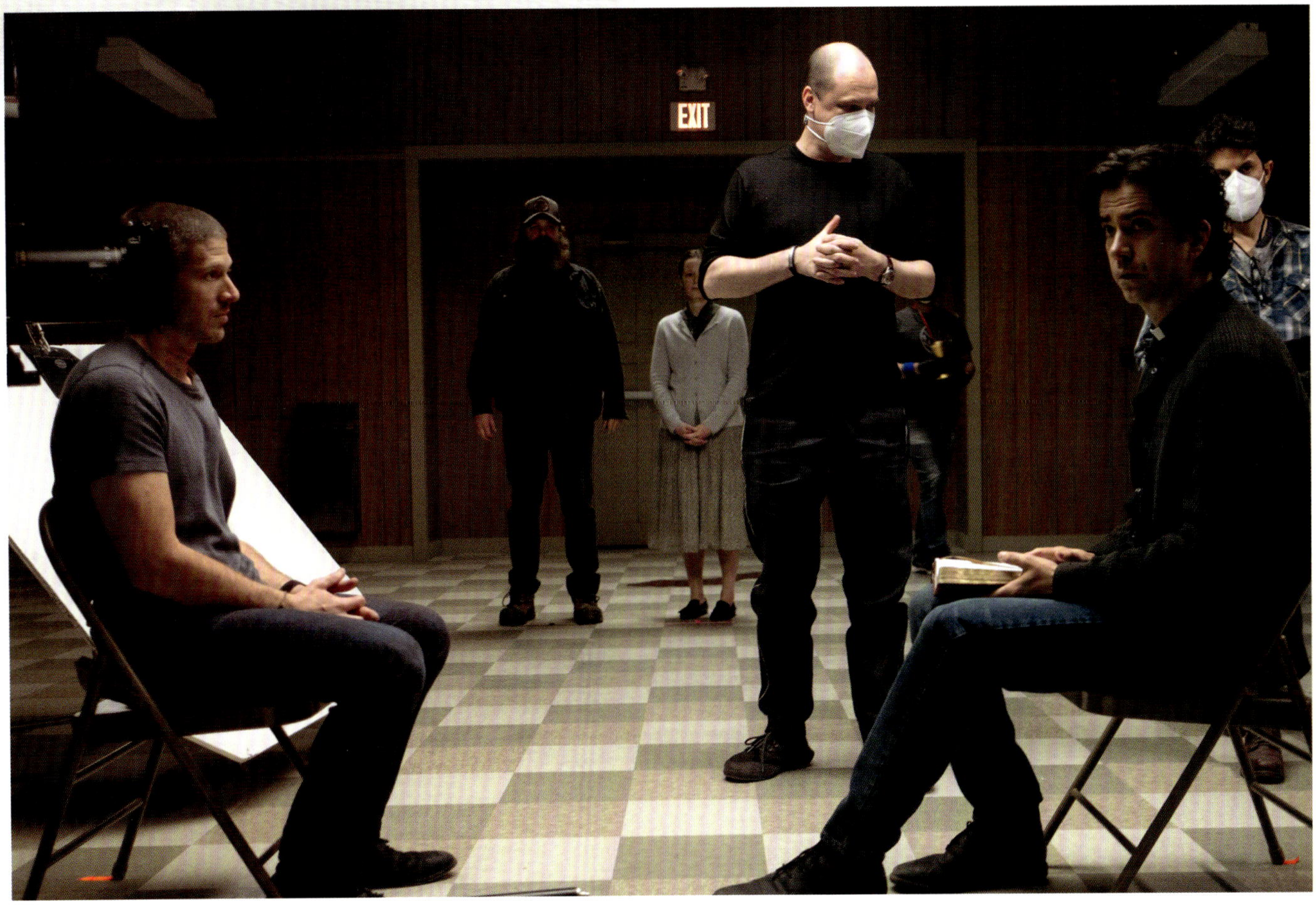

TOP/ Flanagan directs Gilford and Linklater in an AA meeting.

are like, 'You're going to go to some version of Hell' where I have an issue. But Riley believes Father Paul is just trying to help people. And then, where he realizes Father Paul lied to him, it shatters that."

Asked about being fed on by the Angel, Gilford makes a revolted sound. "I don't know how you write that down," he laughs. "The prosthetic on my neck for that bite was disgusting. When Quinton was gnawing at my neck, my neck prosthetic stuck to his prosthetics, so when he pulled away, there were pieces of my prosthetic on his face."

It made for a surreal chat in the greenroom, Gilford recalls. "Quinton is the nicest dude. He's got the makeup on, he's huge, Hamish is in a priest outfit, and Quinton is explaining the difference between the MCU and the DC Universe."

Gilford says that, when Riley turns, "Mike was specific about, 'You're feeling this kind of pain in your stomach,' or, 'The lights are a little brighter.' He holds your hand through it in a way that doesn't make you feel like a puppet, but you feel like you have someone looking out for you to help you do the best you can."

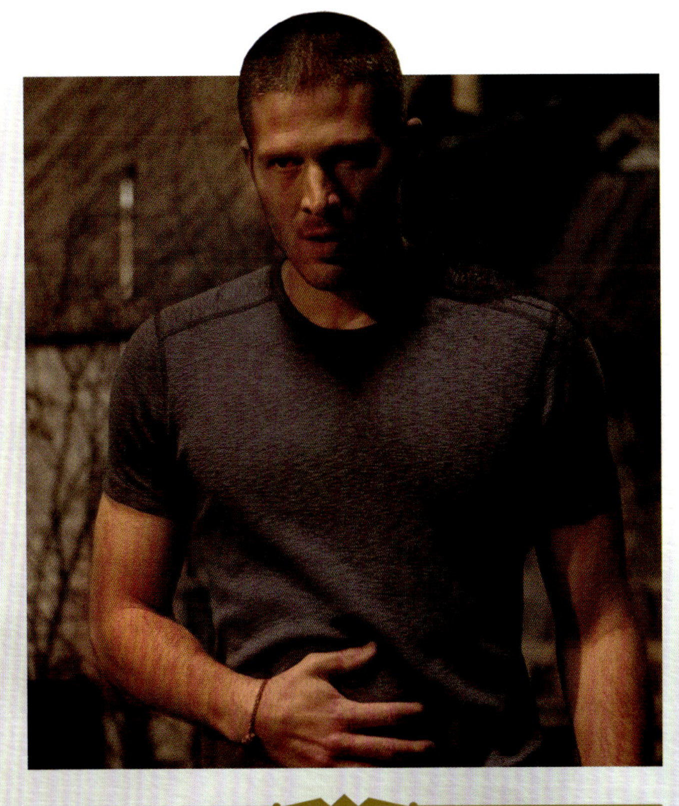

TARA-BETH

EBONY BOOTH

Tara-Beth, played by Ebony Booth, is the young woman accidentally killed by Riley when he drives drunk four years prior to the events of the show. Riley periodically sees her thereafter, bloody and broken.

Flanagan says that he doesn't think Tara-Beth is a ghost, but rather a projection of Riley's guilt. The one possible exception "is when Tara-Beth is restored and pristine, not covered with glass, which any merciful afterlife would have already spared her from. When she reaches down to lift Riley up, that would be the one place where I'd say just maybe that could really be her."

Anderson dressed Tara-Beth befitting "a young, beautiful girl from Chicago. She's very stylish in her leather coat, and she dresses tone on tone, tan and taupe and cream. Of course, she looks like a nightmare."

Raleigh says, "She has hemorrhage contact lenses, and a variety of deep wound prosthetics. Some of it goes into her hair, but most of it was blood dressing with a degree of subtlety. Mike wanted it gory and shocking, without being so disgusting that you couldn't look at it. So, we had to find a balance. All of the glass that's on her is rubber silicone glass, because it obviously has to be safe. They did a little bit of VFX on the glass to give it refraction."

Alvarez explains that the appliances on Tara-Beth are made of Pros-Aide thickened glue substance. "You put a little bit more glue on the top of it, but then it transfers straight to the skin, with just water. You paint all the blood on, and then we'll add fresh blood on set."

Fimognari relates, "Mike wanted Riley to see her bathed in a police/ambulance strobe. That hasn't left him. So, we brought that faint little red and blue flicker, not to the room, but just to her."

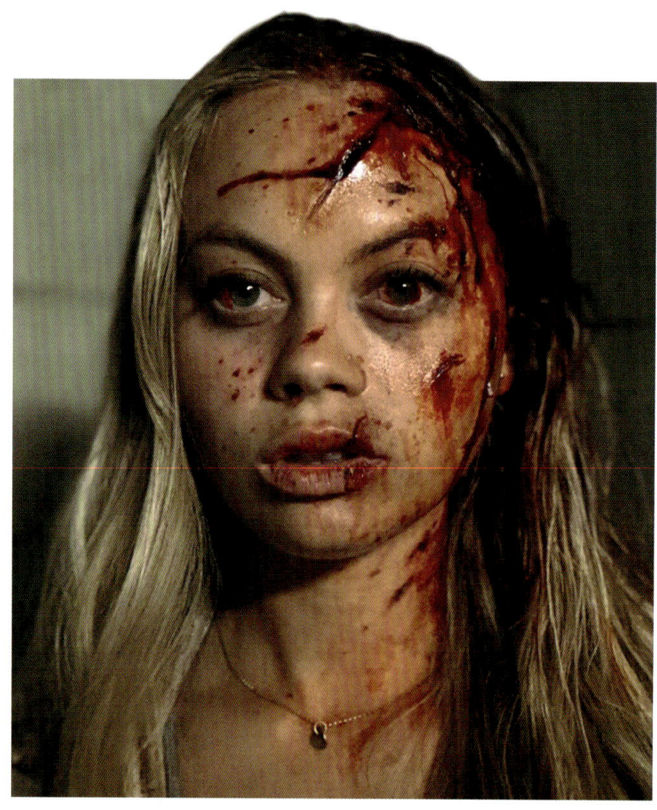

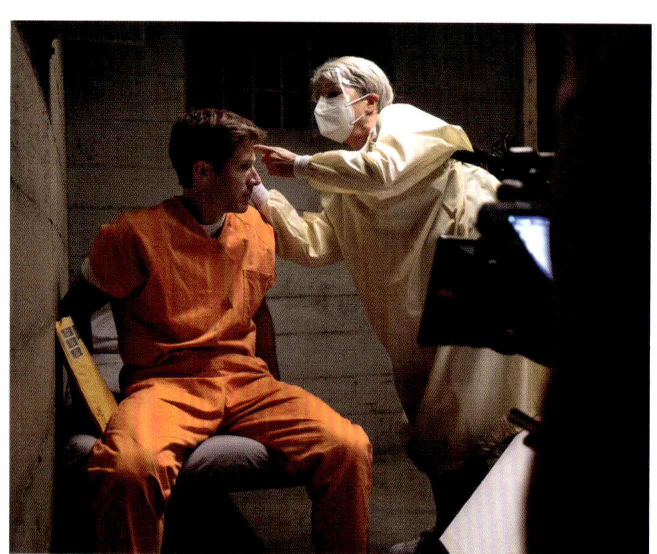

RIGHT/ Riley's victim Tara-Beth appears in his hallucinations.

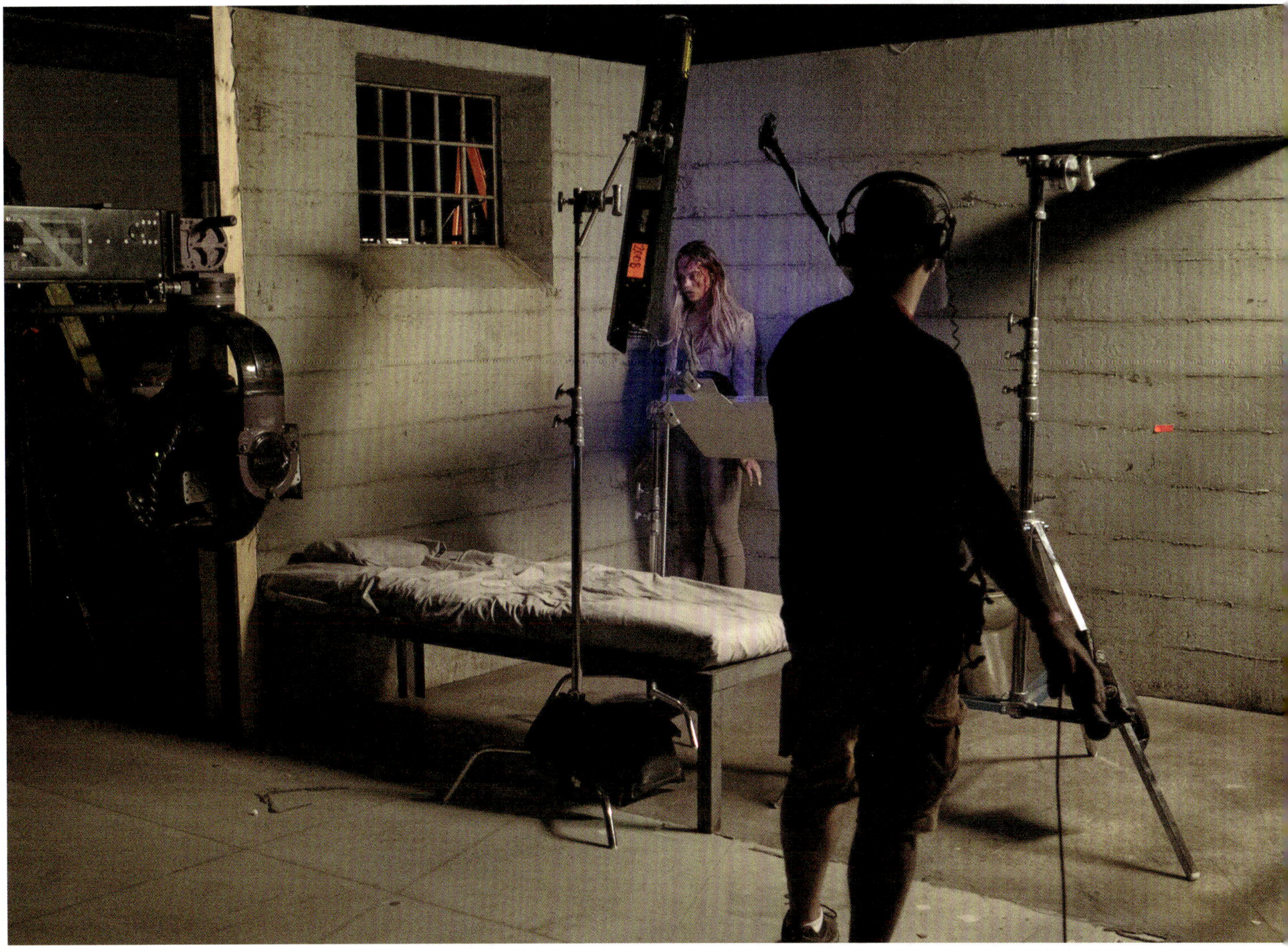

TOP/ Riley's jail cell was built on a soundstage.

BOTTOM/ Tara-Beth extends a forgiving hand to the dying Riley.

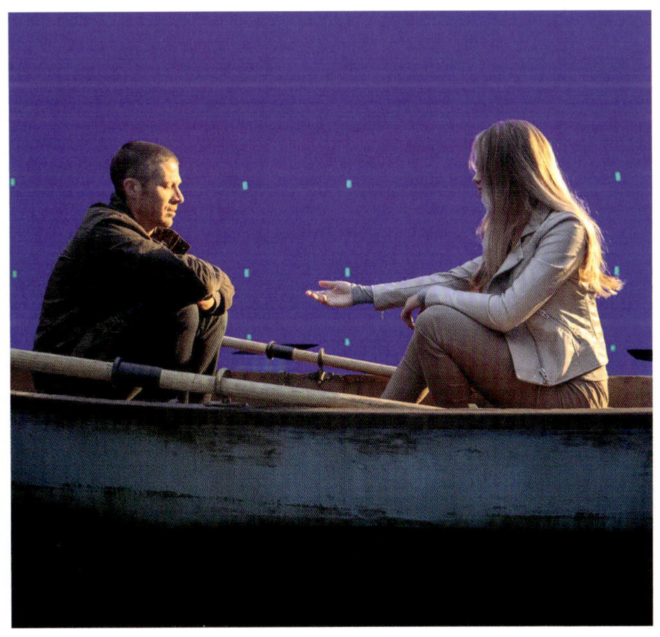

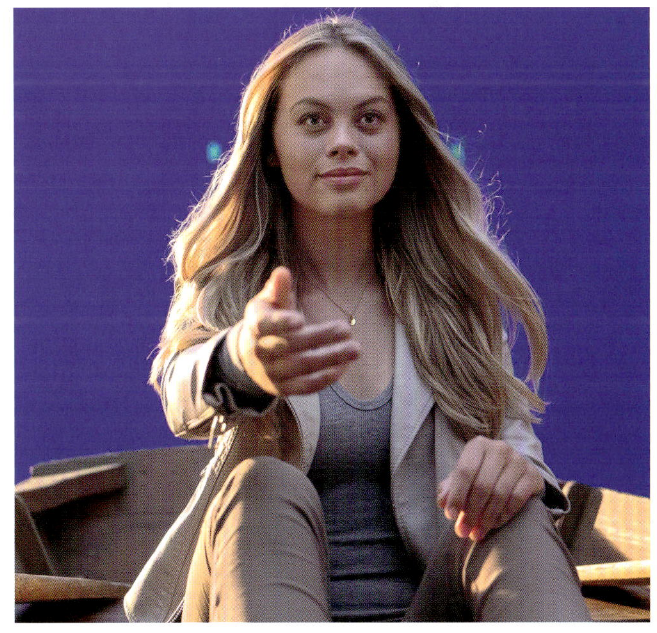

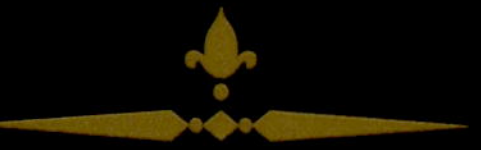

WARREN FLYNN

IGBY RIGNEY

Flanagan says that one of his intentions with Warren Flynn was "the idea that he would demonstrate how a younger generation doesn't have to carry the prejudices of the generation that came before. It was important that Warren was always very inclusive of Ali."

Igby Rigney, who plays Warren, describes him as "a little complicated. He's dealing with family history, and how everything in town is impacted by everything else. Riley is so much older that, at least in my mind, it was hard for them to have that brotherly connection. Ed is very disapproving of Riley's mistakes. So, it's hard to separate his dad's opinions of Riley from his own, until they finally meet. He finds that he likes Riley a lot more than he expected to."

Regarding Warren's parents, "He adores his mom. He's got a lot of love and respect toward his dad, but doesn't totally look past Ed's problems with alcoholism and his temper."

Because they're in a small town, with "limited romantic opportunities," Rigney doesn't know if Warren actually loves Leeza. "He really likes her. He is very upset with her situation. He thinks it's disgusting that someone took away her ability to walk, [but] he doesn't view the chair in a negative way."

With Warren's peers, Rigney relates, "Ooker is his best friend in world, and can sometimes get on his nerves, but for the most part, they're incredibly close. He welcomes Ali partially because his mom would have encouraged him to, and also because, why not? He's a new friend."

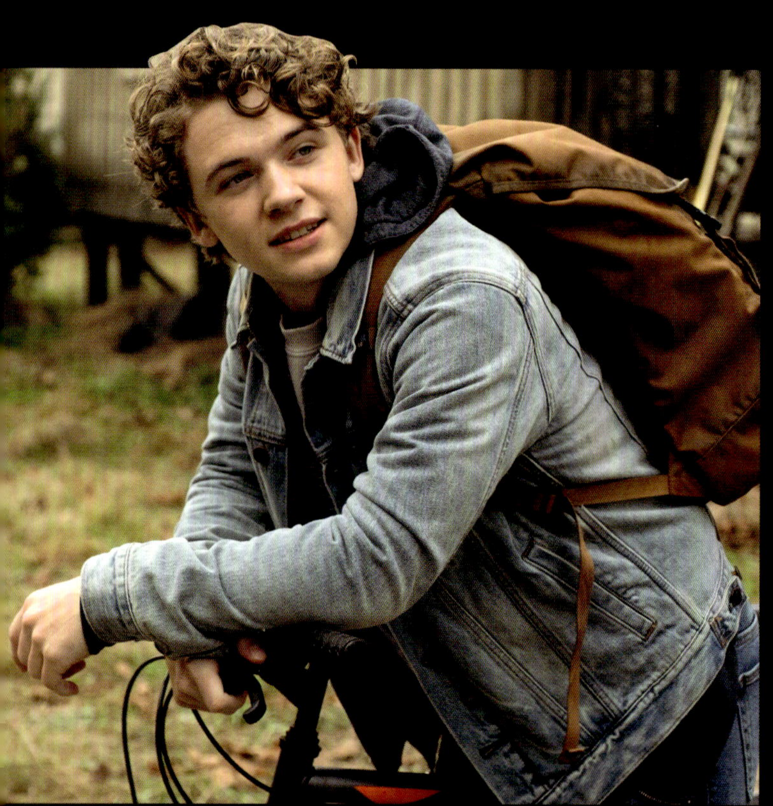

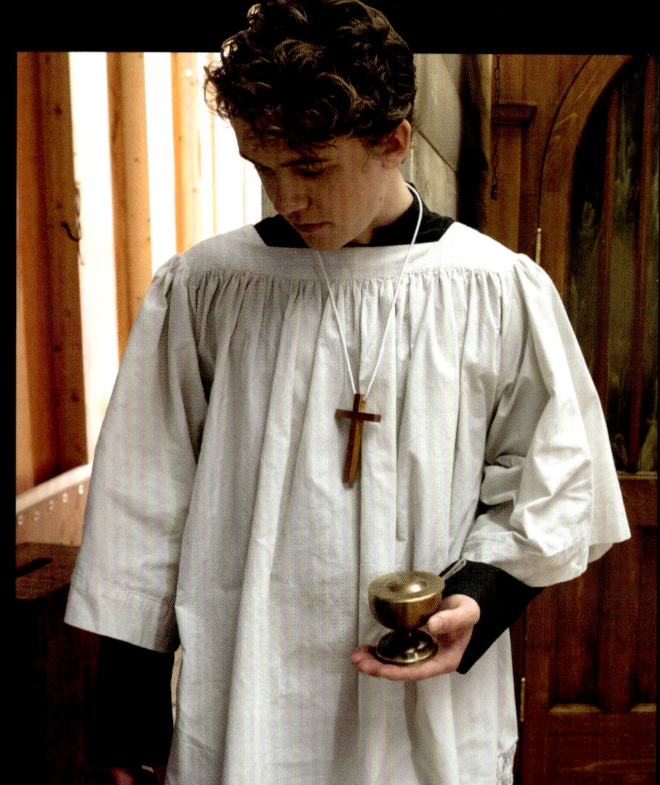

THIS SPREAD/ Rigney: "Warren's doing the altar boy thing to make his mom happy."

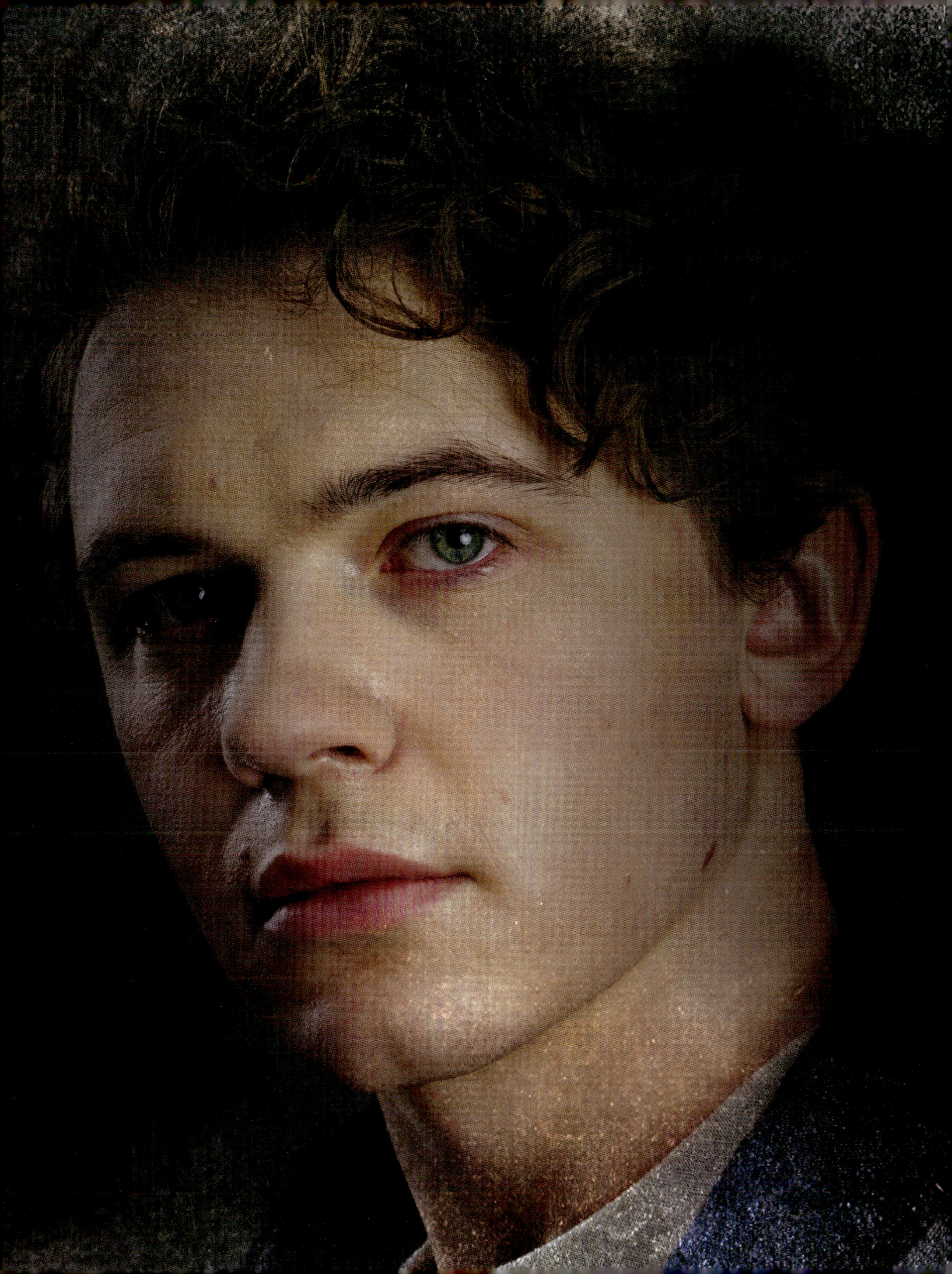

"WE LIKED THE IDEA THAT WARREN WOULD DEMONSTRATE HOW A YOUNGER GENERATION DOESN'T HAVE TO CARRY THE PREJUDICES OF THE GENERATION THAT CAME BEFORE."

MIKE FLANAGAN

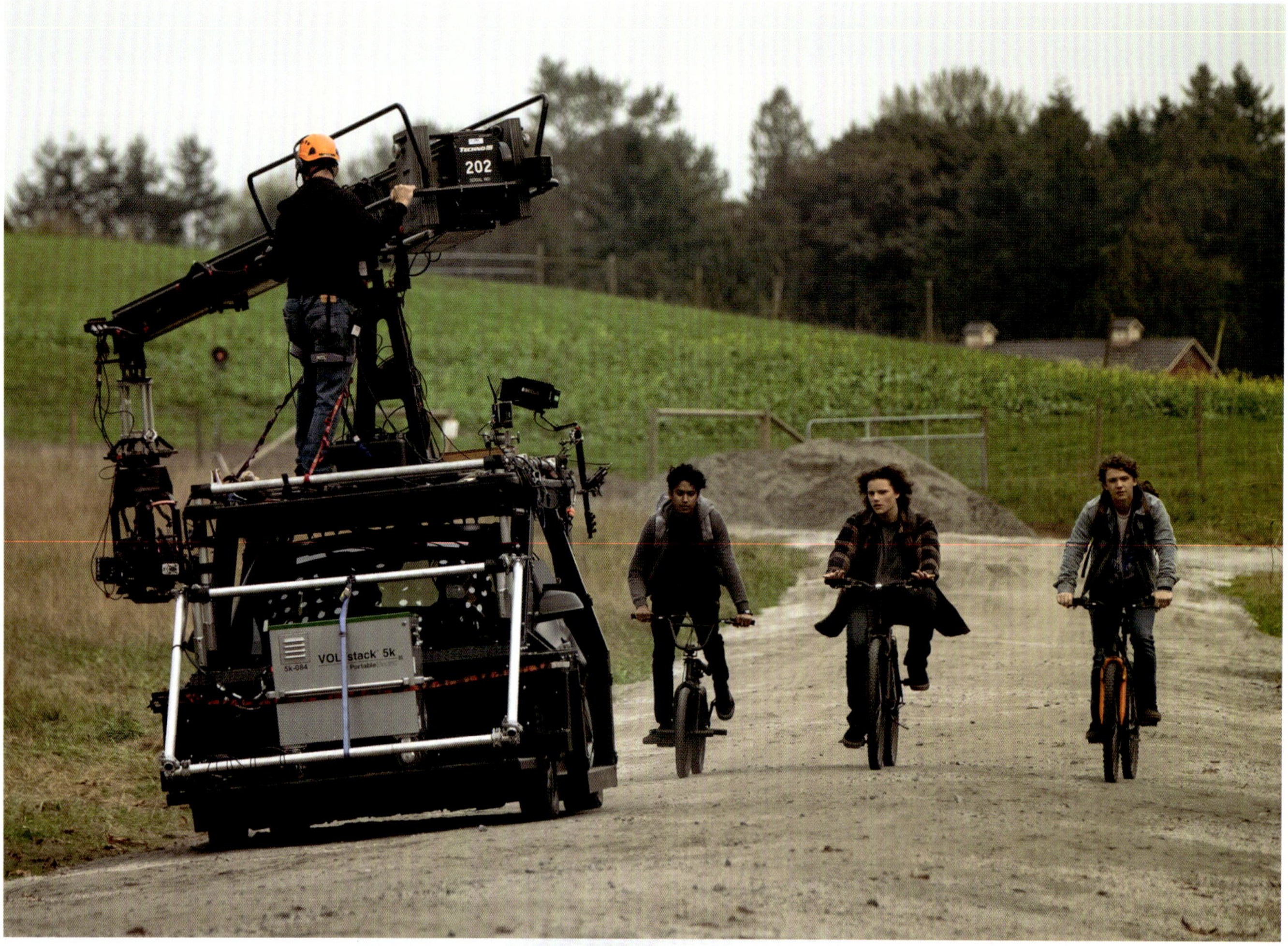

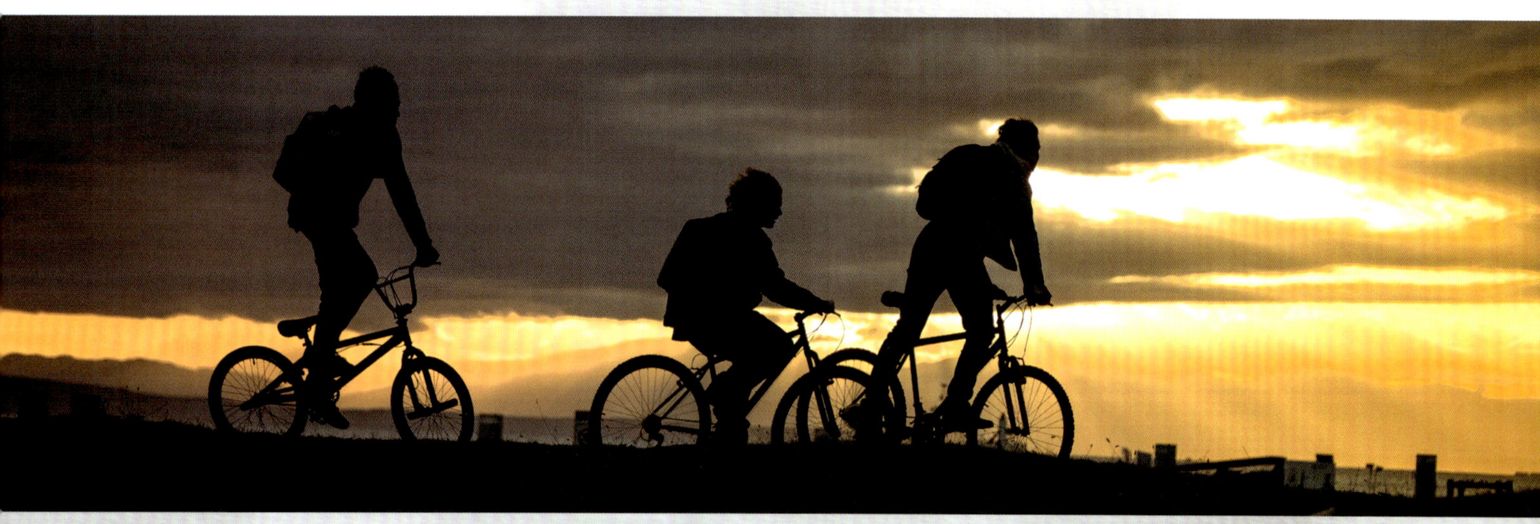

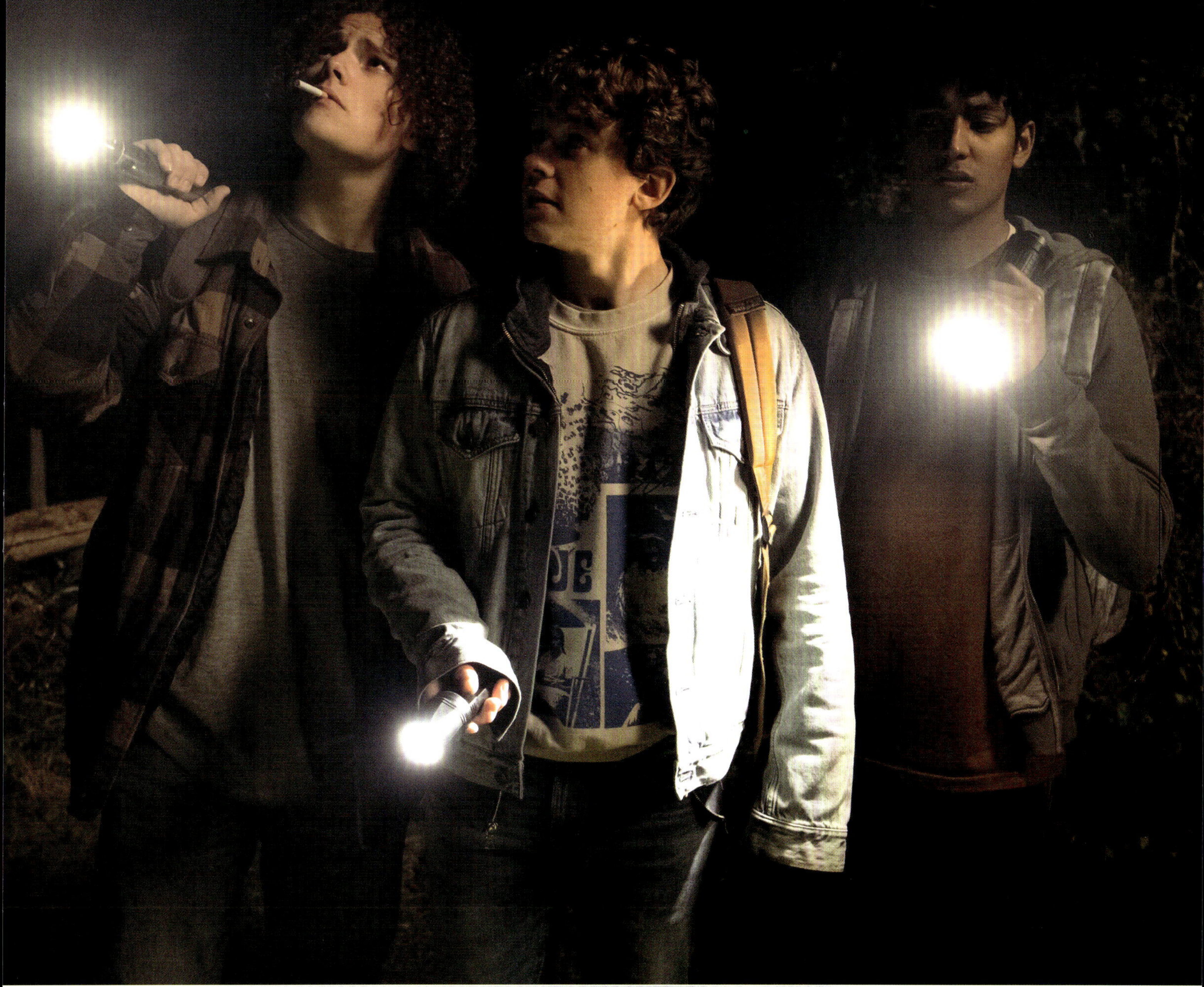

Anderson says that Warren's fashion sense consists of "sweatshirts and t-shirts with prints on them, and a denim jacket that he loved. He also has his smelly work clothes, with his dad, rubber boots and raincoats."

One challenge for Rigney came in a church choral sequence. One of the times I had to sing, I showed up to set not knowing I had to sing. I had about thirty seconds before we started rolling to learn the lyrics. Because I was an altar boy, it would have looked terrible if I didn't know the song."

THIS SPREAD/ (LEFT) Filming boys on their bikes: Aburri, Moffat and Rigney. (TOP) Ooker, Warren and Ali see something eerie in the Uppards.

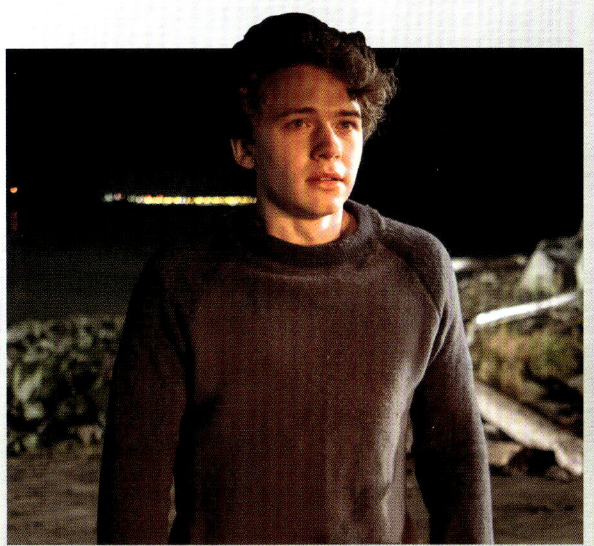

WARREN FLYNN

ANNIE FLYNN

KRISTIN LEHMAN

Kristin Lehman found her character, Annie Flynn, "on the page. My perspective of acting is that you start with the material. I had to conjure archetypes of people that I knew who were older, conservative Catholics, who are all quite loving. But the road map was already written in the dialogue and story setting."

Anderson says that Annie dresses traditionally and sweetly. "Modesty is her thing. She would never wear anything too revealing, or too stylish."

Lehman portrays Annie as someone of sincere religious conviction. "She believes that God loves unconditionally, and she wants that loving freedom for her children who suffer. So, her devout presence at church is part of pursuing freedom from suffering the people she loves."

Annie, says Lehman, "accepts Ed. Their relationship is based on archetypes they've agreed to uphold, in terms of a power dynamic in their relationship. I think [Annie feels] a real acceptance that includes the relationship between Riley and Ed."

Annie slits her own throat to distract Bev from chasing Warren. "It was meaningful to me that she was willing to do that act of self-sacrifice," Lehman says, "so there was real grief and righteousness, but it wasn't hard. It's all acting.""

To facilitate this, Ozzy Alvarez says, Lehman had "a full neck wrap silicone prosthetic appliance that had blood tubing in it. As she comes up to slice her neck, we start pumping the blood."

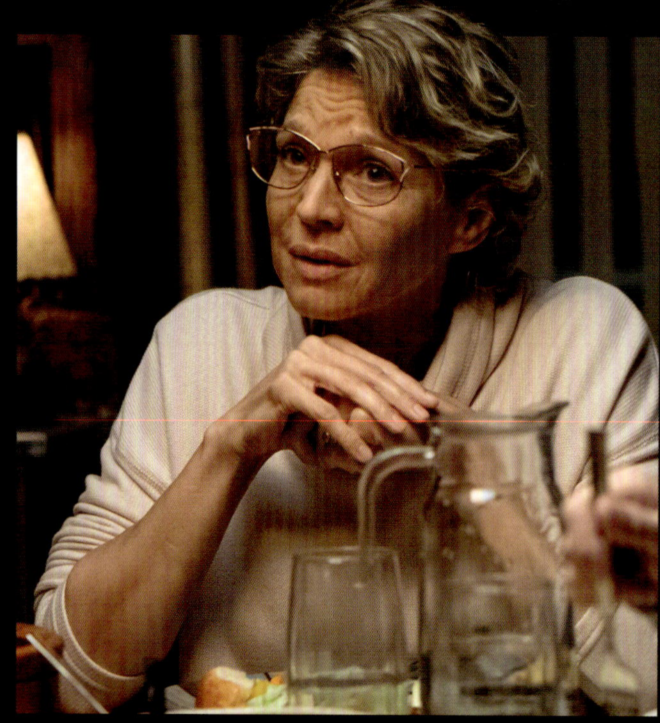

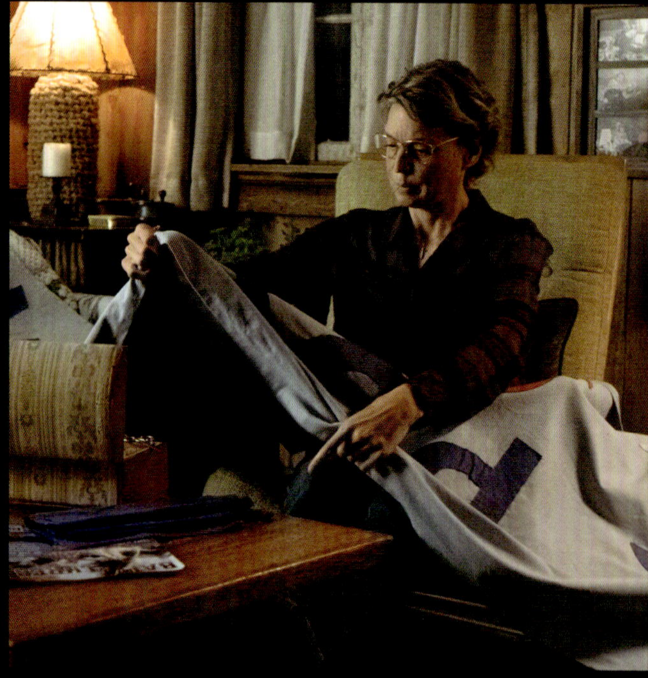

THIS SPREAD/ Anderson: "Annie wants everybody to get along."

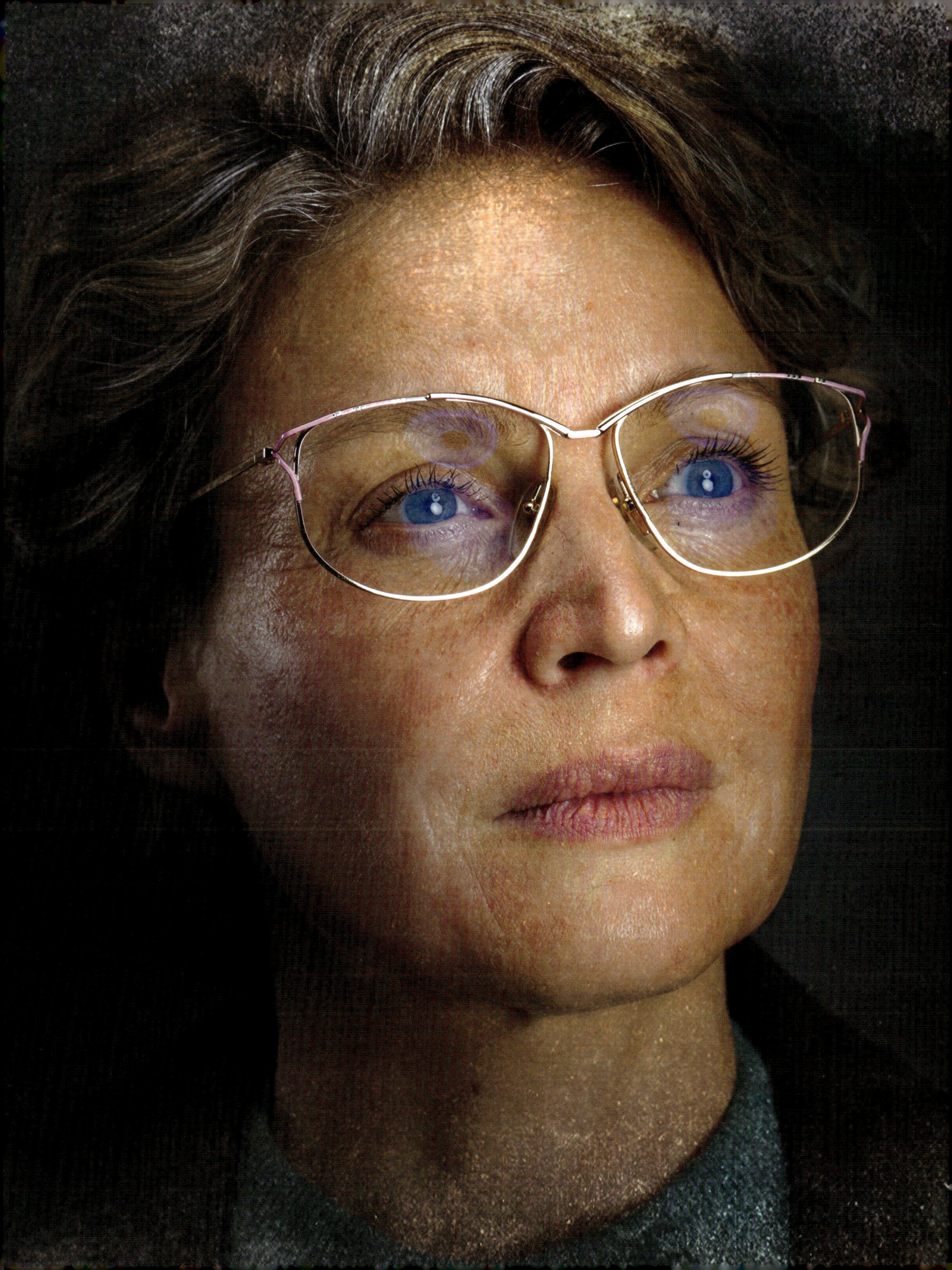

In the final scene, as Annie and Ed wait for the sunrise, Lehman relates, "We were in a muddy, flooded field. The great big wide [shot] when we were trying to get the sunrise/sunset just right, both of us made a fairly rookie mistake, and ended up becoming incredibly emotional in the big wide [shot], and then we were both like, 'Oh, God, we have to move in for our closeup – we're spent from the wide.' But Henry's a joy to spend time with."

Between shots, Lehman recalls, "All of us on the same COVID-19 testing schedule would congregate in a big tent, and play hours of card games. It was wonderful working with everybody."

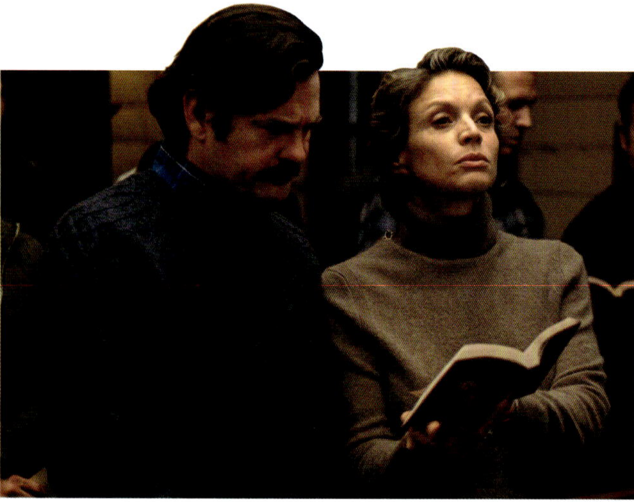

TOP/ Lehman, re Thomas: "We laughed, and faced any difficulties together."

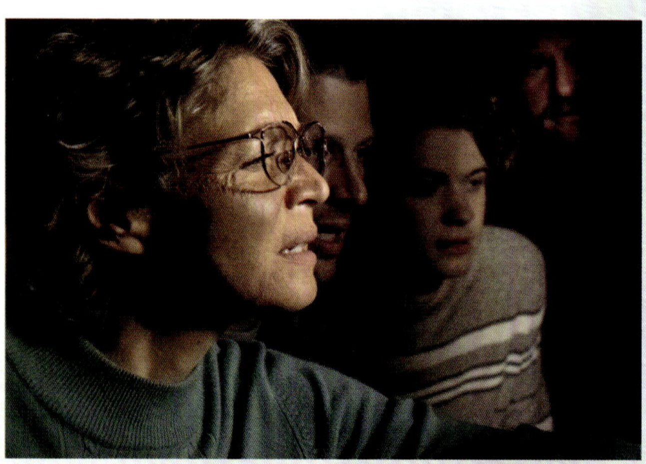

TOP/ Annie and her family peer out their window.

RIGHT/ Lehman: "We had one minute to capture sunrise, which actually was sunset."

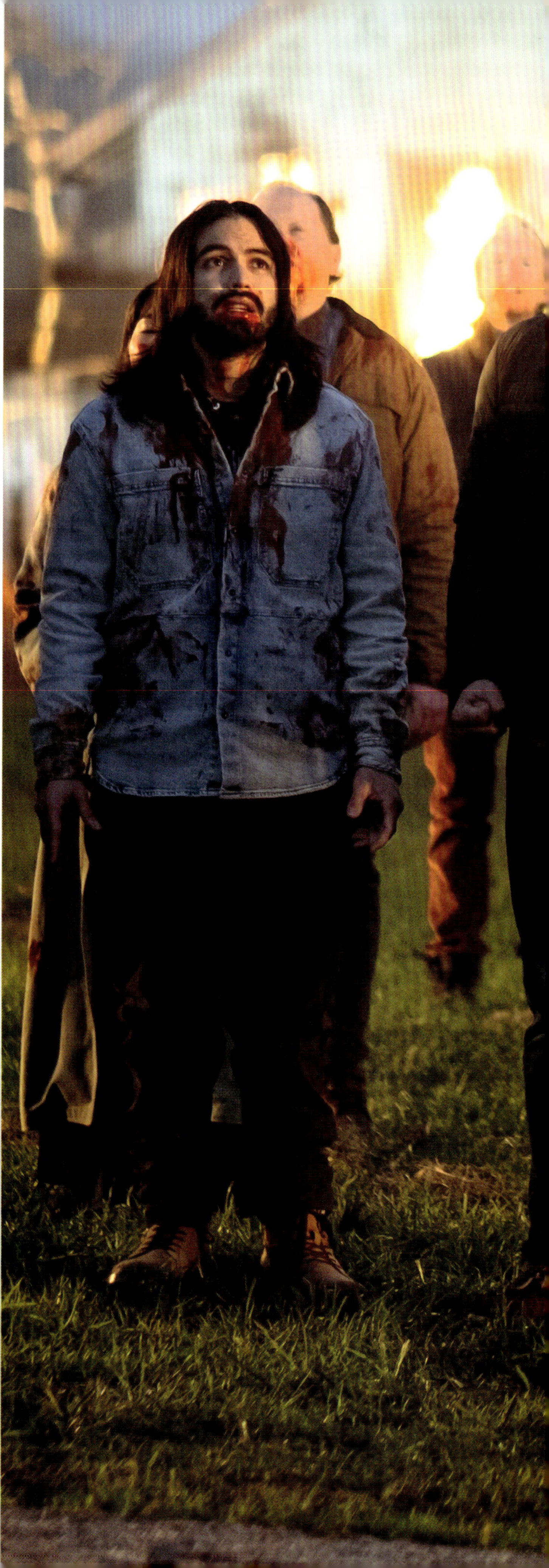

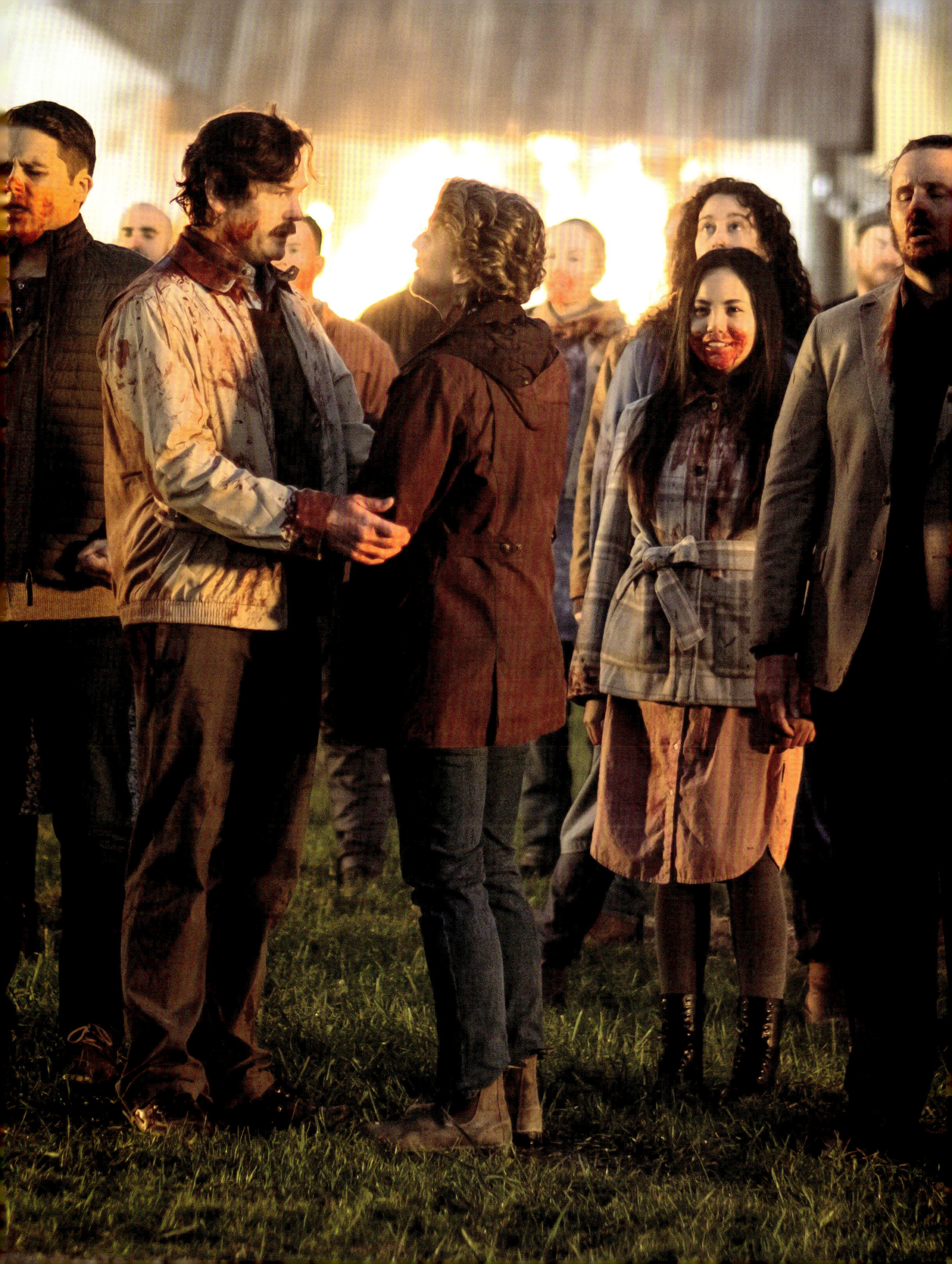

ED FLYNN

HENRY THOMAS

Midnight Mass is the sixth project that actor Henry Thomas has done with Flanagan, following *Ouija: Origin of Evil*, *Gerald's Game*, *The Haunting of Hill House*, *Doctor Sleep*, and *The Haunting of Bly Manor*.

Flanagan says, in creating Ed Flynn, "[He] leapt away from the people that I was basing it on, and more into what I knew Henry could do."

By now, does Thomas even ask to see the script, or does he just sign on whenever Flanagan asks? Thomas laughs. "We have a standing rule that, if I'm available, I'll do it. I trust Mike's taste and judgment."

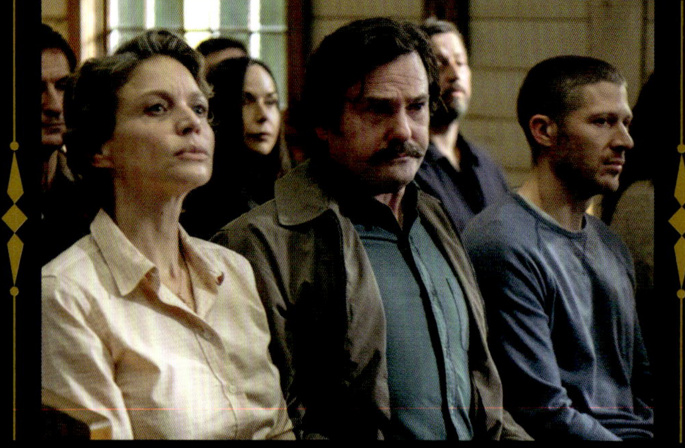

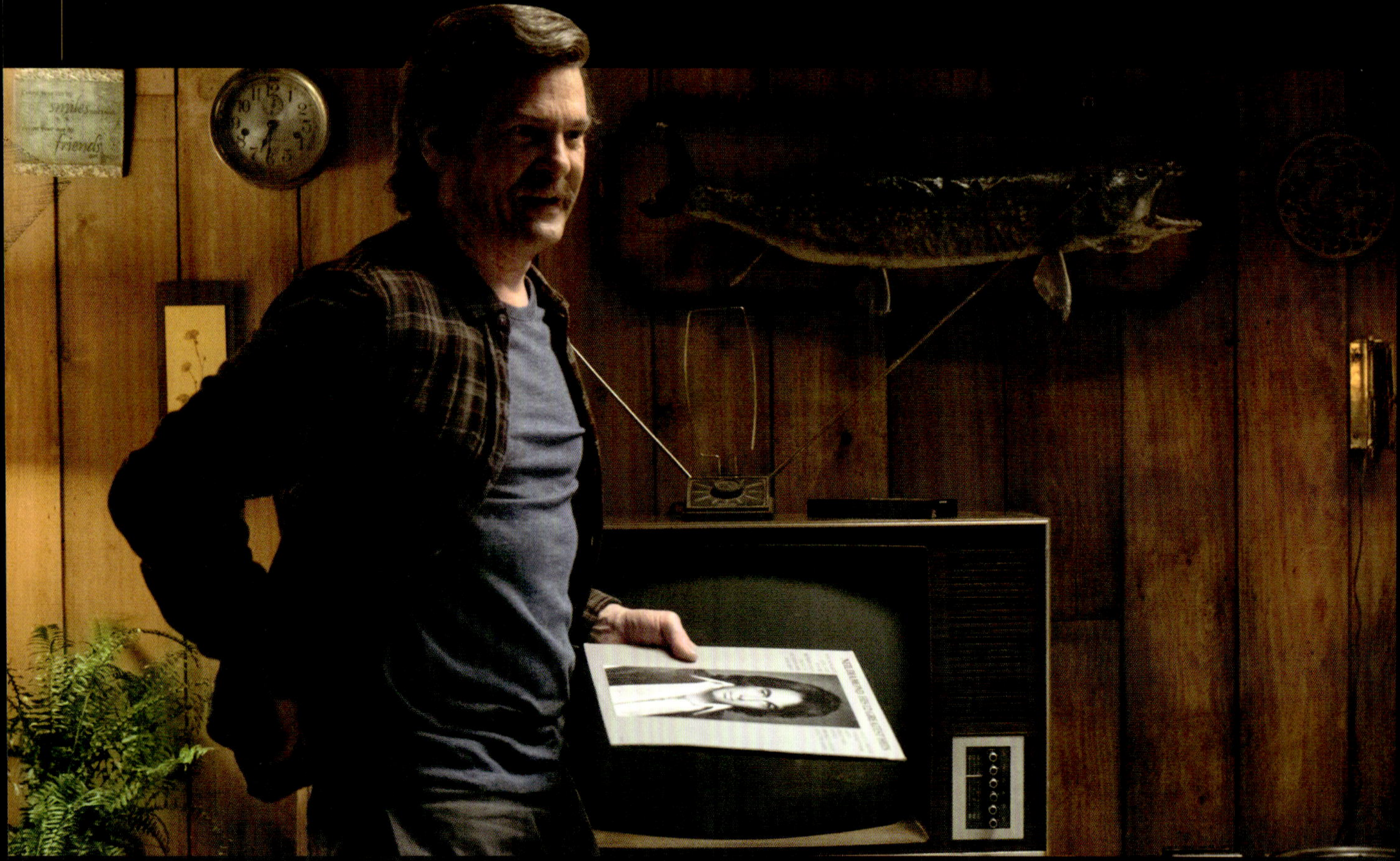

THIS SPREAD/ Thomas: "Ed's kind of the ringleader for the whole community."

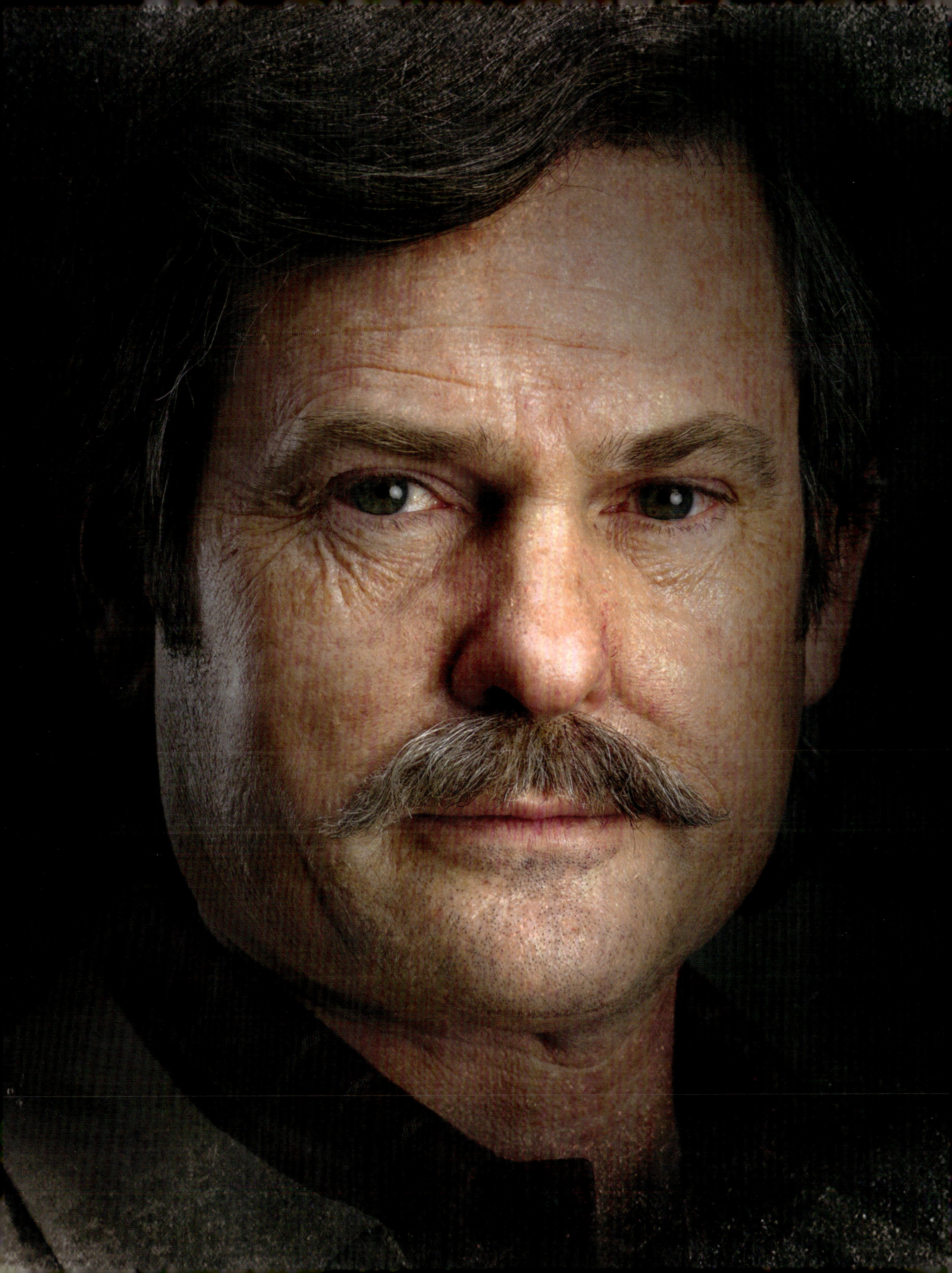

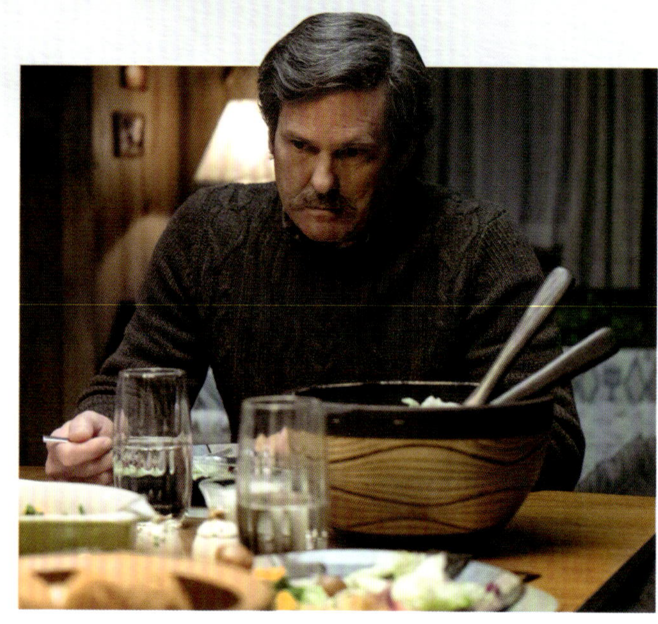

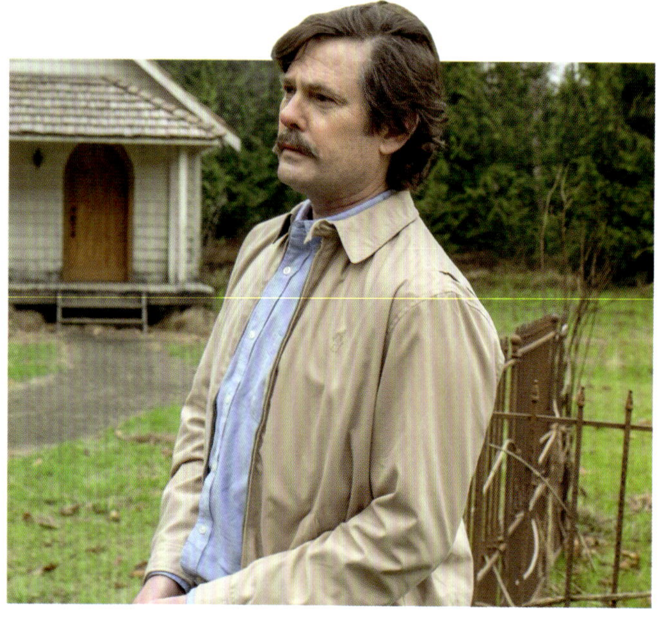

TOP/ Thomas: "Ed's in debt, doesn't have a lot of hope."

BOTTOM/ Thomas: "I think Ed believes in Heaven and Hell."

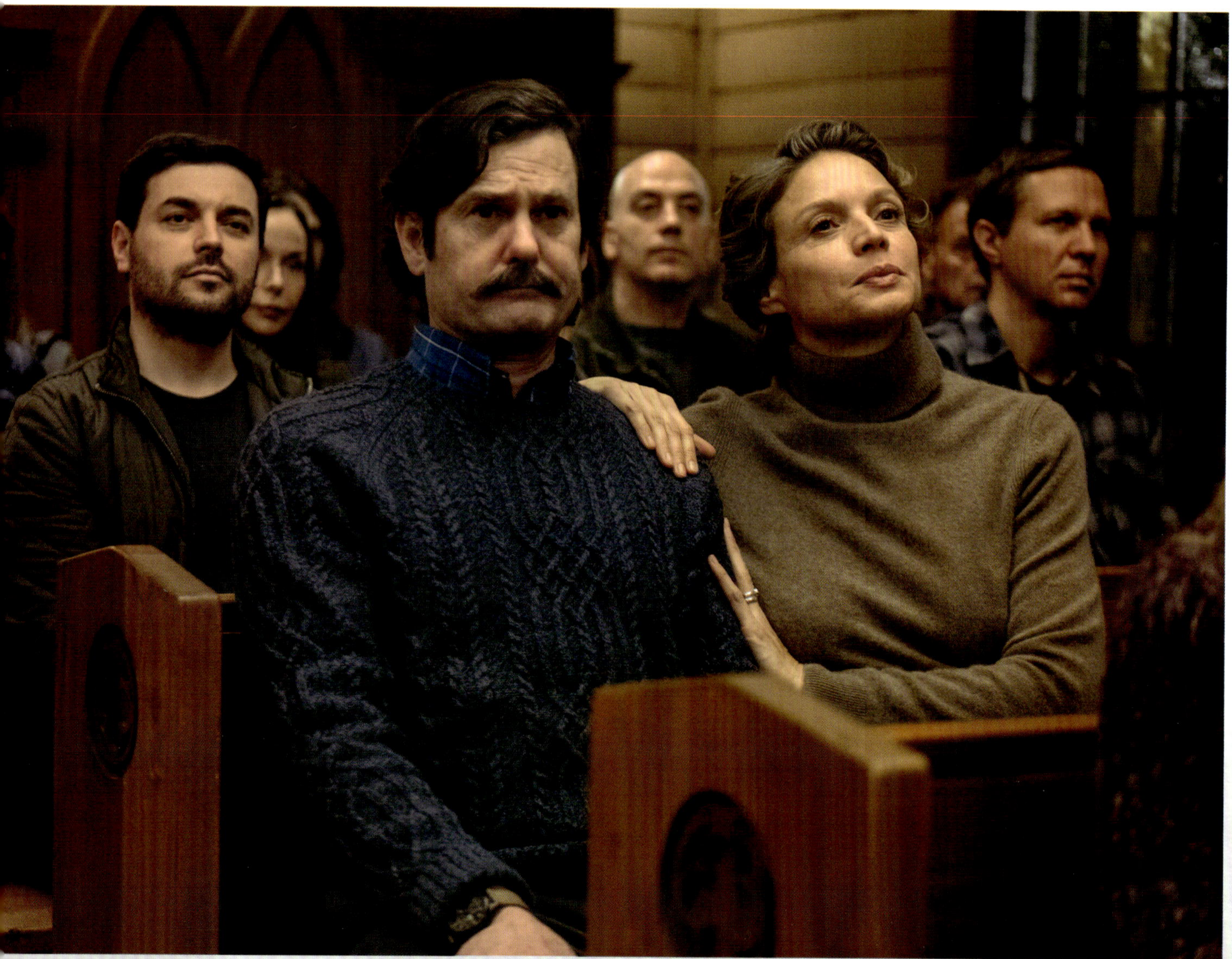

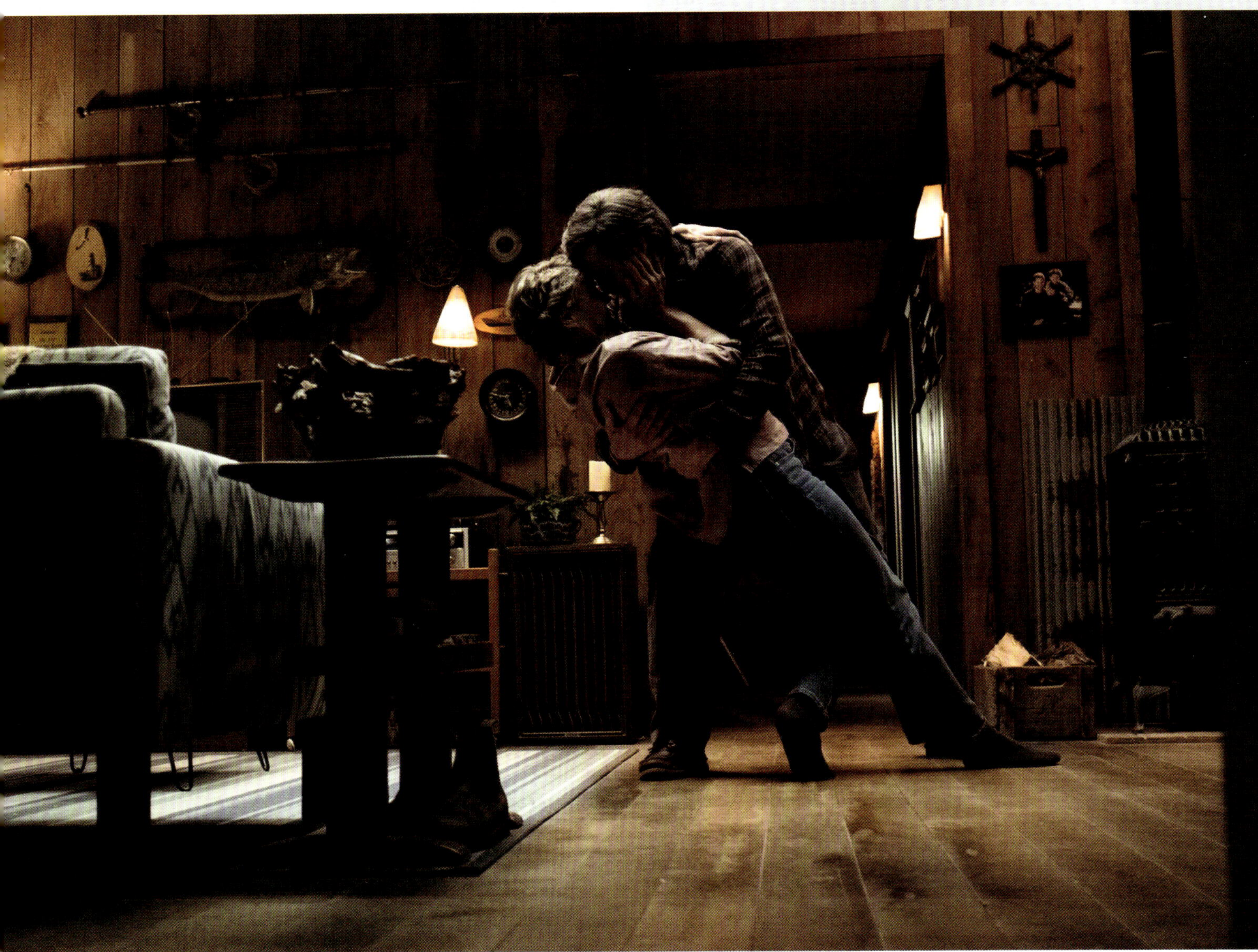

TOP/ Gilford on Lehman and Thomas: "Two of the funniest people I've ever met."

Anderson says Ed's clothes reflect his traditional values. "He wears the same style his father wore, sweaters and button-up plaid shirts [for] church, and then his work clothes, an old fishing coat, and, like every fisherman, a baseball cap to keep the [elements] off his face."

For research, Thomas went "out on a crab boat to learn all the things that Ed would know, and get a feel for the physical work, with the guys who were doing the marine side of the production. It's invaluable to talk to people who actually do the job that your character does."

Thomas says Ed sees Riley as bringing "shame to the family. It's only Ed's personal angst that he's mad about, like most people when they're angry with someone else." Ed sees Warren as "the good boy," and wife Annie "as a saint."

For Ed's older state, Thomas says, "I modeled a lot of my body language off of my father, who worked a blue-collar job until he retired at sixty-five."

Ed's moustache was a prosthetic added by the makeup department, because it would have been problematic to apply the aging makeup around a real one. "My makeup and mannerisms as Ed would make Zach laugh. We had a few times where we could barely get through our scenes together. Sometimes the moustache would pop off on one side from laughing."

Thomas notes that his final scene with Lehman was made more intense "because we were performing in the freezing cold, and the rain, and the wind."

THE MARINA

ACCESS TO THE OUTSIDE WORLD

"There are multiple harbors in Vancouver," Macy says. Fortunately for production, "The one that was nearest our coastal build in Steveston actually had most of what we needed."

This was used as the Crockett Island marina. Arnold relates, "We removed a bunch of their boats, and brought in our own boats and signage, and large square containers called 'fish totes,' which we stacked up to hide various things we didn't want to see. Then we brought in [fake] gas tanks, for the whole fuel/oil fire conflagration."

Arnold explains that the production's marine coordinator helped find the specific vessel for Ed Flynn, as well as the harbor's other craft. "We had to paint them and do various things to make them fit in with the rest of the scheme, and he brought in the passenger ferry boat that people get transported to the island on, and a bunch of pieces of dock, and floating barges."

The barges, Arnold adds, are to accommodate, "cameras, and lighting equipment, and part of the crew. You always need that when you're working on water."

Flanagan speaks with joy of shooting the boat sequences. "I can't believe we pulled that off. I had been told all the horror stories of having multiple vessels with equipment, and crew, and cast out in choppy water, where everyone's going to throw up, and we'd fight for every frame of footage. We had two wonderful days on the water that made for some of the most unique and high-velocity, coolest memories I have of filming anything."

BOTTOM/ The *Island Belle* at Crockett's ferry port.

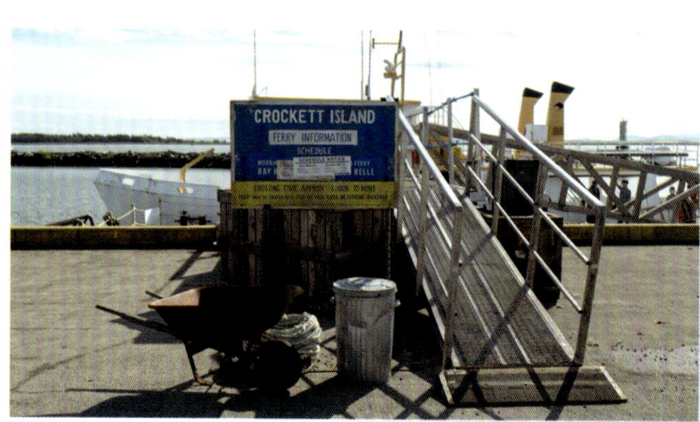

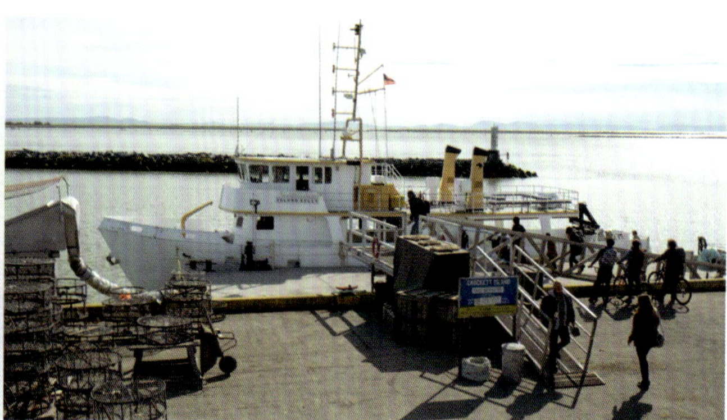

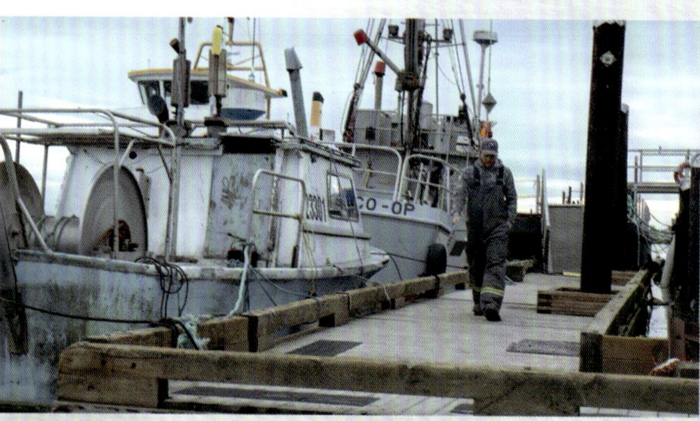

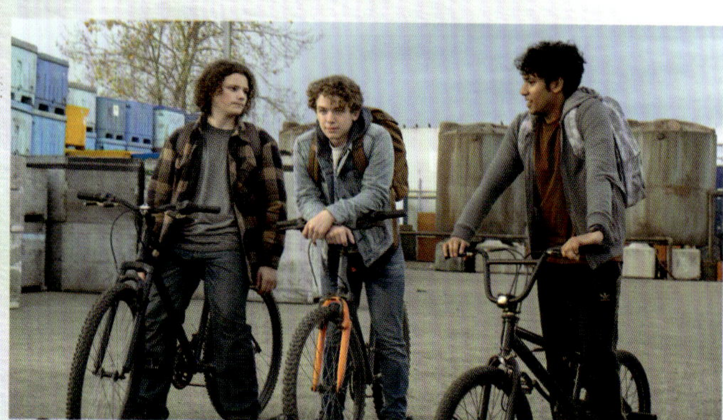

BOTTOM/ Concept art for the *Bay Breeze*.

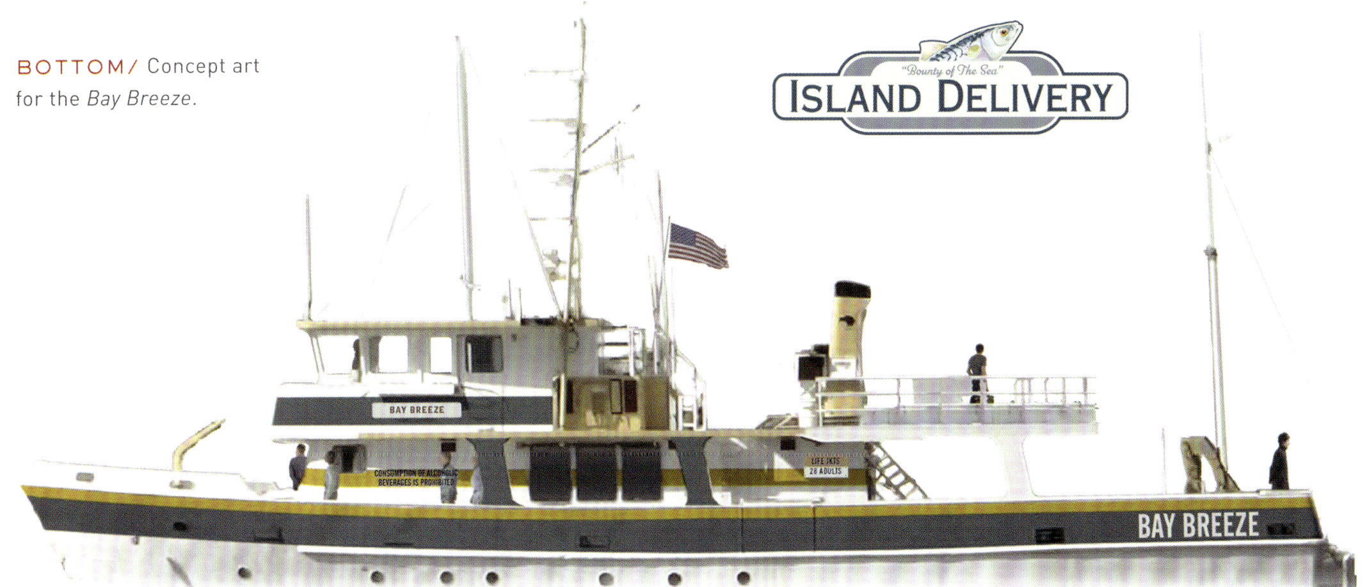

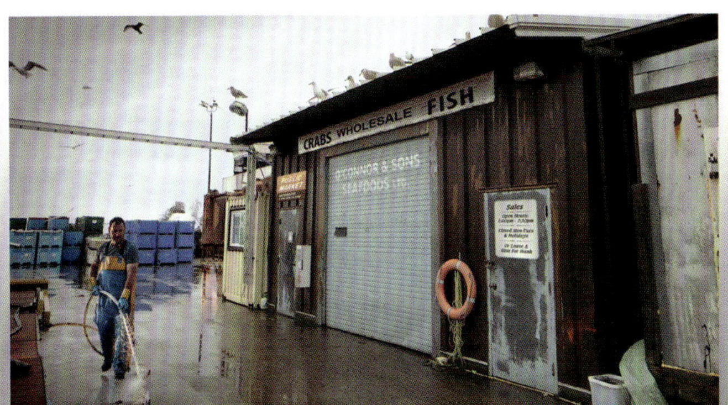

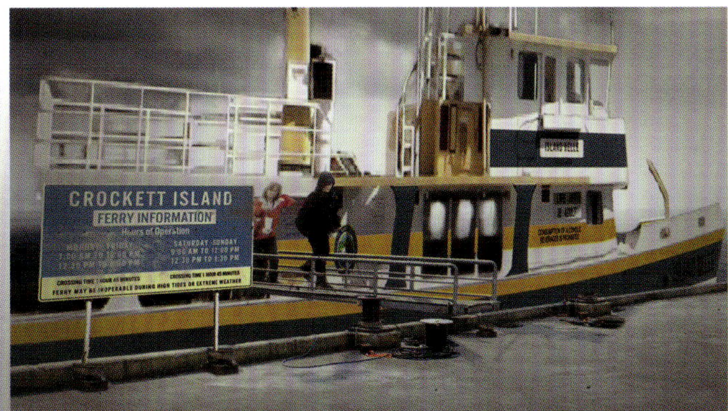

THIS PAGE/ Pre-viz concept art of the marina.

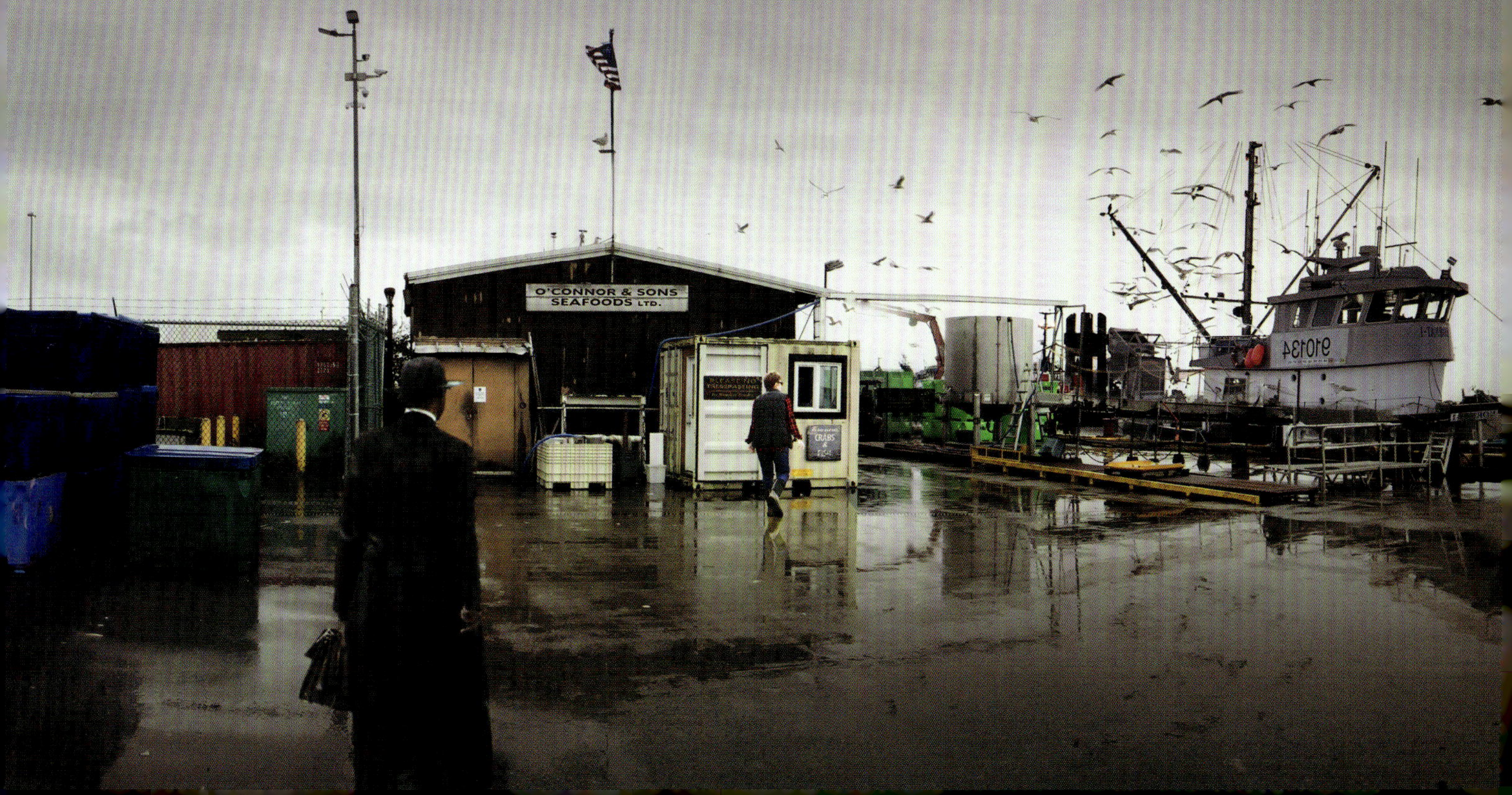

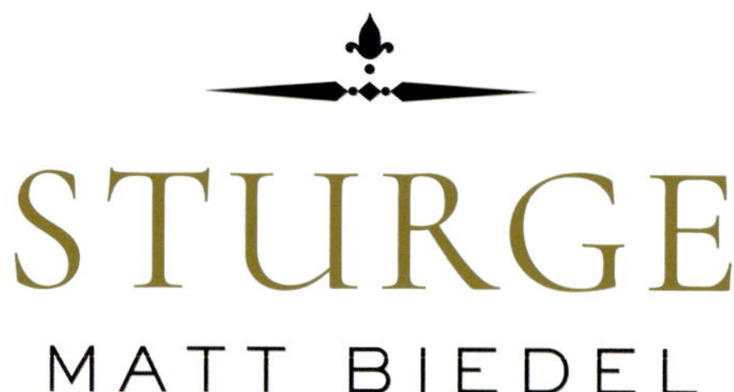

STURGE

MATT BIEDEL

Matt Biedel plays handyman Sturge. "He's not the smartest guy," Biedel says, "but he gets stuff done, he's good with a hammer, and he can figure things out mechanically. He does have his own thoughts, but he's gotten used to doing what everybody tells him to do."

When Bev includes Sturge in her crusade, Biedel opines, "He's never had anything to believe in like this [crusade] before, and it becomes something he can feel pride about. He's suddenly a person who has responsibility."

When Sturge throws a Molotov cocktail, Biedel says, "It was a little nerve-wracking at first. 'How do I throw this so it doesn't catch my sleeve on fire?' But after the first time, those jitters go away."

Anderson says of Sturge's style, "He wears work pants even to church. The only [dressy] thing he does for church is wear a blue Oxford button-down shirt with no tie."

Biedel appreciated Flanagan's notes. For a scene in which Sturge is lying to Sarah and Erin, "Mike said, 'Try it a little less suspicious.' It just flowed after that. He's very positive. And with Ooker at the end, the pseudo father/son moment, I'd built up this scene in my mind. Mike said, 'We don't have a lot of time, so we're going to knock this out in a couple takes.' He took away all that pressure. Both Louis Moffat and I felt wonderful about it. Mike doesn't say a lot, but what he does say is very specific and intuitive."

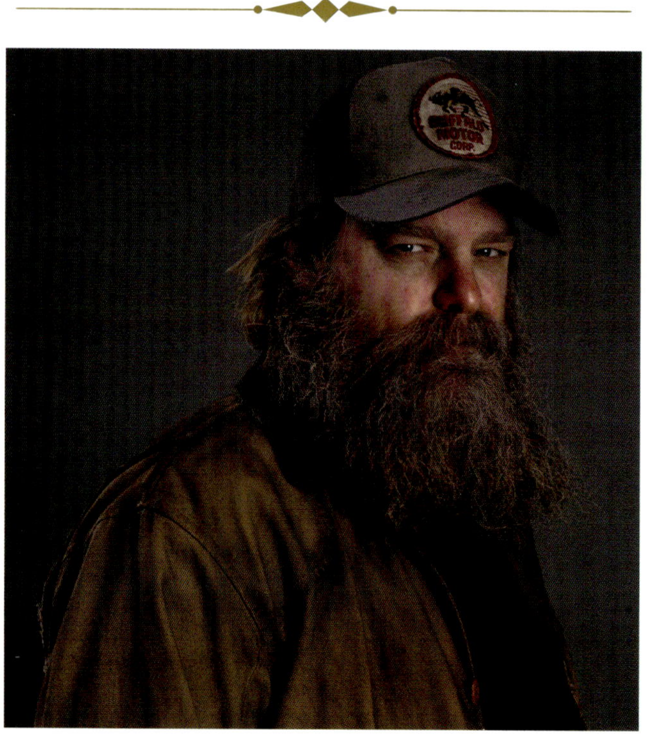

TOP/ Biedel: Playing older "wasn't too tough for me."

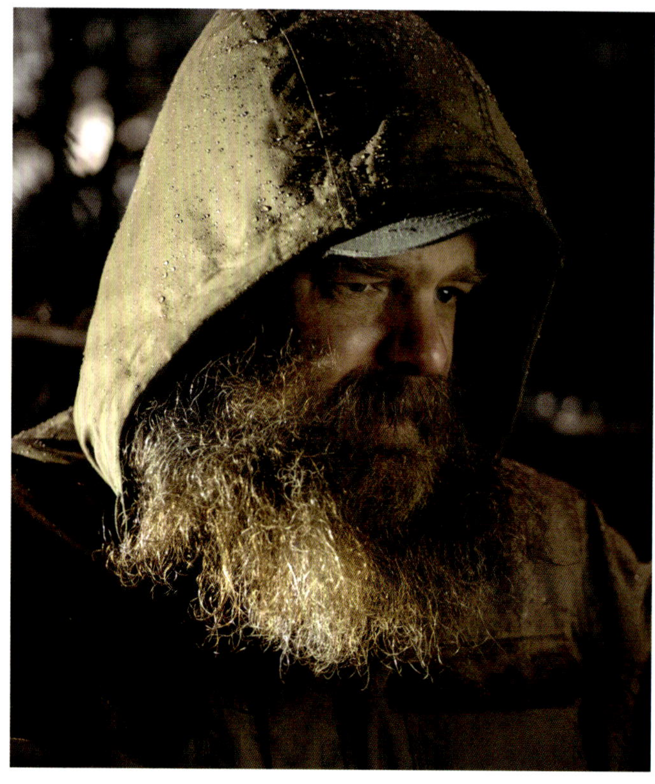

TOP/ Biedel: "I think Sturge is a sweet person inside."

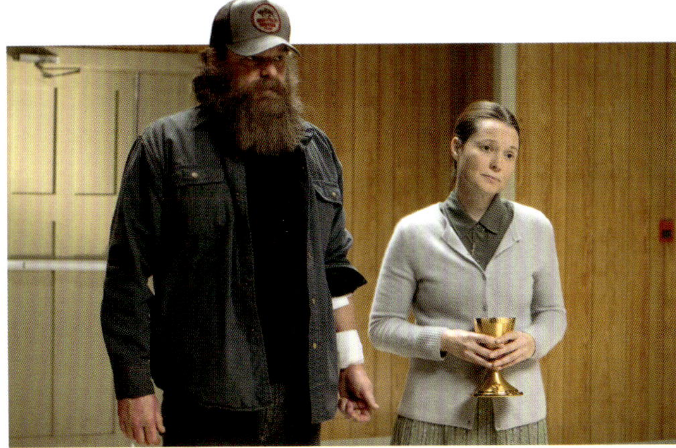

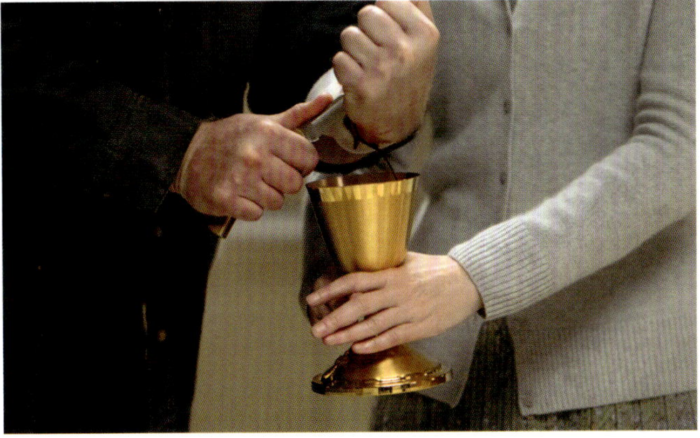

TOP/ Bev helps Sturge prepare to shed his blood for the cause.

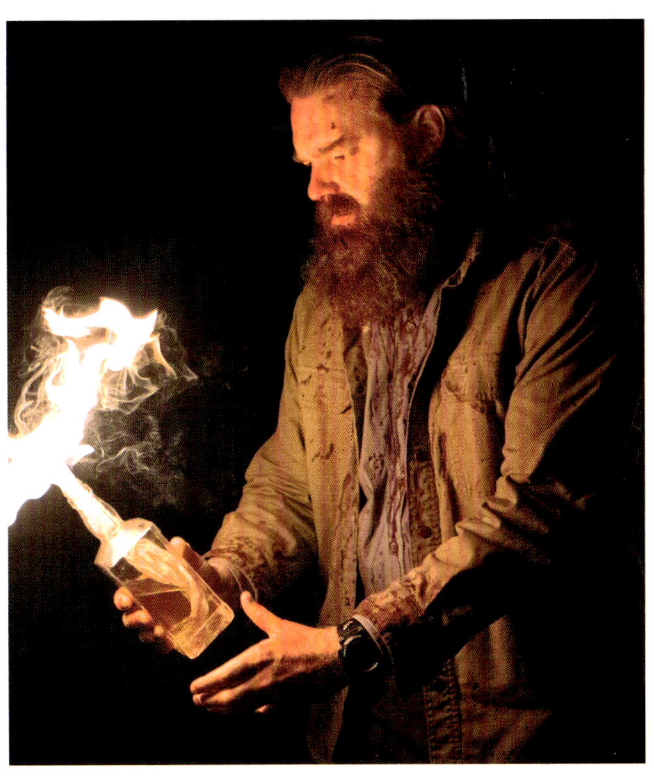

TOP/ Sturge's handyman duties include setting up the church's sign.

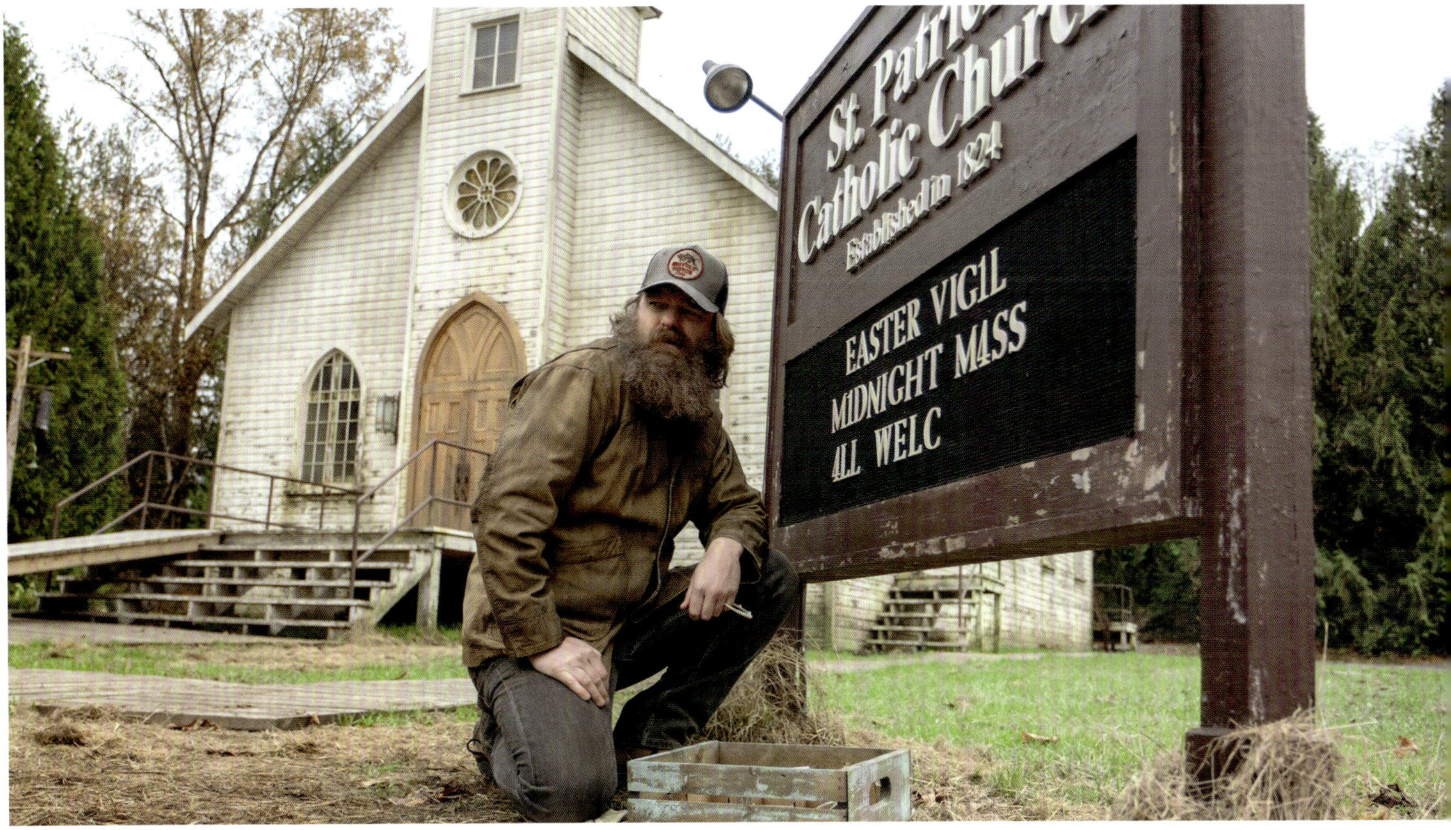

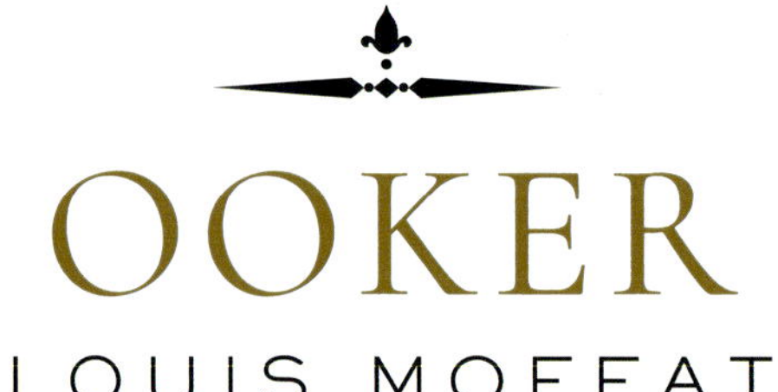

OOKER

LOUIS MOFFAT

Ooker, played by Louis Moffat, is Warren's friend and fellow altar boy. Ooker resents Warren's newer friend Ali. Per Flanagan, "Ooker represented the old guard, a kid who had no reason to give Ali the hard time he gives him, but does anyway, based on learned behavior."

Moffat is English, but says his American accent "came naturally." He initially auditioned for Warren. When he and Rigney compared their tryout tapes, Moffat saw "where Igby meant a line innocently, I was more conniving. Ooker is a bad influence on Warren. But Warren calls Ooker on his bullshit."

Weed-selling Bowl, Moffat believes, is who Ooker really respects. "I think they're the secret best friends. That's what Ooker wants to be when he's older, which is a sad aspiration, to be a drug dealer on the island."

Moffat misstepped when the boys moved a canoe. "It was dark, and I put my whole leg in the water," he laughs.

Moffat's favorite scene was "super-sad, where I'm talking about how I killed my mother. I don't know why that would have been my favorite, but I nailed it to what I wanted, so it made me feel like I was meant to be there."

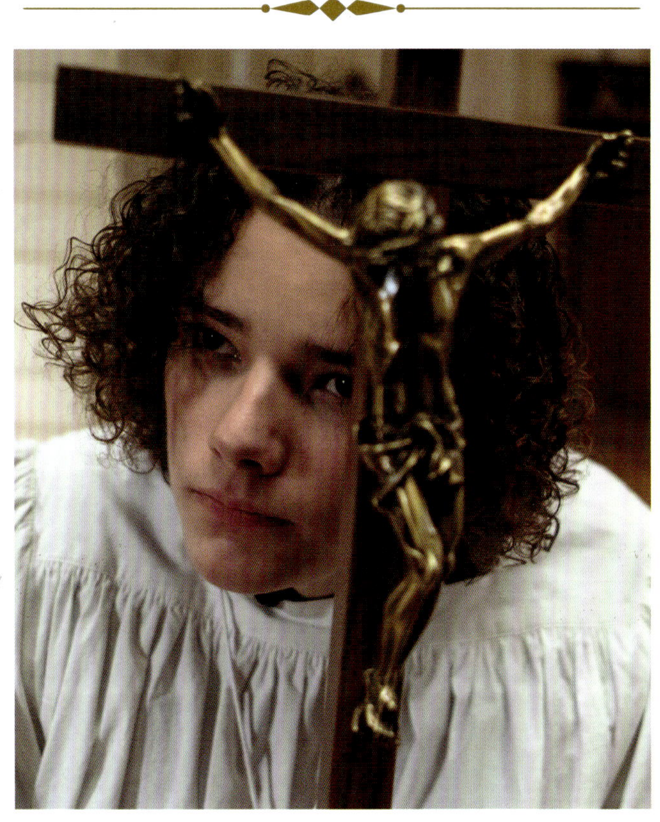

TOP/ Moffat: "I don't think Ooker has much belief."

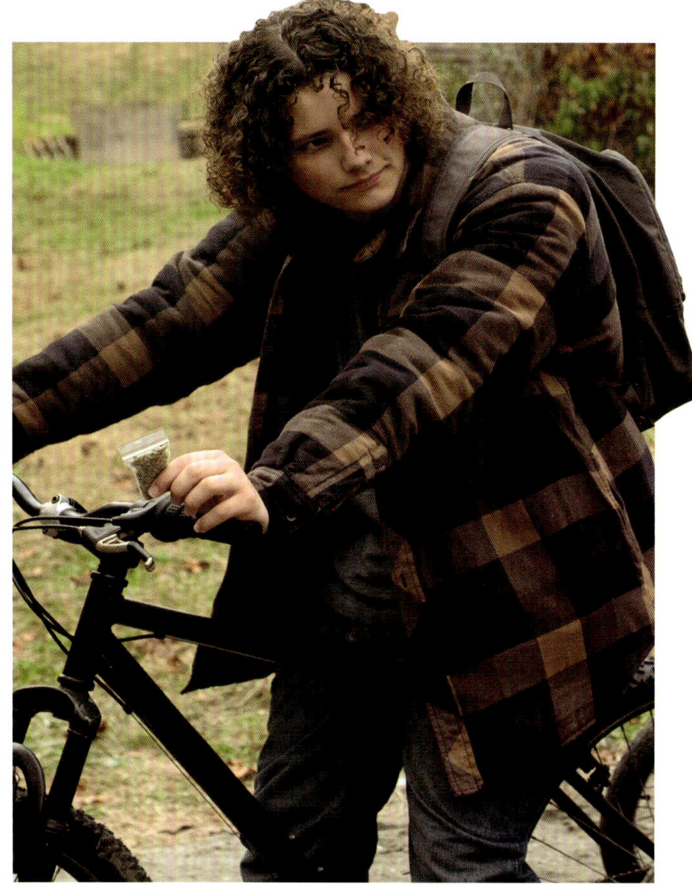

TOP/ Moffat on Ooker, re Crockett: "I think he's comfortable there in some respects."

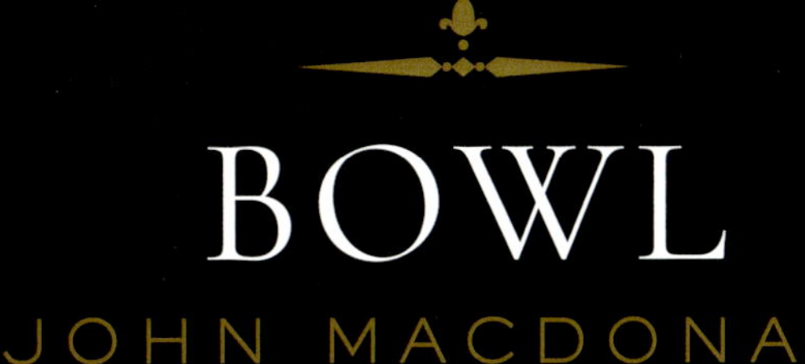

BOWL

JOHN MACDONALD

Bowl, real name Bill, is played by John MacDonald. Bowl is close with his mother Joanie (Patricia Drake), sells weed to Warren and Ooker, and helps out his pal Joe Collie. Then Bowl becomes one of the Angel's first human victims.

MacDonald gave Bowl a back story. "He's working at a sawmill off-island, trying to make ends meet for his family, because he's the breadwinner. I wanted to go against that idea that he's just a stoner."

MacDonald enjoyed shooting the Crock-Pot-Luck in the town square. "Everybody in the cast was there, and me and [Drake] were hanging out between takes."

Bowl sees Joe mourn the dying dog Pike. "That was the same day, at the end of filming the festival. I'm really sad for Joe, because I know he's going down to rock bottom. I don't want to end up in his shoes."

MacDonald also plays Bowl's days-old corpse. "That was fun; it was a big ordeal, too, because it took about four hours to get the makeup on, a lot of blood and bite wounds. My body had lost color, and all this blood had dried and scabbed over. When people watched the playback, they were saying, 'Well, that was disturbing'."

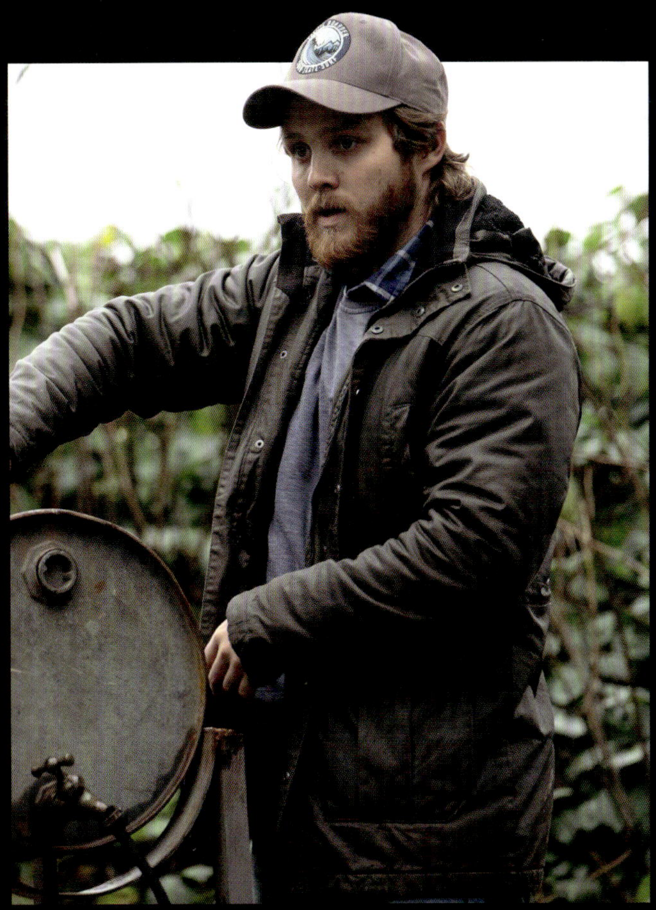

TOP/ Bowl helps out around Joe Collie's trailer.

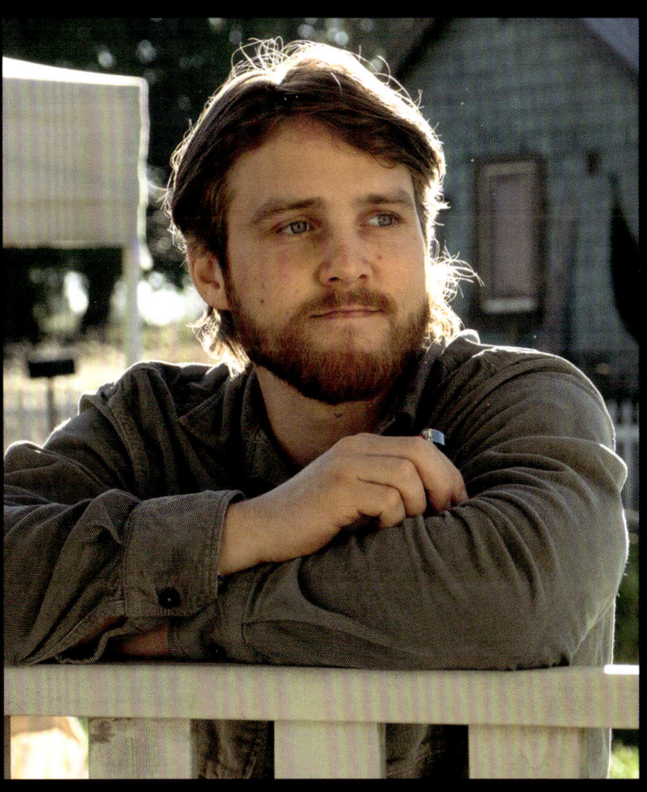

TOP/ MacDonald, re Bowl's friendship with Joe: "He's almost a father figure to me."

LEEZA SCARBOROUGH

ANNARAH CYMONE

Annarah Cymone plays young Leeza Scarborough, who lost the use of her legs six years earlier after being accidentally shot by Joe Collie. Leeza regains the ability to walk due to drinking the Communion wine (Angel blood); when she realizes what's behind the miracle, she is relieved at the end to be paraplegic once more.

"What [Cymone] does in her performance is awfully compelling," says Macy. "I find how Leeza starts and how she finishes to be a fascinating arc that you don't see so often."

Cymone says, "One of the cool things about the way it was written, and the way that we were able to bring it alive on screen, is that there's a lot of strength in her, especially in the way she finds faith as a way to become a better version of herself."

Books and videos aided Cymone's research for the role. "I read *Life on Wheels*. And I watched a lot of people who are Leeza's age, sixteen, who make vlogs, or just tell stories about what they went through."

The rough terrain on location necessitated an electric wheelchair, Cymone explained. "Mine was called the Jazzy, and it had the joystick." She tried out a regular wheelchair in Vancouver, prior to production, "and sometimes Igby would come with me, and we'd be Warren and Leeza, and he'd push me around. But the non-electric chair was impossible in the sand."

Cymone believes Leeza found a more contemplative view of life in the chair. When she's able to walk again, she is happy, but she's "confused about God's will for her."

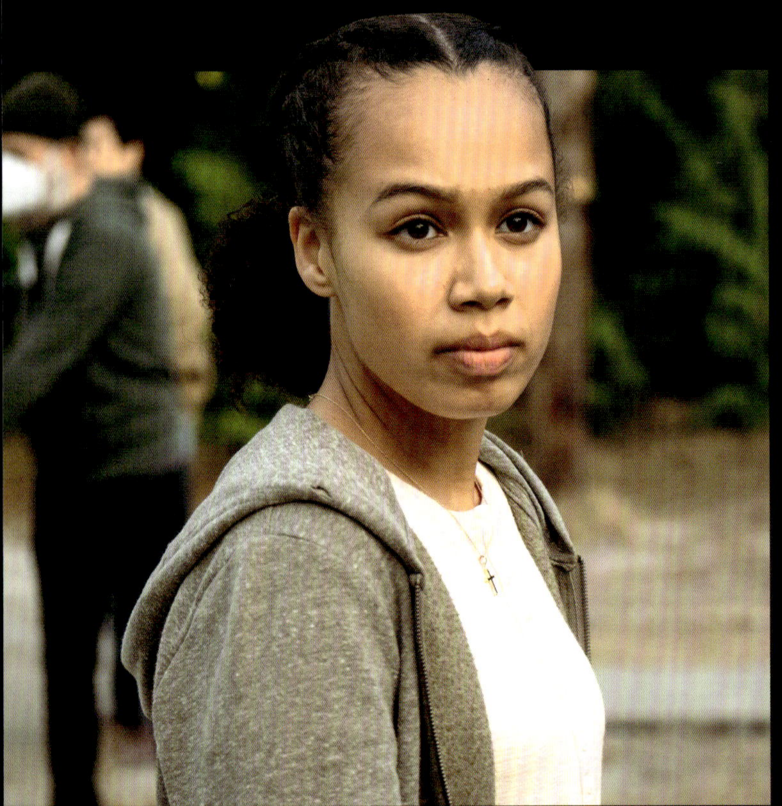

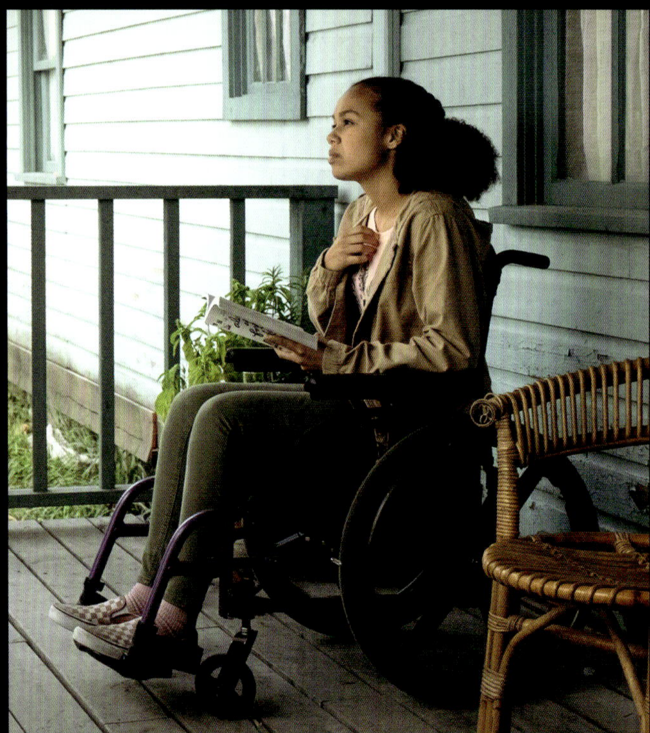

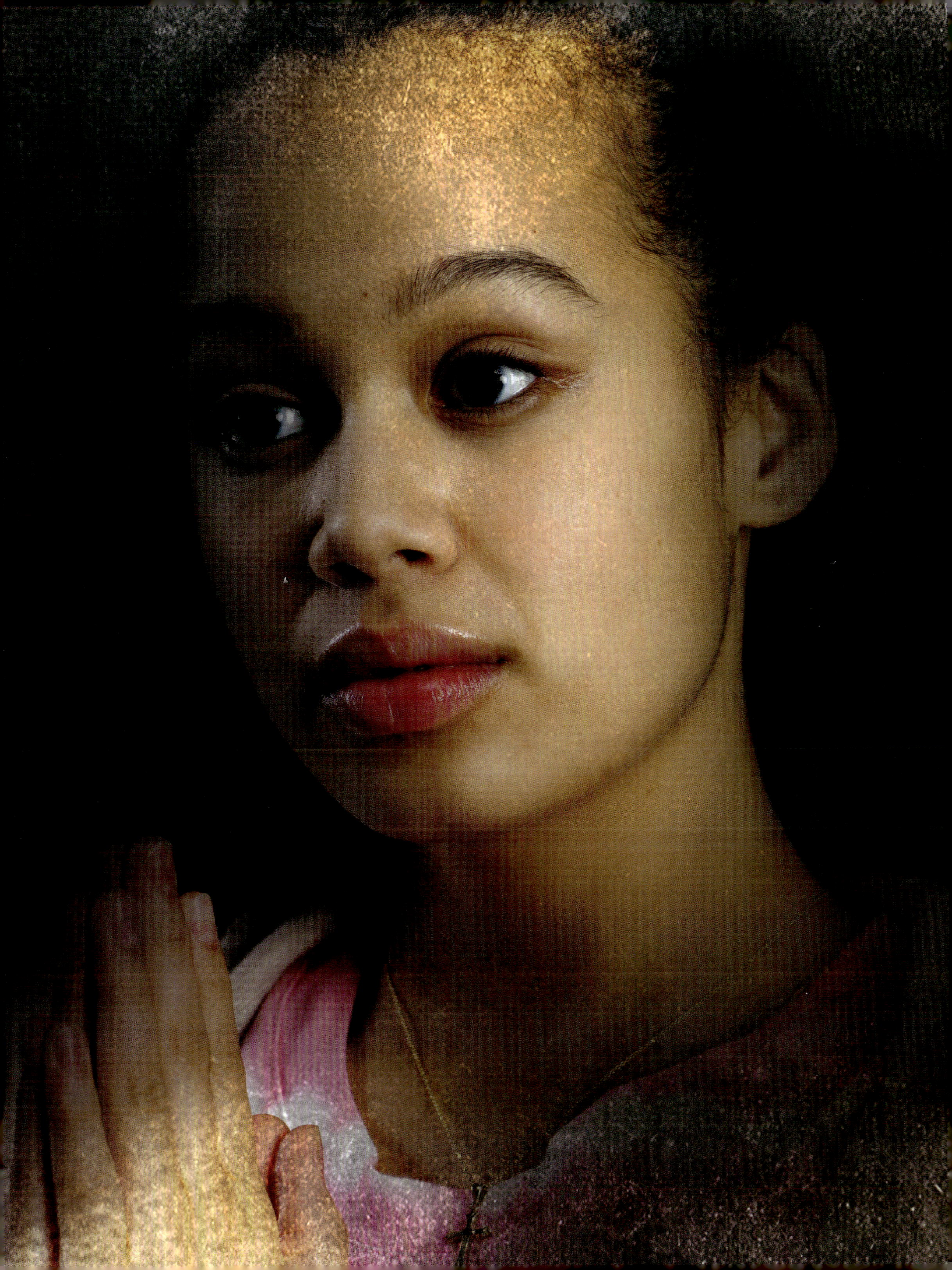

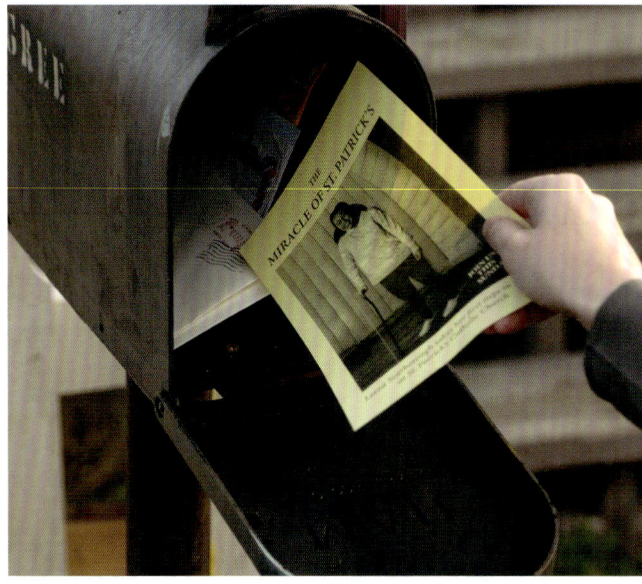

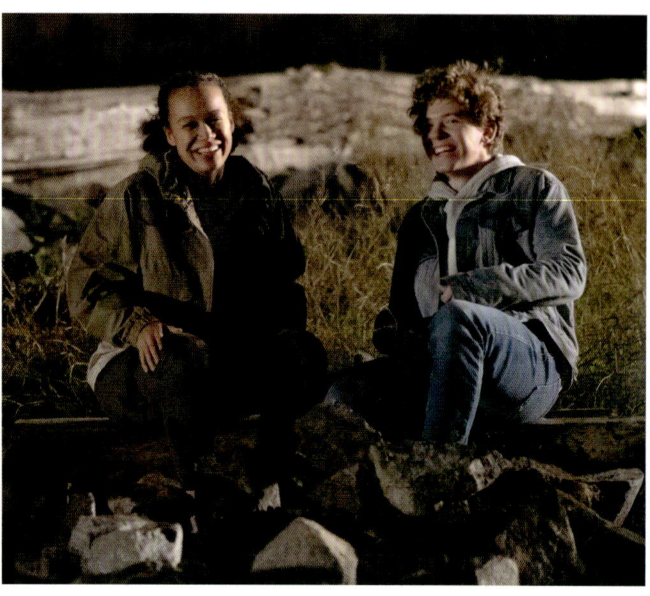

TOP/ (LEFT) Flyers spread word of the miracle at mass. (RIGHT) Leeza and Warren share a light-hearted moment.

BOTTOM/ The youth of Crockett Island on an outing.

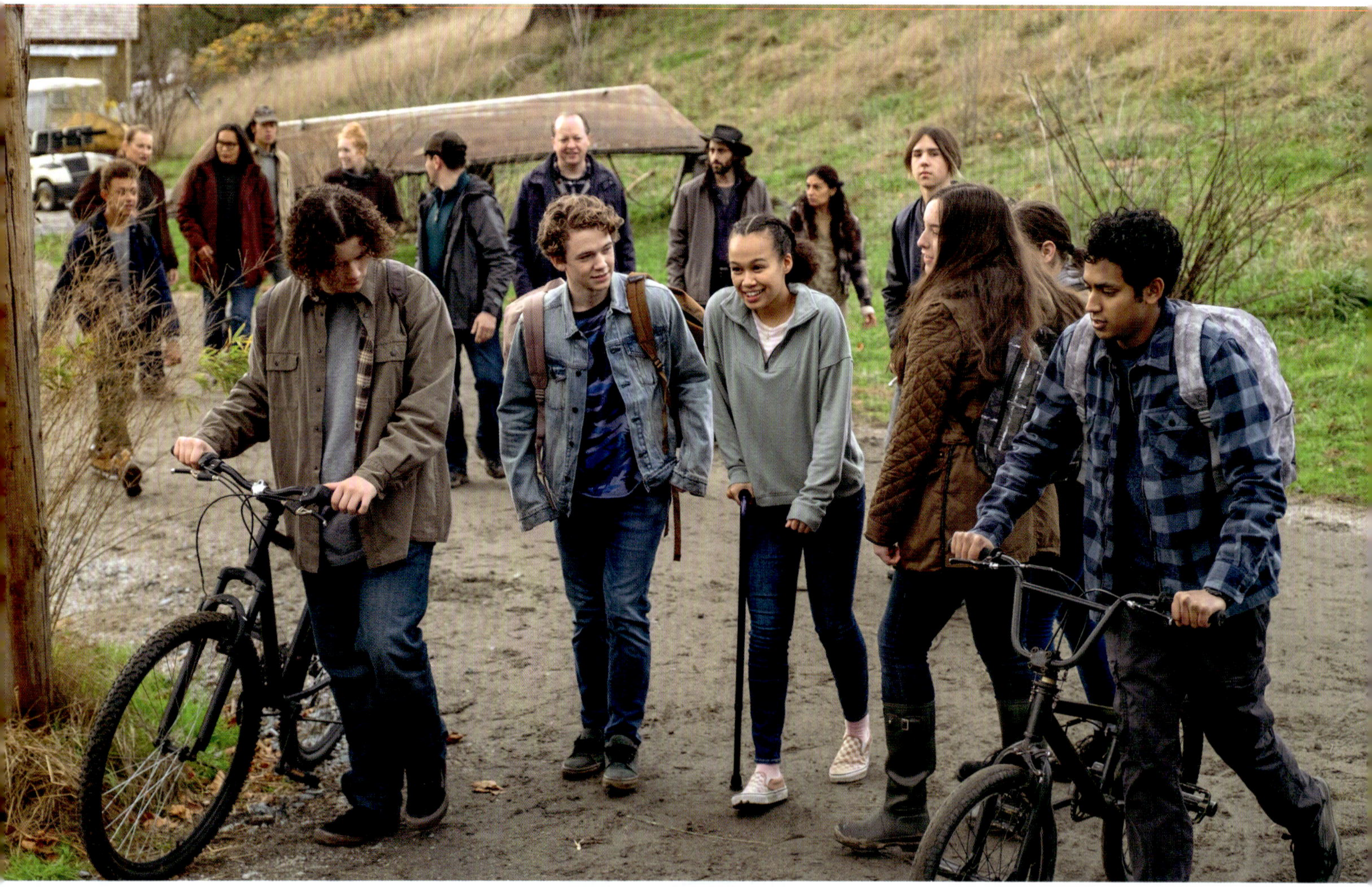

"SHE DOESN'T FIND IT AS A WAY OF BEING DISABLED AT ALL. SHE FINDS IT AS A WAY FOR HER TO SEE A NEW VERSION OF LIFE. WE FOUND A WAY TO FIND POWER IN HER SITUATION."

ANNARAH CYMONE

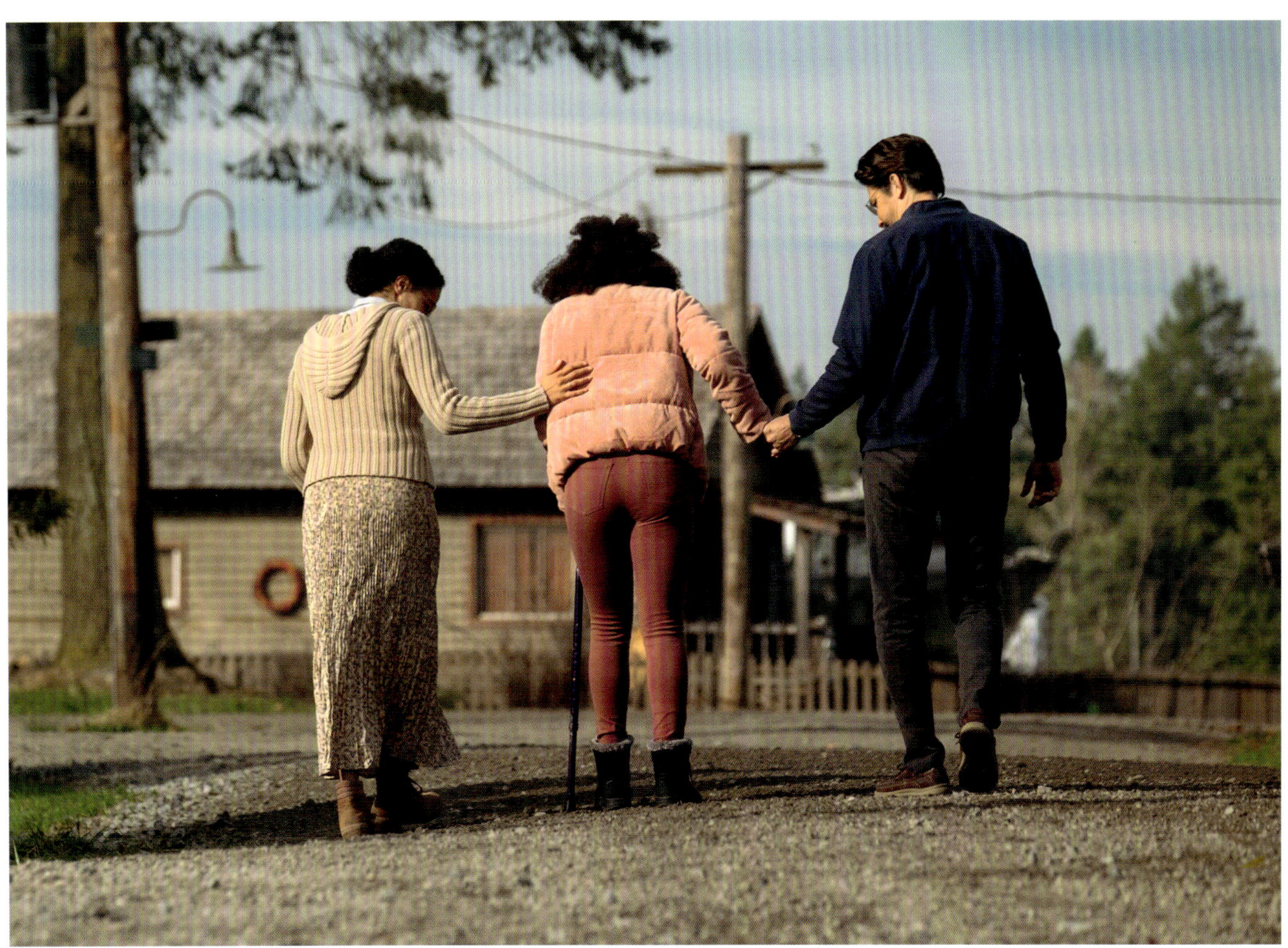

Leeza has a speech about forgiveness, which she delivers to Longstreet's Joe. Cymone says, "That was terrifying in the best way possible, because that monologue was beautifully written. A lot of Mike's direction was, 'Just take your time.' And Robert's the best scene partner to have. That's one of my favorite scenes, because it's a turning point for her as well, that she's forgiving [the man who disabled her]. And Robert does such a beautiful job. Your heart breaks for him."

There are parallels that Cymone sees between Leeza's specific experiences and what the town goes through. "Pre-vampire, she's very close to her parents. And she's very close to a lot of the town. The church is where she finds peace. The scene where the whole church is trying to turn people into vampires, that was one of the hardest to shoot, because she does have such a deep love for [her fellow congregants]. But she has to find a way to be okay with letting go, which is similar to what happened when she lost her feeling in her legs."

Leeza's feelings about Warren are "puppy love," says Cymone. "She's also very protective. In the last episode. It's kind of a role reversal – and I love it that it was written this way – where the girl has to do all these things, because the guy's in such shock. She's already been through a trauma, so she's finding a better way to cope."

TOP/ Leeza's parents, Dolly and Wade, help her adjust to walking again.

WADE SCARBOROUGH

MICHAEL TRUCCO

Michael Trucco, who plays Crockett Mayor Wade Scarborough, first worked with Flanagan (and Macy, Siegel, and Sloyan) in *Hush*.

Trucco remembers Flanagan showing him a fully-edited sequence that had been shot only the day before during *Hush*'s production. "I knew at that point that Mike is an overachiever. He shoots something, goes home, and he's already editing. I don't think he sleeps."

Trucco researched the various stages of age so he could play them authentically. "My father's friend has a condition called Dupuytren's contracture, where the tendons in your hands curl up, usually the last two fingers. I [decided], 'I'm going to play Wade with this condition on his right hand.' Over the course of the episodes, it gets better."

Flanagan says he loved this "incredible detail that Michael came up with on his own, and threaded consistently through it."

Wade is profoundly impacted by his daughter's situation, Trucco notes. "Leeza has a great speech about the day that she was shot. 'My father screamed and made sounds I've never heard him make before.' So, I have to go to a really dark place to imagine what it would be like to watch your child be shot right in front of you. It definitely informs the character."

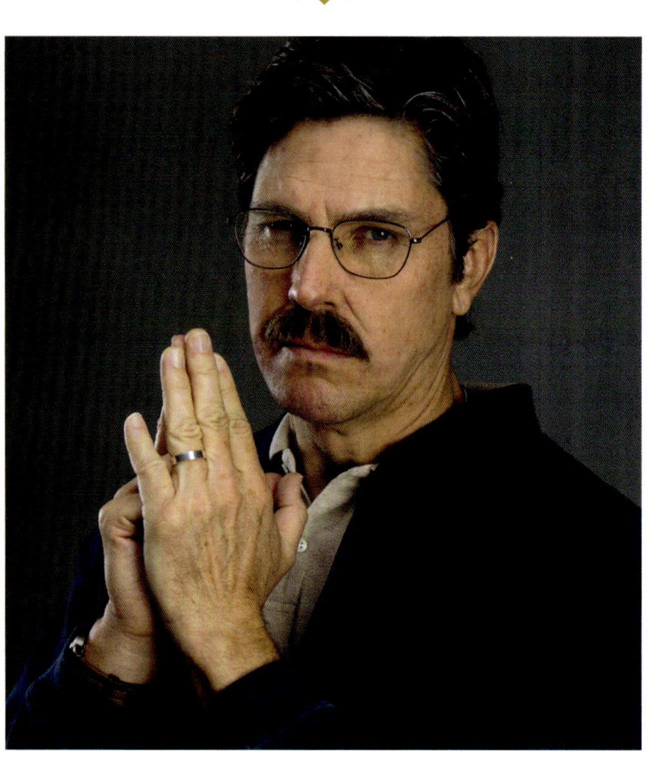

TOP/ Trucco: "In Wade's mind, being mayor is very serious."

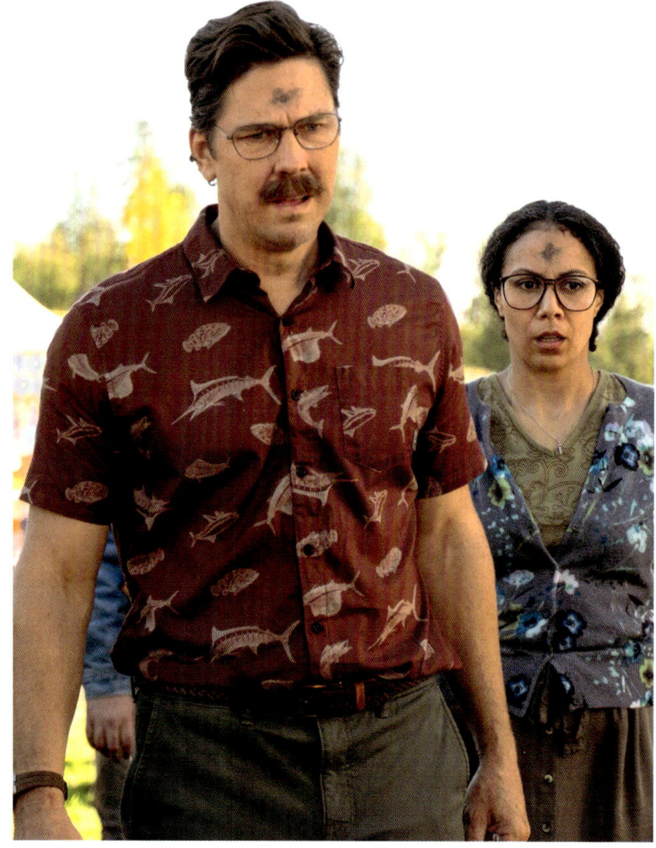

TOP/ Wade and Dolly Scarborough on Ash Wednesday.

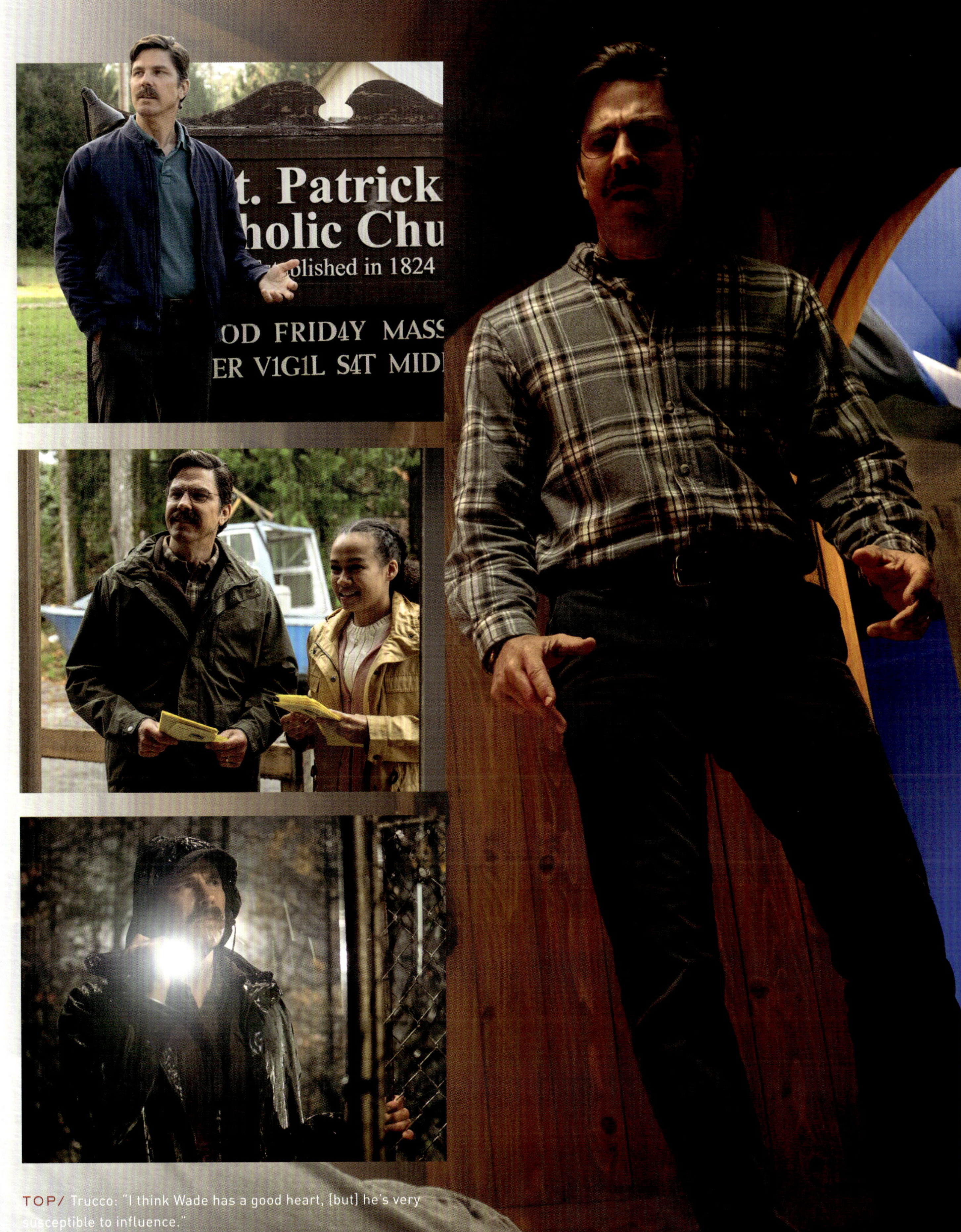

TOP/ Trucco: "I think Wade has a good heart, [but] he's very susceptible to influence."

DOLLY SCARBOROUGH

CRYSTAL BALINT

Crystal Balint plays Dolly Scarborough, wife of mayor Wade, mother of Leeza.

Balint and Trucco conferred during pre-production about their married characters, and how their daughter's shooting impacted the family. "He was really collaborative," Balint says. "[Wade] worked harder at seeing the positive. Dolly fell into this cycle of shame and darkness."

Balint researched cults, even listening to a recording of the Jonestown mass suicide. "It's haunting. It's a study in this culture of a hundred-percent belief. The Crockett community find themselves in a similar situation."

Balint describes enacting the poison's effects in the church. "It's [like] Alka-Seltzer tablets, they put it in a water bottle, and give you a blood goo. They call, 'Action', you quickly put it in your mouth, and swish it around. It doesn't taste great, but I love being able to spit out this awful goo, have it running down your face, and see it coming out of other actors. It makes it more real."

Co-composer Grush remembers that Balint asked if she could sing harmony for the nighttime procession through town. "It was beautiful." Balint has been singing from a young age. "I have sung hymns. But learning the hymn lyrics, which are challenging, it's like singing Shakespeare."

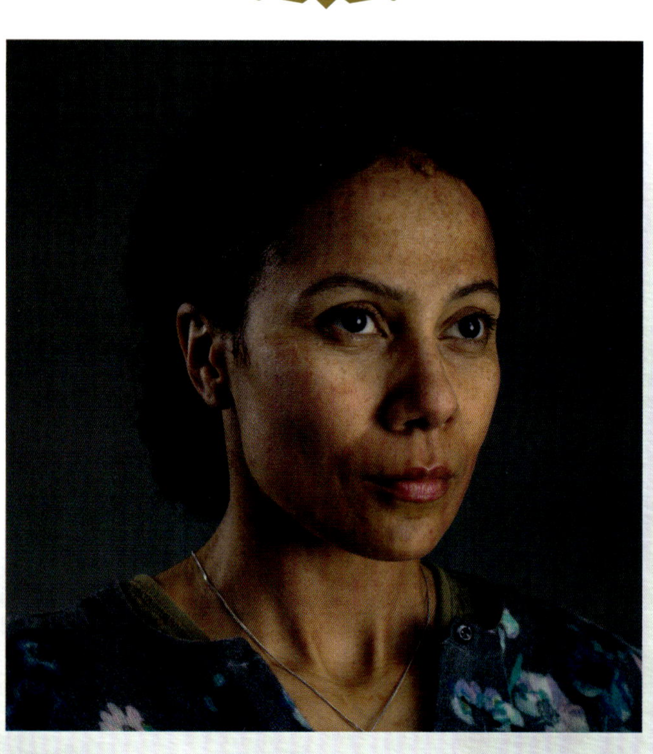

TOP/ Balint: "[Leeza's injury] affects Dolly in innumerable ways."

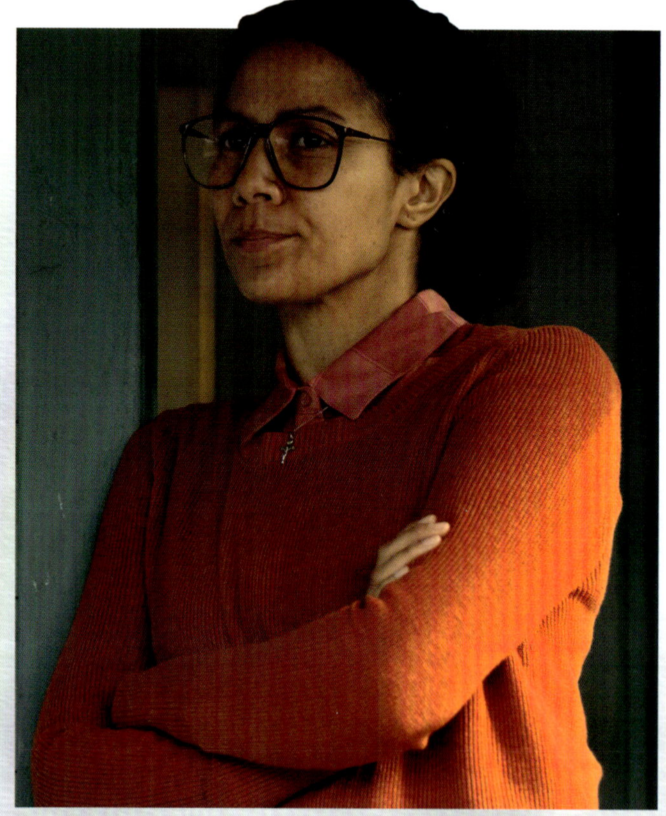

TOP/ Balint: "Michael [Trucco] and I talked about what keeps our characters there [on Crockett]."

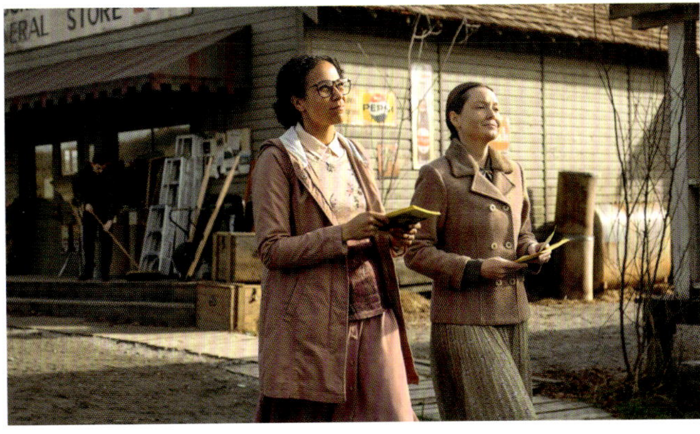

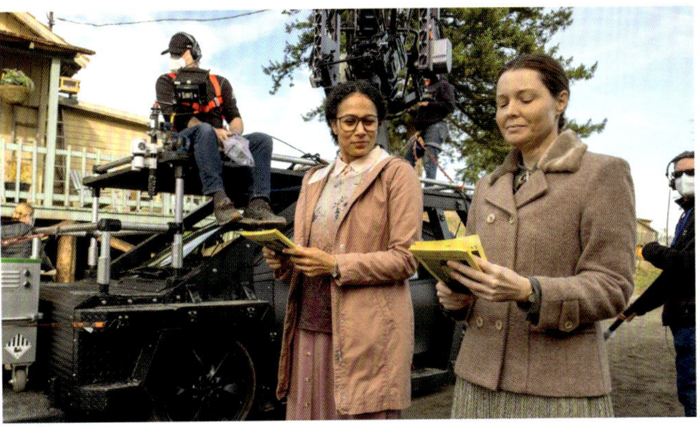

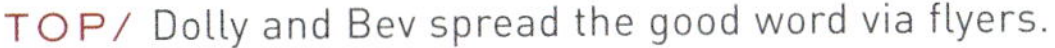

TOP/ Dolly and Bev spread the good word via flyers.

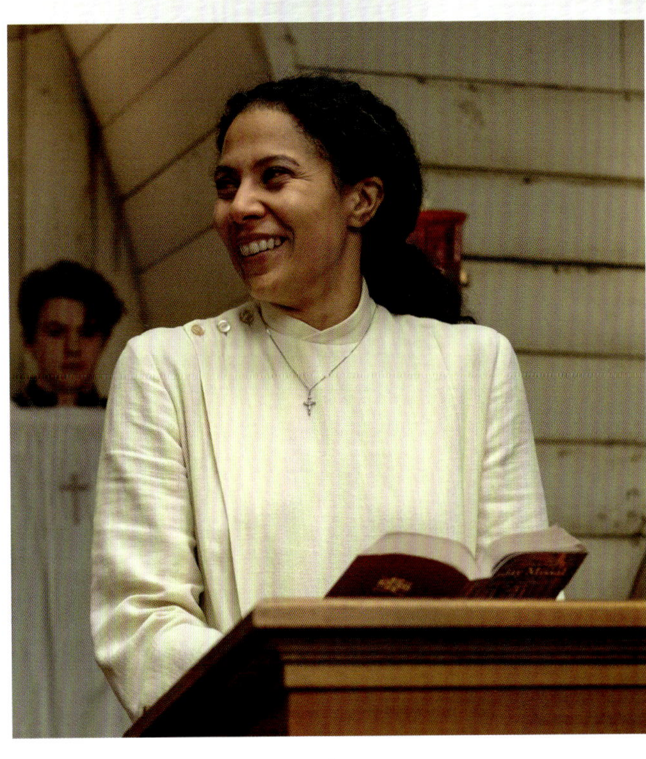

TOP/ Dolly leads the congregation in a hymn.

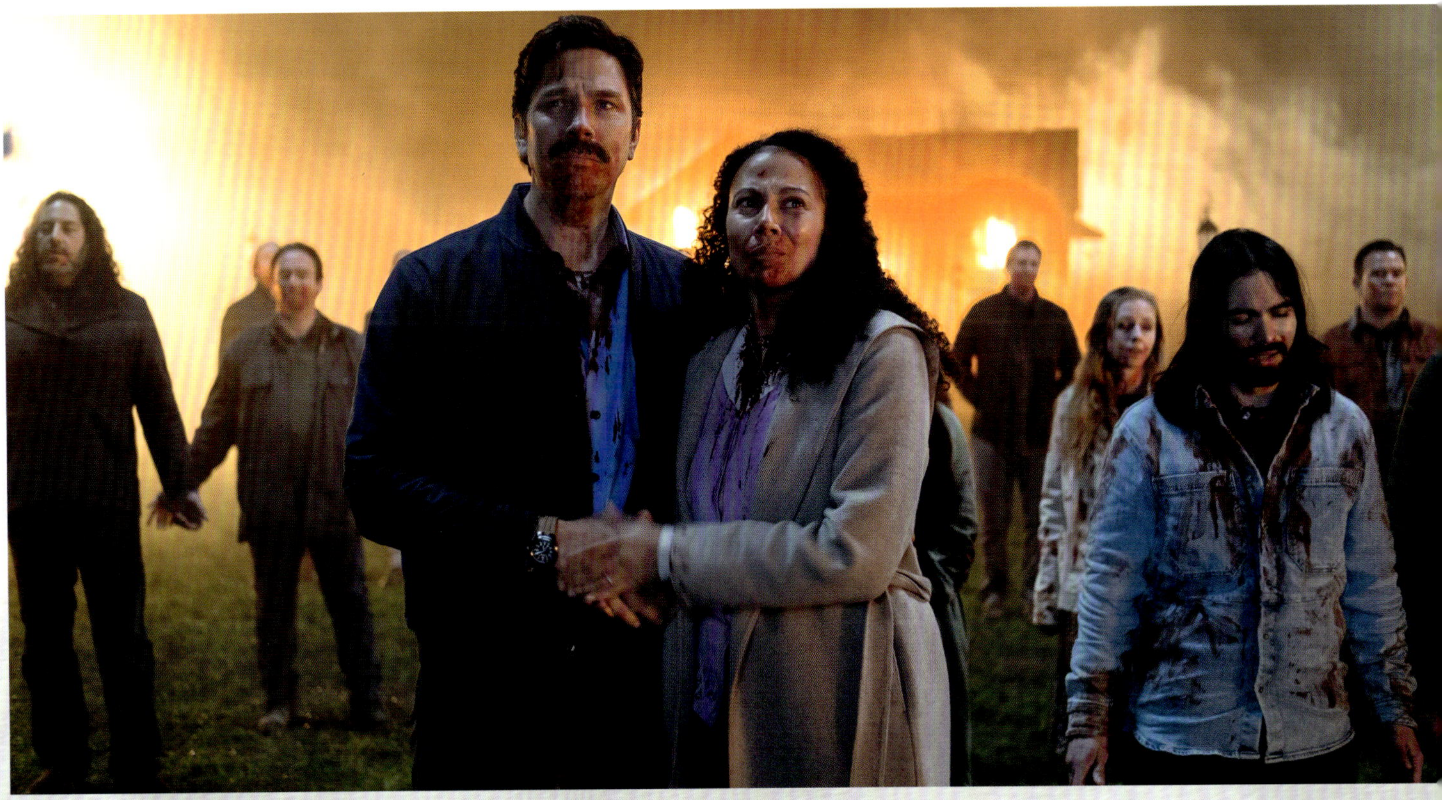

TOP/ Wade and Dolly await the sunrise, knowing their daughter is safe.

SARAH GUNNING

ANNABETH GISH

Dr. Sarah Gunning, Crockett's resident physician, is played by Annabeth Gish, who worked with Flanagan and Macy in *The Haunting of Hill House* and *Before I Wake*.

Flanagan says that Sarah's presence on the island is "a direct manifestation of her love for her mother. Otherwise, Sarah would be in a much more metropolitan environment. That's something I love. Sarah is there by choice. That gives her a clarity, and an agency, that a lot of other characters don't naturally have."

Gish agrees. "The driving impulse for her to come home was her mother. Sarah left, got educated, and was living her best life, until she [needed] to take care of her mom."

Anderson says, "Sarah fits in a city that's livelier than this island. She's not dressing to show off, but she's a little more stylish than the other ladies. She has a linen coat that she's decided is her lab coat. She has an alternative idea about the way women should dress."

Sarah is Erin's obstetrician. For authenticity, Gish consulted her own gynecologist, via Zoom. "'How do you hold the wand for the ultrasound, where are you feeling, what are you feeling for?' We also had an on-set [med tech] consultant, Katherine Kadler. I'm indebted to her."

Gish appreciated Sarah's constant fight for science and logic. "It was a rigorous mantra in my mind. 'It has to make sense. How does this make sense?' That was hard for me, because I'm always like, 'Oh, Leeza's walking. Cool, mystical!'"

Gish also made a point of learning what she was talking about when Sarah explains erythropoietic protoporphyria, her theory of why some blood dissolves when exposed to sunlight.

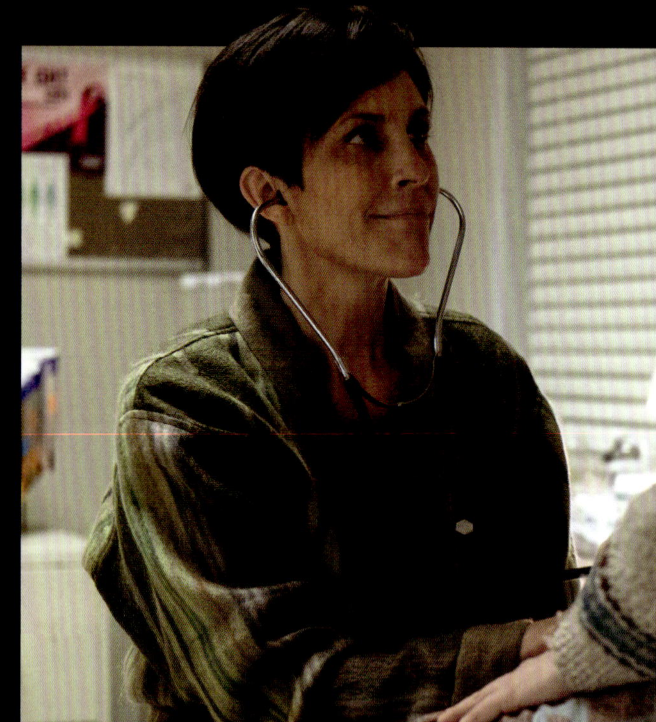

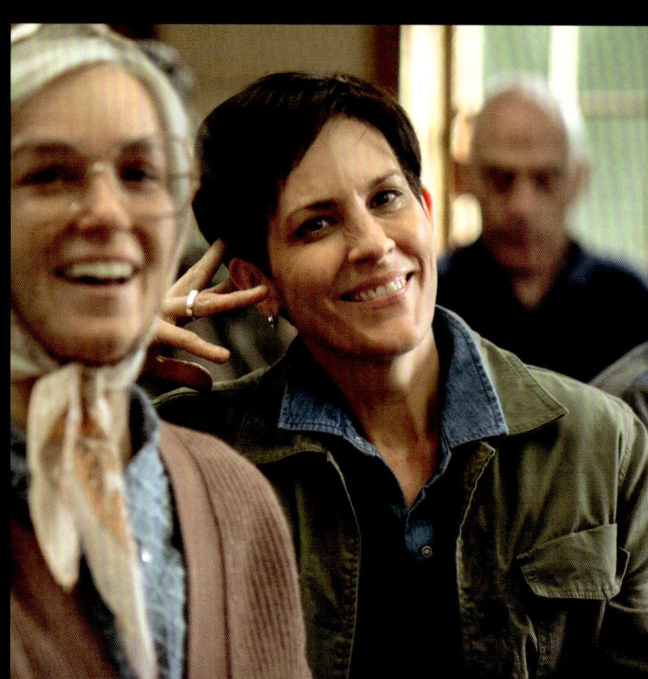

THIS SPREAD/ Dr. Sarah Gunning at work, and out with her beloved mom.

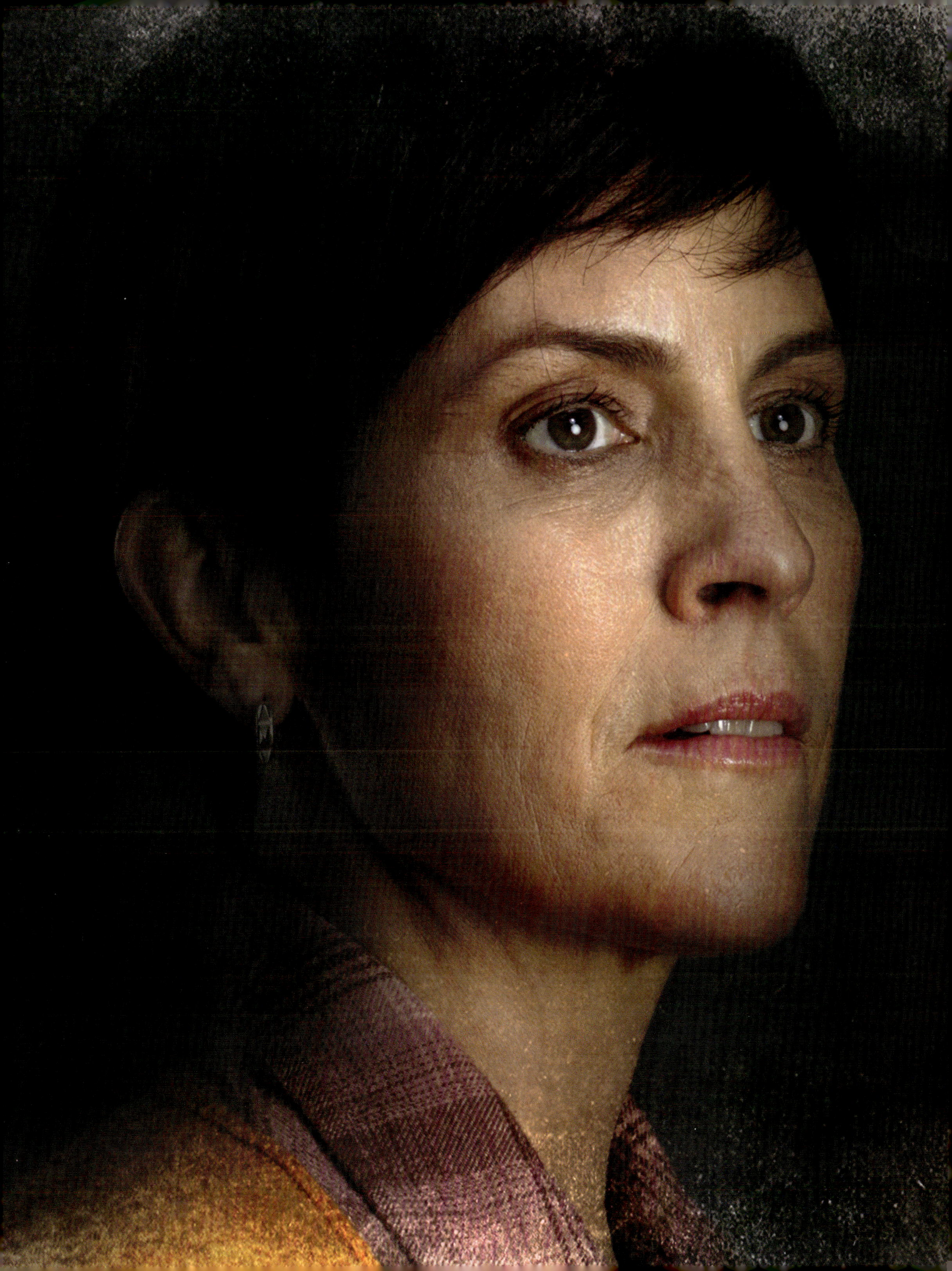

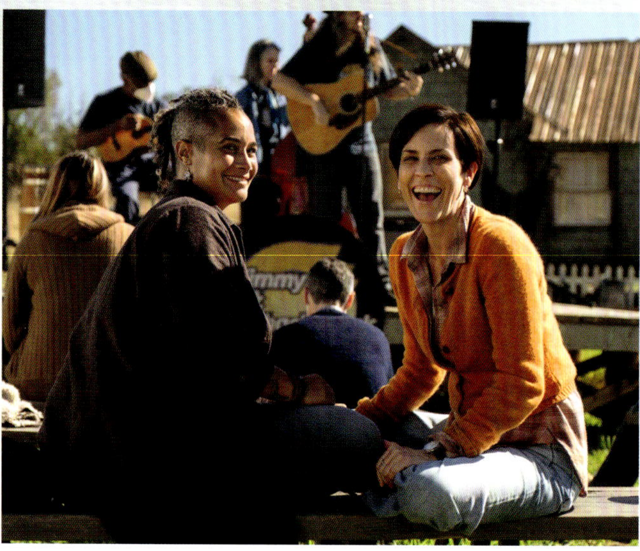

TOP/ Sarah with her date at Crock-Pot-Luck.

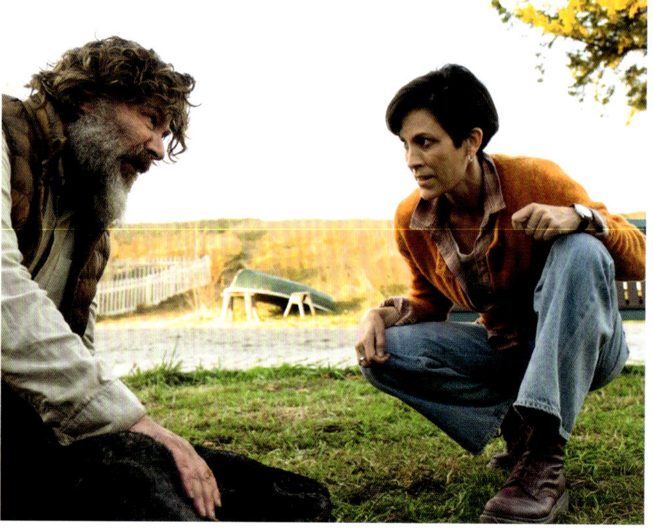

TOP/ Sarah examines Joe Collie's dog, Pike.

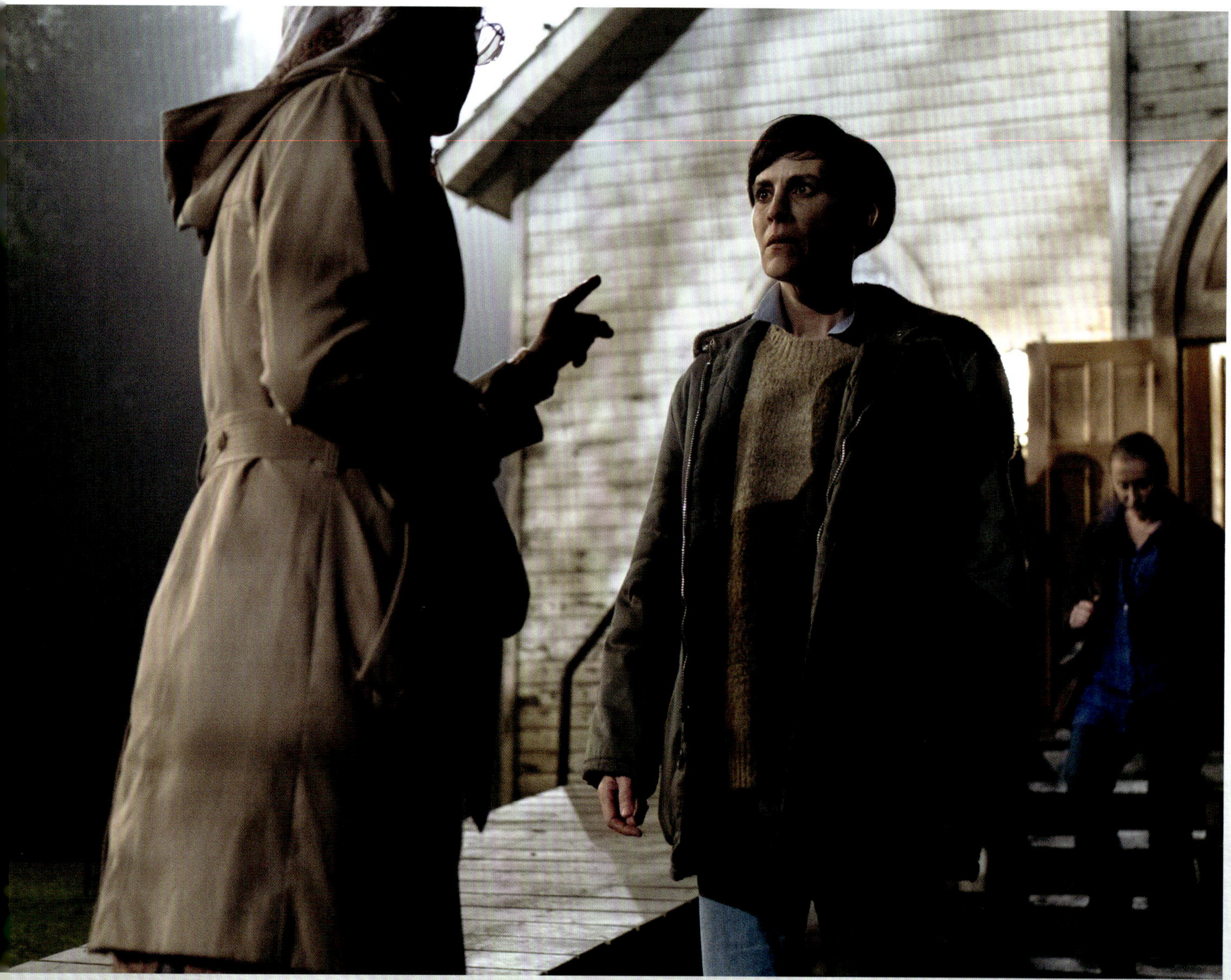

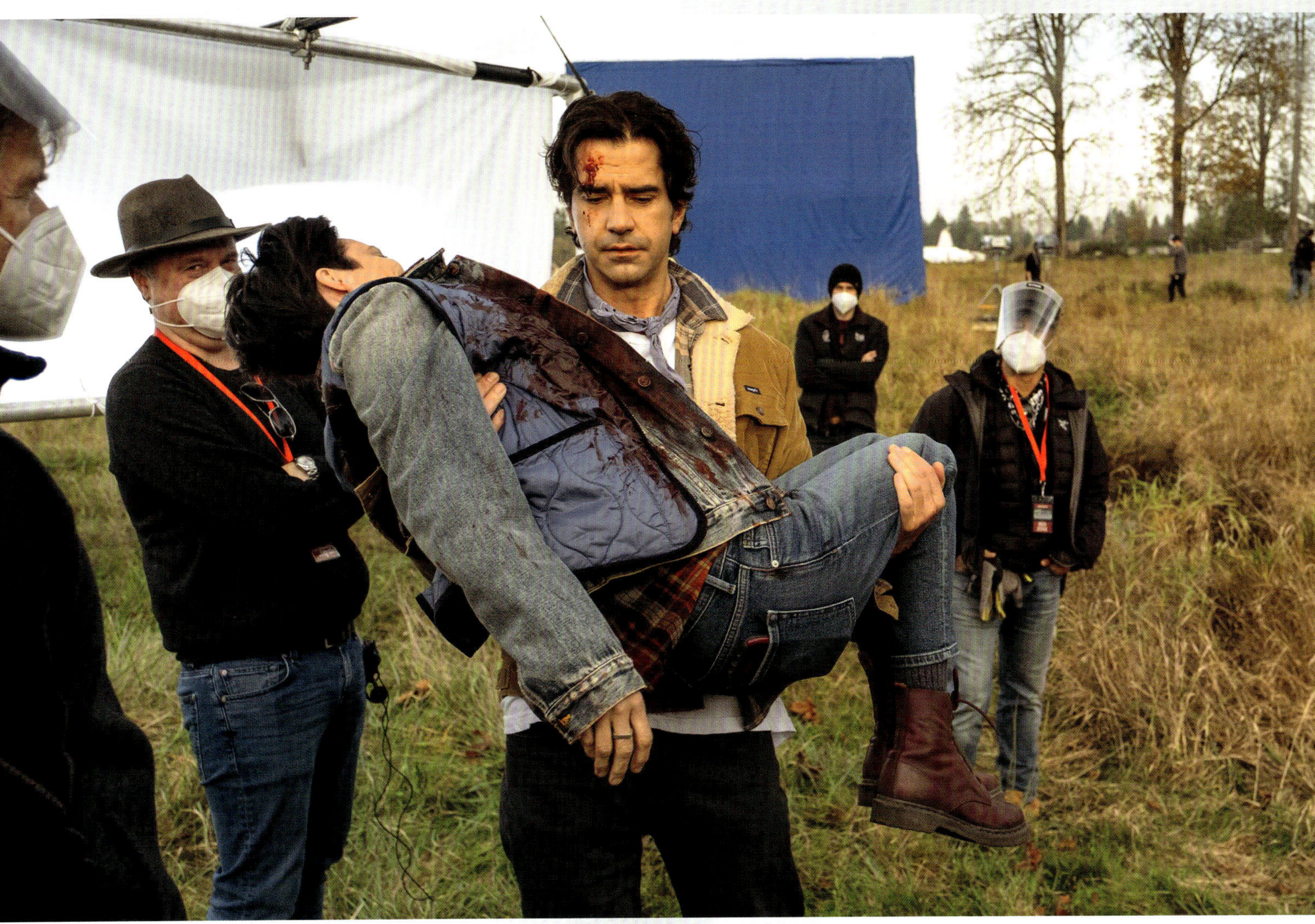

TOP/ Linklater and Gunning rehearse Father Paul carrying Sarah's corpse; (from left to right) first assistant director Morgan Beggs, executive producer Trevor Macy, and stunt coordinator Lauro Chartrand-Delvalle look on.

"To have a chunk of material that is so rigorous that you can't just learn your lines the night before is freaking lovely," Gish enthuses. "I had to learn scientific medical terminology, with laser-like focus. The Ignaz Semmelweis monologue is and will be forever known by every member of my family, because I would be saying this over and over, to be able to have it on the day." She also likes that Sarah's sexuality is matter-of-fact. "Sarah is gay. It's just there."

On working with Essoe, who plays Sarah's mother, Mildred, Gish says, "The aging makeup on Alex was phenomenal. The visual alone dropped you into a scene. Alex is an old soul herself. At the same time, she's rooted. When Mildred comes out of her dementia, and sees me for the first time in years, it's beautiful. There was a real passage of energy between us."

Gish loved getting to perform with other women. "Most of my scenes were with Alex and Kate. We allowed space for each other's processes, we took back seats when someone else needed to shine. It was a lovely dynamic."

The last scene Gish did in *Midnight Mass* is Sarah's death. "I'm not good at stunts. I had to have intense instruction from our stunt coordinator on how to take a hit from a shotgun. But the symbolism of getting shot and killed on your last night, in a church, after this year-long commitment to a show, with your mother and father, it's so symbolic. And, everybody was sad to wrap up this show. We were all tired, and relieved, because nobody freaking got COVID-19."

"When Father Paul accepts Sarah, the real redemption comes when she spits out the blood. She could have saved herself. But Sarah holds this moral code, and she refuses Catholicism and she refuses vampirism. She is a fulcrum, she's this steady piece. And I'm so thrilled I got to play her."

MILDRED GUNNING

ALEX ESSOE

Mildred Gunning, Sarah's mother, is played by Alex Essoe, who had worked with Macy and Flanagan on *Doctor Sleep* and *The Haunting of Bly Manor*.

Raleigh explains Mildred has five age stages. "At her [oldest], she's completely covered in prosthetics: silicone forehead piece, cheeks, eyebags, stretch and stipple around the eyes, upper lip, lower lip and chin, full neck, hands, and contact lenses for arcus senilis. The next step, we were able to switch the hands to stretch and stipple. The face prosthetics are sculpted to look a bit younger. Her next stage down is the same level of prosthetics that everyone else on the show is in at their oldest."

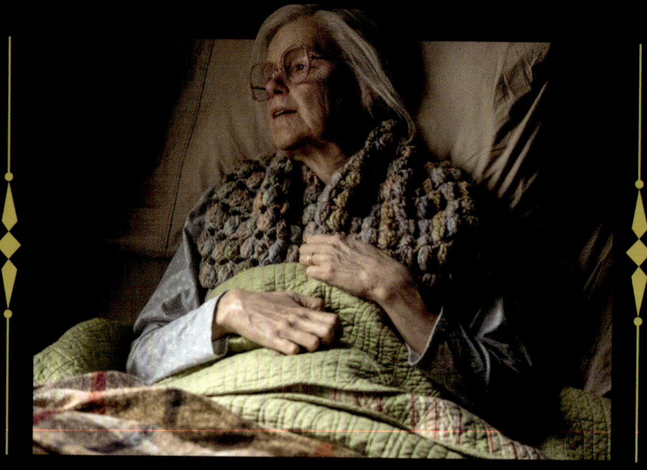

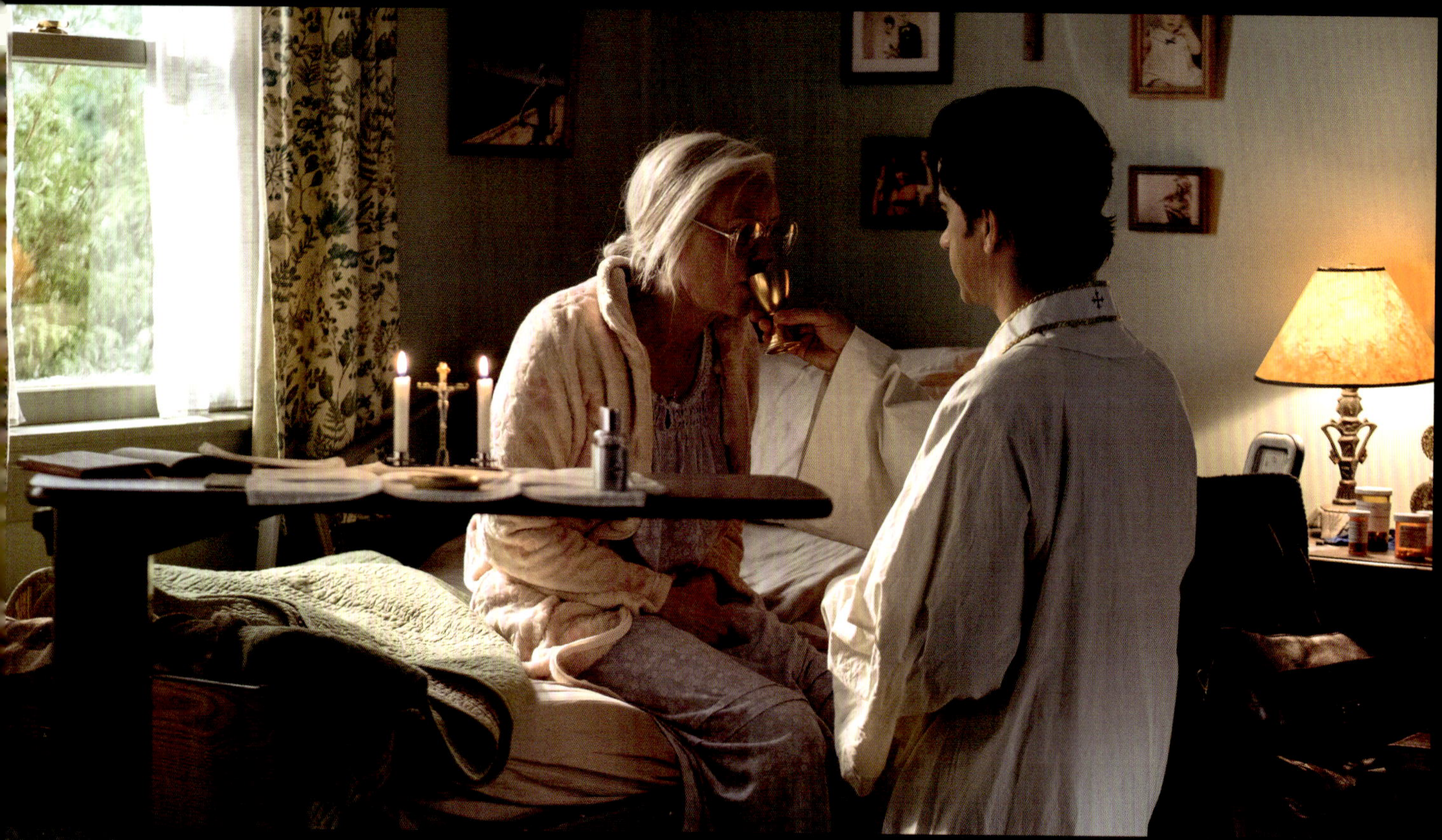

TOP/ Mildred receives Communion at home from Father Paul.

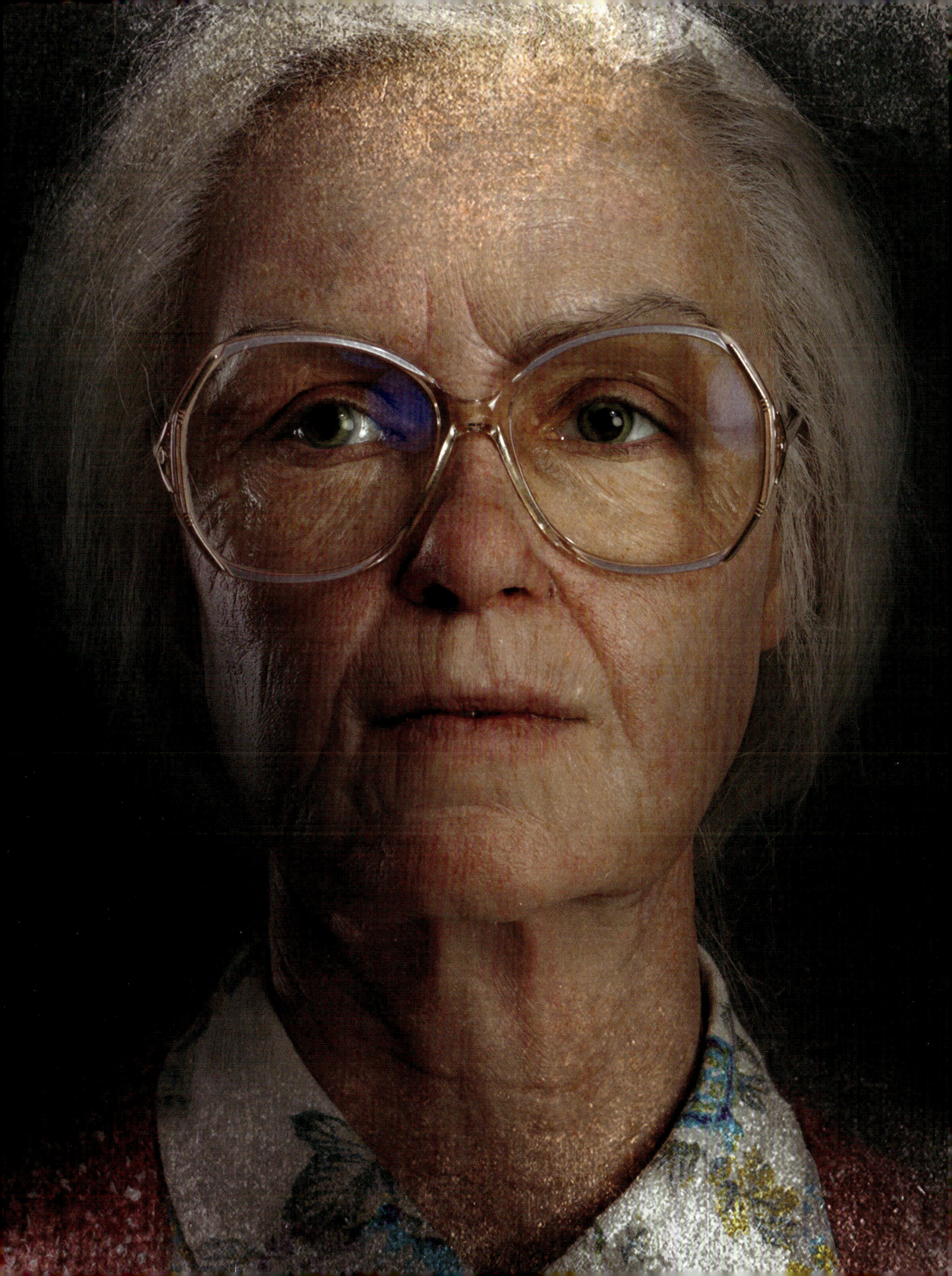

"A COMMON ARGUMENT AMONG ACTORS IS, IS PERFORMANCE FROM THE OUTSIDE IN, OR THE INSIDE OUT? I FIND IT'S BOTH. EVERY ASPECT [INCLUDING PROSTHETICS] INFORMED MILDRED."

ALEX ESSOE

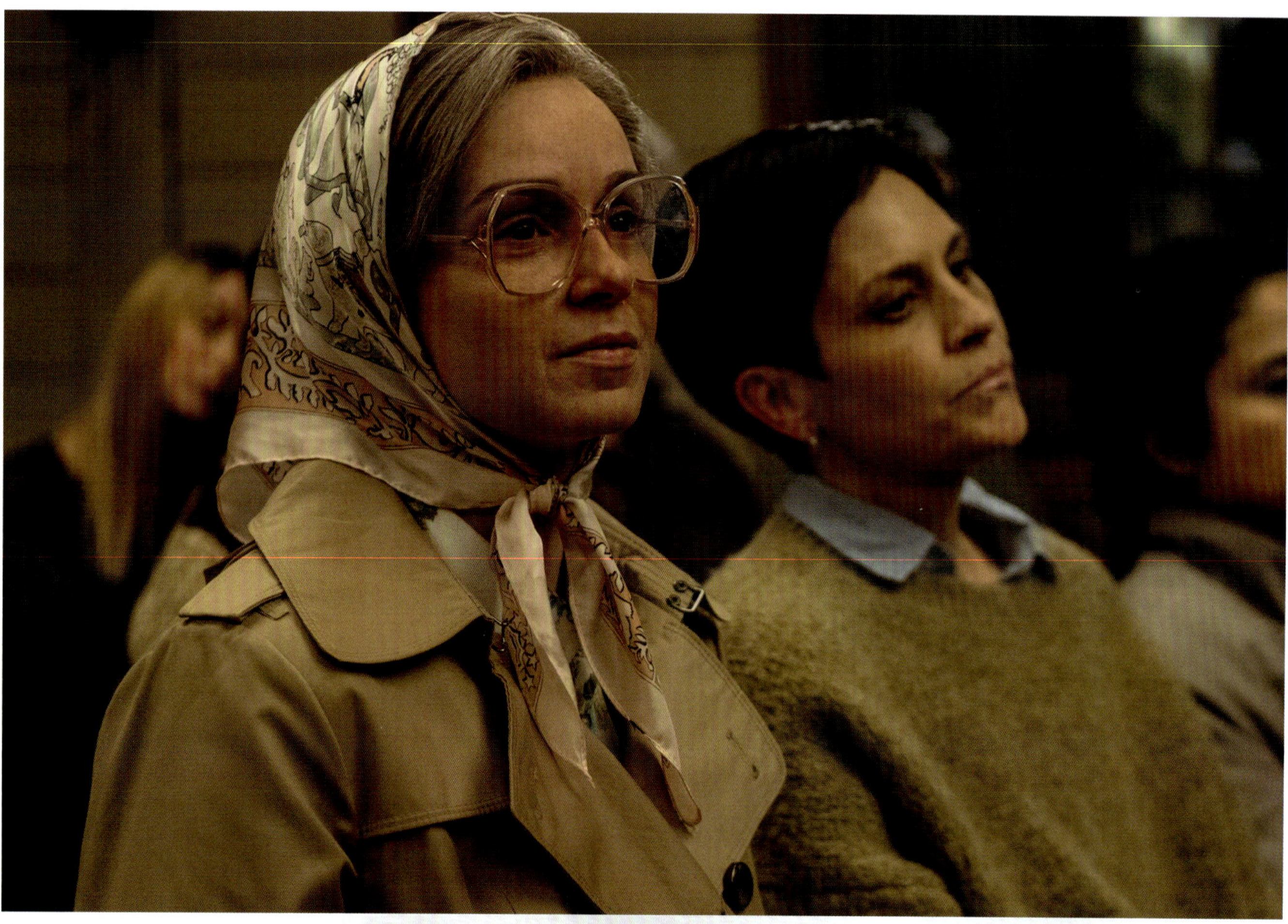

TOP/ Mildred, with Sarah, gazes at her old love in church.

Essoe has never played a character so old before. "It's the whole reason that I wanted to act in the first place, to challenge myself. It was exhilarating, but also heartbreaking. I was terrified. It's easy to do badly."

The weight of the prosthetics helped, Essoe adds. "You feel that tiredness, that frailness. And the makeup team were so meticulous. It was perfection."

Flanagan notes, "[The prosthetics] didn't seem to limit her face mobility. Alex is that good."

Essoe credits Flanagan's direction. "He gave me practical notes, 'Don't shake so much,' and, 'Make her voice deeper'."

For research, Essoe watched videos of older people, and worked with actor Terry Notary, "a genius movement instructor. He helped me with what it's like to have Alzheimer's. It was literally sitting and being present, like a lens through which I see everything and nothing at the same time."

Essoe found playing the middle stages trickier than the oldest. "Obviously, I know how to be my own age. Extreme older age, there's something to anchor me. But the in-between stages, there are tiny details that start to change."

Anderson discusses Mildred's costume arc, from robe and slippers to her old dresses to her youthful appearance. "Even though the styles of her dresses are the same as earlier, she looks way chicer. That was fun, to show the progression of her growing younger. Her colors are lighter in the beginning, and go darker. In the end, she and Father Paul look like they belong together."

Since Essoe is slightly younger than Gish, how was it playing Sarah's mother? "We would joke about it. But Annabeth is easy to love. I don't have children, but I have maternal instincts, and she's such a generous actor that it was easy to see her that way."

Essoe says her favorite scenes as Mildred include "when her dementia dissipates, and she looks at her daughter as an adult and recognizes her for the first time in a long time." Also, "When Father Paul is talking about why he did what he did, and how he wanted to be with us, and we have that exchange about this is the way it's supposed to be. Another big moment is when she goes to church, and hears him talk about fighting, because she realizes this is about him, and all the people that are here, and not about God. Which is what happens, I believe, with many ideologies. It dawns on Mildred, 'This is totally toxic, and everyone has been brainwashed into thinking that their biases are divine'."

The scene where Mildred dissuades Paul from bringing Sarah back as a vampire "is a tough one, because I don't want my daughter to die, but I also don't want her to come back as a monster. When Sarah spits out the blood, as much as it rends my heart, I'm so proud of my daughter for being consistent with her principles."

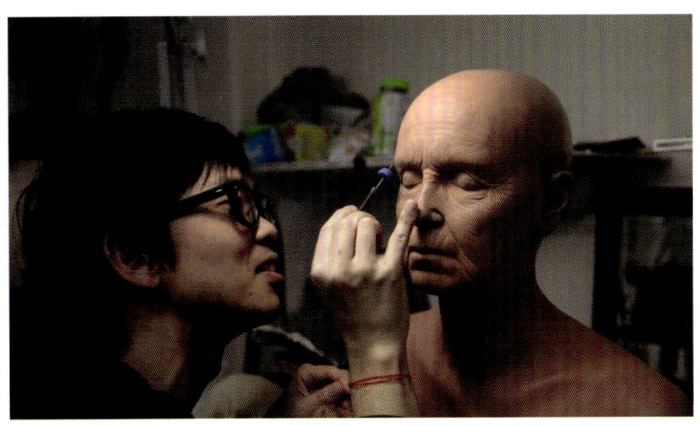

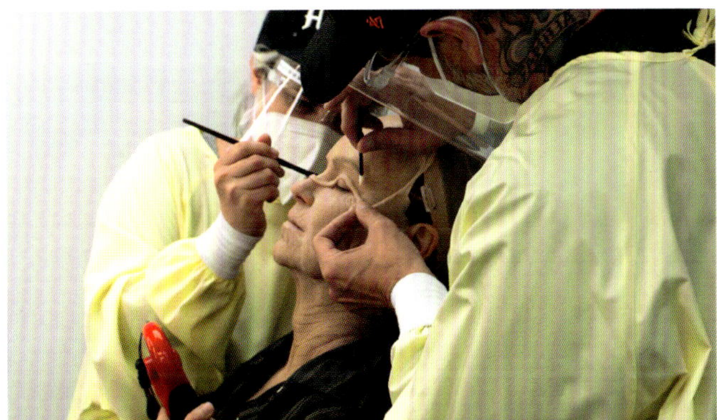

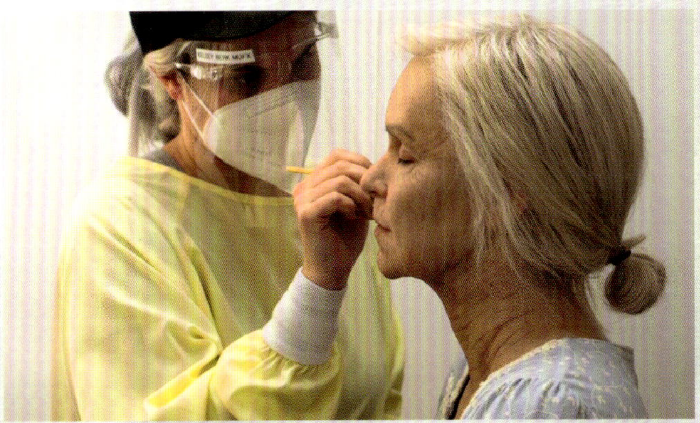

TOP/ Essoe undergoing the aging makeup process for Mildred, with the middle-stage result to the right.

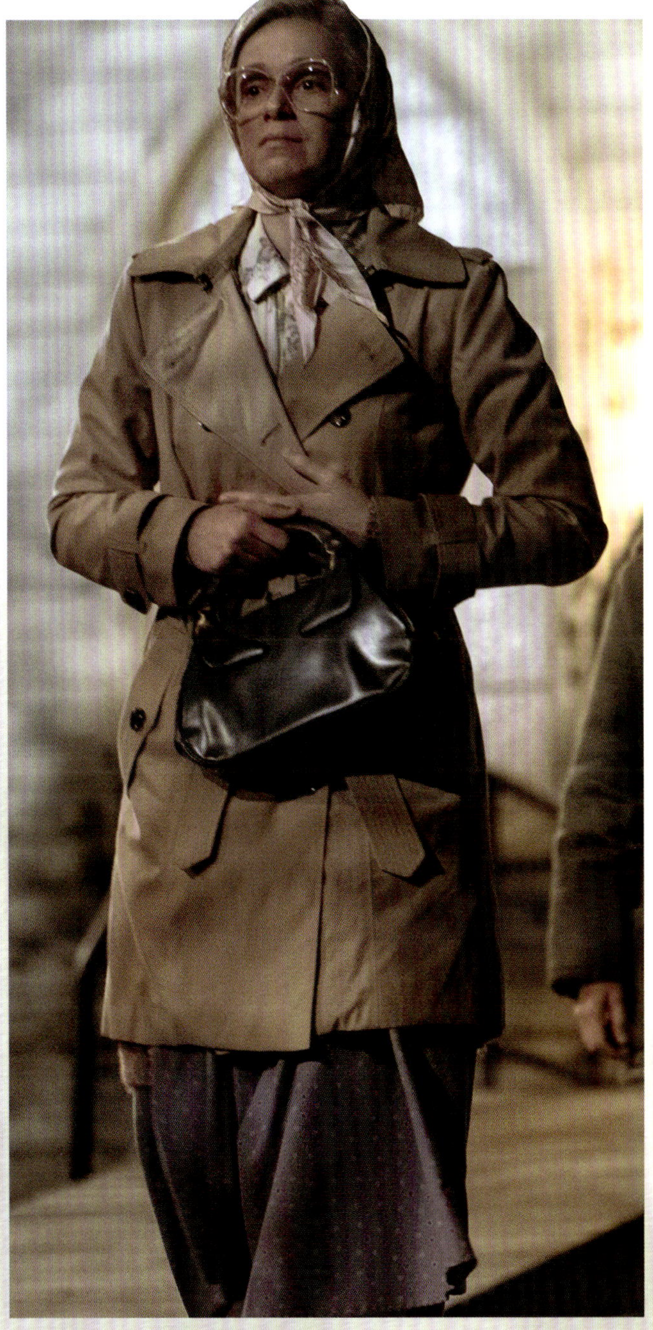

SARAH'S HOUSE

HOME AND RESEARCH LAB

Dr. Sarah Gunning's medical office is in her home, which she shares with her elderly mother Mildred. Arnold relates, "Sarah's house is really her mother's house." In decorating it, "I went kind of neutral. It's green and restful. It had to be a business and a residence. It has bedrooms upstairs, and downstairs. They brought in an actual hospital bed [for Mildred] into the living room. There's a side section of the house, with a separate entrance, where Sarah has her office."

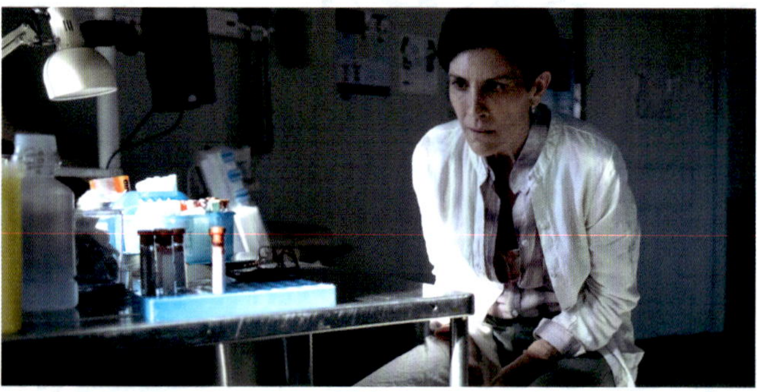

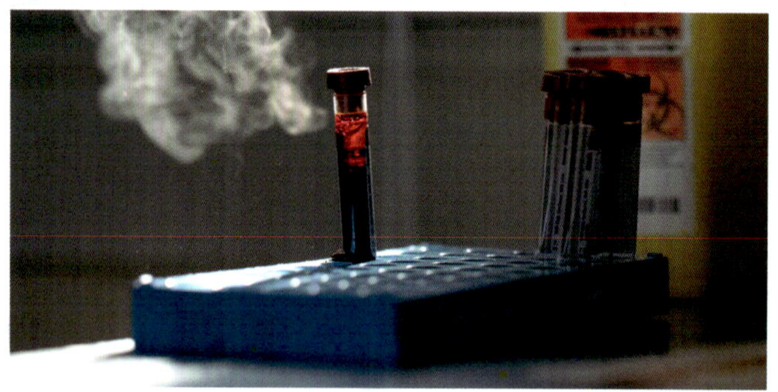

THIS PAGE/ (TOP) Sarah runs her blood experiments. (BOTTOM) Essoe and Gish rehearse with Macy and Flanagan in Sarah's office.

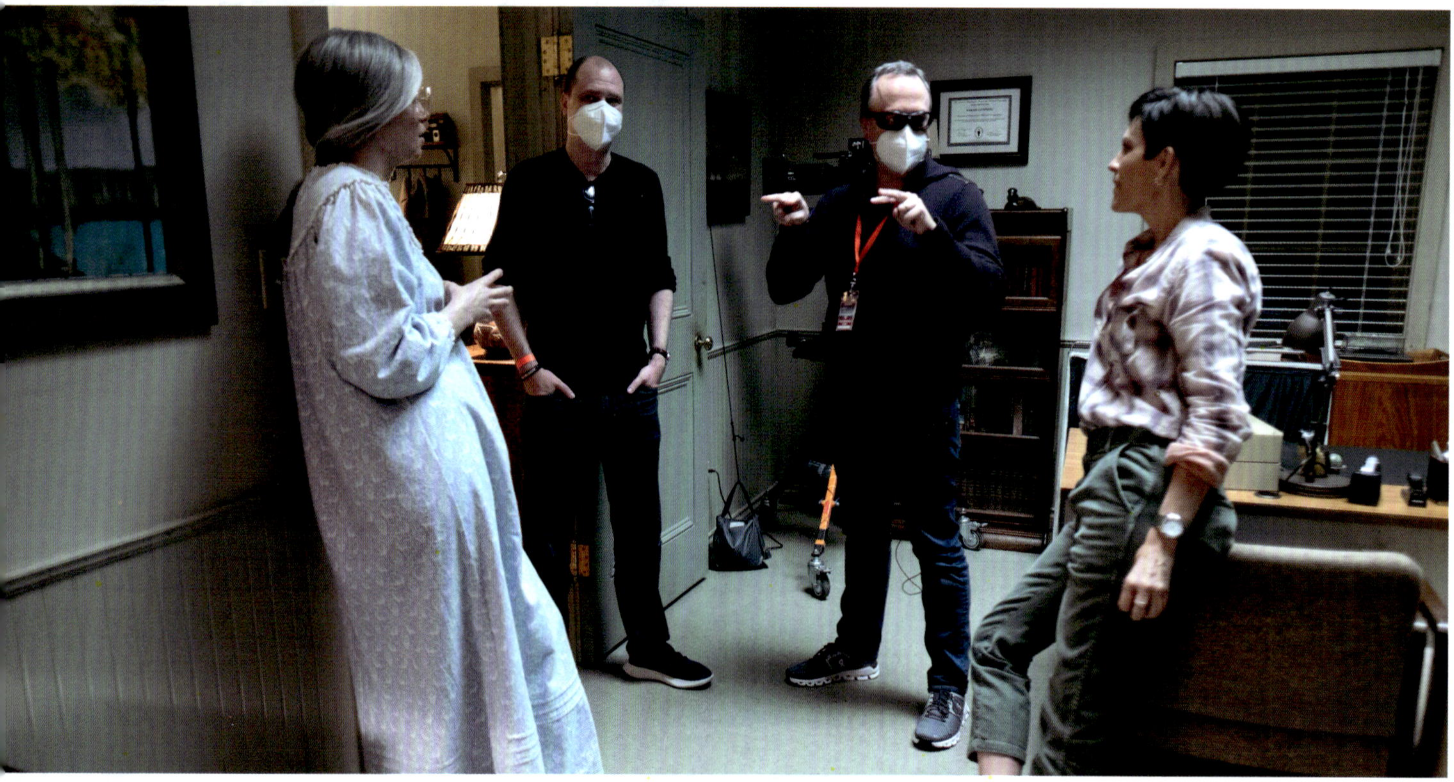

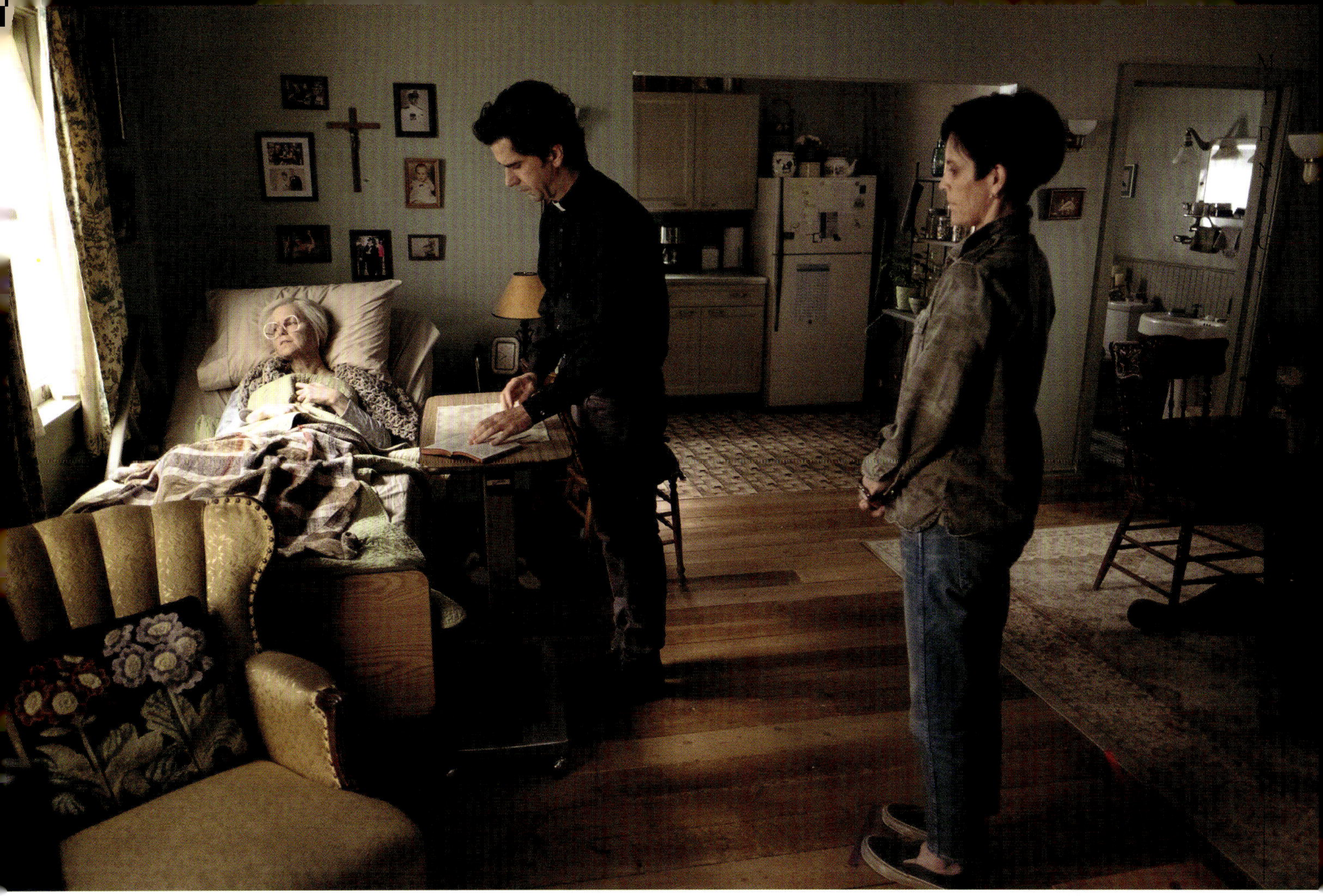

TOP/ Mildred, at her oldest, is visited by Father Paul as Sarah watches.

The furnishings are largely from Mildred's era. Essoe says, "The set dec felt so personal. I was able to form a relationship with all the little knick-knacks and décor. It was easy for me to attach memories and history to those things."

Gish says she found she needed to spend time in Sarah's office, "to own the space. Wardrobe and set are external, but they really do inform my way into a character. There were always multiple pairs of boots, umbrellas, island raincoats. On Sarah's desk, there was one of those old metal Rolodexes, like my grandmother had. There were these antiquated artifacts that spoke to how this island was stuck in time, and therefore so susceptible to this stylized religious rhetoric."

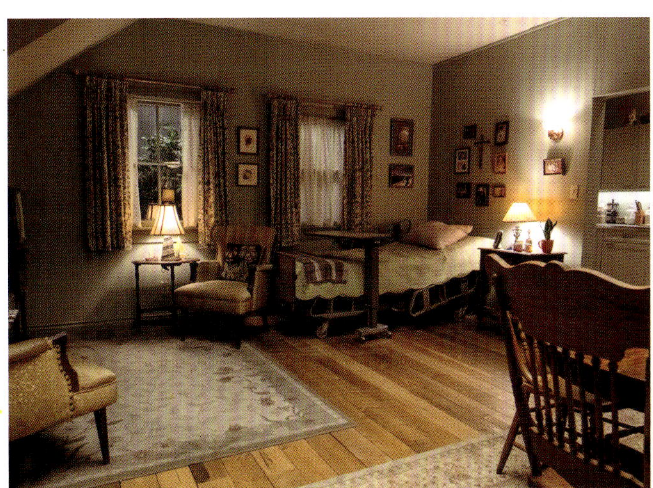

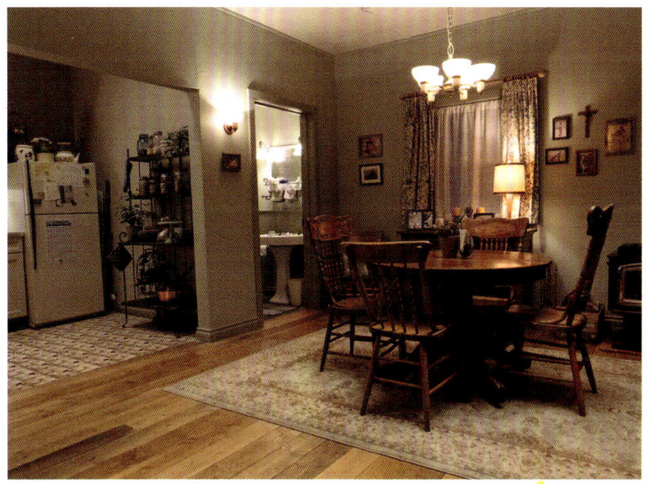

TOP/ Sarah's living room doubles as Mildred's bedroom.

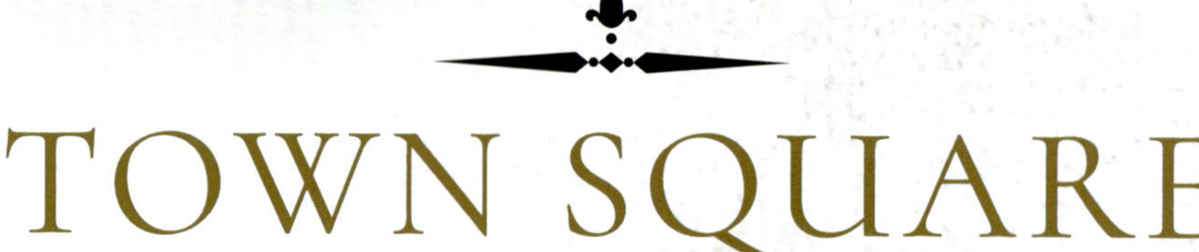

TOWN SQUARE

THE HEART OF CROCKETT

The Crockett Island town square was built at Anderlini Farm in Langley. It was, Arnold says, "a space that we needed quite a large area for. It had to be flat. There's a boardwalk that goes around the perimeter. There were boardwalks everywhere, just because it was a muddy world out there. It's an area where people would congregate for events and just for restful contemplation. So, there are park benches and, because we were shooting at night quite a bit, we put in lampposts, just to give it some light. We put in this monument in the middle, [of] sailors who had been lost at sea, with a flagpole, and there was a gazebo."

For story purposes, Arnold continues, "Certain things had to be near other things. The general store had to be right there by the town square. Certain people needed to live near it, and other people needed to live distances away, so that when they walked to school, they had to go by certain other houses. So, it dictated quite a bit of the geography of how things were laid out."

Fimognari says, "The town square is the workhorse of the show. There is a lot of character connection that happens around the town square, between Erin and Riley, between Riley and Joe Collie. It's where the community comes together for their potluck. And it's also the ending, where they all come back together, and see the sunrise. So, it truly is what the town square was meant to be. It's a gathering place for its people."

The town square goes through a number of different looks, Fimognari adds. "We went for a sunny day for the potluck, so we're getting everybody together, and seeing Father Paul interact with everybody. We had a lot of long walks through the town that pass the town square, and when the town has its power, all the streetlights are alive, and it has a cozy feeling to it. It feels like it's a community that cares about each other, and it's struggling, but it's still staying connected."

Then, when the power is cut, Fimognari says, "You have a candlelit vigil going through the town, there's an eerie beauty, that then turns ominous when you take even that light away, and turn it into an inferno. So, it's one of those beautiful expressions of a space, just based on time of day and conditions of lighting

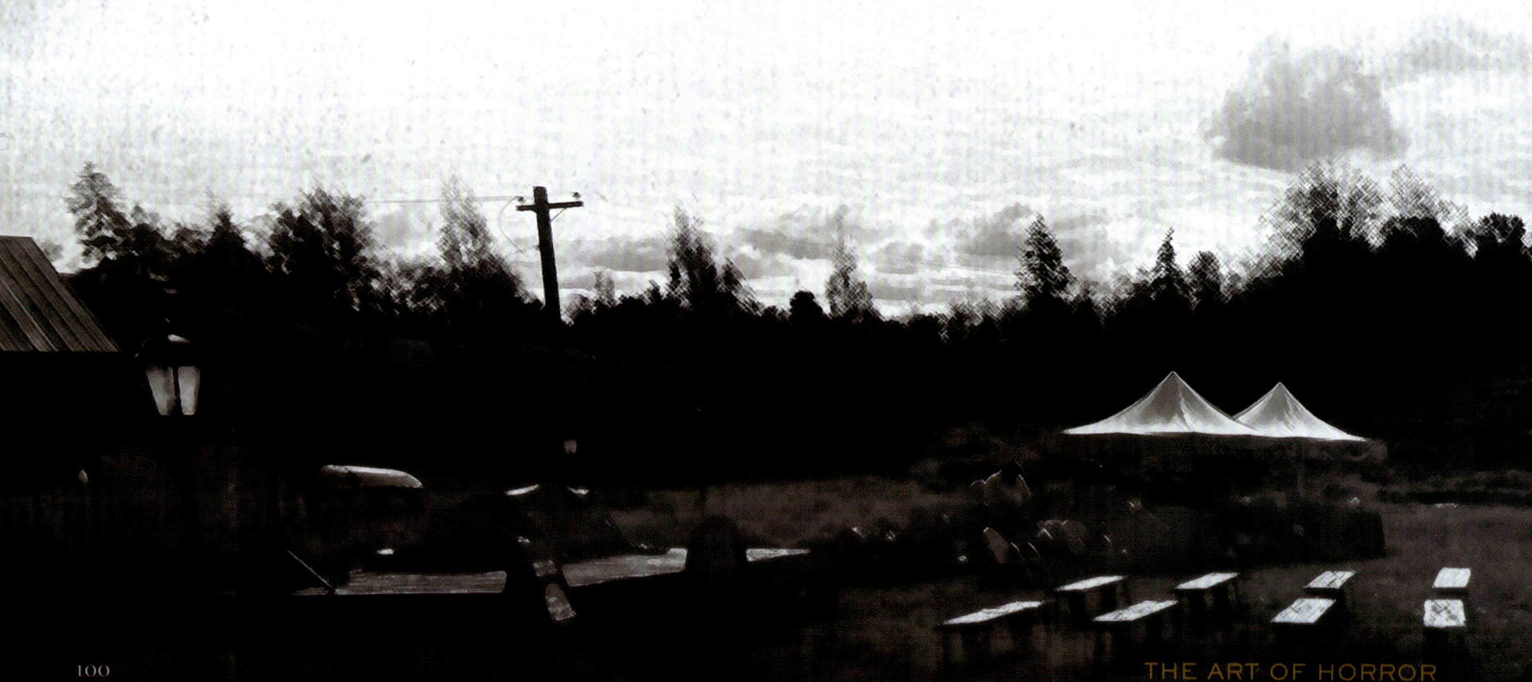

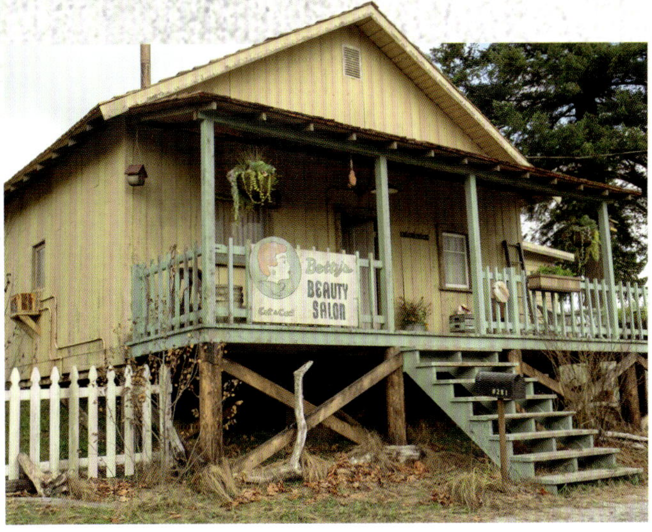

TOP/ Crockett Island's Beauty Salon.

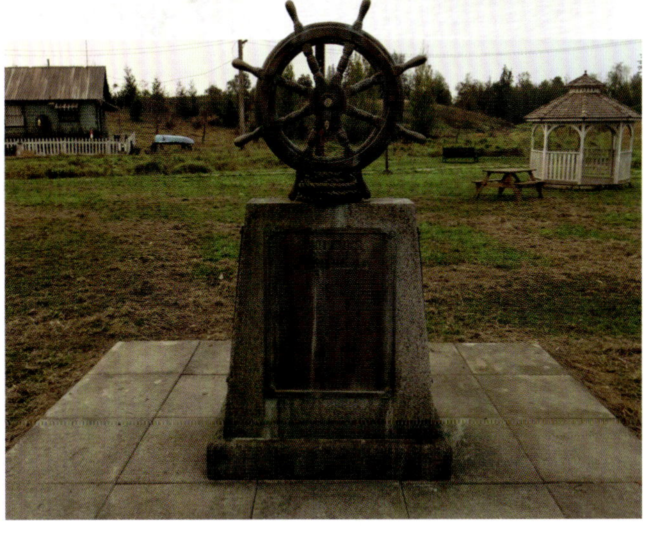

TOP/ The town monument to sailors lost at sea.

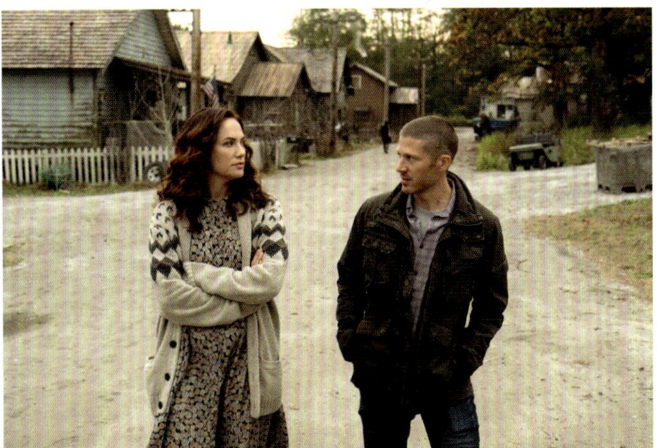

TOP/ Erin and Riley go for a walk.

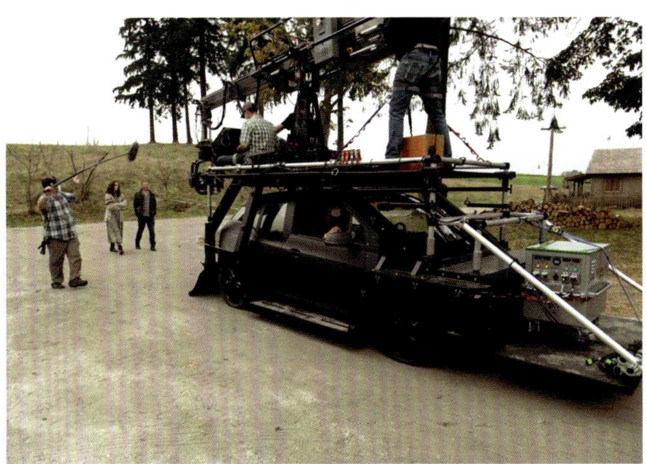

TOP/ Camera mounted on truck to move with Erin and Riley.

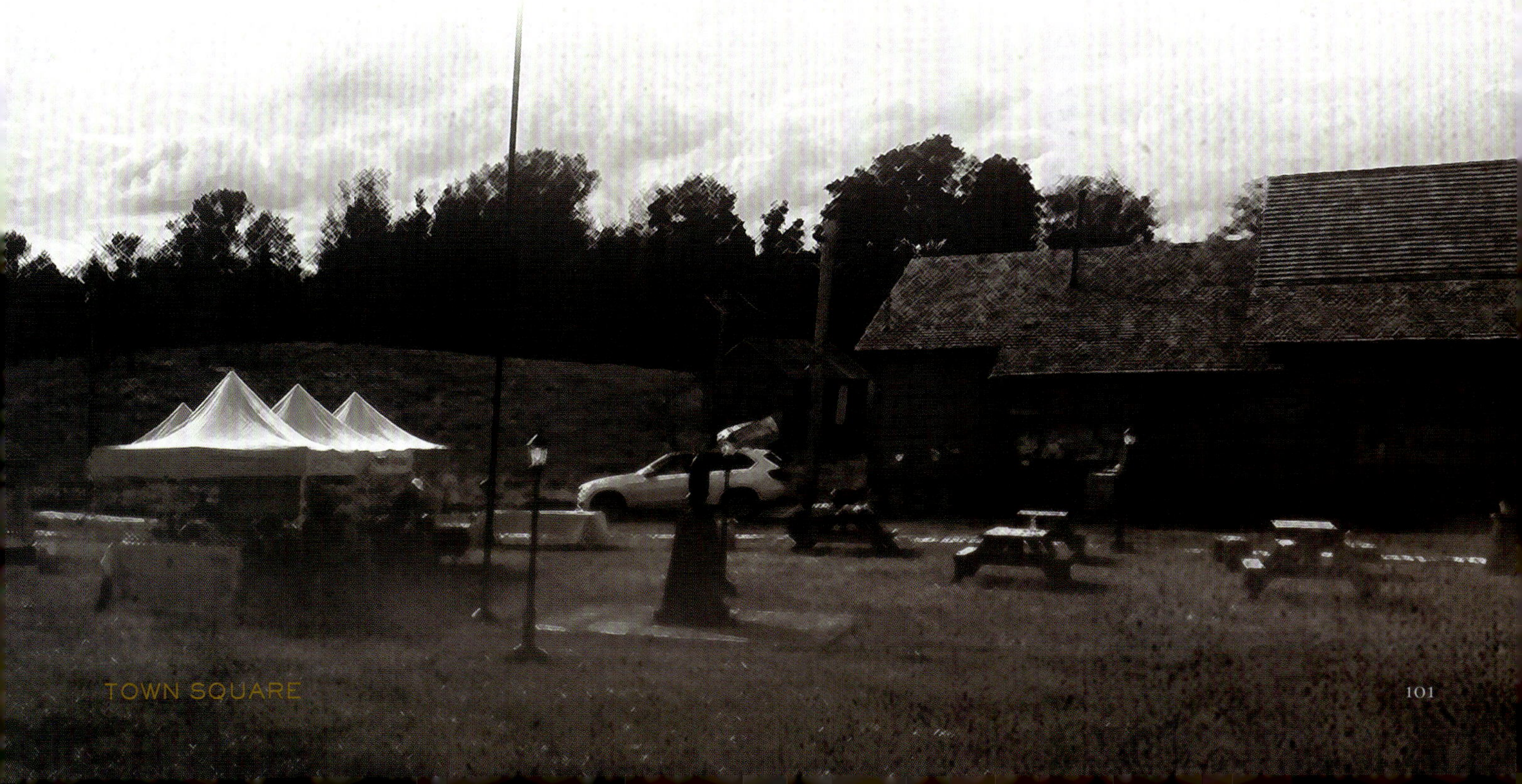

TOWN SQUARE

> "I'VE NEVER WORKED WITH PEOPLE LIKE THIS. EVERYTHING THEY MADE WAS SO AMAZING, AND FROM SCRATCH, AND IT LOOKED SO REAL... YOU JUST BOUGHT IT."
>
> ZACH GILFORD

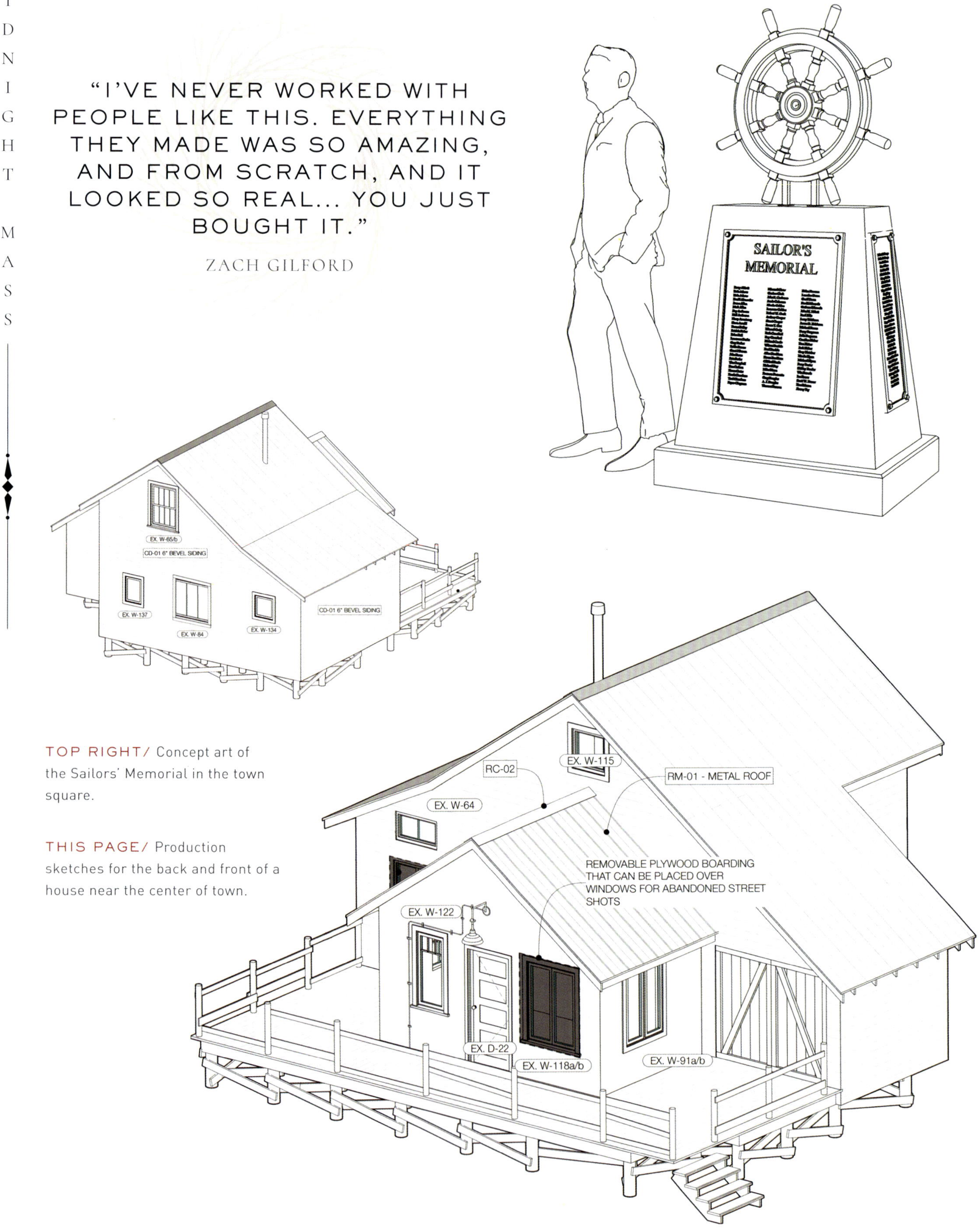

TOP RIGHT/ Concept art of the Sailors' Memorial in the town square.

THIS PAGE/ Production sketches for the back and front of a house near the center of town.

that we have to control. And because we knew the shots, and because it's very carefully scripted how light interacts with each, our lighting design took that into account, and we had special looks associated with the town prior to having fire, that fire including the candlelight, and then the town after having fire, and that fire including the candlelight."

When the fire is not directly in frame, Fimognari explains that the look of something burning and flickering off-camera is achieved by "a mix of having our lights, and a fire effect, like a flame bar, close by."

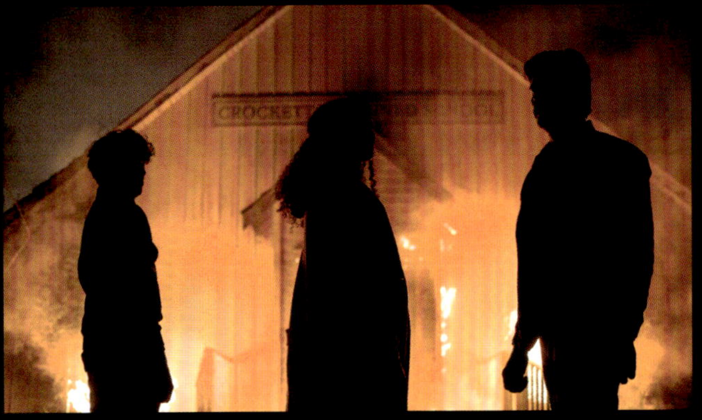

TOP/ Ali, Dolly and Wade outside the burning school.

BOTTOM/ Leeza and Warren flee the flames and the vampires.

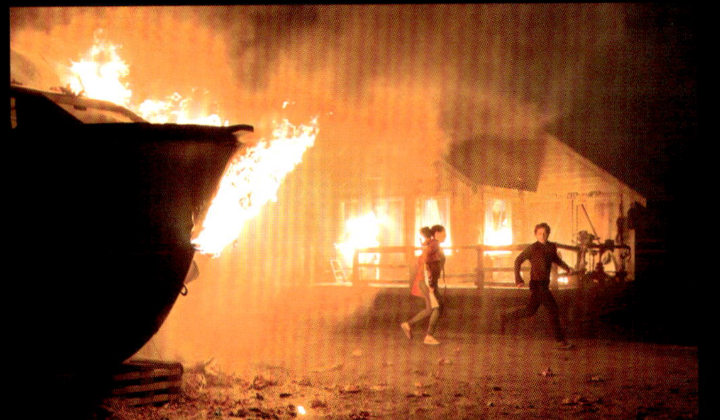

BOTTOM/ Erin Greene's house, completely engulfed in fire.

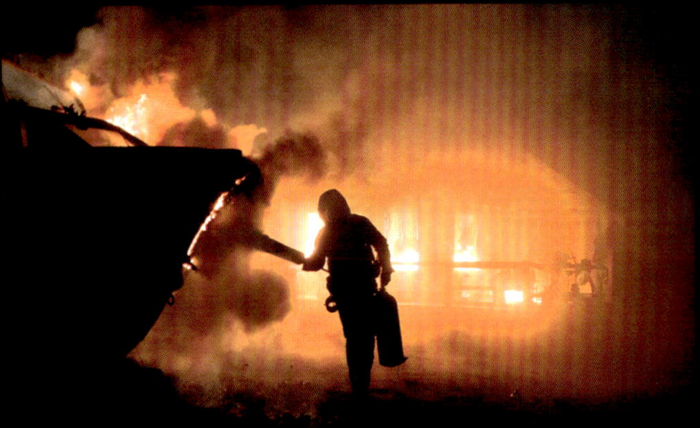

TOP/ A SPFX assistant uses a fire extinguisher on a blazing boat.

CROCK-POT-LUCK

THE YEARLY PARTY

The town square is transformed into a festival space for the annual Easter Crock-Pot-Luck, with a makeshift bar, a buffet line, craft vendors, and more."

Arnold explains, "The bar was a couple of very large planks, stretched across a couple of old-time wooden barrels. We built a stage, because we had a band that was there. The buffet tables were just large folding tables. I don't know that we had a really defined dance area, but we had booths with local artisans and/or merchants, who sold honey, and candles, and flowers, and cotton candy, and things like that."

On stage, co-composer Andy Grush performs, in character as church organist Timmy. "I play the acoustic guitar and sing three cover songs at the Crockpot."

It had been scripted that John MacDonald's character Bowl would be eating cotton candy, but MacDonald laughs, "I just smoked. I did a lot of smoking, actually. It's not quite the same thing. They were just herbal cigarettes, too, so I wasn't killing myself." If he'd had to eat throughout the festival shoot, "I would have been really full."

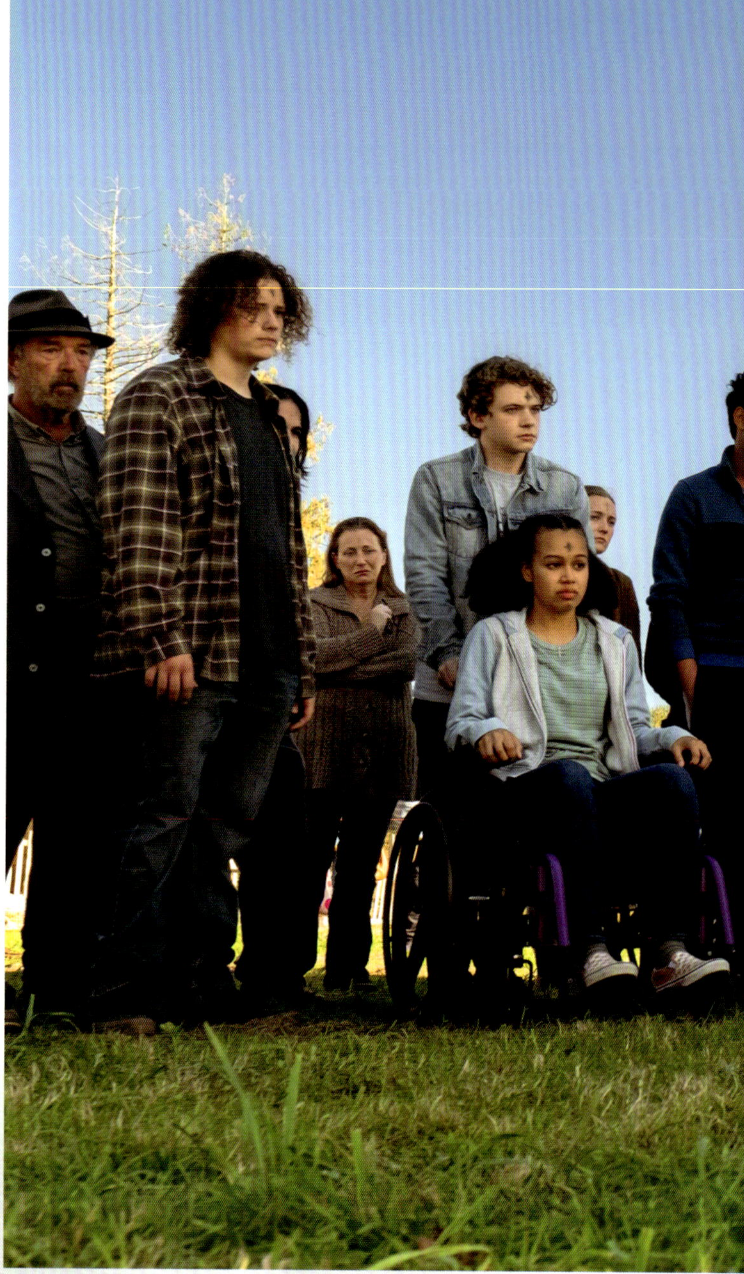

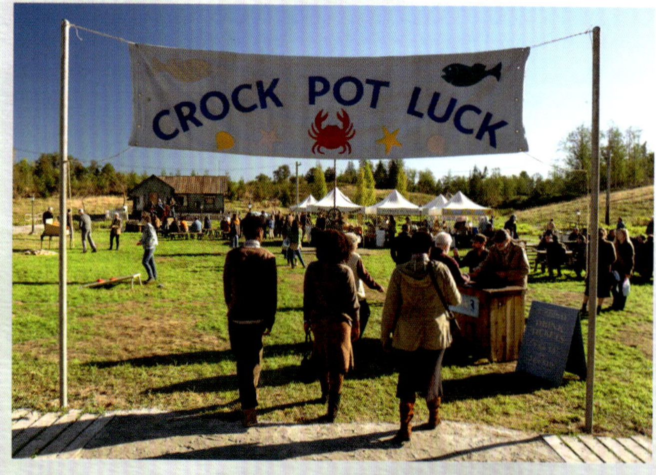

THIS SPREAD/ (TOP) The Crock-Pot-Luck scenes include the entire cast, plus one hundred extras. (BOTTOM LEFT) The residents of Crockett arrive for Crock-Pot-Luck. (BOTTOM MIDDLE) Father Paul under a pop-up tent awning. (BOTTOM RIGHT) Hassan, Wade, and Dolly enjoy the festivities.

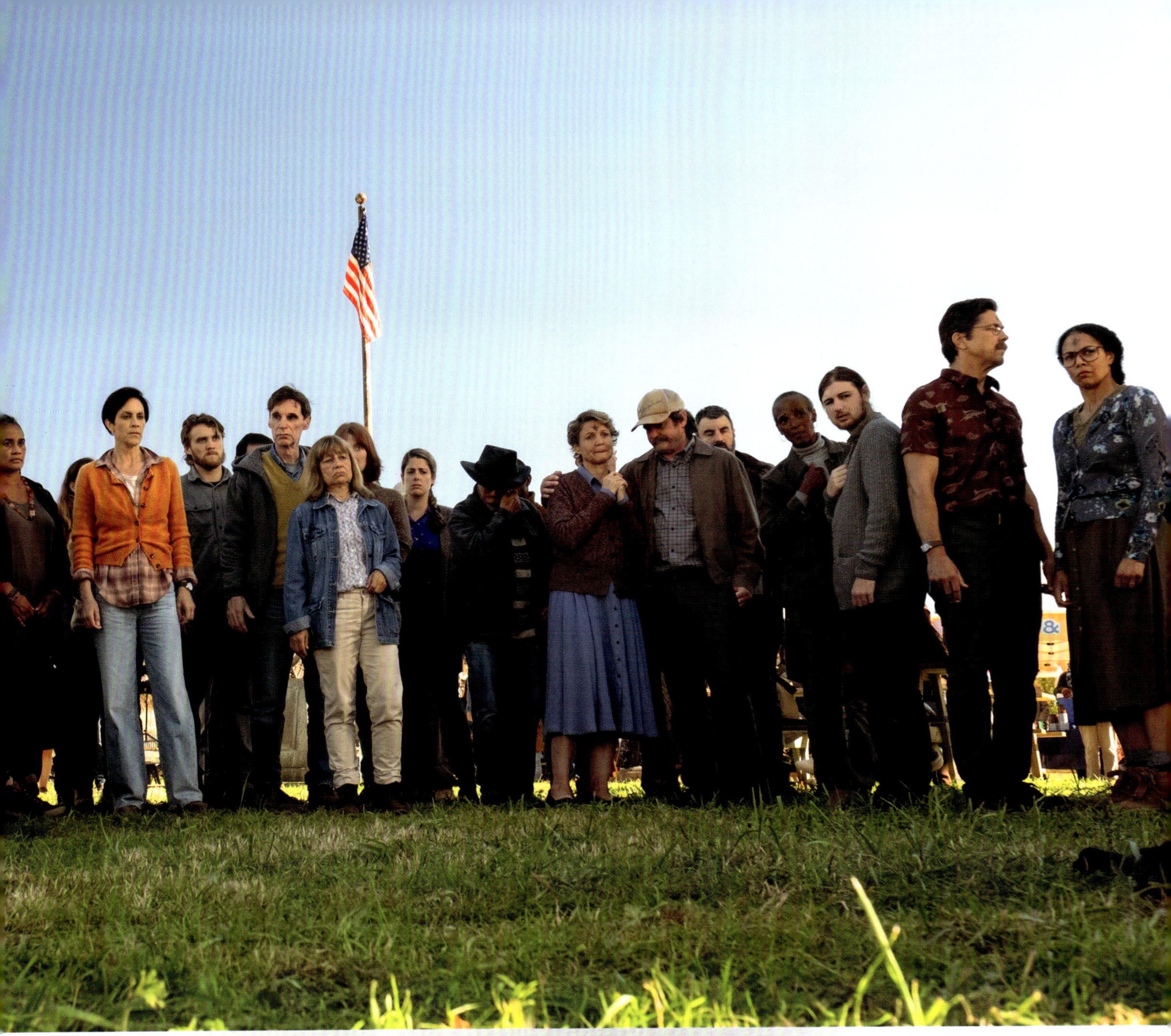

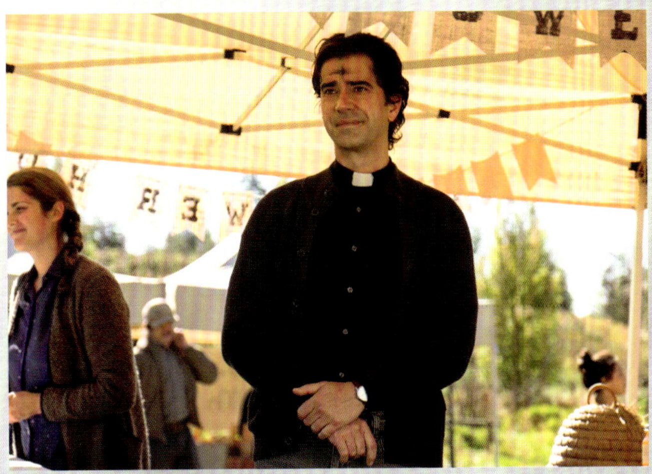

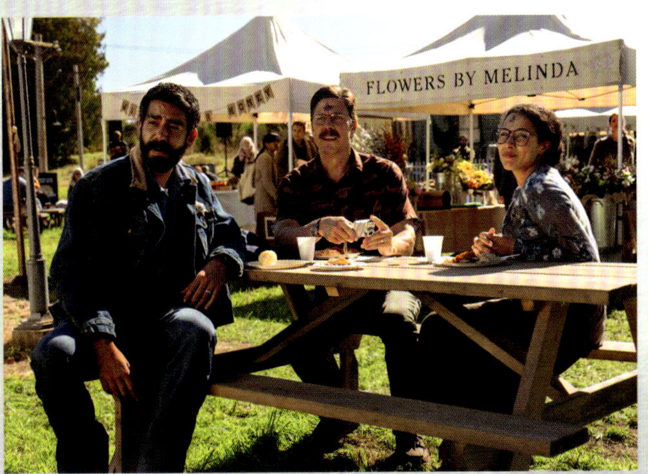
FLOWERS BY MELINDA

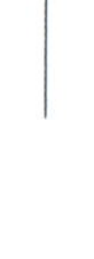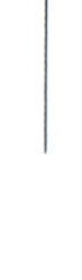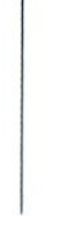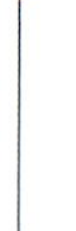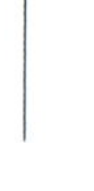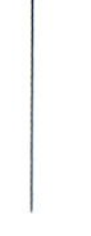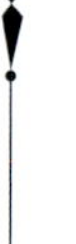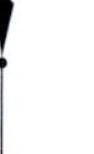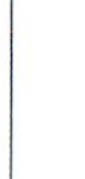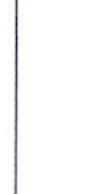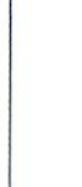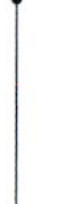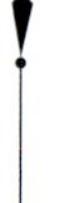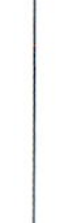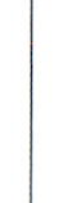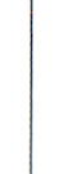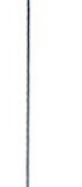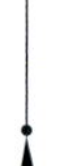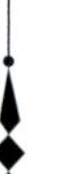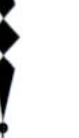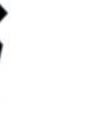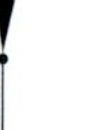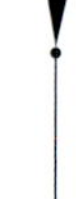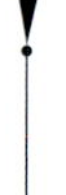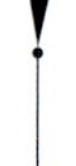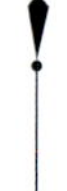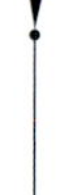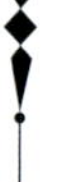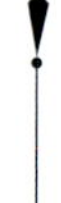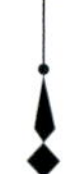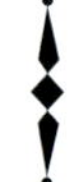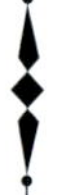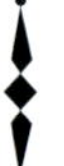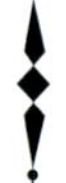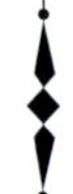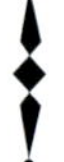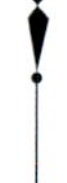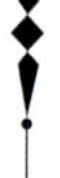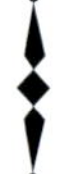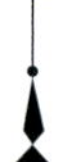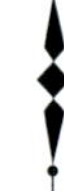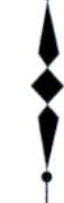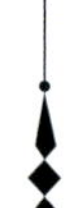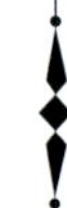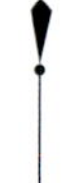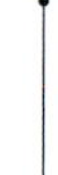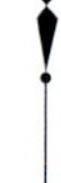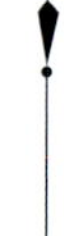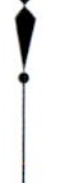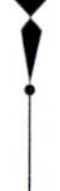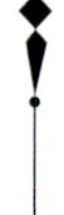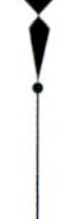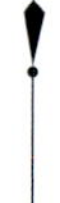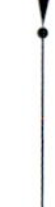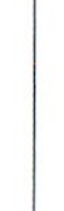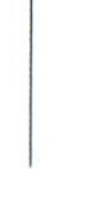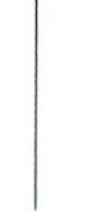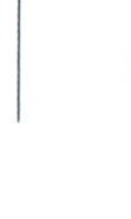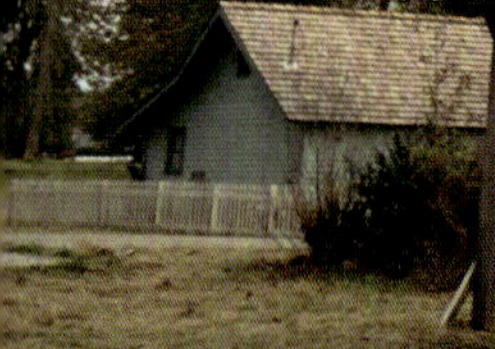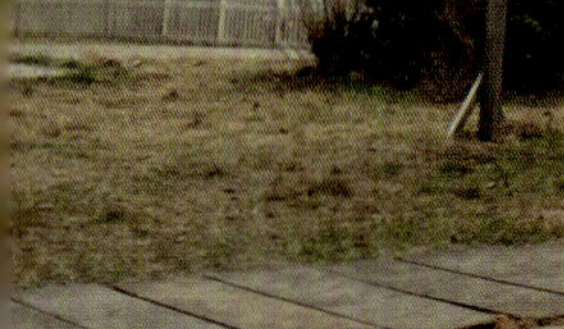

CROCKETT SCHOOL

LESSONS AND CONTROVERSY

The exterior set for Crockett Island's small school was built on the farm, as part of the town, with the interior constructed on stage.

Arnold explains that initially, production had planned on re-using the school interior for the recreation center, but that wound up getting its own set. "The footprint of the school was quite small. I think there are only a dozen kids in each room, so not very many desks." There are two separate classrooms, though. "We had a hallway down the middle."

Balint was impressed by the set. "You open a locker, and the locker is dressed. 'Okay, they dressed one locker. Great, just in case someone opens the locker.' No. Every single locker was dressed with details. That does thirty or forty percent of the work for you, when you're on a set where things are real."

Siegel says, "In the schoolhouse set, there is a back office, and the supply closet. The art department had filled that full of tiny little things. One of my favorite touches is, pinned up on Erin's side of the desk are all these notes from students, saying, 'Thank you, Ms. Greene.' And on Bev's side, there are just Bible verses."

BOTTOM/ The Crockett Island schoolhouse – note the ramp installed for Leeza.

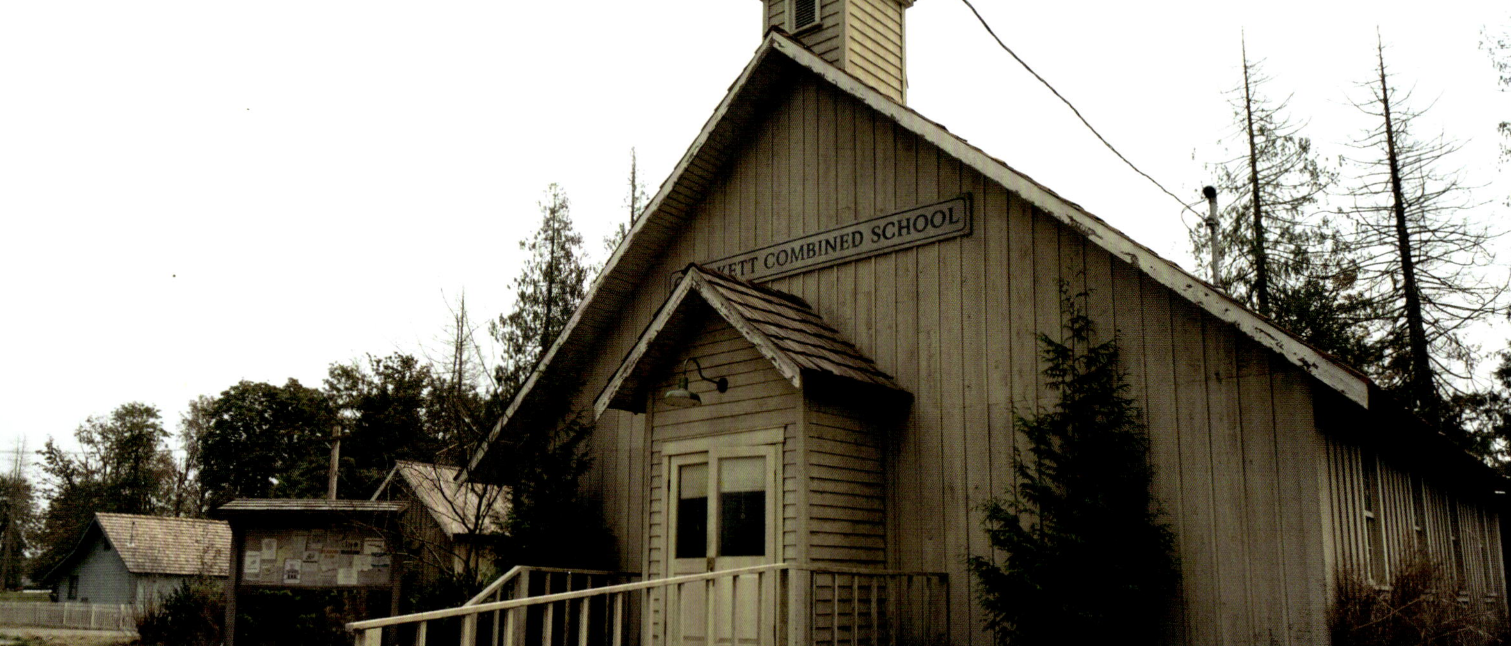

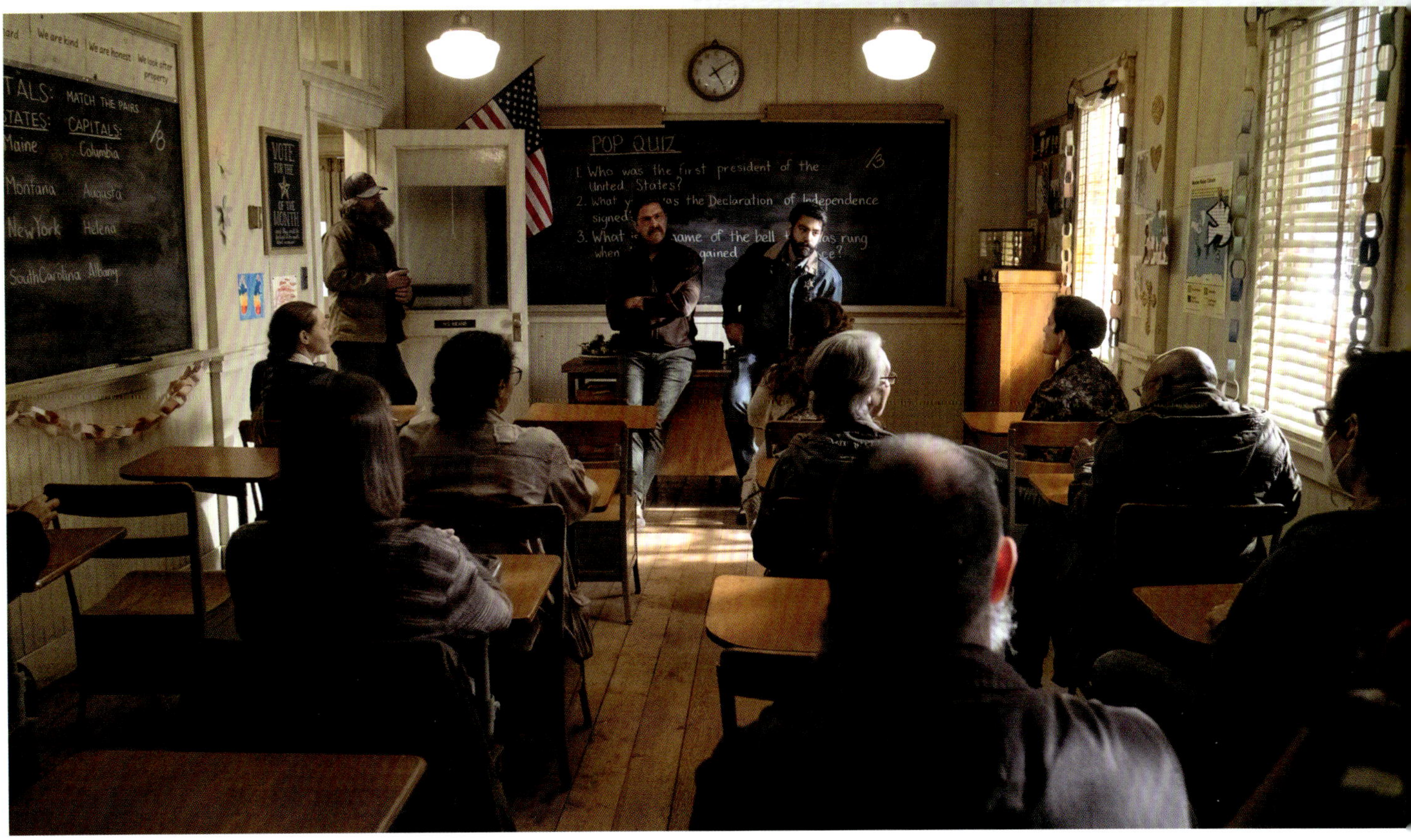

TOP/ Sturge watches as Wade and Hassan address a PTA meeting.

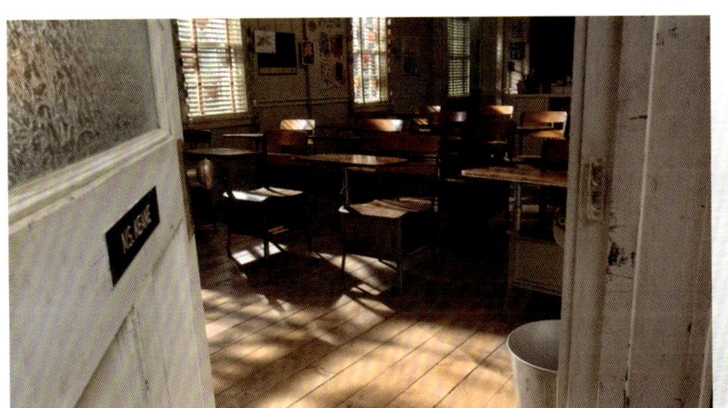

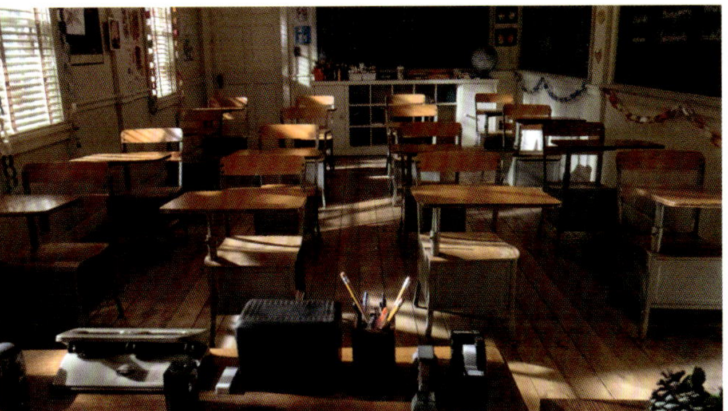

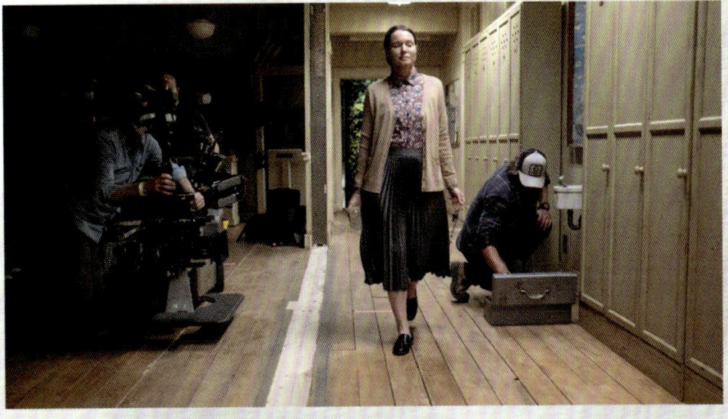

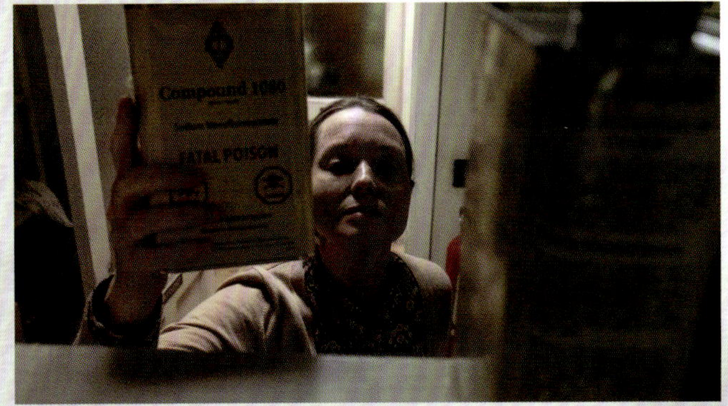

TOP/ Bev fetches rat poison from the school supply closet.

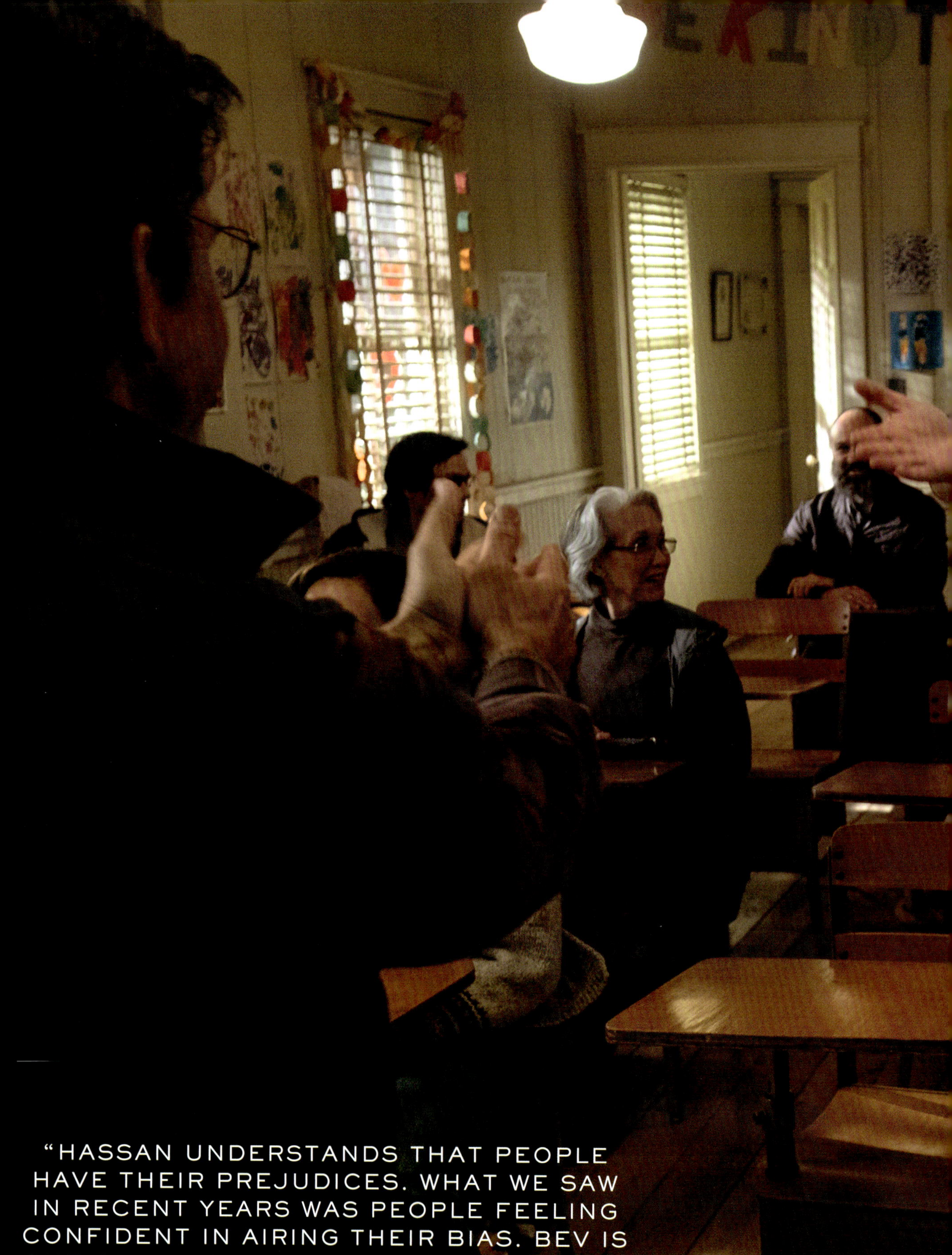

"HASSAN UNDERSTANDS THAT PEOPLE HAVE THEIR PREJUDICES. WHAT WE SAW IN RECENT YEARS WAS PEOPLE FEELING CONFIDENT IN AIRING THEIR BIAS. BEV IS ONE OF THOSE - SHE DOES NOT HIDE IT."

RAHUL KOHLI

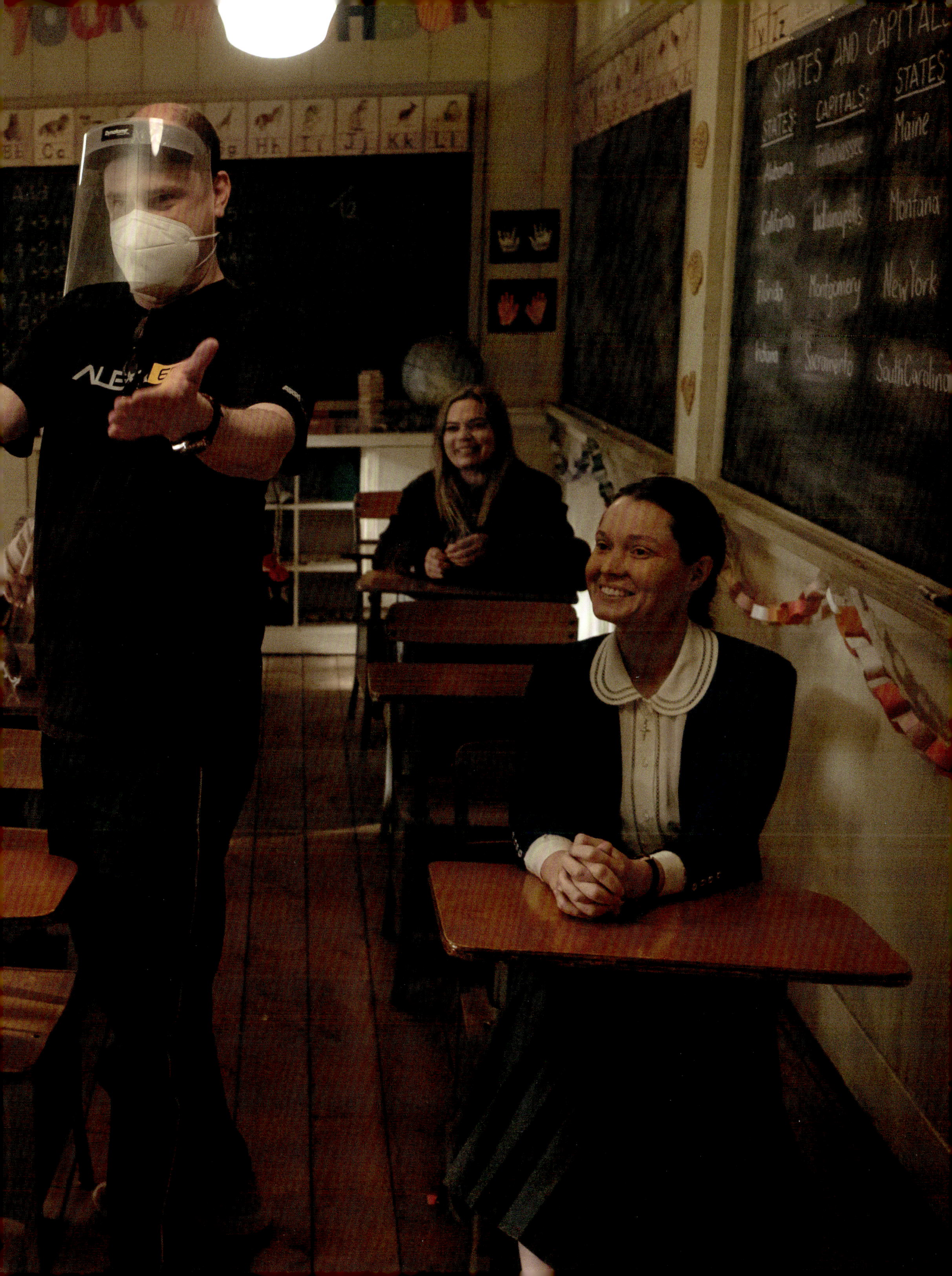
STATES AND CAPITALS
STATES:
CAPITALS:
STATES:
Maine
California
Indianapolis
Montana
Florida
Montgomery
New York
Sacramento
South Carolina

JOE COLLIE

ROBERT LONGSTREET

Robert Longstreet plays Joe Collie, the island pariah since he accidentally shot Leeza Scarborough six years ago. Flanagan says he paralleled Joe and Leeza with Riley and Tara-Beth. "The difference is, obviously, Tara-Beth didn't survive. But Joe is a potential future for Riley. I love symmetry in story structure, and that gave me a great opportunity to have Riley sit, essentially, with his future. You'll notice that it's Riley giving Joe words of comfort and encouragement, not the other way around."

This is Longstreet's third project with Flanagan, following *The Haunting of Hill House* and *Doctor Sleep*. Gish, who played Longstreet's character's wife in *Hill House*, says, "Robert's this magical, eccentric genius of an artist. I love Mike for capitalizing on him."

Longstreet says that he thinks Joe was alcoholic even before shooting Leeza. "The backstory that I made up for him was that he was a fisherman who had to go on disability. When he fired the gun, he was in an absolute blackout, ranting – which isn't [in the script] – but never meaning to hit anybody."

Joe stayed on Crockett as penance, Longstreet believes. "He could have gotten out, and started a new life somewhere, because he's actually an intelligent, viable human being, who's just so wounded. Being universally hated ground him down to nothing. He's stagnated into utter inertia."

Joe's closest companion is his dog Pike, played by Chico. Longstreet says, "The trainer, Paul Jasper, was incredible. I think it's really going to look like he's my dog. I had [dog] treats, and took Chico around. He was such a puppy that you had to be really mellow, because he was always ready to play. That looks terrifying, because he's an enormous dog."

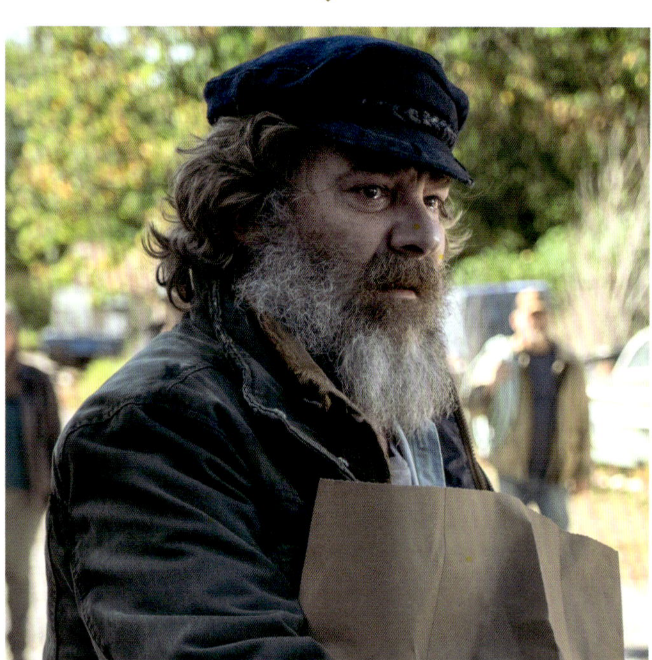

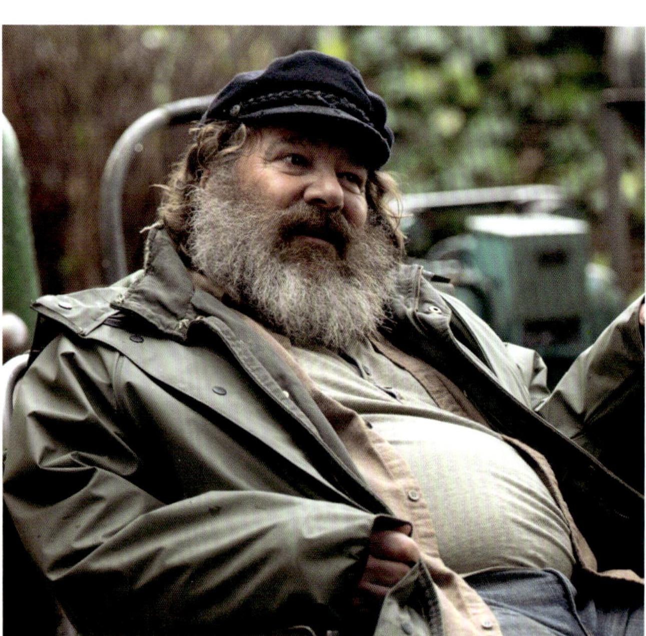

RIGHT/ Joe Collie relaxing outside his trailer.

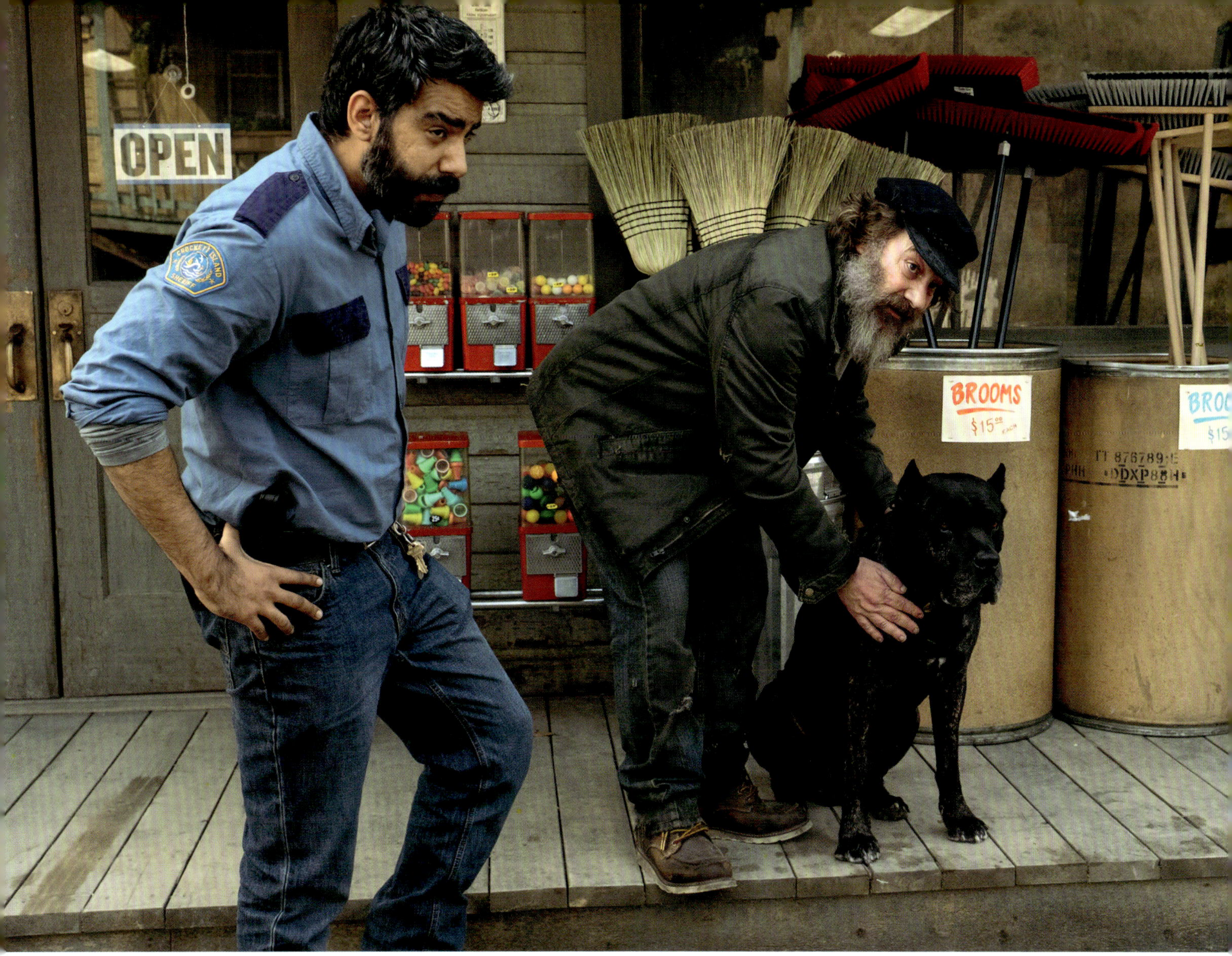

BOTTOM/ Chico as Pike, walking with Robert Longstreet as Joe.

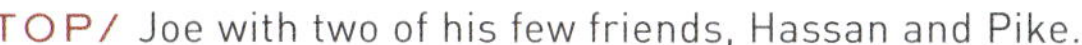

TOP/ Joe with two of his few friends, Hassan and Pike.

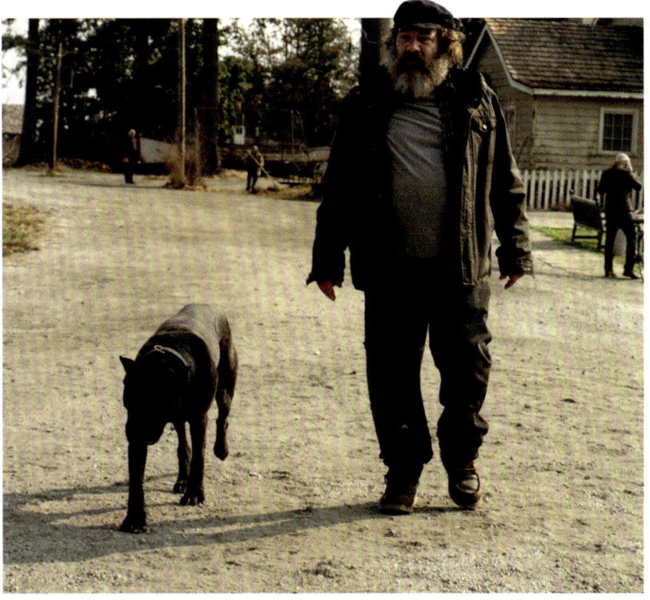

Bev intentionally poisons Pike, who dies in Joe's arms. Raleigh explains that Fractured FX got Chico's exact dimensions, then did a sculpture, made a mold and built a Pike replica puppet "from the ribcage up" for closeups, with foam rubber skin and hair applied with a flocking gun.

On-site, Alvarez laid on the ground, with one arm inside the puppet to control its face. Kelsey Berk handled the tubing for blood and vomit, and a third puppeteer maneuvered the paws via marionette rods.

Longstreet says the puppet "looked so real that I just dissolved. We would switch back and forth from the puppeteered dog to the real dog, and he would lick my face every time, like, 'It's okay.' That broke my heart, too."

Other actors were likewise moved. Aburri relates, "I looked at Robert's eyes, and I cried."

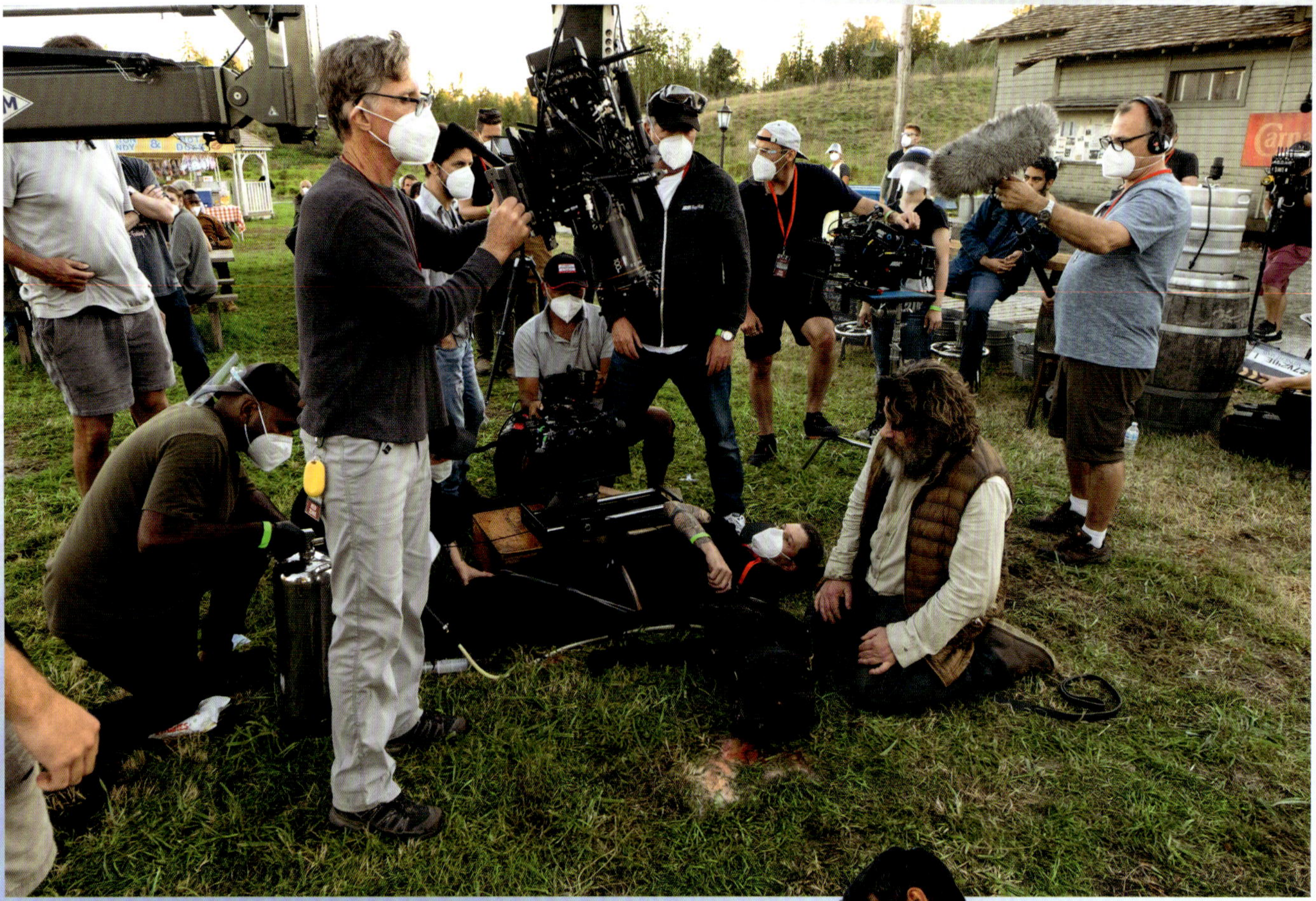

THIS PAGE/ Filming the death of Pike.

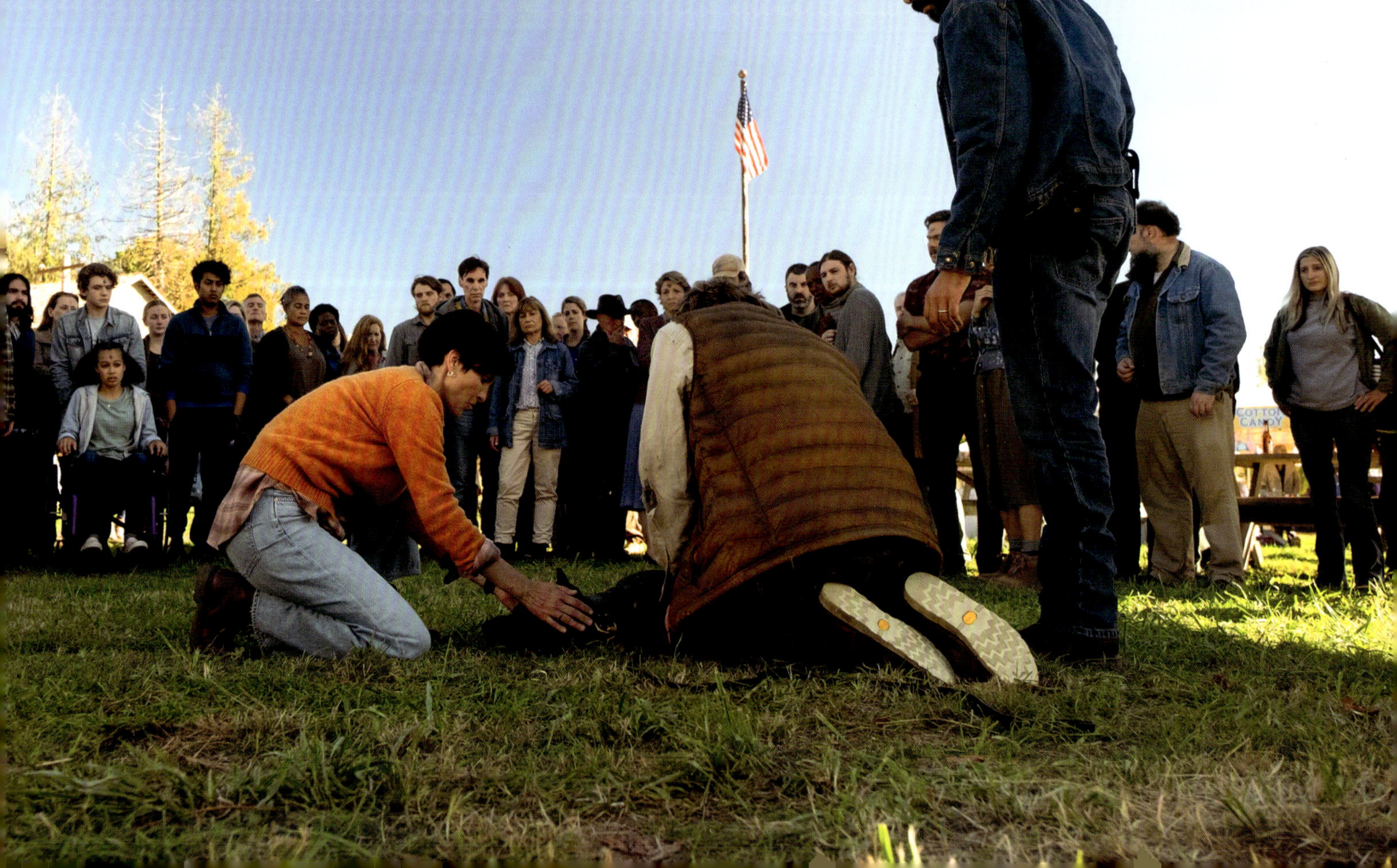

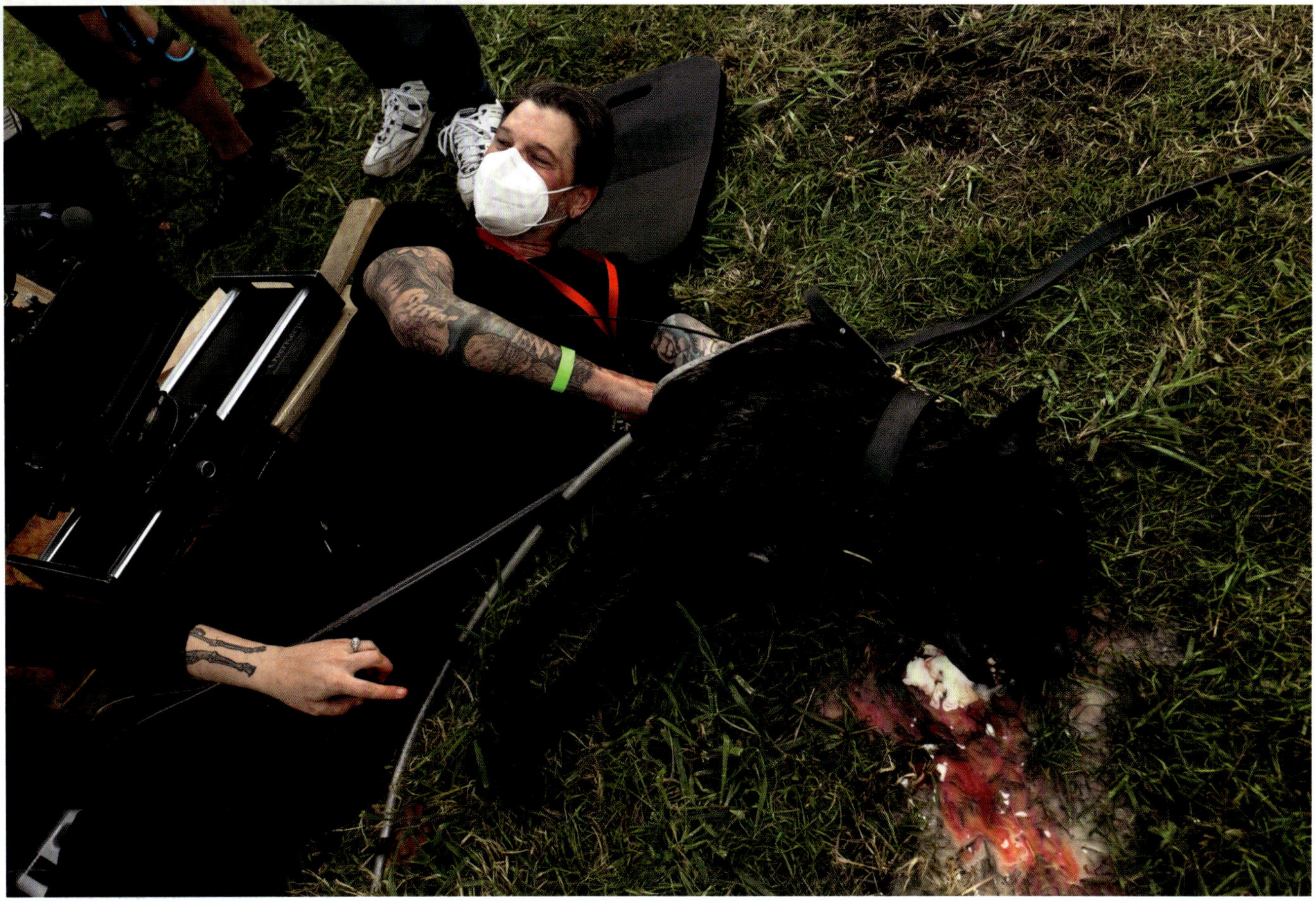

TOP/ "Ozzy" Alvarez operates the Pike puppet.

In Leeza's monologue where she forgives Joe, Longstreet says Cymone "was so brilliant" when the camera was on her that he feared he'd cried himself out before the turnaround. "Mike did a great trick. He said, 'We got it. Let's do where she comes in the door, ten seconds, we'll cut.' And then he didn't cut. With the pressure off, I got it all back."

Joe has his own monologue about his sister. Longstreet says, "She's probably the last person I ever heard say, 'I love you' to me. I was just so into my own shit that, even when I knew she was sick, I couldn't visit her."

When he sees his AA sponsor Father Paul drinking what looks like wine, "I'm trying to make no big deal of it," Longstreet says. "I'm so disappointed in him."

But it's much worse than that. "He's hugging me and not letting go. Hamish was playing it creepy, and it was chilling my blood."

Longstreet reckons that Midnight Mass is overall "the most emotionally naked and devastated I've ever been on film."

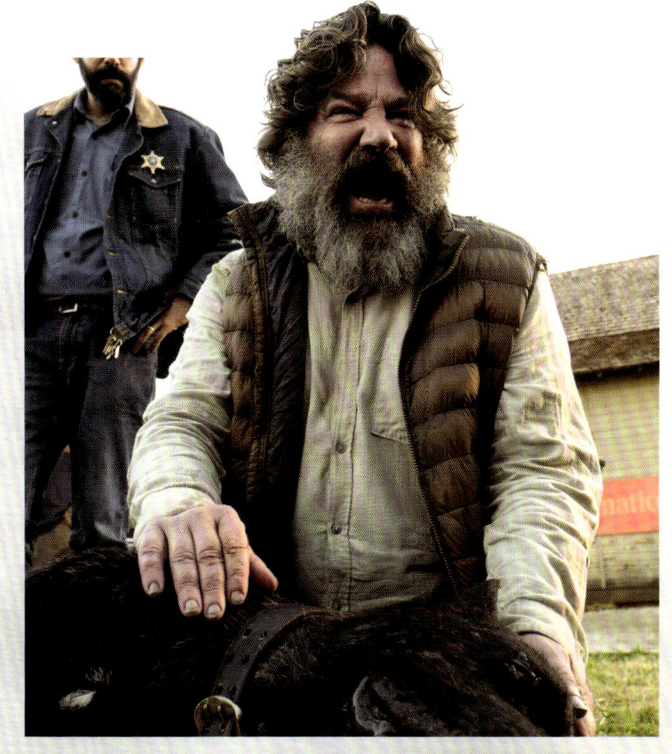

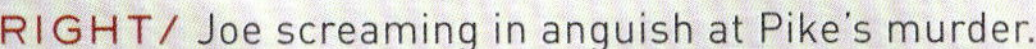

RIGHT/ Joe screaming in anguish at Pike's murder.

JOE'S TRAILER

A LIVED-IN TRAGEDY

Longstreet says Joe Collie's trailer "was claustrophobic, full of crap, and so sad. It helped my character, where I would look at that, and go, 'That's all you fucking deserve'."

"Joe Collie's trailer is meant to be in a very separate space," says Arnold. "We shot at the farm in an isolated area, in a blackberry bramble. There are castoff pieces of lawn furniture, and other equipment. He has a generator there to supply his electricity, because he's not on grid. So, there are oily rags, and gas cans, and all kinds of flotsam, like getting on the way to homeless clutter."

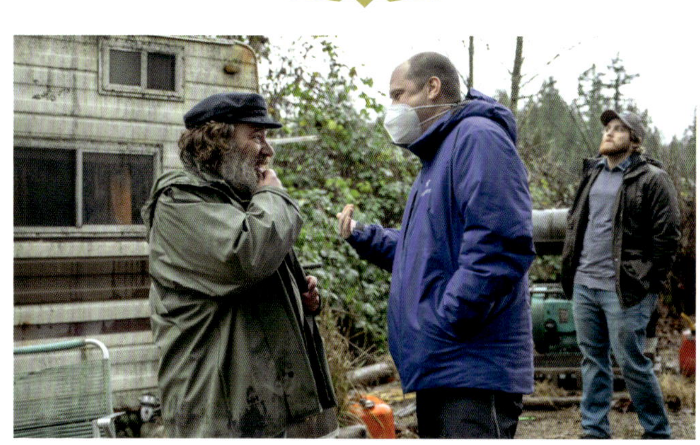

THIS SPREAD/ Joe Collie's self-hatred expresses itself in his home.

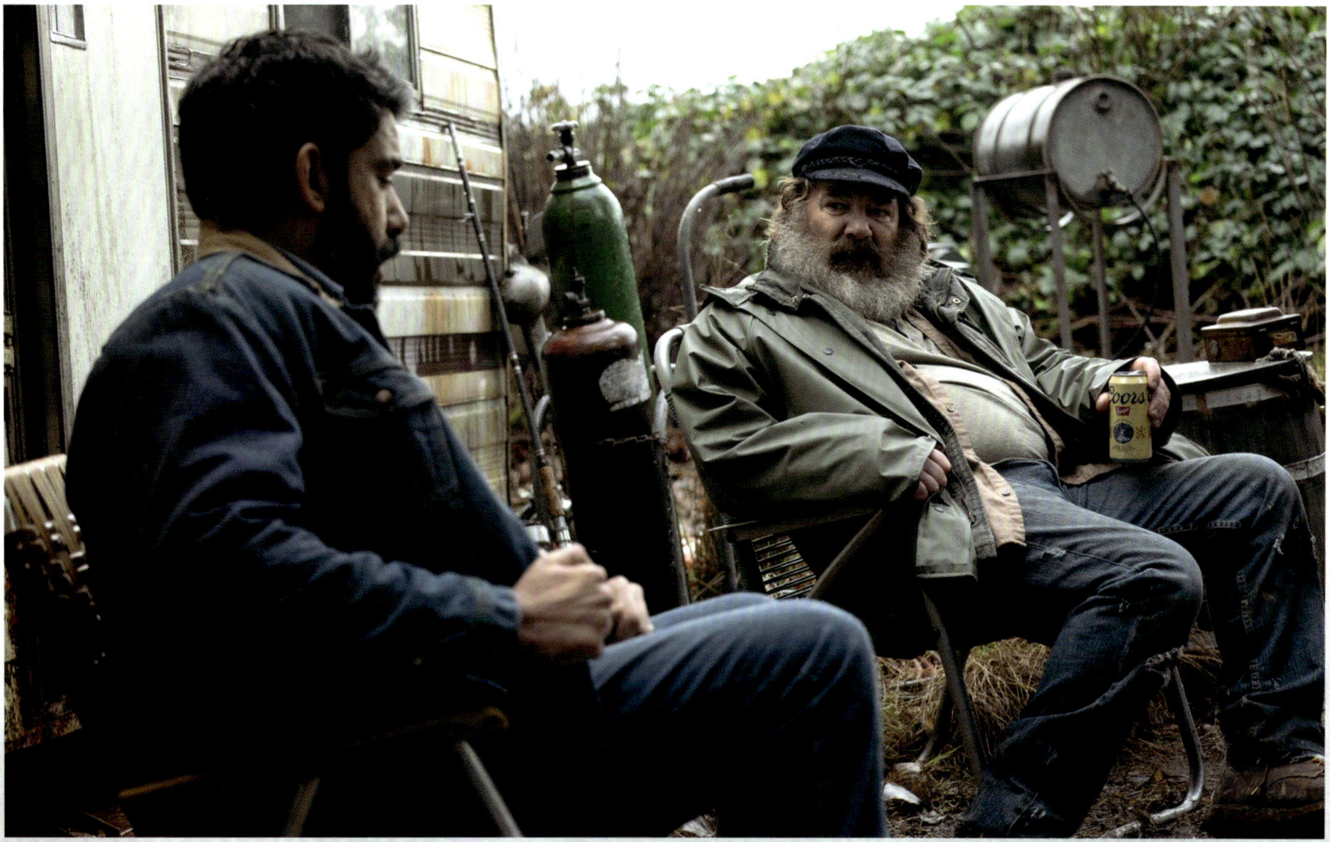

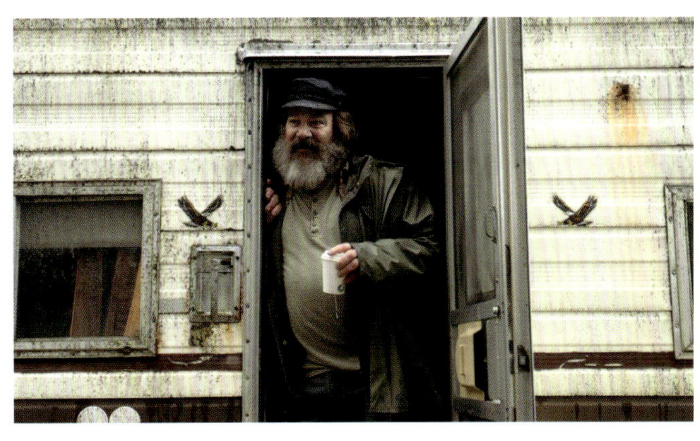

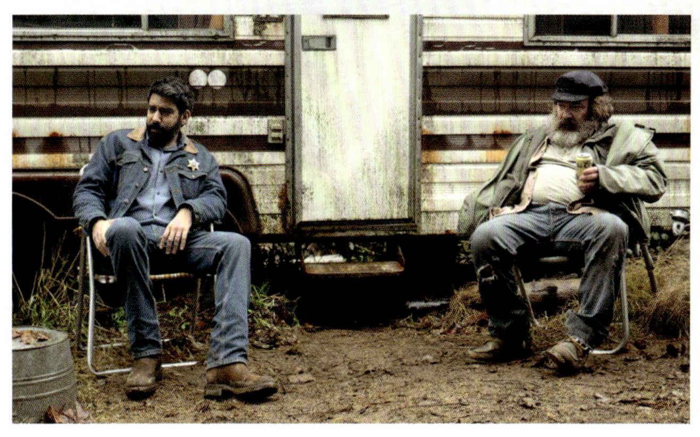

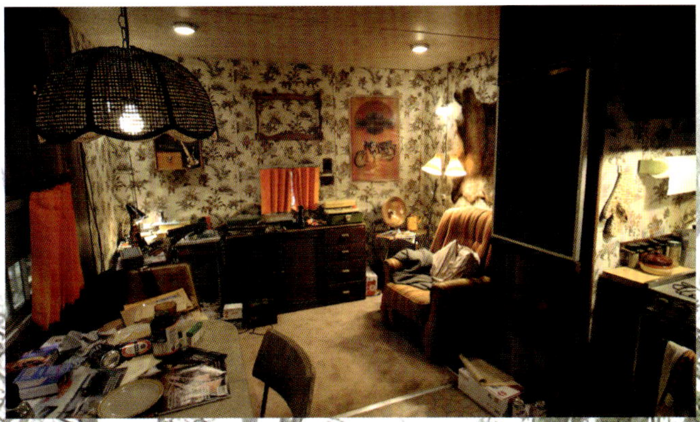

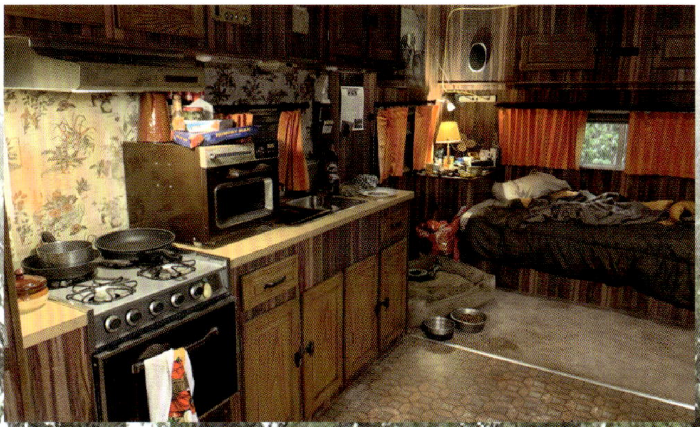

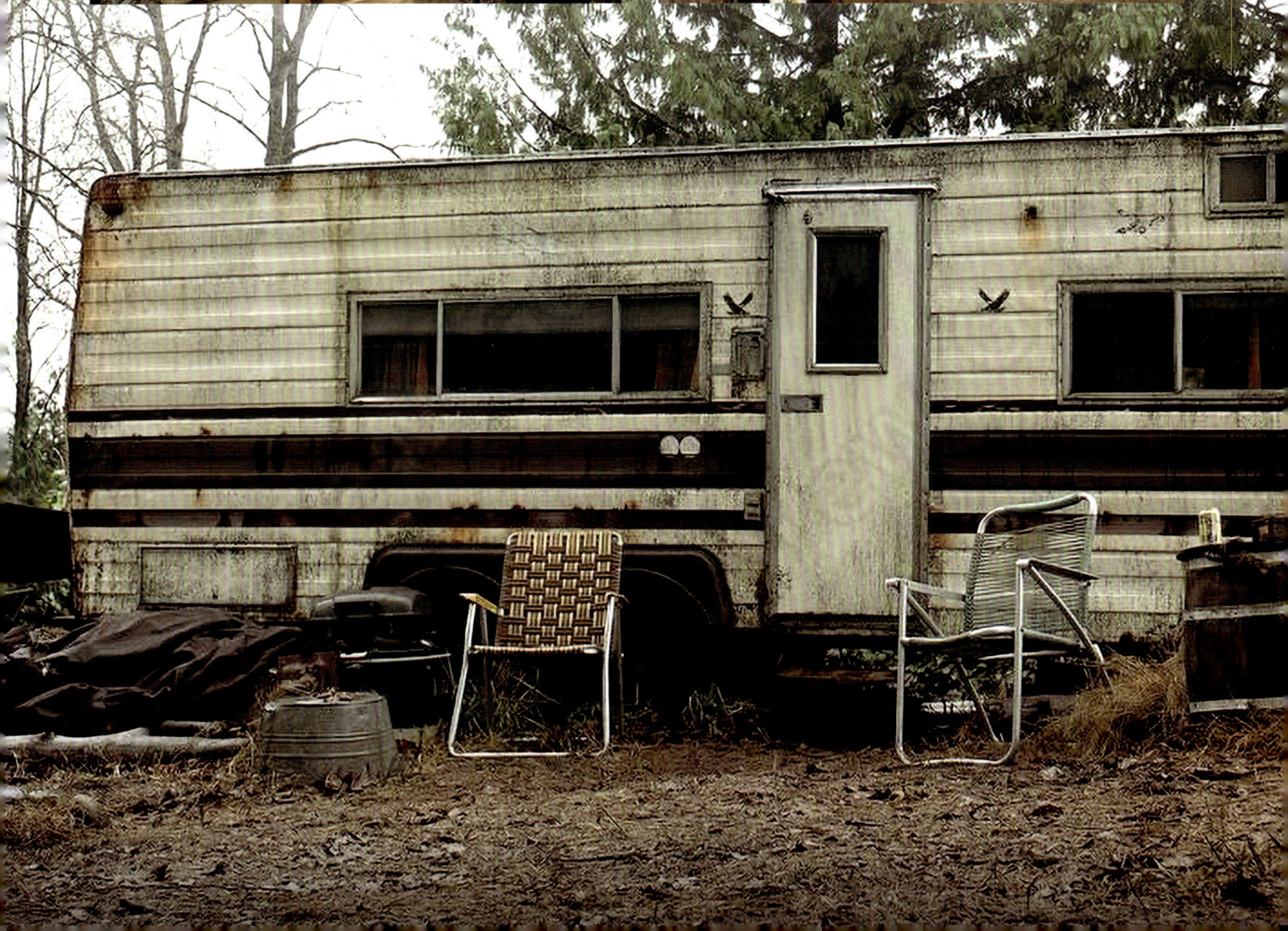

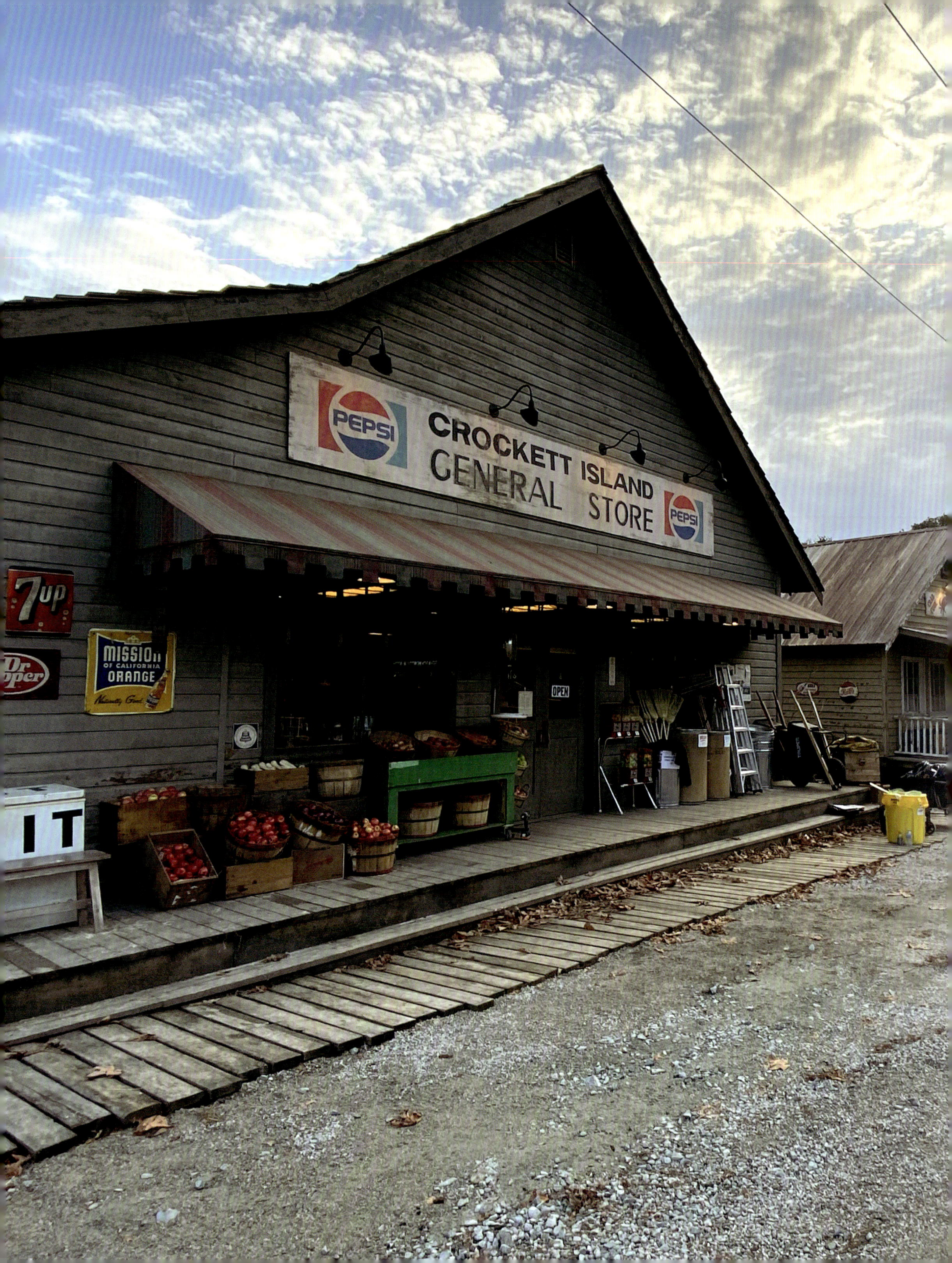
PEPSI
CROCKETT ISLAND
GENERAL STORE
PEPSI
7up
MISSION
OF CALIFORNIA
ORANGE
OPEN

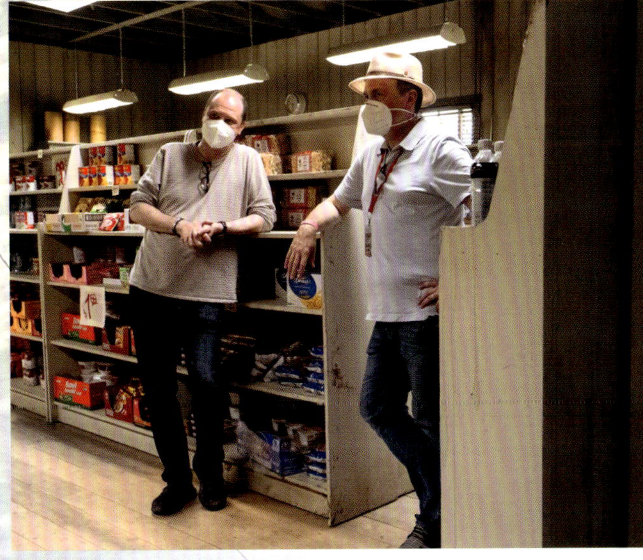

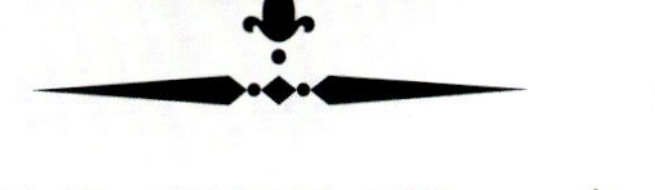

GENERAL STORE

RETAIL AND LAW

Arnold reveals, "The only big set that was finished inside and out was the general store. That was completely built and dressed on the location."

This was partly because much of the interior can be seen from the exterior, and partly to accommodate action between the store and the sheriff's office.

For the store's contents, Arnold relates, "Because this is a maritime place, we had things that were related to fishing, and working on the water, basic food staples, and a little hardware, wheelbarrows, brooms, and trash cans, because this is where you get everything in town."

Cymone says she didn't have any scenes in the store, but went in a few times. "The design was beautiful." It also felt real. "I didn't take any, but people were taking gummies and chips," she laughs.

Kohli admits to being one of the culprits. "People were lifting items from the shop, much to the dismay of the set designer. I'm a good boy. But I developed this idea for anyone who has a Flanalogue [Kohli's term for a monologue written by Mike Flanagan] – when it's your day, you get to act up. So, I did my Flanalogue, lifted a pack of Skittles, and was challenging our a.d. [assistant director] Morgan to do something about it, because I was obviously stealing in broad daylight. I popped one Skittle in my mouth, and broke my crown. That became the karmic story for why you shouldn't shoplift in the grocery store."

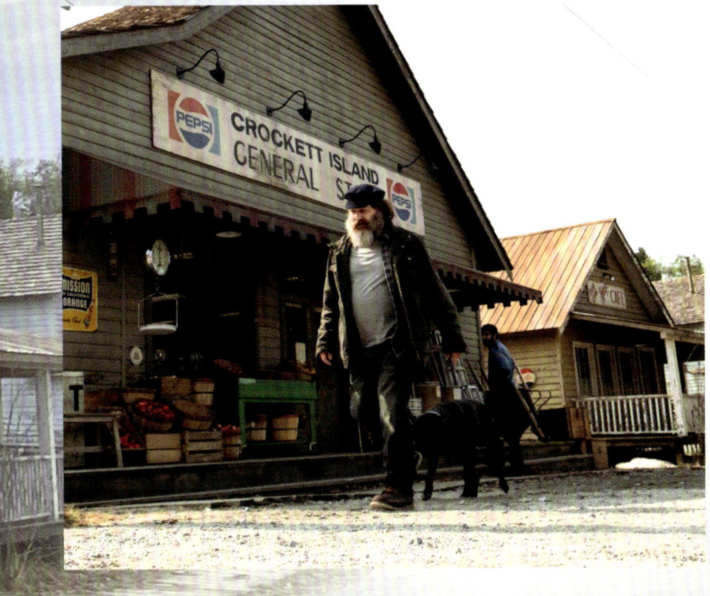

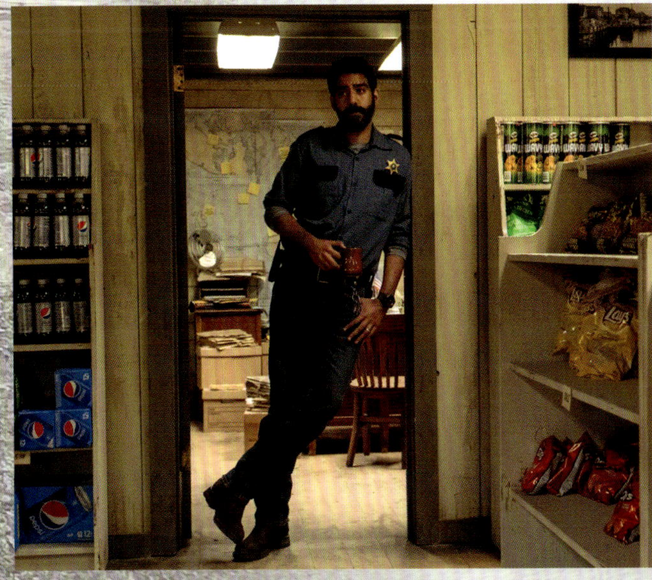

THIS PAGE/ (TOP) Flanagan and Macy hang out in the General Store. (MIDDLE) Joe Collie leaves the store with Pike. (BOTTOM) The sheriff stands in the doorway between the store and his office.

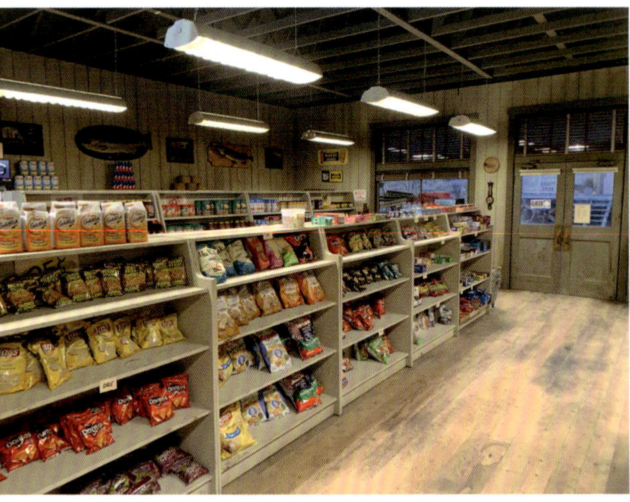

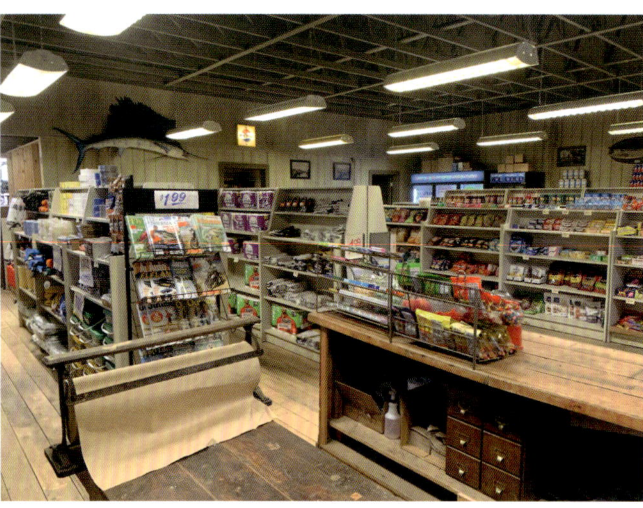

TOP/ (LEFT) The store's snacks were a temptation for cast and crew. (RIGHT) Behind the counter – brown wrapping paper and cleaning supplies.

BOTTOM/ The sheriff's office, with a view of both store and jail cell.

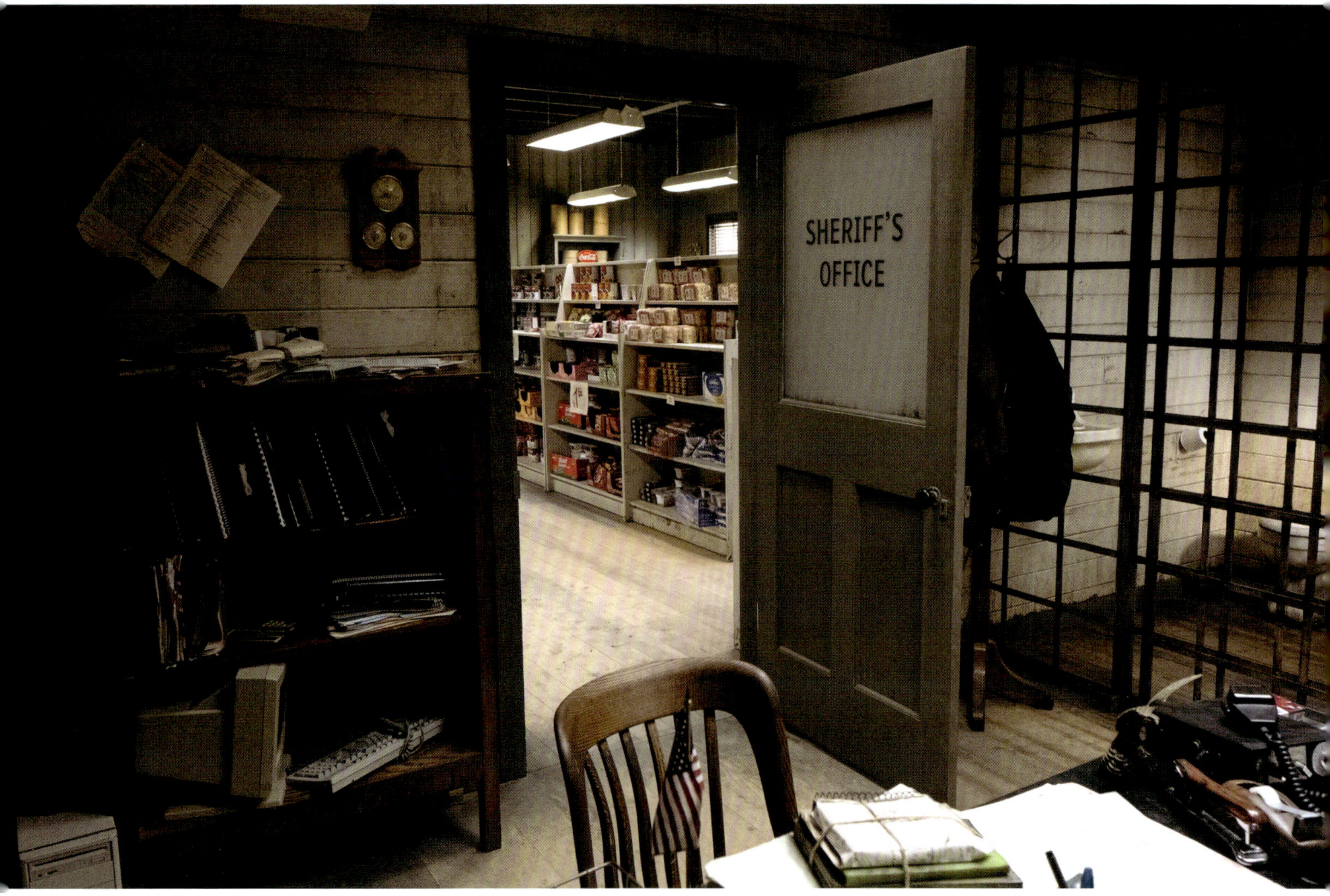

SHERIFF'S OFFICE

Arnold says, "The sheriff's office is a little room in the back of the general store. When the door is closed, it's very separated, but when the door's open, you can see into the general store, and vice-versa. There's a formal jail cell. Those criss-crossed bars were something that was done a long time ago in jails. I thought it was an interesting, different look."

Arnold adds that he was very specific about the maps in the office, "and how the maps should be laid out. We produced all those maps. We're pretty specific about the paperwork in the office, too. Some of it is specific to island culture: cases of missing boats, the person who drowned falling overboard."

Longstreet says the jail helps the relationship between Joe and Hassan. "I would bet that, in a perverse way, Joe wound up there a couple of times just seeking comfort. 'Let's have our buddy the Sheriff take us to where it's clean, and people are nice to me'."

BOTTOM/ Even on a small island, law enforcement involves a lot of paperwork.

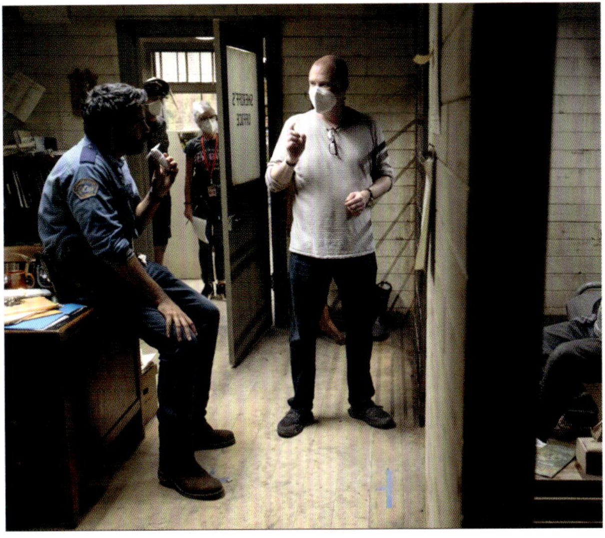

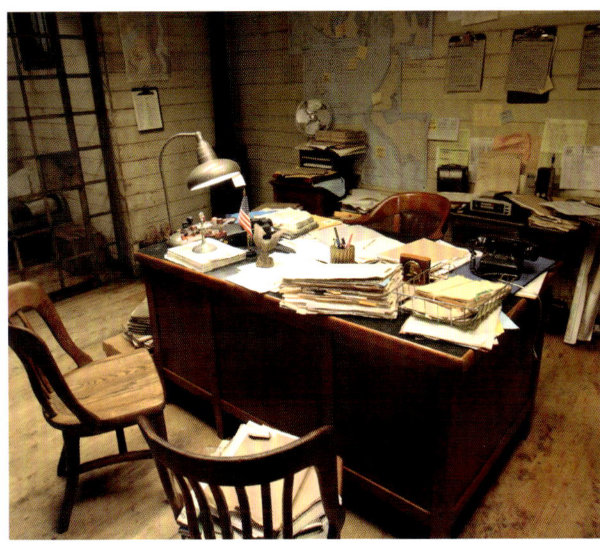

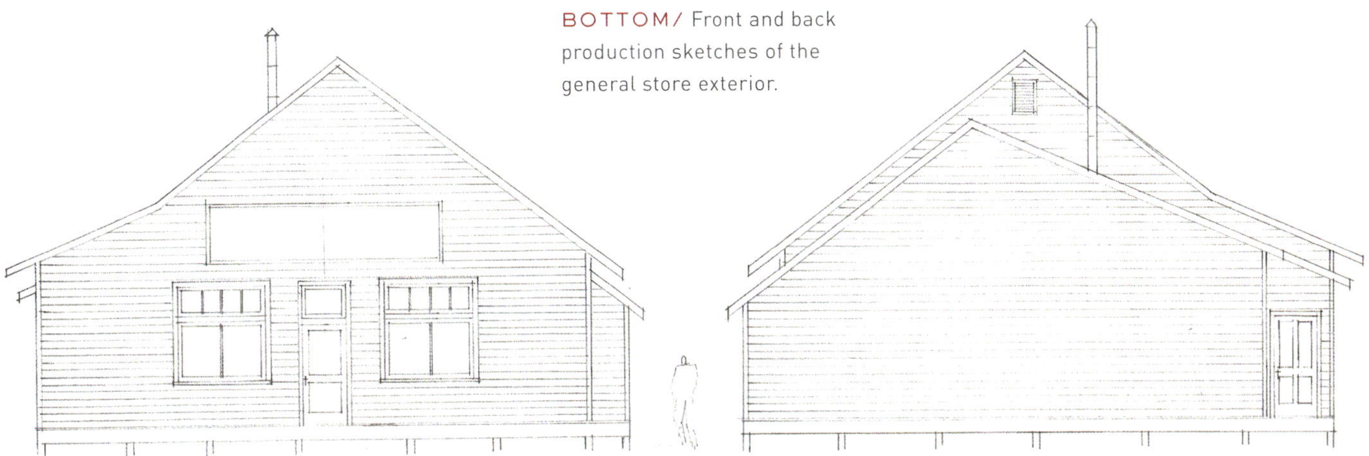

BOTTOM/ Front and back production sketches of the general store exterior.

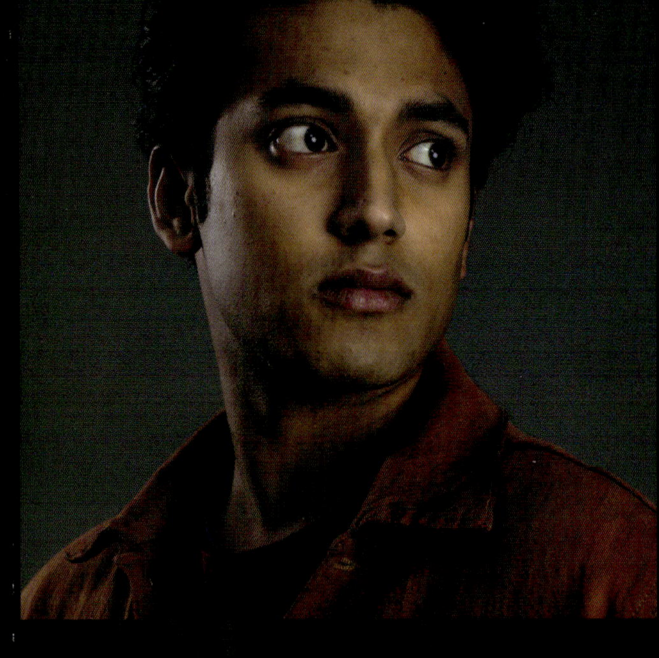

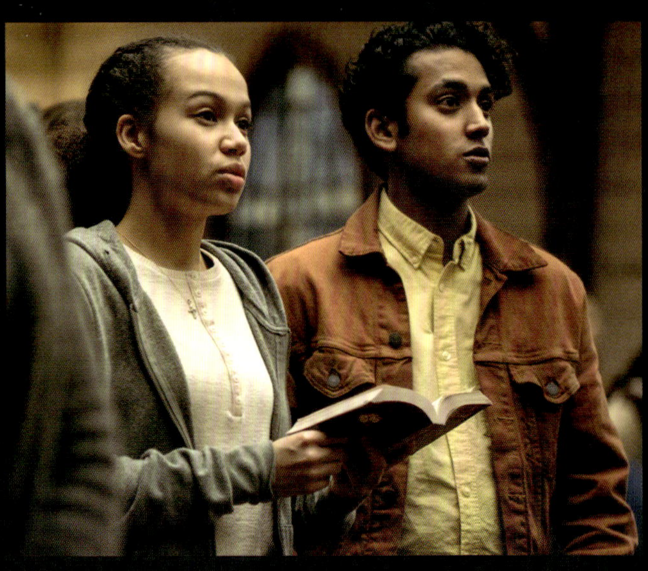

Flanagan says, "We loved having a character that would kind of be living out the tensions that Hassan was living, but in the much smaller social circle of Warren and his friends."

In Aburri's view, "Ali's just an everyday kid, trying to find his way in the world. But he has a strict father. I think it's a natural coming of age, but it's in this weird setup, where all these crazy things happen, and that has a completely different result on his overall mindset throughout the show.

"At the start, he's trying to fit in. He was never really deep into his own faith that he was born and raised in. I don't think he understood it. Ali enjoys the way Father Paul explains Christianity. [Seeing Leeza walk] was the factor that pushed him to, 'Well, maybe I should just go for it'."

But, Aburri continues, "Before he resurrected, Ali was either looking at things from his father's perspective, or from his own perspective. He could never combine them together. I think he reawakes to the truth. He wasn't a guy who ate meat, so he's not the type of person who would go cannibalistic. He has his own values, and [after resurrection] he understands what the truth is, and where his father is coming from."

Aburri loved working with Kohli. "When the cameras turn on, and he's in character, I see my father in him, exactly the way my father would behave with me. But off-camera, he's just like a cool friend, like a big brother. Also, I've seen Rahul on *iZombie*, and I was like, 'Man, it would be cool to work with him one day.' I'm blessed."

THIS SPREAD/ (LEFT) Ali becomes curious about Catholicism. (RIGHT) Hassan and Ali, dying differently as the sun rises.

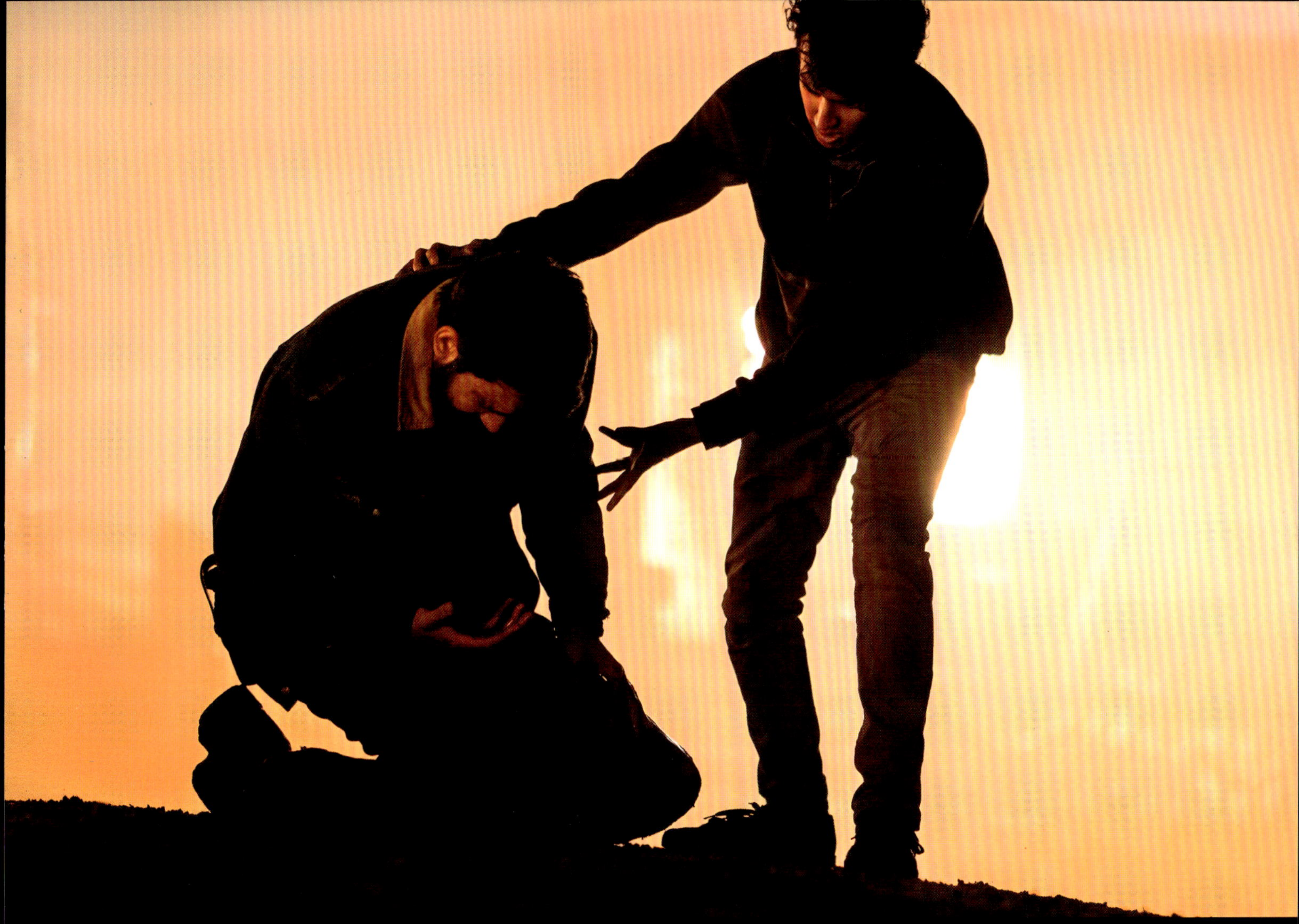

Aburri was raised as an observant Hindu, which meant that he had lots of experience with religious ritual, but none with Muslim prayers. He says on-set advisor Mohamad Hajem "was great. He taught me all the prayers, step by step. It was almost like dance choreography. I was able to get the steps down fairly easily, because I was doing prayers since I was a kid, and it came back for me."

For Ali's look, Anderson says, "He's probably a little cooler than the other kids in this town, because he's a transplant from New York. So, he has cooler track pants, cooler sportswear than the [other] kids. I still had to tone down everything, because I'd rather not have it about the clothes."

Aburri got to select Ali's bike, a BMX. "Ali was born in New York, and I thought Ali would be the guy who rides bikes. We actually did a day of training on bicycles in the park, so I had a lot of fun riding around."

At the end, Ali prays with his dying father on the beach, awaiting the sunrise. Aburri says, "That was probably the most emotional scene I've done throughout my acting career."

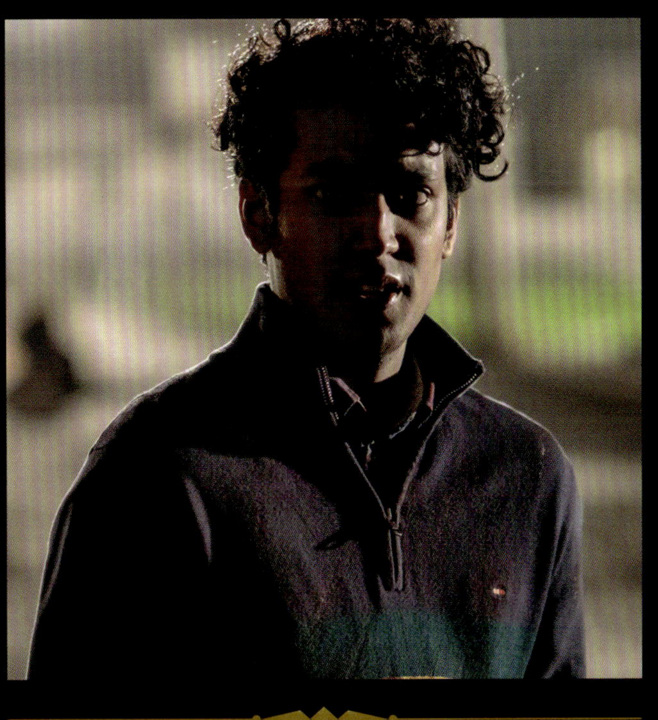

Rahul Kohli plays Crockett's sheriff, Hassan Shabazz. When Kohli was acting in *The Haunting of Bly Manor*, Flanagan reveals, "After his second episode, I said, 'I think you might be a fantastic choice for Sheriff Hassan'."

Kohli says, "Mike took me through the pitch, the story and the character. I said, 'This is one of the best things I've ever heard. Do not offer this to another actor, it's mine.' I'm a huge Western fan. Mike has taken the archetypal American hero, the sheriff, and fused that with modern-day America's biggest [perceived] threat, the bearded brown Muslim man. One big draw was the idea of playing those in one person."

Flanagan says, "In a small-town-under-siege story, the sheriff's meant to embody and protect not only the town itself, but the values of the town. I thought that was a wonderful opportunity to represent Islam in a way that isn't often done. That was important to Rahul, and to myself."

For research, Kohli conferred with his lifelong friend, Mohamed Bouissa, a devout Muslim who became an official consultant on *Midnight Mass*'s depiction of Islam. (Since Bouissa is based in the U.K., Mohamad Hajem was brought in to be the on-set consultant.) Kohli recalls, "I asked him, 'When you were a teenager, what would you have wanted to see from a badass Muslim sheriff?'" Kohli says Bouissa wanted him "to look like a leading man as much as humanly possible, while still portraying Islam." Kohli grew a beard, and was given a subtly Western look, with boots and plaid shirts.

"Mike was interested in speaking to Mohamed," Kohli says, "so I put the two together. Mike started sending drafts to Mohamed. 'Is this correct?' Nothing was overlooked. Most of it, Mike had found already."

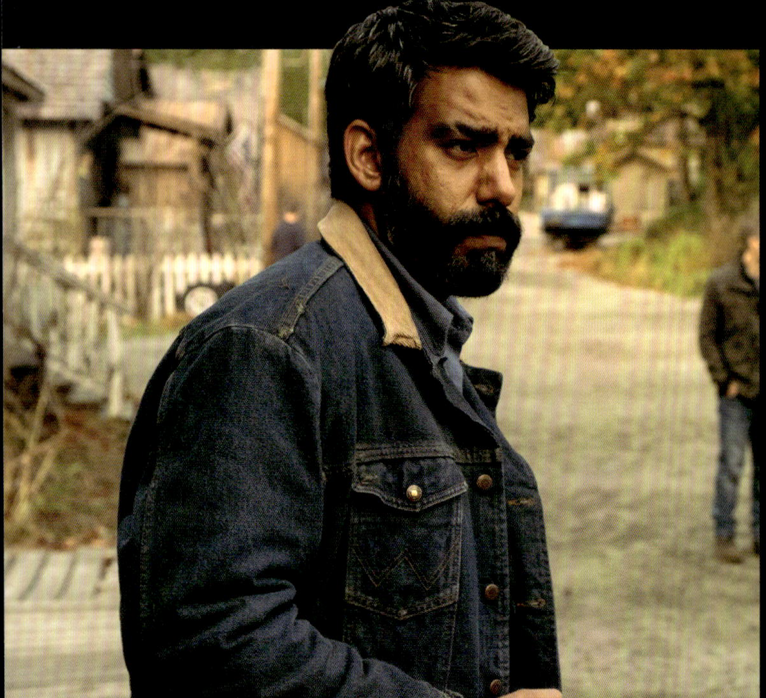

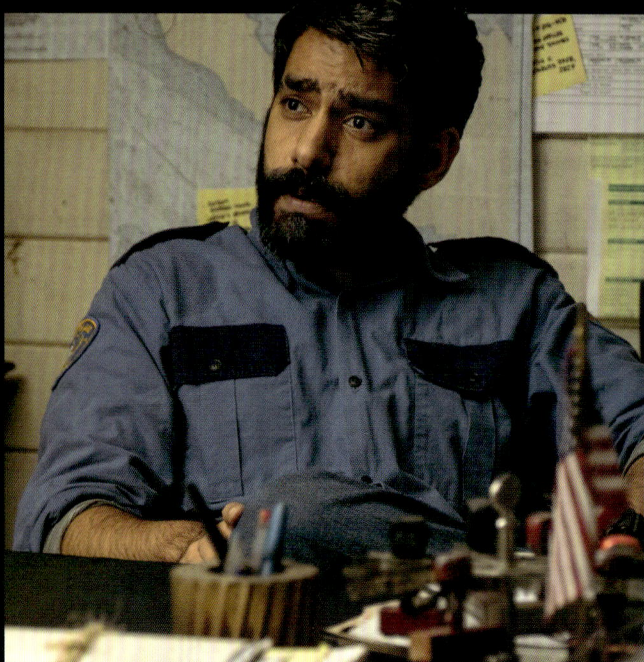

THIS SPREAD/ Sheriff Hassan, on the street, and behind his desk, in uniform.

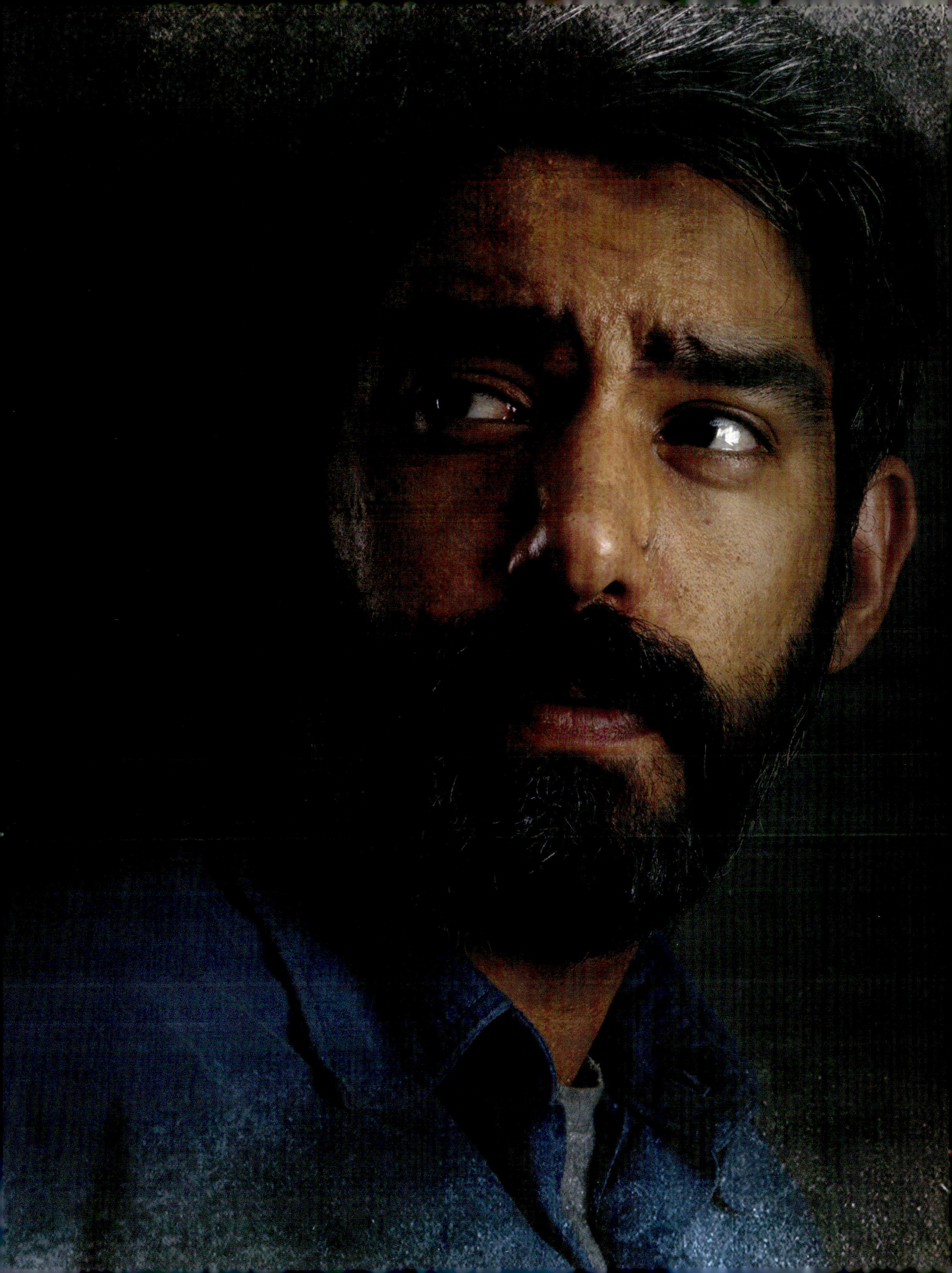

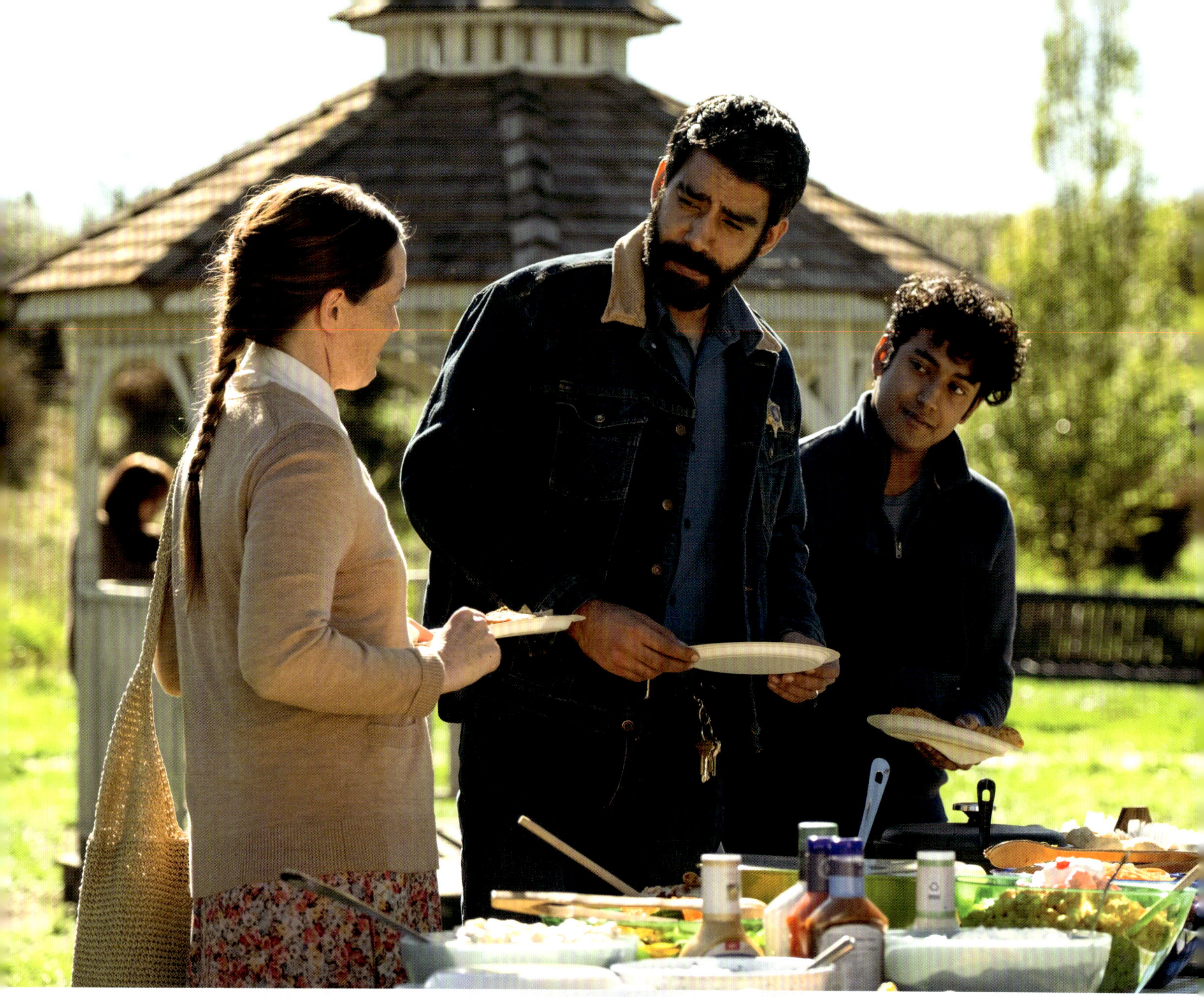

TOP/ Bev, Hassan, and Ali at the Crock-Pot-Luck buffet line.

Bouissa "massaged a story beat," Kohli adds. Originally, "Hassan finds the Bible in Ali's school bag, and is upset. Mohamed said, 'This wouldn't be an issue. Most [observant] Muslims are well-versed in the Bible.' Together, Mike and Mohamed then turned that into a more informed portrayal of what Islam is, [demonstrating] a lot more synchronicity and acceptance of all religions."

Kohli's research took him on a Netflix-arranged LAPD ride-along. His reading about Islam brought him to Malcolm X and Black Lives Matter. At that time, "The character was just called Sheriff Hassan. When Mike and I were talking, I said, 'What if we give Sheriff Hassan Malcolm X's last name, Sheriff Hassan Shabazz?'"

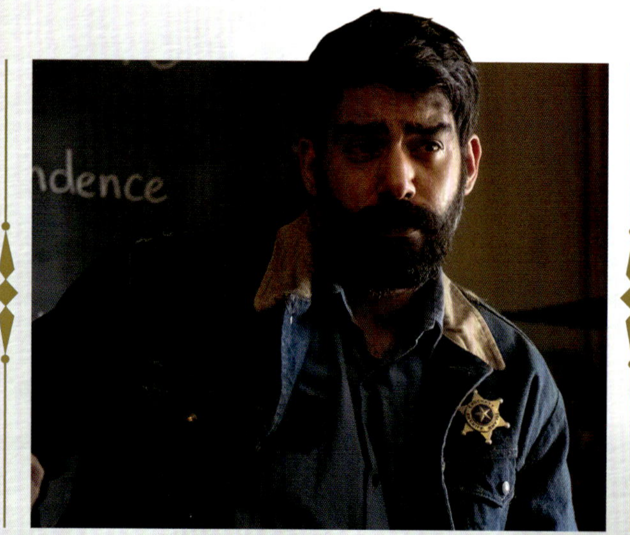

"WHEN I WAS ON THOSE SETS, I FELT LIKE THEY WERE EXACTLY WHAT I HAD PICTURED, ESPECIALLY THE JAIL CELL."

RAHUL KOHLI

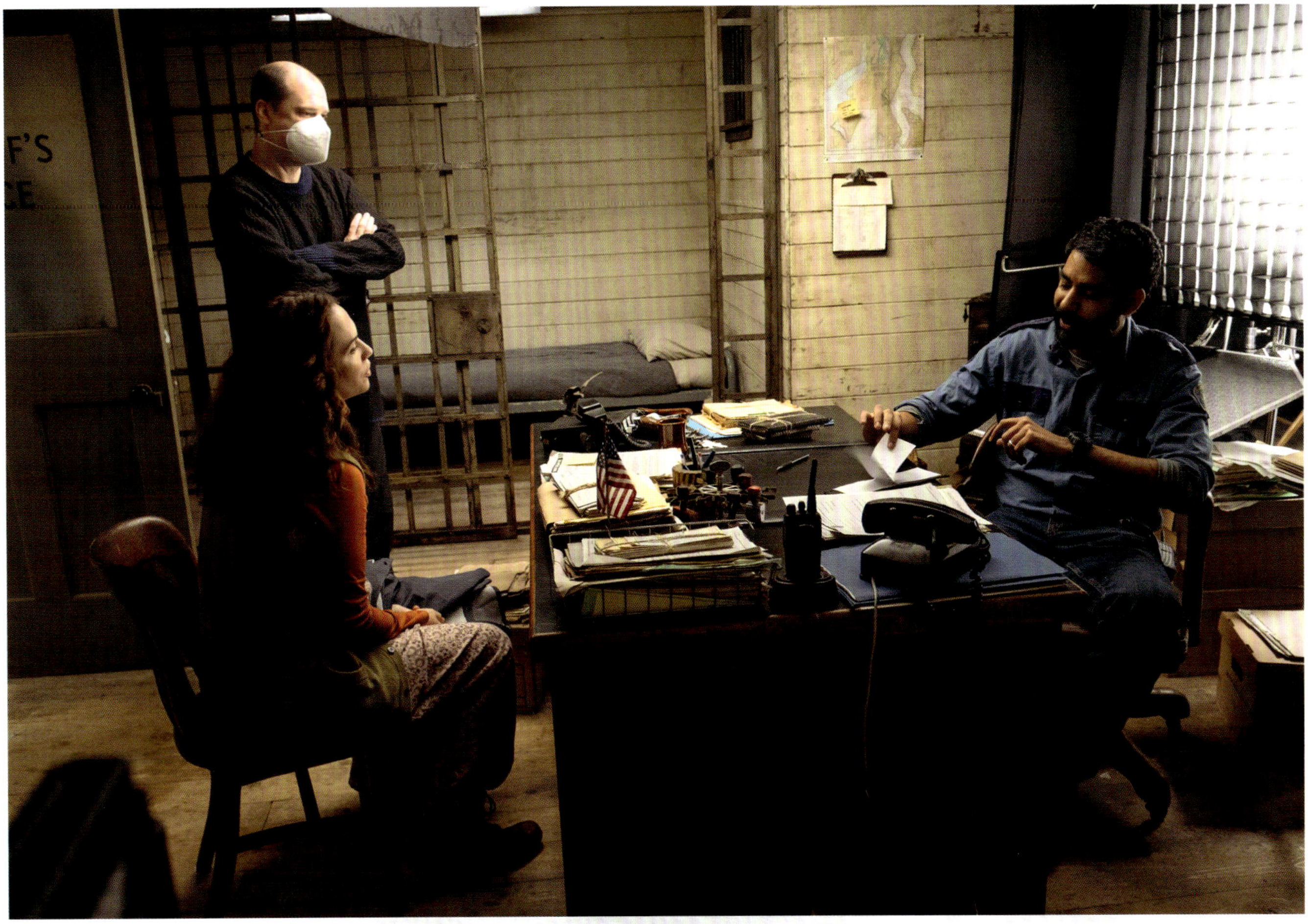

THIS PAGE/ (TOP) Siegel, Flanagan, Kohli. (BOTTOM) Ali mourns his father.

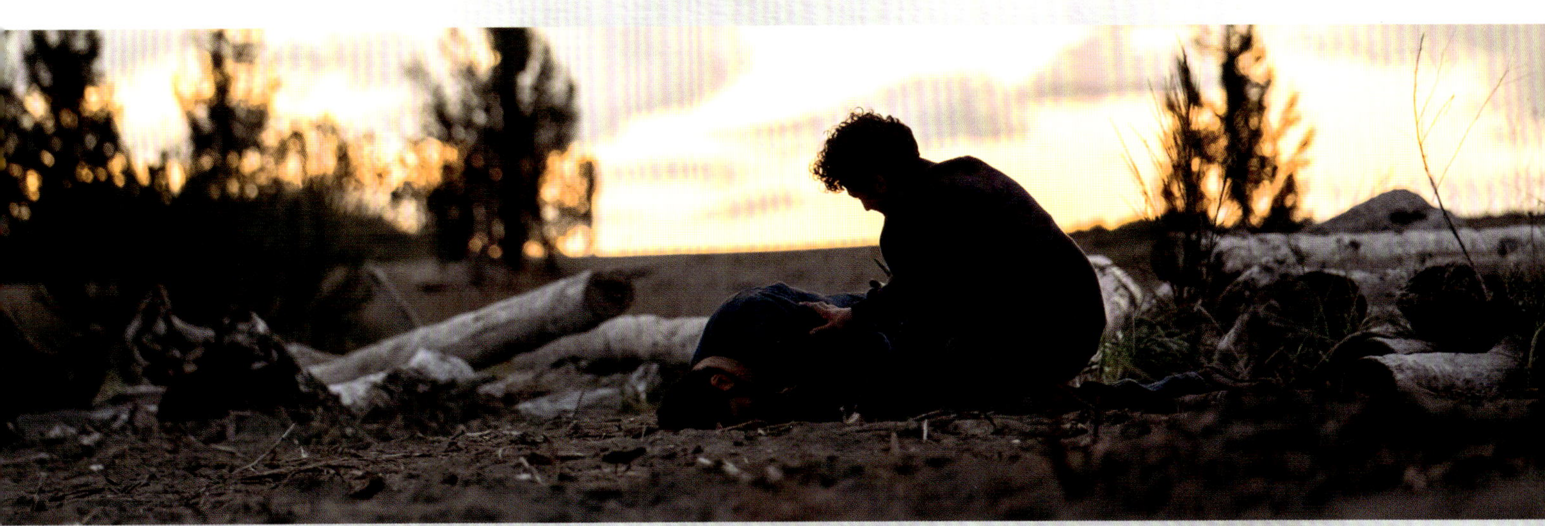

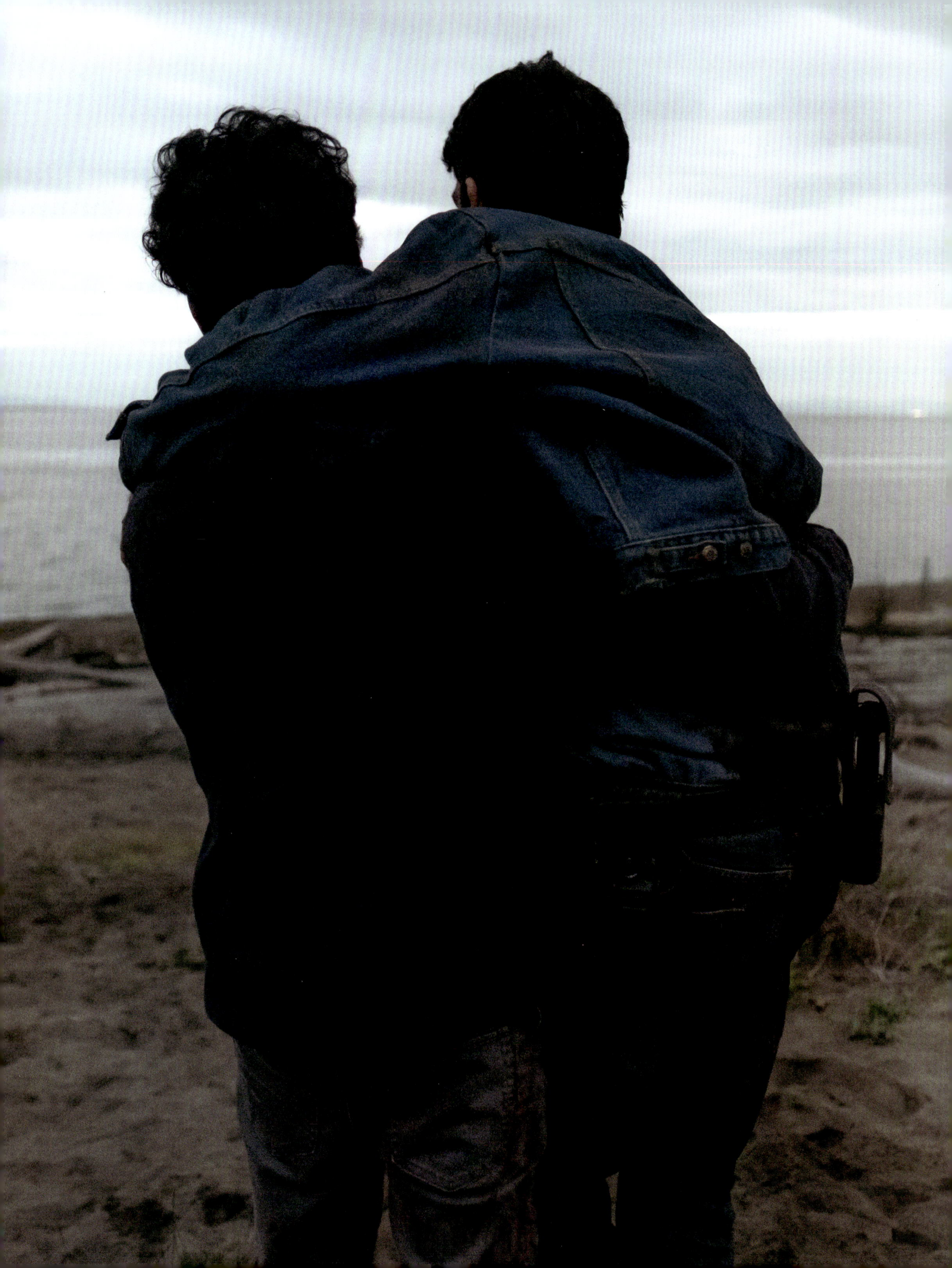

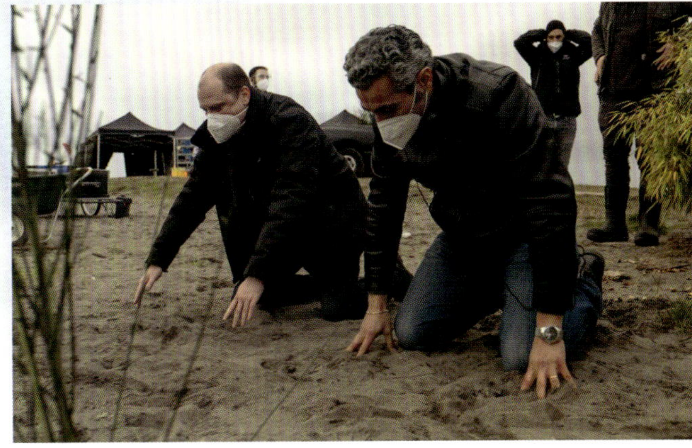

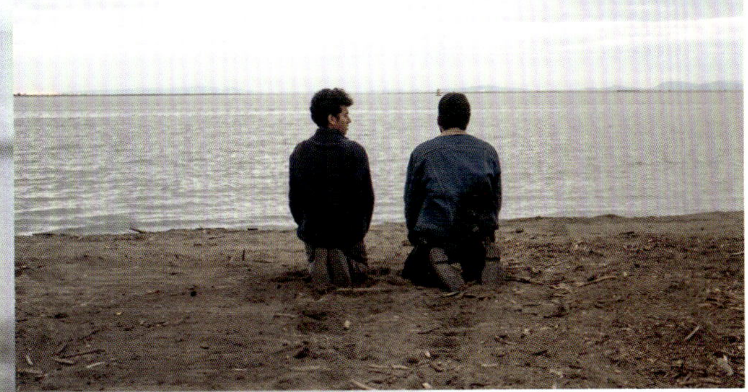

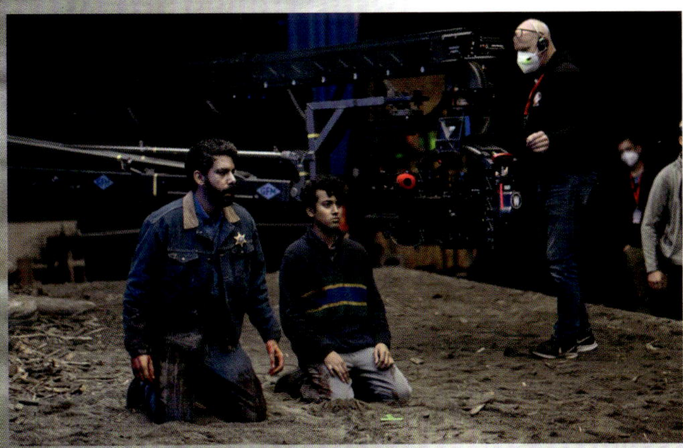

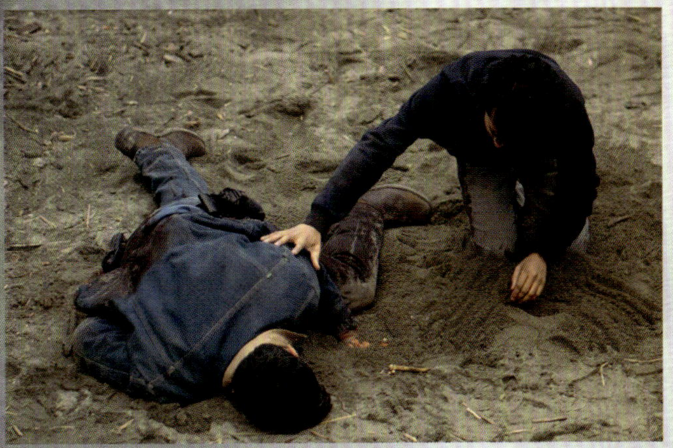

But, Kohli surmised, because everybody called him Sheriff Hassan, Hassan was the surname. "Mike said, 'No. Hassan is his first name. He extended an olive branch to everyone. They're calling him Sheriff, and then first name, like [Sheriff Andy on] *The Andy Griffith Show*.' So, Shabazz is Ali and Hassan's last name."

Flanagan says, "We also loved Hassan as a single father. That explained a lot about his faith, his need to try to pass it on to his son. Some of my favorite scenes are in that gentle father/son tension."

Midnight Mass is the first time Kohli has played a father; Ali is one of Rahul Aburri's first professional acting jobs. That difference in experience, Kohli relates, "the energy that we had around one another, helped us play [the relationship]. I thought of Hassan as a Leo, a lion protecting his cub. His sole mission is really Ali."

Stage monologues usually get months of rehearsal. But "The scary thing with doing [a Flanalogue] is, nine times out of ten, Mike's not going to break it up. The monologue is just going to exist as it is, with a slow push-in. I love Mike's words. They flow fantastically."

Kohli had input into Hassan's fight in the church, although of course Flanagan and the stunt coordinator had ultimate say. "I was like a kid in a candy store. My first blocking was, how do I get up with three people pinning me down? And then I knock those three dudes down."

Getting shot on-screen, Kohli says, is "the most fun I've ever had. I've had all these dreams of things I want to do in my career, and one of them was having a blood bag explode on me."

"WE WANTED HASSAN TO BE THAT STRONG CHARACTER THAT YOU EXPECT FROM THE SHERIFF IN A STORY LIKE THIS."

MIKE FLANAGAN

THIS PAGE/ Rehearsing and filming the final prayers of Hassan and Ali Shabazz.

ST. PATRICK'S CHURCH

KEEPING THE COMMUNITY TOGETHER

Crockett Island's St. Patrick's Church, Arnold observes, "is the center of the community. It keeps everybody together."

Production needed to have complete control of the church within and without, says Macy. "We built the interior on the stage, and the exterior at the primary location."

The design, Flanagan relates, "is informed by the chapel at a parish in Bowie, Maryland, called Sacred Heart. It's one of the oldest Catholic chapels in North America. I was an altar boy there as a kid. I tilted toward design elements that reminded me of that – I gave Steve photographs."

Unlike many exteriors, which only had their immediate entryways dressed, Arnold explains, the church exterior had the full vestibule built inside it, "because they needed shots of people going in and out."

The church interior, Arnold continues, "had to be plain, bleak and isolated, so I went toward a simple wood, almost Shaker-like quality. We designed and built the pews, the pulpit, the altar, every stick of light fixtures, everything in that space." Siegel notes that she was especially impressed by the original, unique wooden carvings of the Stations of the Cross.

BOTTOM/ Side view of St. Patrick's, plus edge of the graveyard.

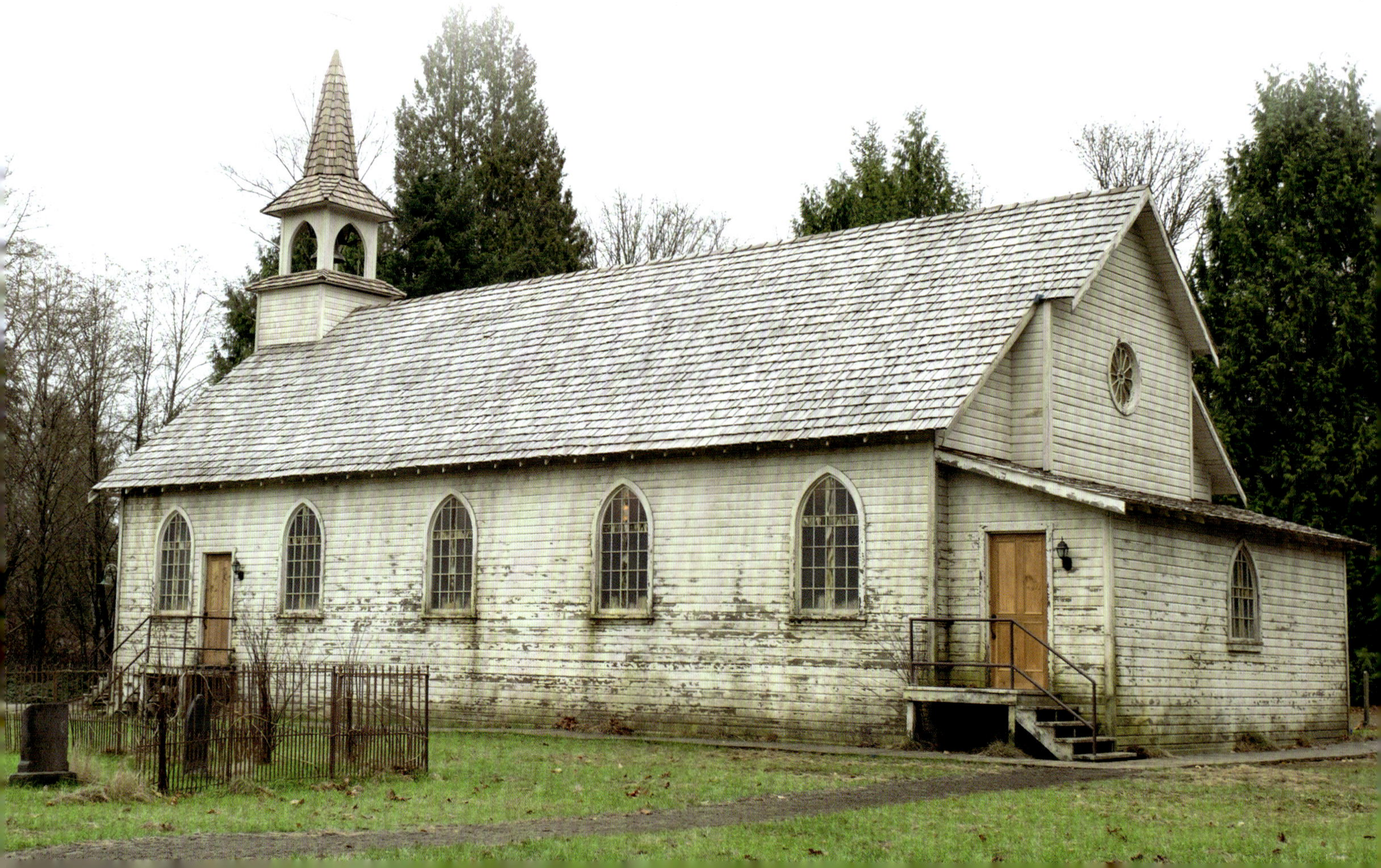

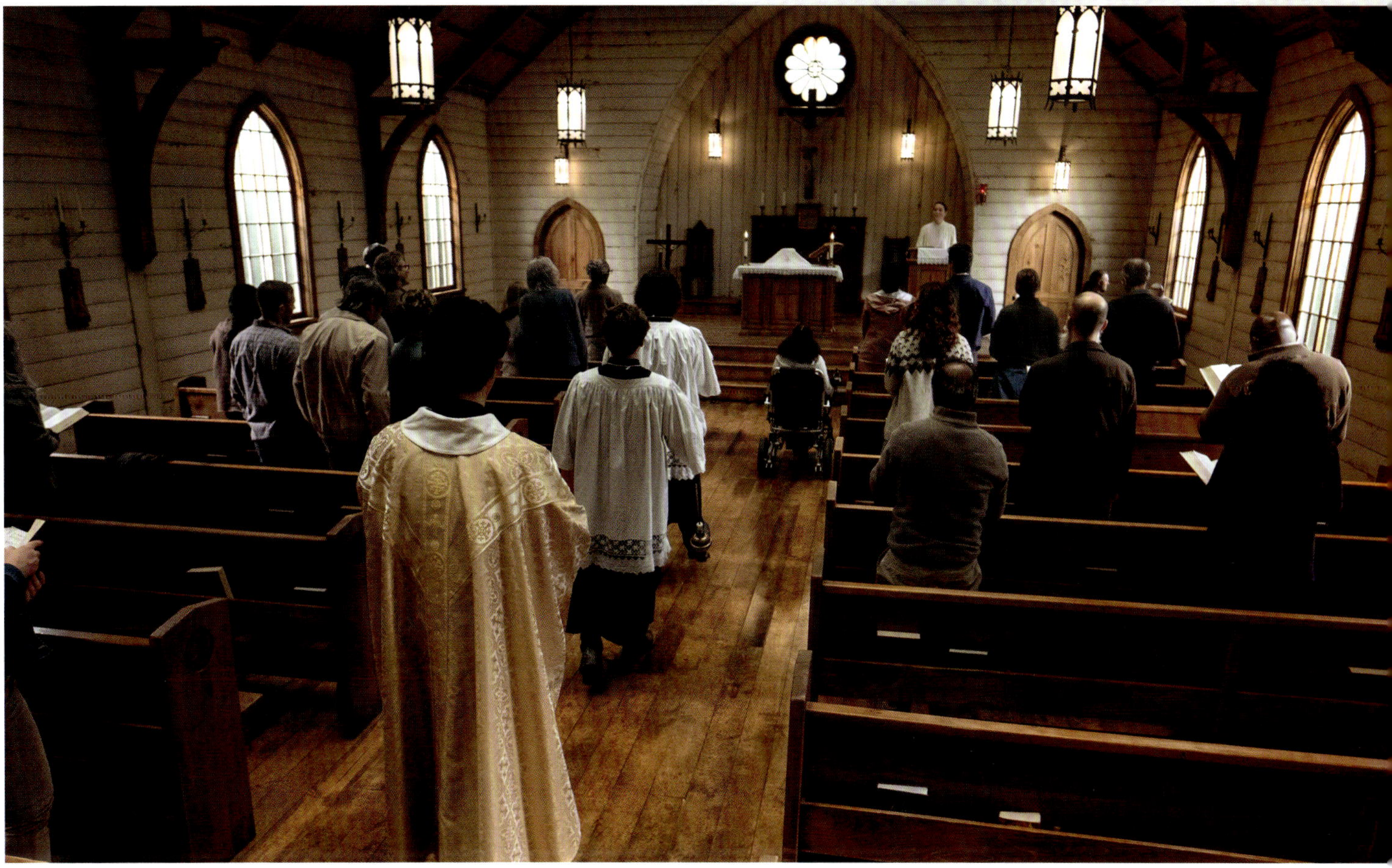

THIS PAGE/ The church interior on a soundstage, and the exterior on location.

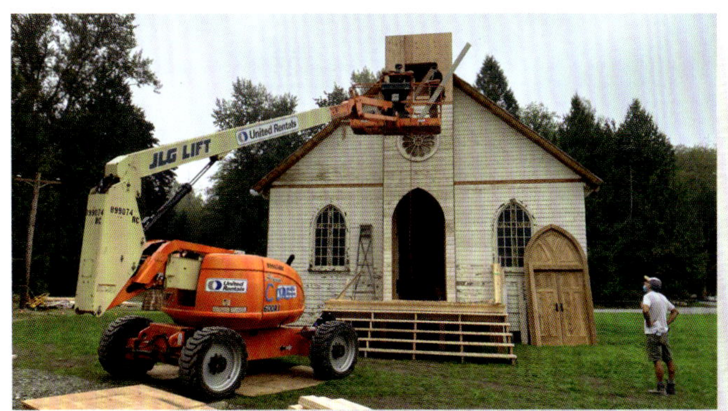

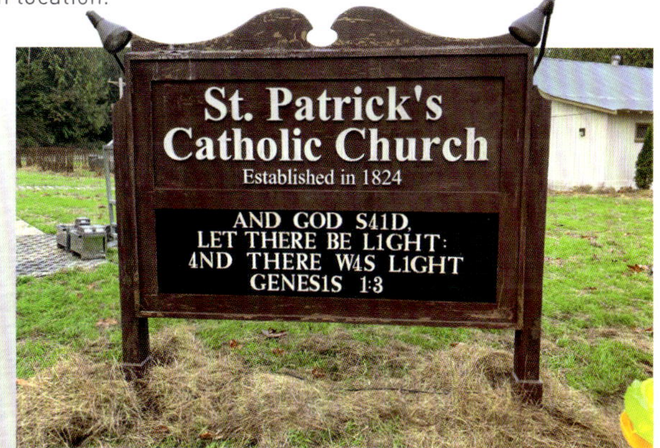

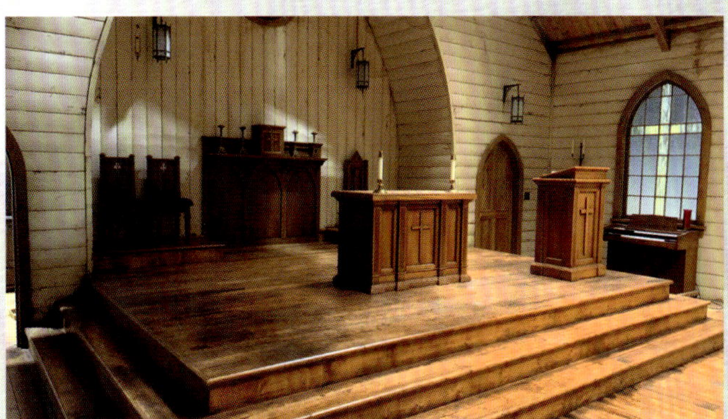

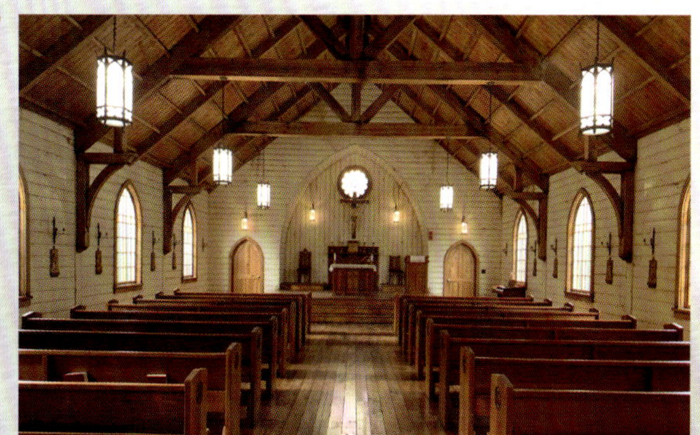

“I DREW AND DESIGNED EVERY SINGLE HOUSE, EVERY SINGLE [ELEMENT] - THE CHURCH, THE INTERIOR, THE EXTERIOR. I DID ALL THE INITIAL STUFF IN PENCIL AND PAPER.”

STEVE ARNOLD

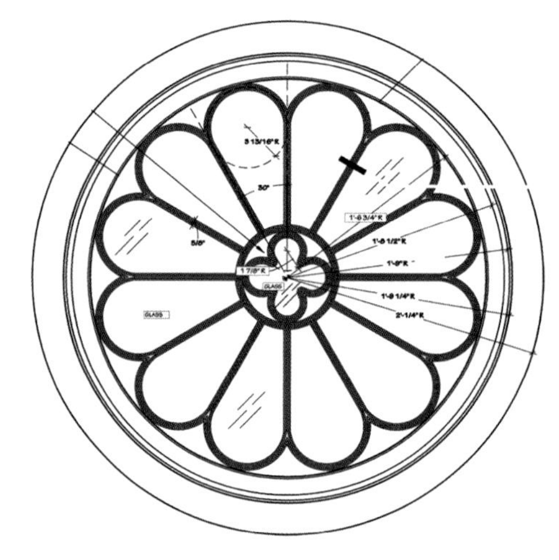

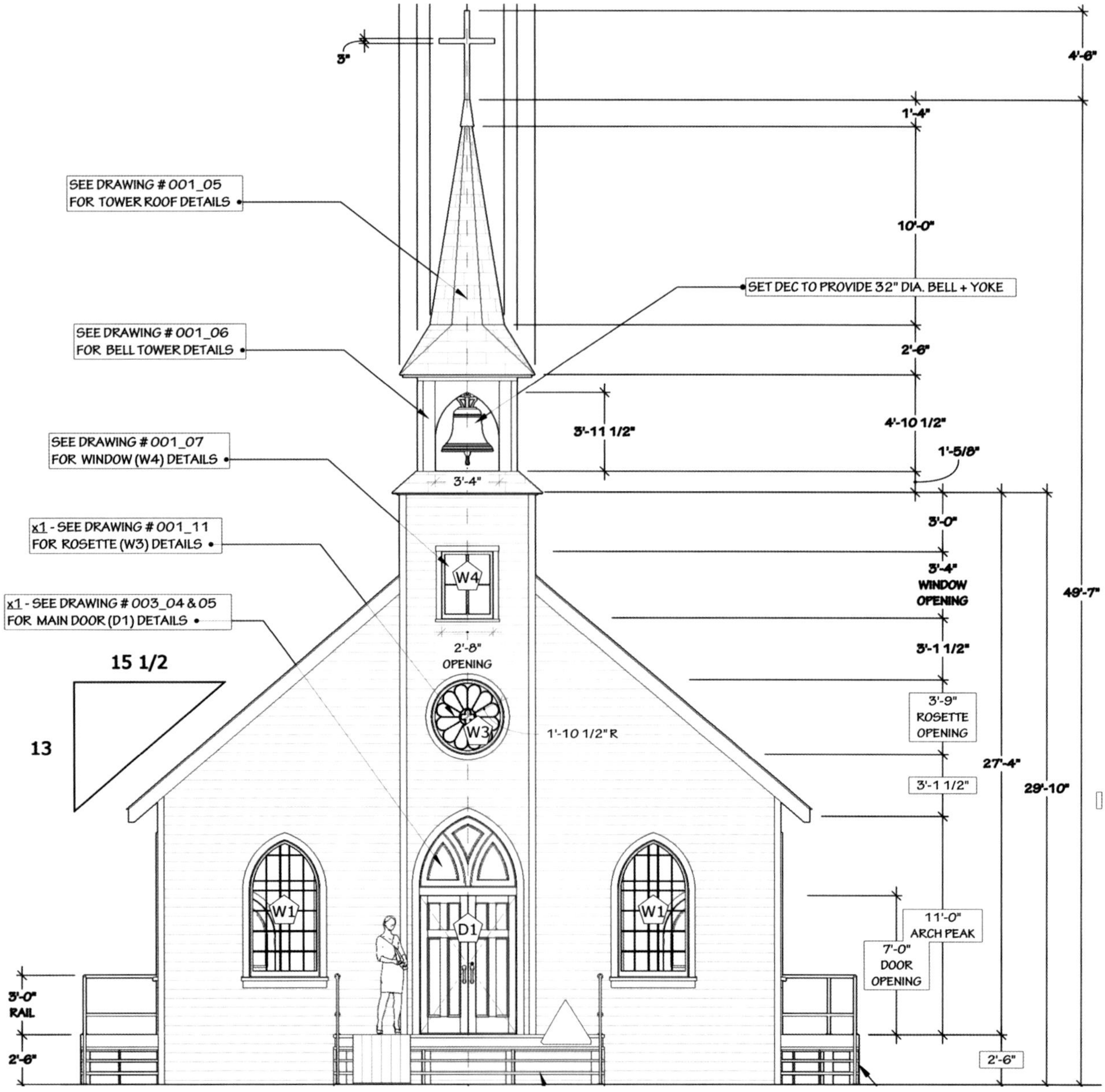

3"
4'-6"
1'-4"
SEE DRAWING # 001_05 FOR TOWER ROOF DETAILS
10'-0"
SET DEC TO PROVIDE 32" DIA. BELL + YOKE
SEE DRAWING # 001_06 FOR BELL TOWER DETAILS
2'-6"
3'-11 1/2"
4'-10 1/2"
SEE DRAWING # 001_07 FOR WINDOW (W4) DETAILS
1'-5/8"
3'-4"
x1 - SEE DRAWING # 001_11 FOR ROSETTE (W3) DETAILS
3'-0"
W4
3'-4" WINDOW OPENING
x1 - SEE DRAWING # 003_04 & 05 FOR MAIN DOOR (D1) DETAILS
49'-7"
2'-8" OPENING
3'-1 1/2"
15 1/2
3'-9" ROSETTE OPENING
13
W3
1'-10 1/2" R
27'-4"
3'-1 1/2"
29'-10"
W1
D1
W1
11'-0" ARCH PEAK
7'-0" DOOR OPENING
3'-0" RAIL
2'-6"
2'-6"

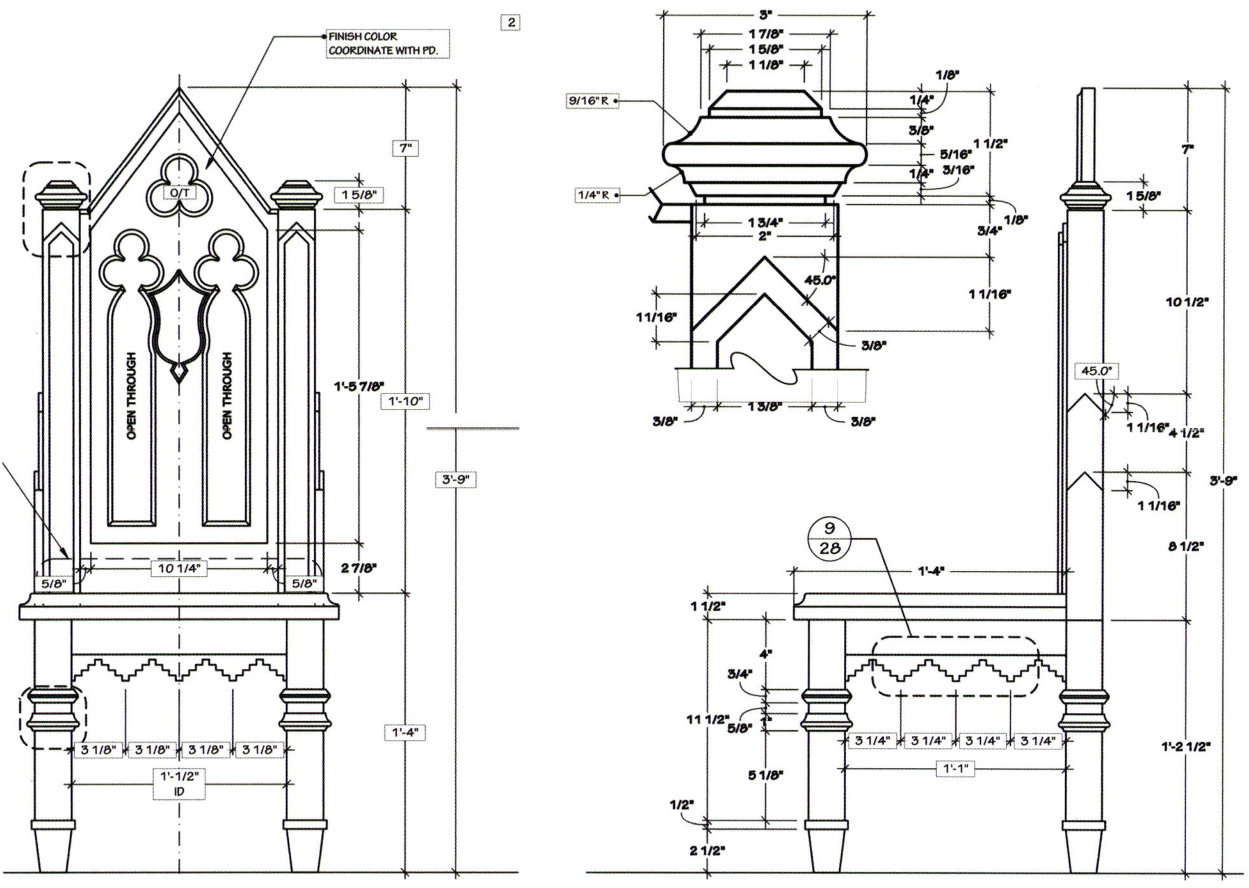

THIS SPREAD/ Every single building and prop was measured down to the millimeter by the production department before being built.

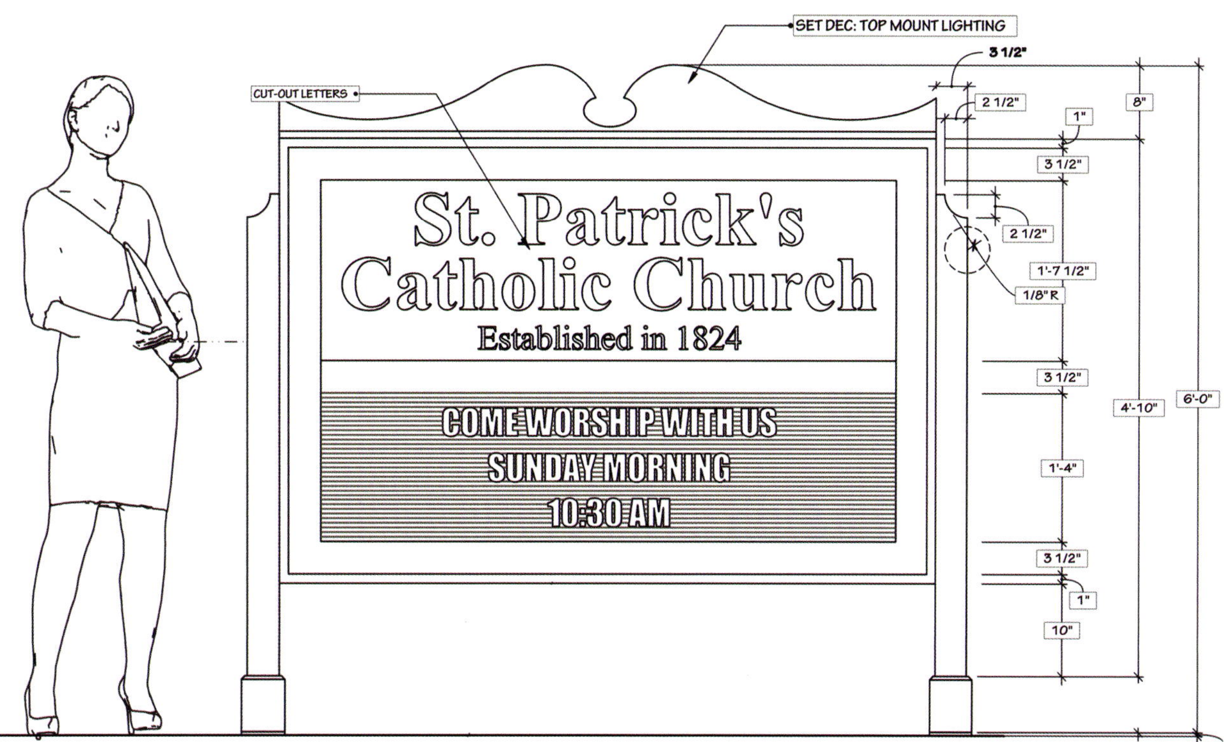

Rigney opines, "Listening to Hamish do the sermons, it felt like a holy place, at least in a film world sense." The parishioners all sing hymns in church. "Mike had conveyed to us early on that he wants the singing in the church to sound natural and not overly produced," says Grush. "So, we prepped for all situations. But it worked out nicely. Being up there, I was able to work with any of the cast members who needed help. Taylor and I reached out to everybody in advance. Different cast members had different requirements for different songs."

Grush created custom guide tracks, "where I could help with lyrics, or make sure there were indications of the key that they'd be singing in. I wanted to make sure the actors were not worried about the songs. So, in some cases, we practiced for two months on a certain hymn. Everyone did a great job."

Sloyan says she's grateful that Grush was there. "He piped a lot of the lyrics into little earwigs for us, so we could concentrate on what we were doing, and not be panicked for what the next line was. I am not a skilled singer at all. I told Mike that. We both thought that Bev might not be good, but she's loud. We did have some wonderful singers." Lehman agrees. "You're singing hymns you don't know, but then you've got Andy, who is an incredible musician, but also an excellent person to spend time with, guiding you through it."

In his onscreen role as Timmy the organist, Grush is killed in the church. "I was bloodied up in makeup, and I laid down on the floor. Henry Thomas walked up to me, shook his finger, and said, 'Rookie'," Grush laughs. "Because he knew that I was going to lay on that floor for fifteen minutes, until they actually shot the scene. Whereas Henry and the other actors stood up and comfortably waited until they were ready to call 'Action,' before they laid down."

"ON OUR SHOW, OUR PHILOSOPHY WAS MORE PPE RATHER THAN A CRAZY AMOUNT OF TESTING."

JENNA IRVINE

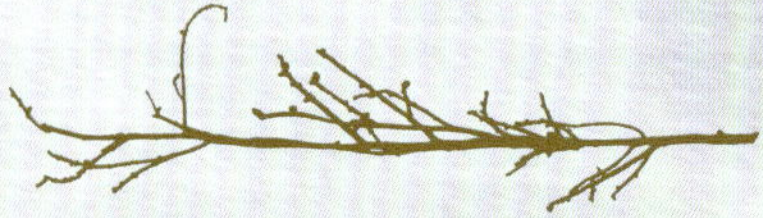

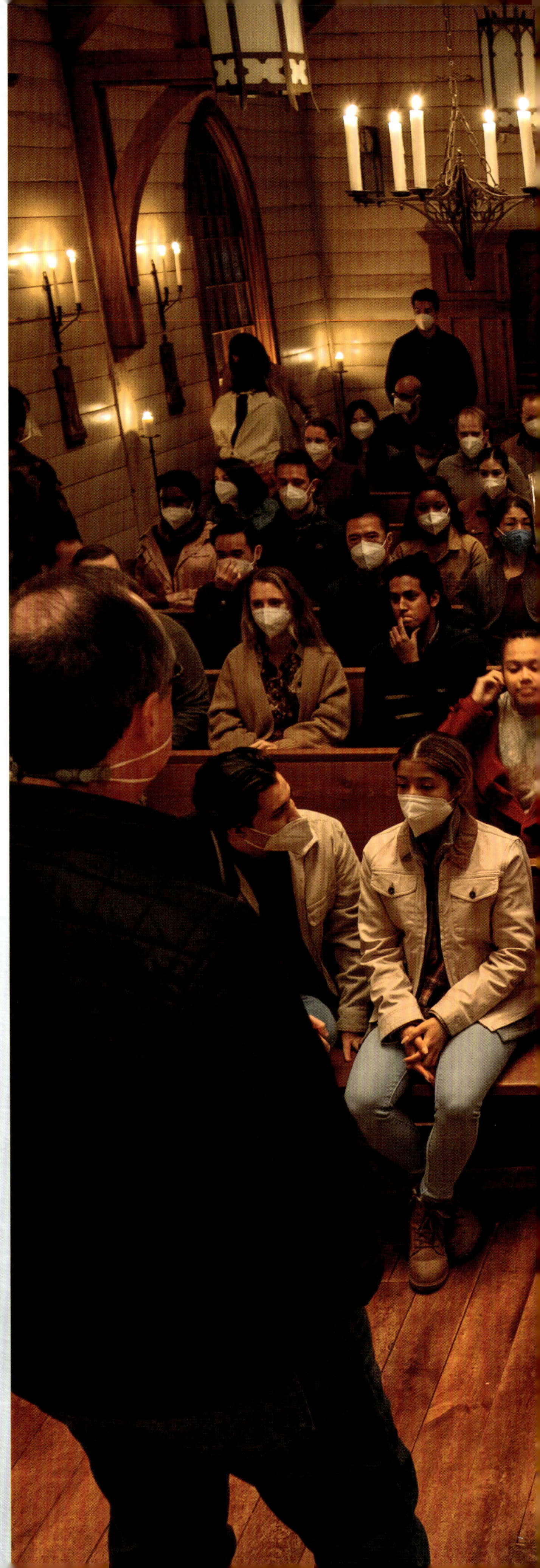

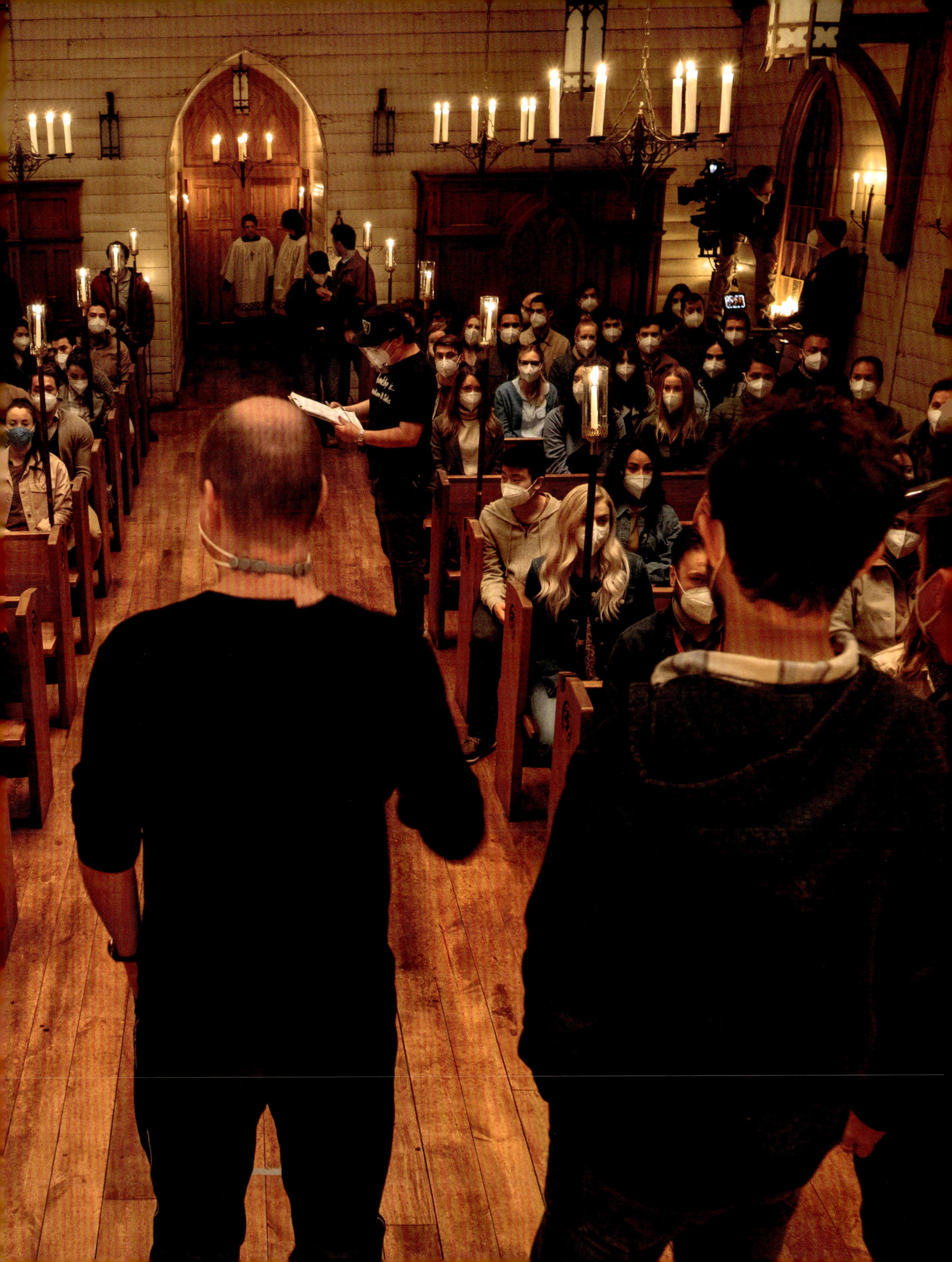

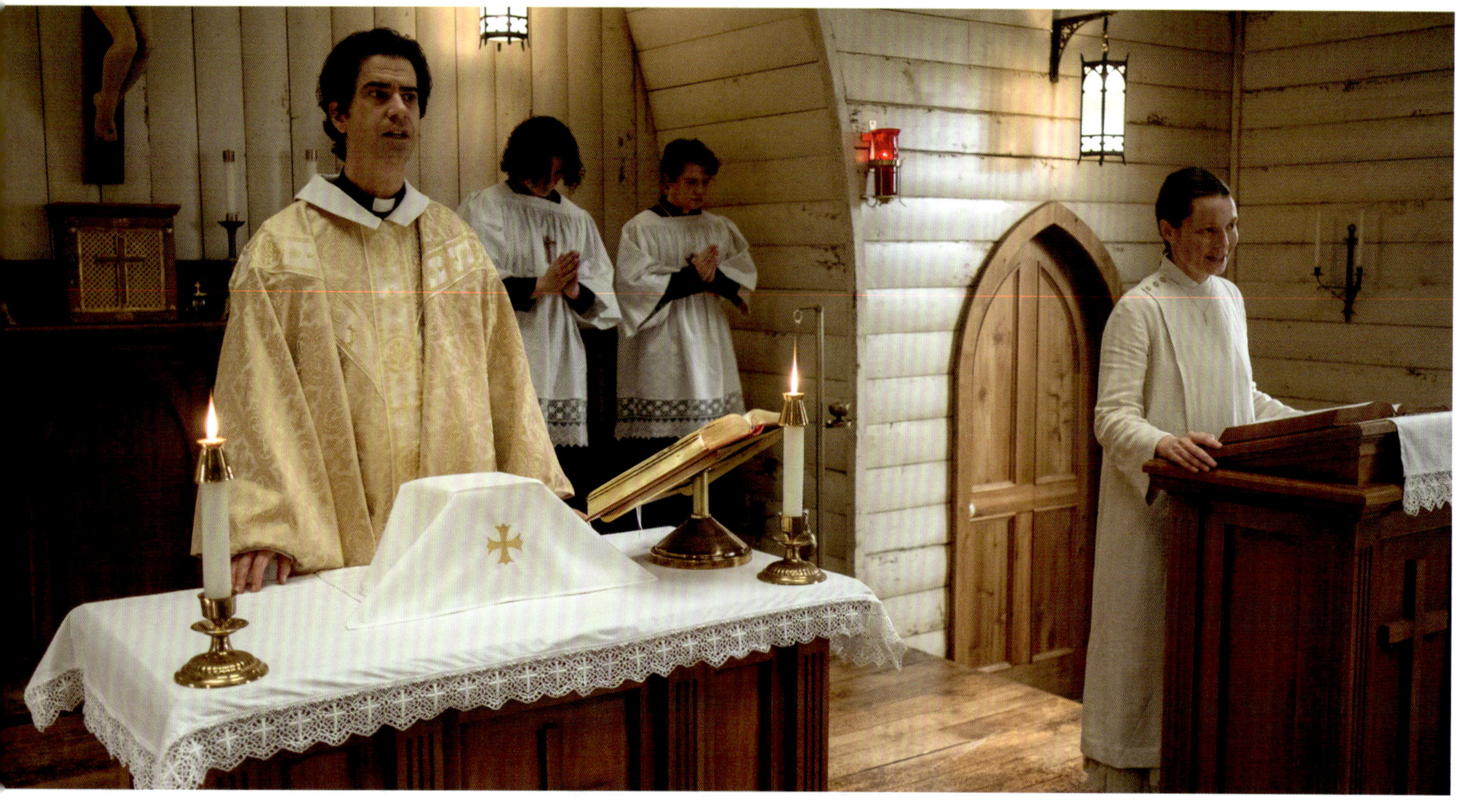

TOP/ Father Paul and Bev commence mass, with altar boys Ooker and Warren participating.

Raleigh points out, "All of the biting had to be planned out to make it COVID-19-friendly." Also, "Some bloods we can't put in the mouth, because they have some alcohol that causes it to dry [for] coagulated blood. Then we have flow blood and dressing blood that has soap in it, so you can't ingest that."

Alvarez says the mouth blood was "a water-based Karo syrup. I don't recommend drinking it, but it's not going to make you sick."

Rigney says of the melee, "There's a part where Michael Trucco is attacking this other parishioner. It's disgusting and gruesome and terrifying, and filming it was frickin' nuts."

Fimognari says, "The designer and Mike wanted a lighter-toned room, which looks fantastic when it's clean and have bright sunlight coming through." For the candle-lit Midnight Mass, In pre-production, we tested the sensitivity of lenses, and the Alexa camera, and found a pairing that allowed us to light, mostly, with

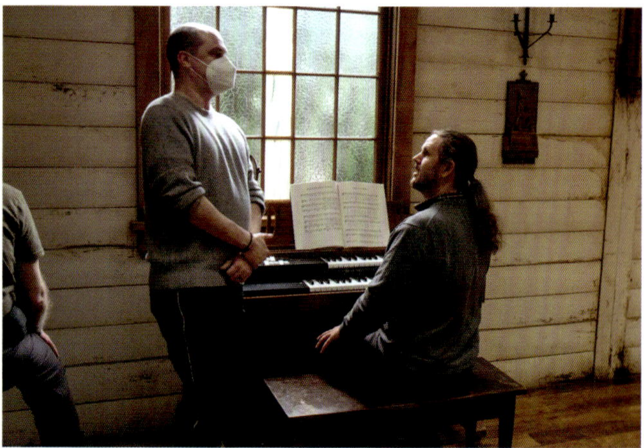

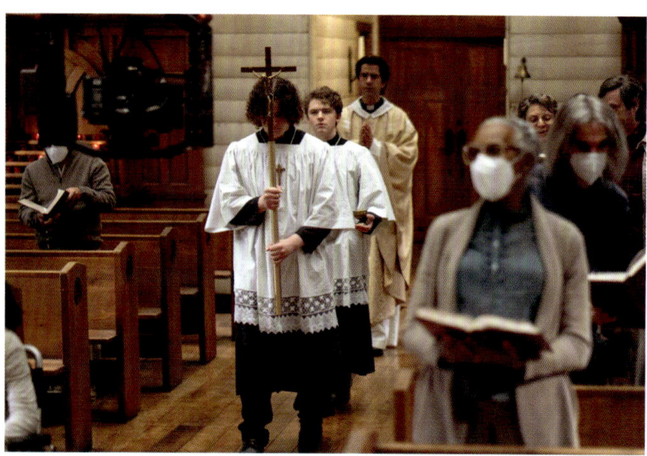

TOP/ Flanagan rehearsing with Grush at the organ; the formal procession.

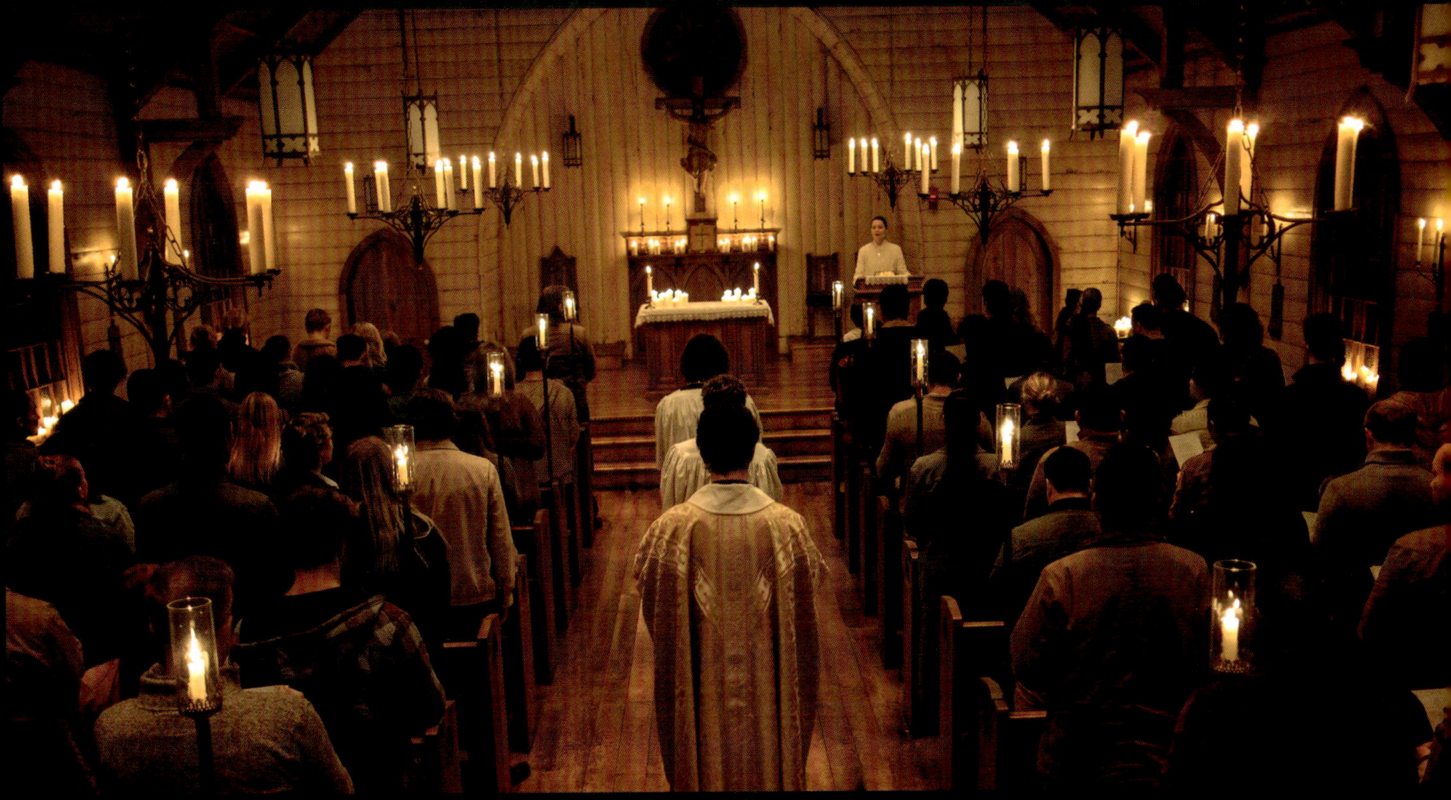

TOP/ The church interior, illuminated by candlelight for the Midnight Mass.

candlelight. We augmented that with our lights above, and a wash of the proper color, but a lot of the time, the light from their candles on their faces is just the candlelight. We had flame bars to give the reflections in the actors' eyes, and you can feel that the flicker is natural. There was actually quite a bit of movie lighting, but the candles gave that a place to feel honest."

Asked if anything surprised him, Flanagan says, "The Mass sequences. They were very surreal. I was grateful that a Catholic priest came in to be a consultant. The authenticity of the Mass was something that we put a lot of effort into. Watching how quickly the actors adapted to it, smelling the incense, hearing the music, that transported me into my childhood in a way I didn't expect. When I would walk on set, if I passed the altar, there were times where I felt the need to genuflect, because it was like muscle memory, from growing up as an altar boy."

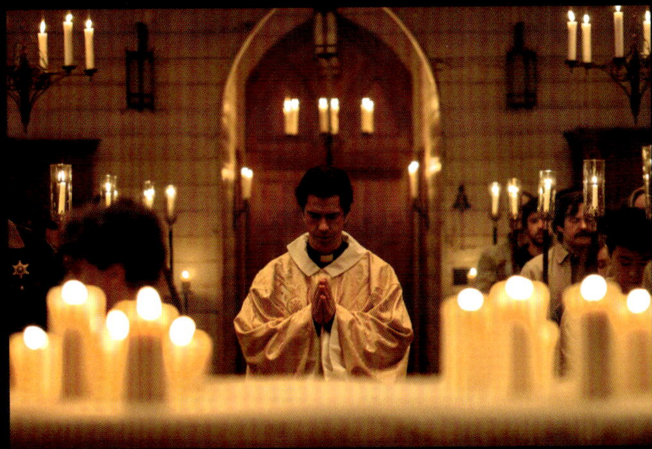

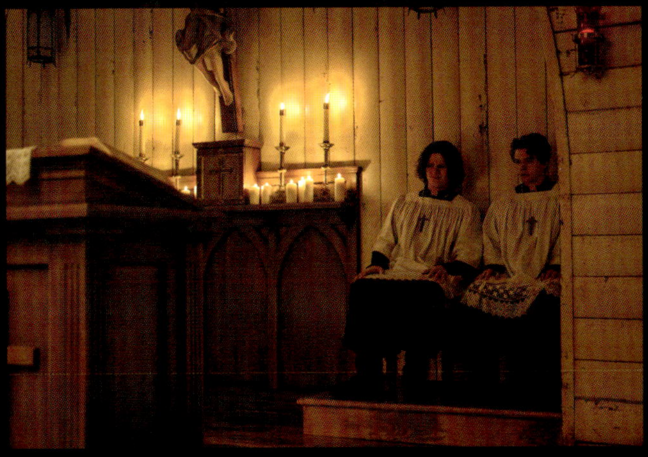

TOP/ Father Paul kneels before the altar; Ooker and Warren observe from the alcove.

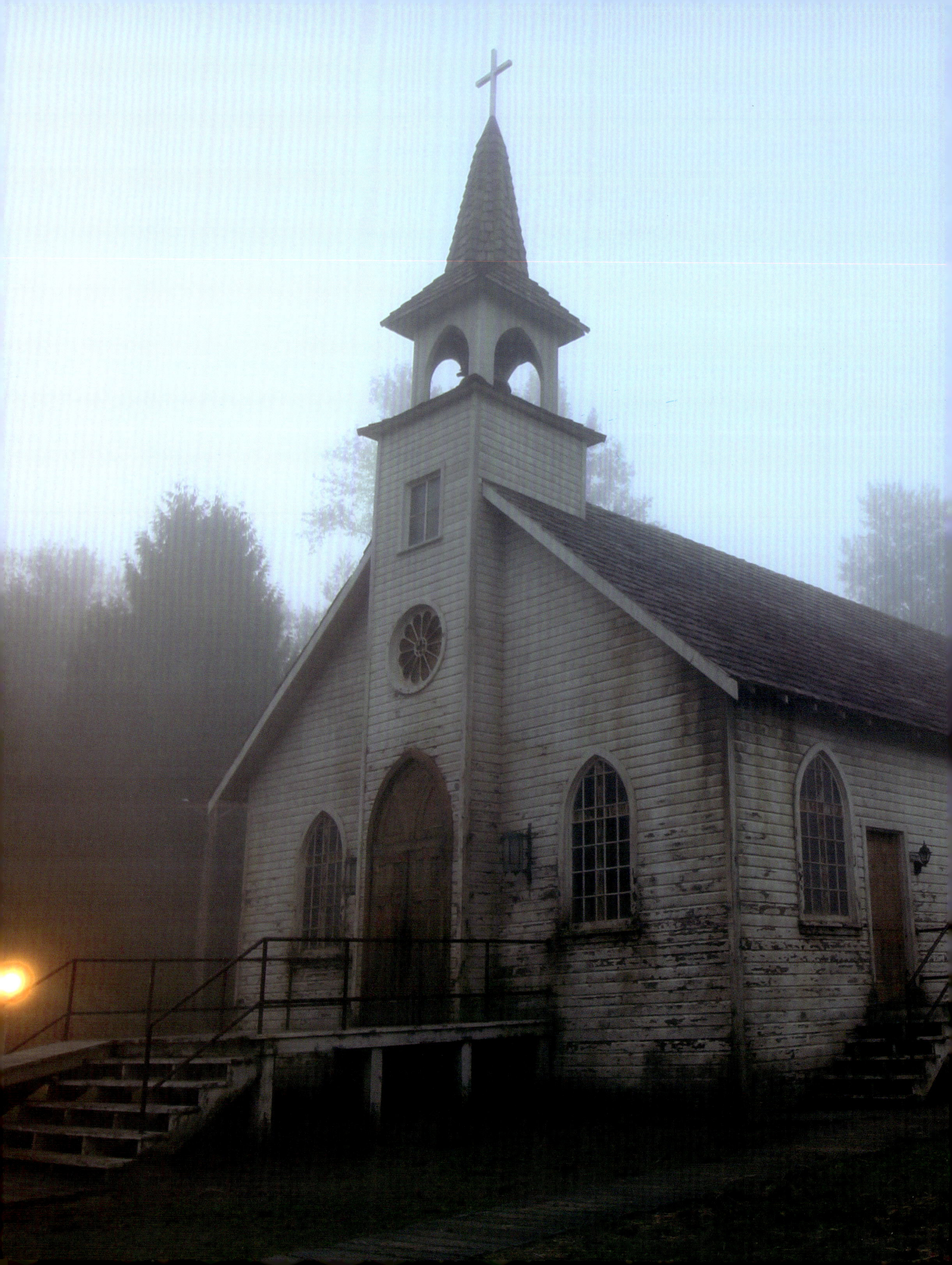

"BEV SAYS 'THE DOORS ARE ALWAYS OPEN... IF PEOPLE DIDN'T COME, THAT'S NOT MY FAULT.' [SHE FEELS] THAT... IF YOU DIDN'T SET FOOT IN CHURCH, SHE DOESN'T HAVE EMPATHY."

SAMANTHA SLOYAN

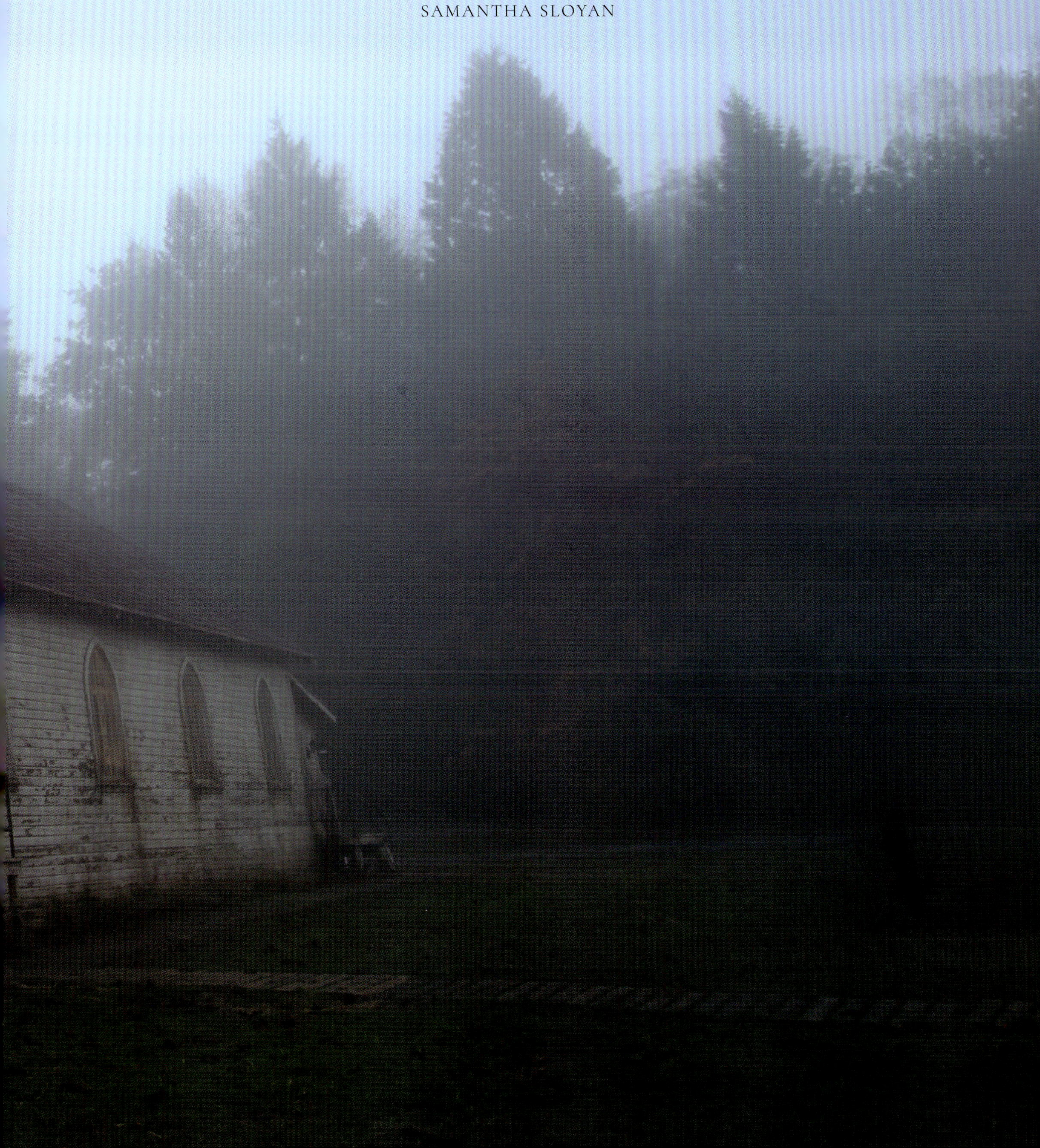

RECTORY

FATHER PAUL'S HOME

Father Paul lives in the church rectory. "I kept that Spartan," says Arnold. "Mike wanted it plain and simple, but he wanted the bedroom to have some specific hobby-related touches. Of course, it's supposed to be Monsignor Pruitt's home, who's an older gentleman. We decided he was a stamp collector, and he's also interested in baseball. So, we went with those two looks. The front area has his little desk, and there's a combination living room/kitchen. The walls are wood plank, and we found some great old furniture for him. There's not a lot of iconography, just a few crosses, few verses that were framed, and a photograph of the current Pope."

Fimognari says he calls the rectory "The Swiss Army knife of our sets, because it had probably the most shots, and most [camera] angles, and it was one of the smallest sets. We had trapdoors in the floor for cameras. Every wall and every ceiling had to fly [be movable]. It starts out as a little safe spot for Father Paul, and then becomes a place where he's afraid of the light, so he has to close all the curtains. So, we changed the look of that space over the course of his relationship with light. It's one of the few sets in the story where I used haze, because I wanted to see the particles in the light, so I could see a beam of light come through a window, and see his interaction with that."

The church has a churchyard cemetery, built by Arnold's team. "A lot of the headstones are in the very old style," Arnold explains, "because this place has been there for who knows how long. And it's got a wrought-iron fence around it."

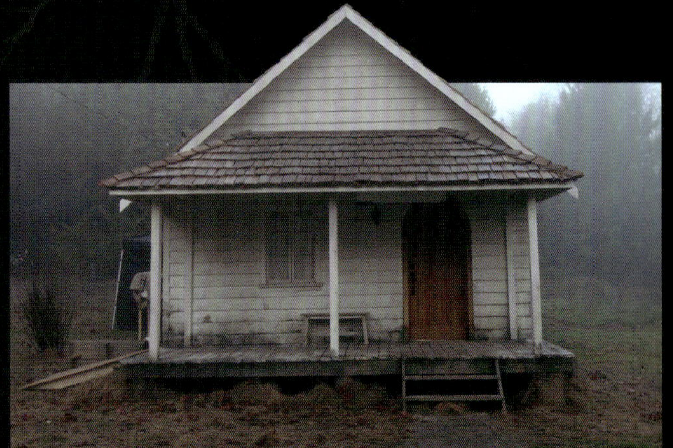

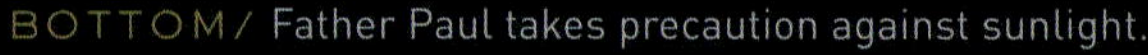

BOTTOM/ Father Paul takes precaution against sunlight.

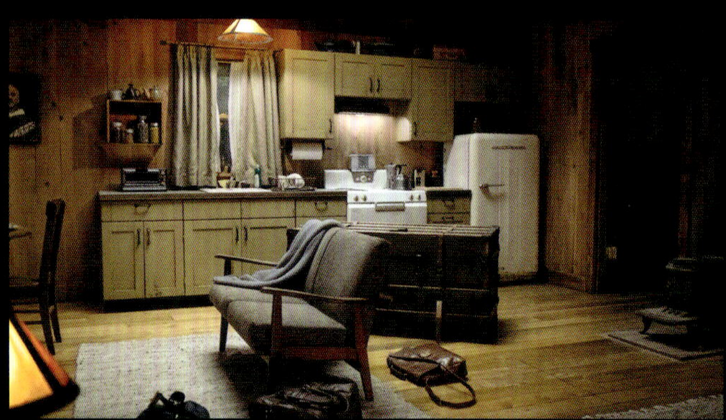

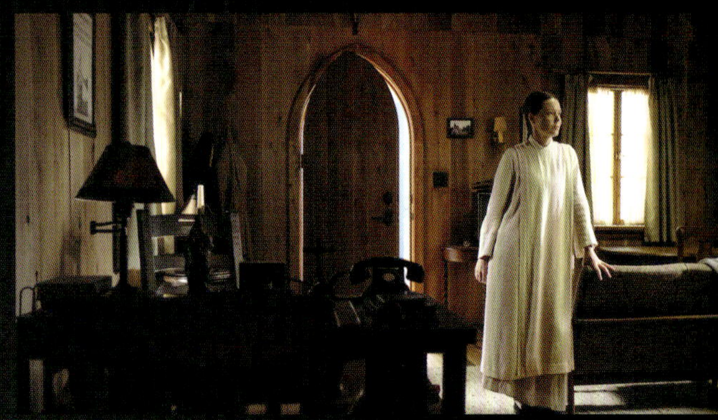

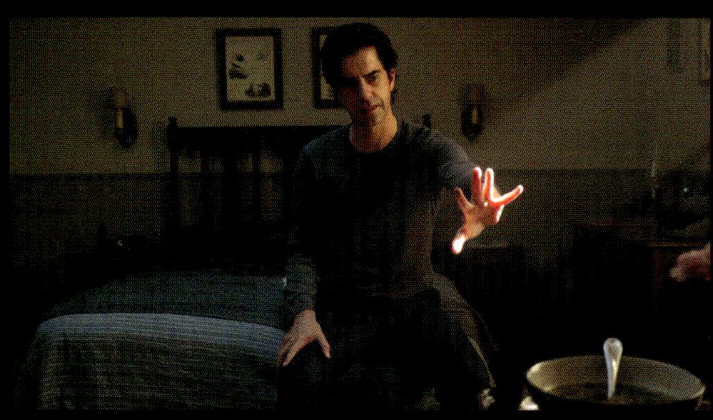

REC CENTER

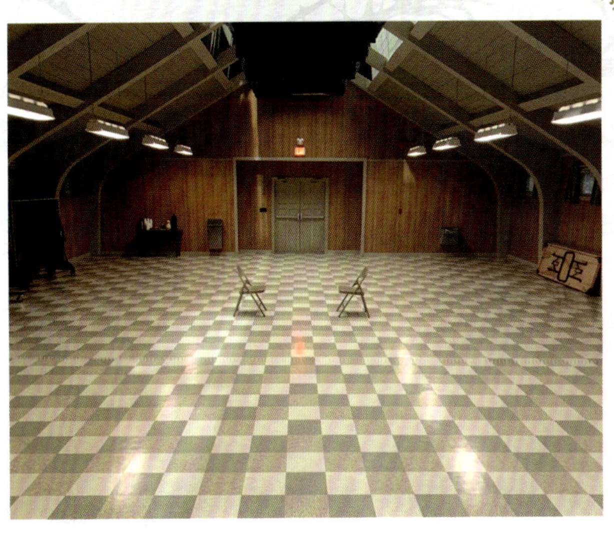

Bev has decided the town should have a recreation center named for Monsignor Pruitt. It's where Father Paul holds AA meetings. Several people suspect Bev of pocketing money from the building. Arnold says "Mike decided it should look a bit spiffier and newer than the rest of this town."

Arnold adds that there was discussion about how close to being finished it should look. In the end, "It's almost painted inside, but there's a little more paint work that has to go on, and ladders, and buckets, and paintbrushes, and rollers. We don't actually see anybody do that work."

BOTTOM/ Riley drinks from the chalice under the watchful eyes of Sturge, Bev, and Father Paul.

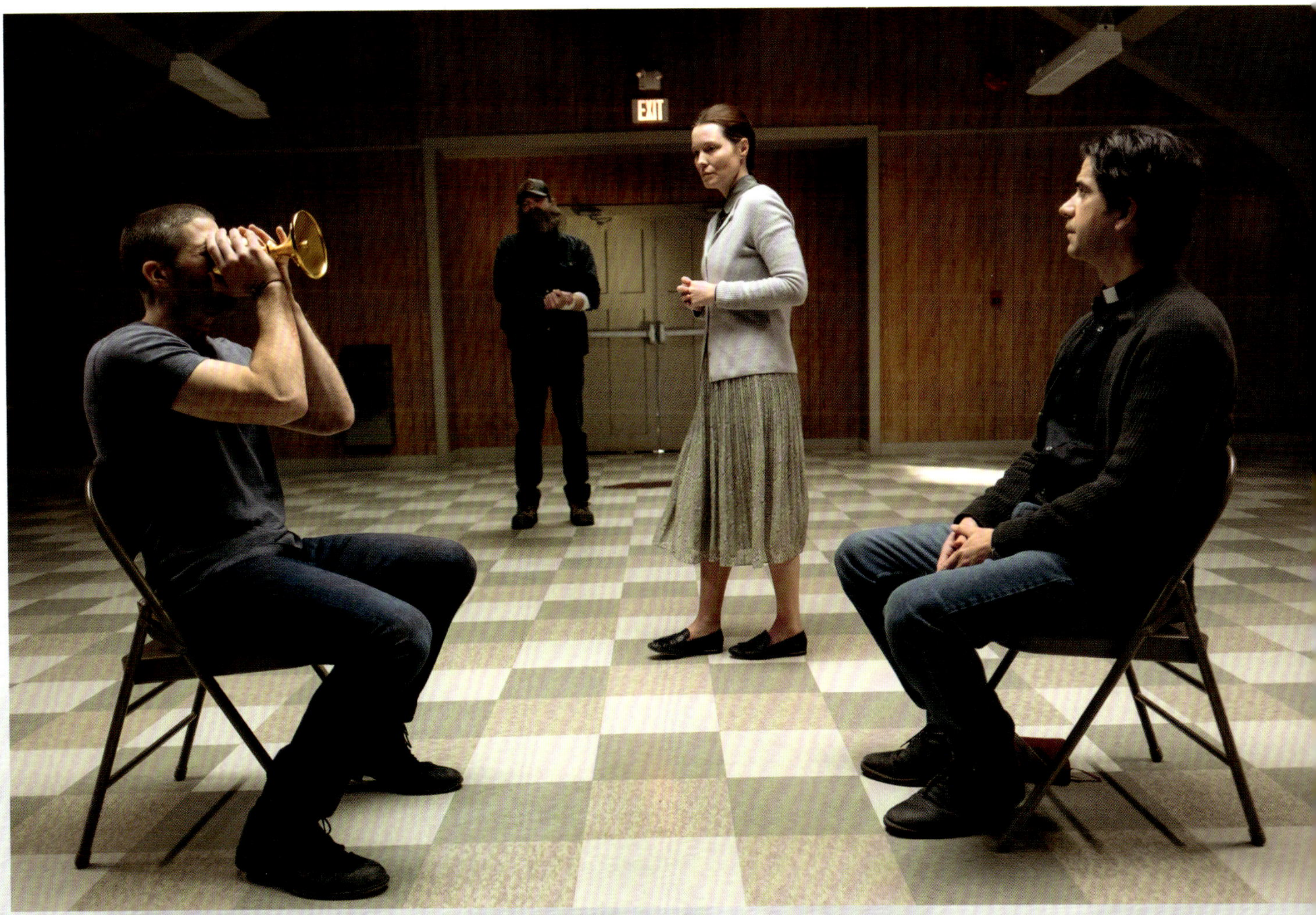

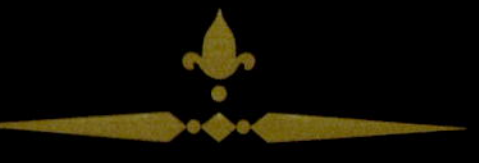

BEV KEANE

SAMANTHA SLOYAN

Samantha Sloyan plays devout Bev Keane. The events of Easter Week bring out Bev's most fervent beliefs and monstrous cruelty.

Sloyan previously worked with Flanagan and Macy on *The Haunting on Hill House* and *Hush*. The latter was where Sloyan first heard of Midnight Mass, as a book her character was writing.

Flanagan says of Sloyan's Bev, "It's my favorite performance in a show where I adore the performances across the board. She's giving a face to a part of human nature that unfortunately we will always be empowering."

"She's an awful human being," Sloyan observes of Bev. "I look for ways to find the person, so you're not just playing a villain. Bev was lonely, and felt isolated. That's why she clung so closely to religion, and to the power she had gained within the church on this island. It was a way that forced people to include her. Instead of that making Bev sad, she blamed everyone else for it. When she was judging everybody, she felt like she had control over not wanting to be a part, because she was better than [them]."

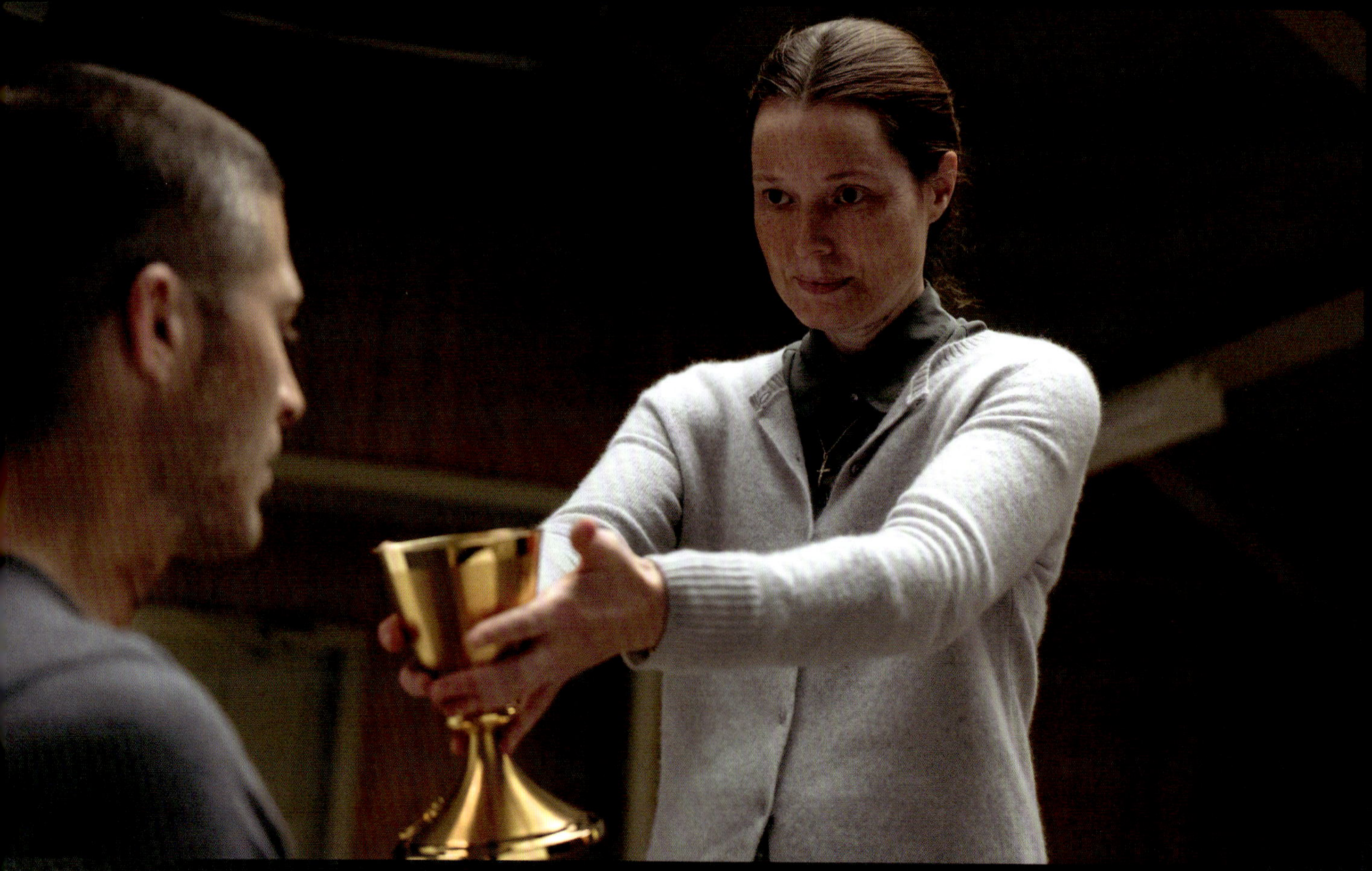

TOP/ Bev offers Riley the life-changing drink, sure she's doing right.

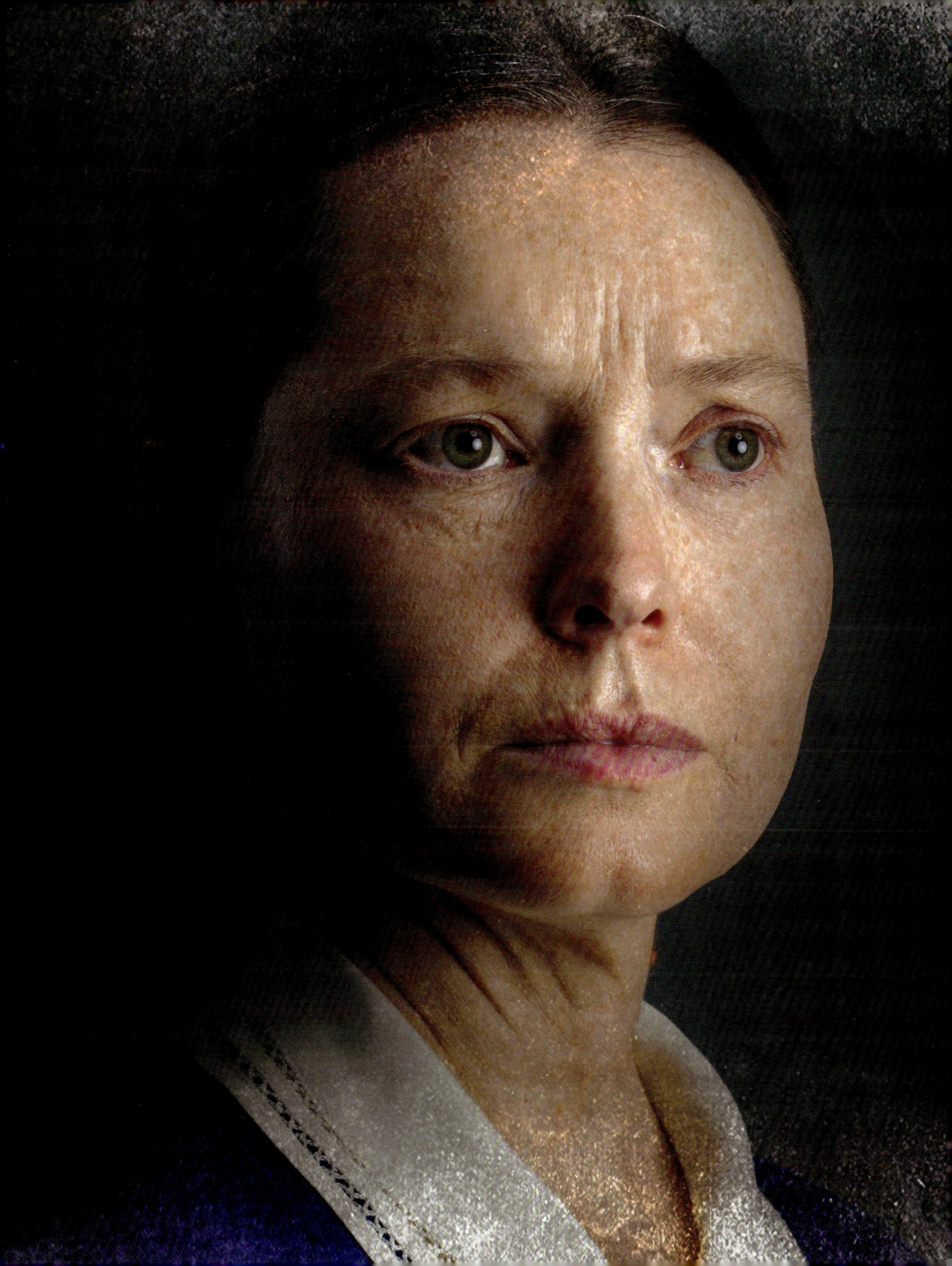

Bev's personality expresses itself in her wardrobe, says Anderson. "Even though there's a modesty about her, like the others, there's also a sense of being proper. She's one of the only ones who put an outfit together, because she thought of herself as the face of the church, like Father Paul."

The style doesn't change as Bev begins to de-age. "The reason that I didn't do an arc in her clothes," Anderson explains, "is she's becoming more of who she is, as opposed to becoming younger."

Sloyan agrees. "She just had better posture than I did, and clung to herself tightly. Those weren't so much age choices as Bev choices."

Bev divides people into categories, Sloyan relates. "She respects Father Paul, and there is this love of him, as this bringer of this world she feels like she knew was always there."

Sloyan adds that Bev has particular dislike for Joe Collie and Sheriff Hassan. "She finds Joe's inability to get over his own human sickness distasteful. And she has very little understanding of Hassan's religion, just that it isn't hers."

Kohli opines, "Sam was incredible. I'm six-four. Sam is five-foot-something. Bev is bigger than Hassan could ever be, far more intimidating."

BOTTOM/ Bev dying defeated, repudiated, and alone.

Bev changes somewhat after the Mass. "The first scene that I shot was where Sturge and I are throwing Molotov cocktails into the Flynn house," Sloyan recalls. "I was playing it with ferocity. Mike led me into a softer certainty, that I was just joyous. We were going to spread the Good Word."

When Bev realizes that Father Paul no longer agrees with her, Sloyan believes, "Her heart breaks. She gets herself off of that by reminding herself that this is the way that God wrote it. So, it was almost cementing even further her beliefs."

What is Bev feeling when she realizes she can't escape the sunrise? "Mike has this wonderful beat," Sloyan recalls, "where she watches the sheriff and Ali praying, and being able to see that they were just as human as she was, and their faith was faith, as her faith was faith. She has the terror, she feels all those feelings, but absolutely no ability to process them in this second – it's not like she's looking back on this. And then she tries to bury herself. She's still trying, up until the last second, to get out of this."

"One of the most futile ways I can imagine someone dying," Flanagan observes with a laugh. "That gave me enormous satisfaction."

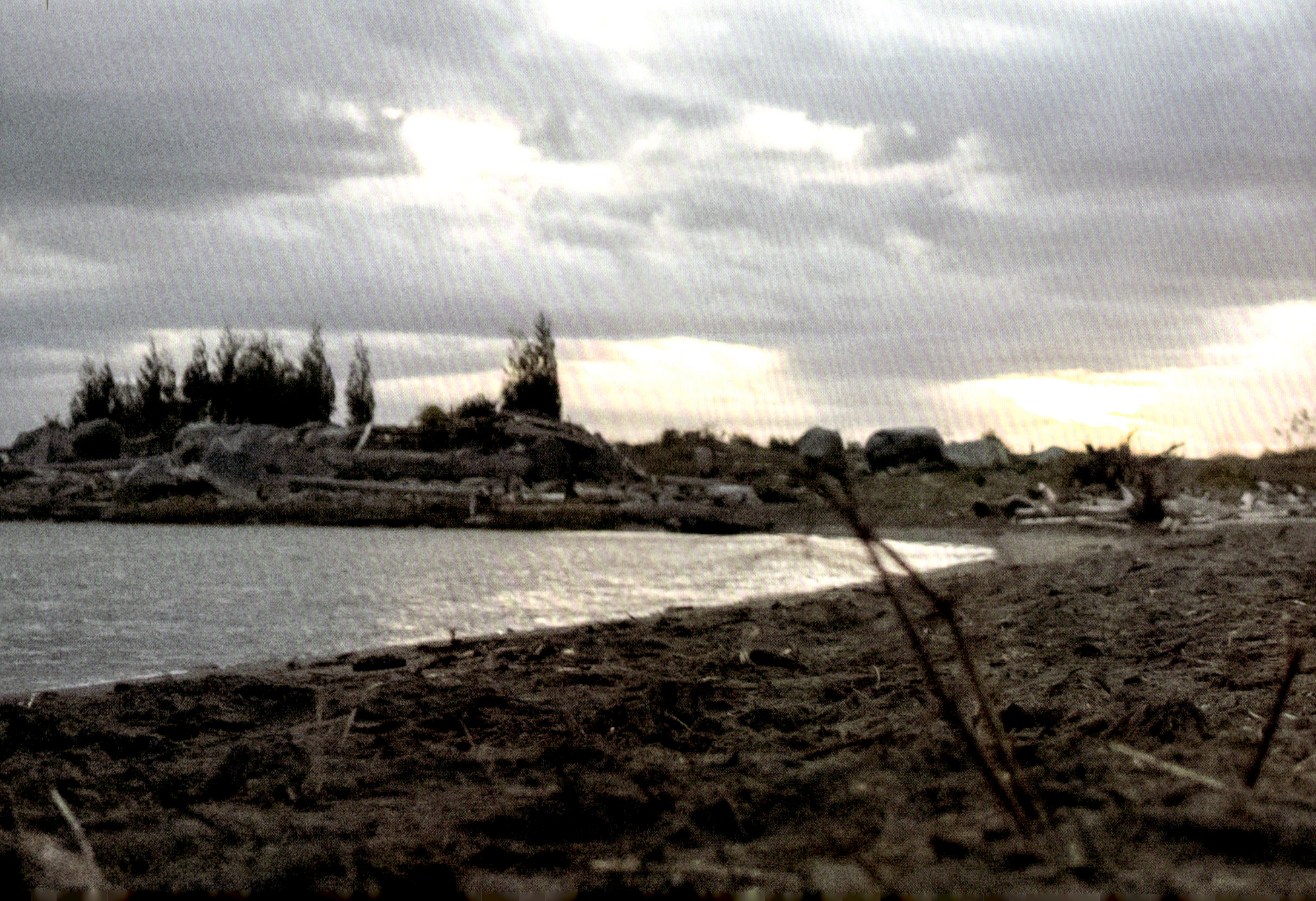

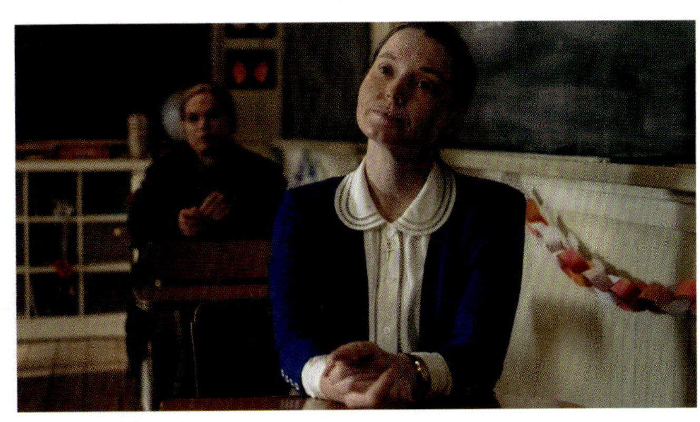

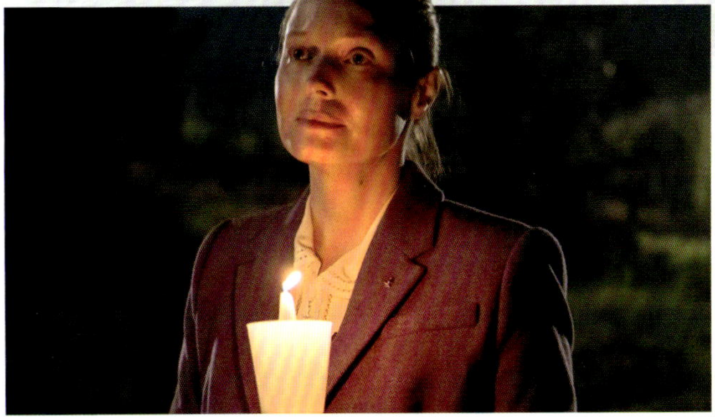

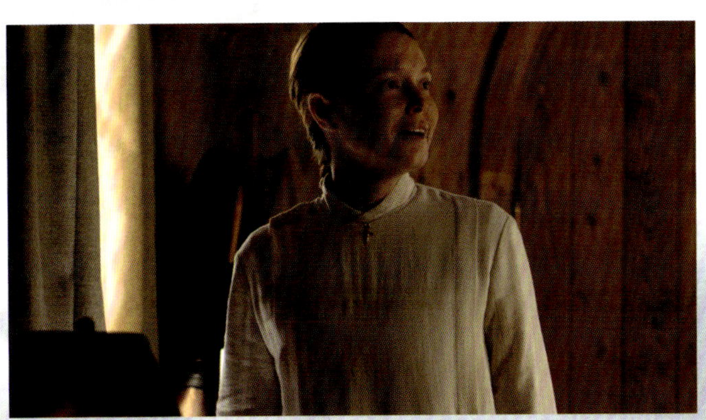

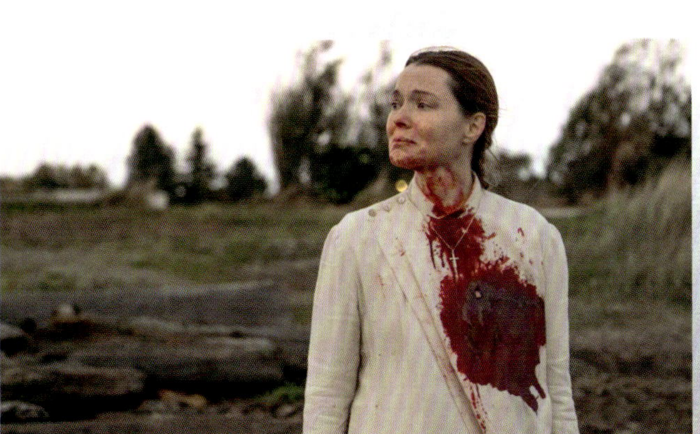

TOP/ Four phases of Bev (clockwise from TOP LEFT): smug, fervent, joyous, and lost.

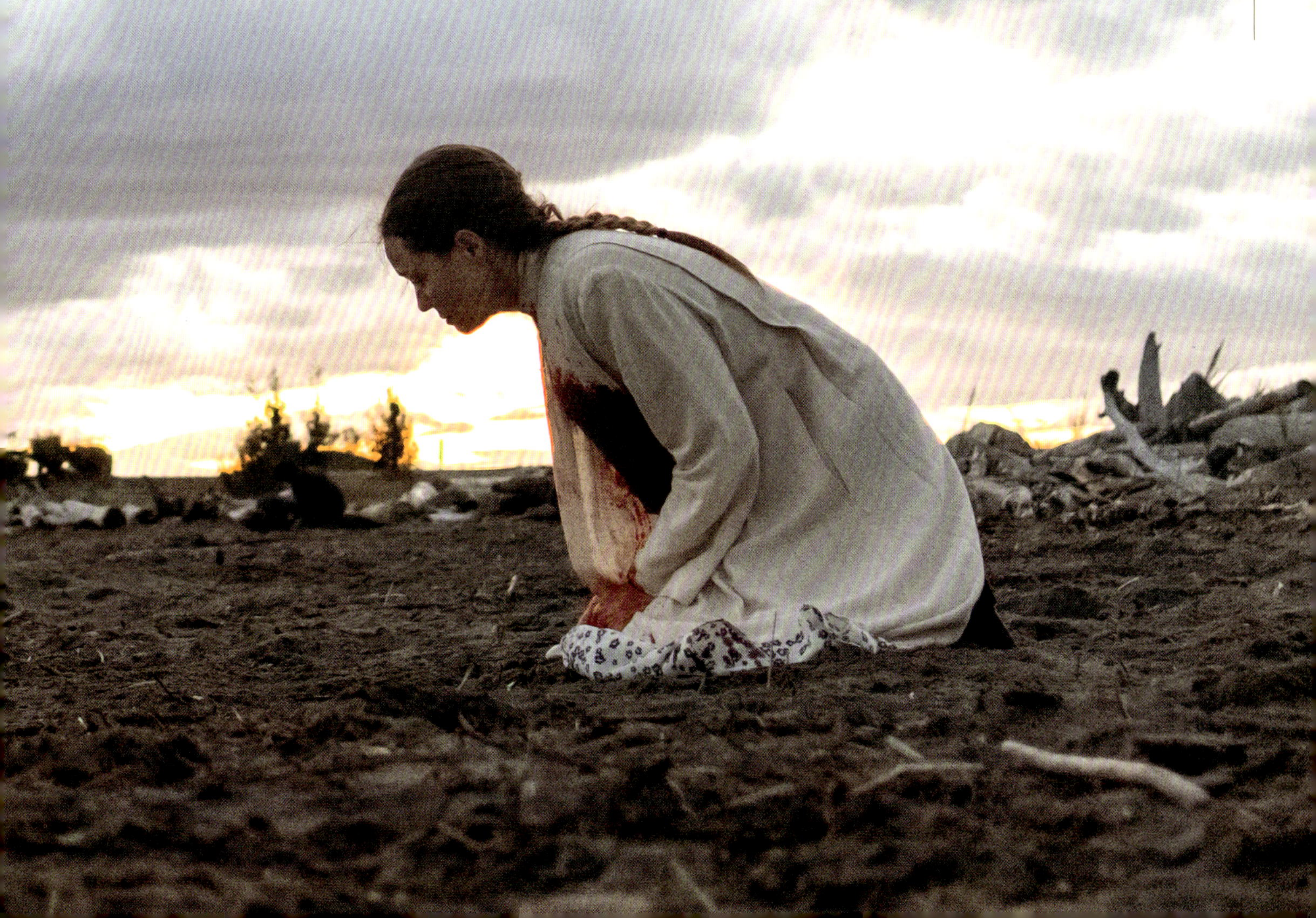

Hamish Linklater plays Father Paul, really Monsignor Pruitt, who has regained his youth after discovering an 'Angel'. Father Paul has apostolic intentions when he shares the miracle of the 'Angel' with his Crockett Island congregation, but finds himself justifying murder…

Macy says, "I think the character that surprised me the most was Father Paul. The way Hamish played him, this is a very compassionate, empathetic, human being, with a lot of love in his heart, but who can do despicable things."

What's it like playing an old man in a young man's body? "I thought about it a lot, and then was weary from the curfew, and just let that weariness go in," Linklater laughs. "Imagining having an arthritic, rickety body, what a jolt it would be to suddenly be in a pony's body. I imagined putting an older head into a young body. Also, there is a thrill to the vampire experience. Everything looks brighter and clearer."

Costumer Anderson initially thought Father Paul's clothes would hint at his real age, but Flanagan wanted him to have a more modern sensibility. "And more real," says Anderson. "There are scenes where he wears a shirt with a hoodie and jeans, because he wanted to be viewed as a young priest."

Once violence ensues, why doesn't Father Paul stop what he's doing? Linklater says, "My character has justified this through Scripture for each move he's making. His point of view is not the same as Bev's. Hers is fascist: the chosen are the chosen, the rest are dross. My guy believes that everyone will be brought along into the glory of God."

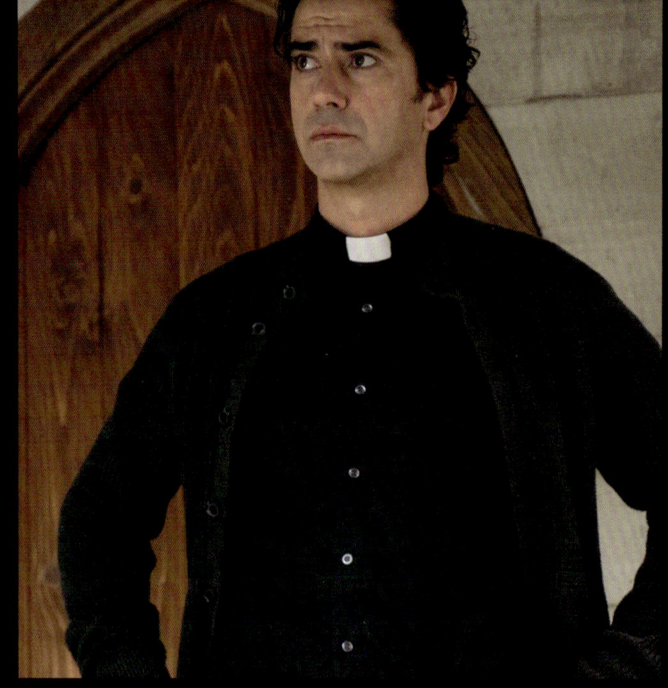

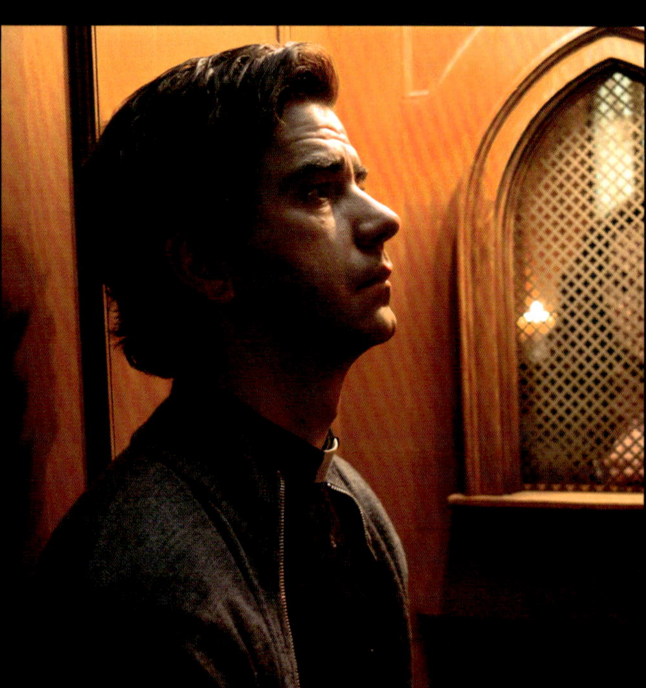

RIGHT/ Father Paul in church, and taking Erin's confession.

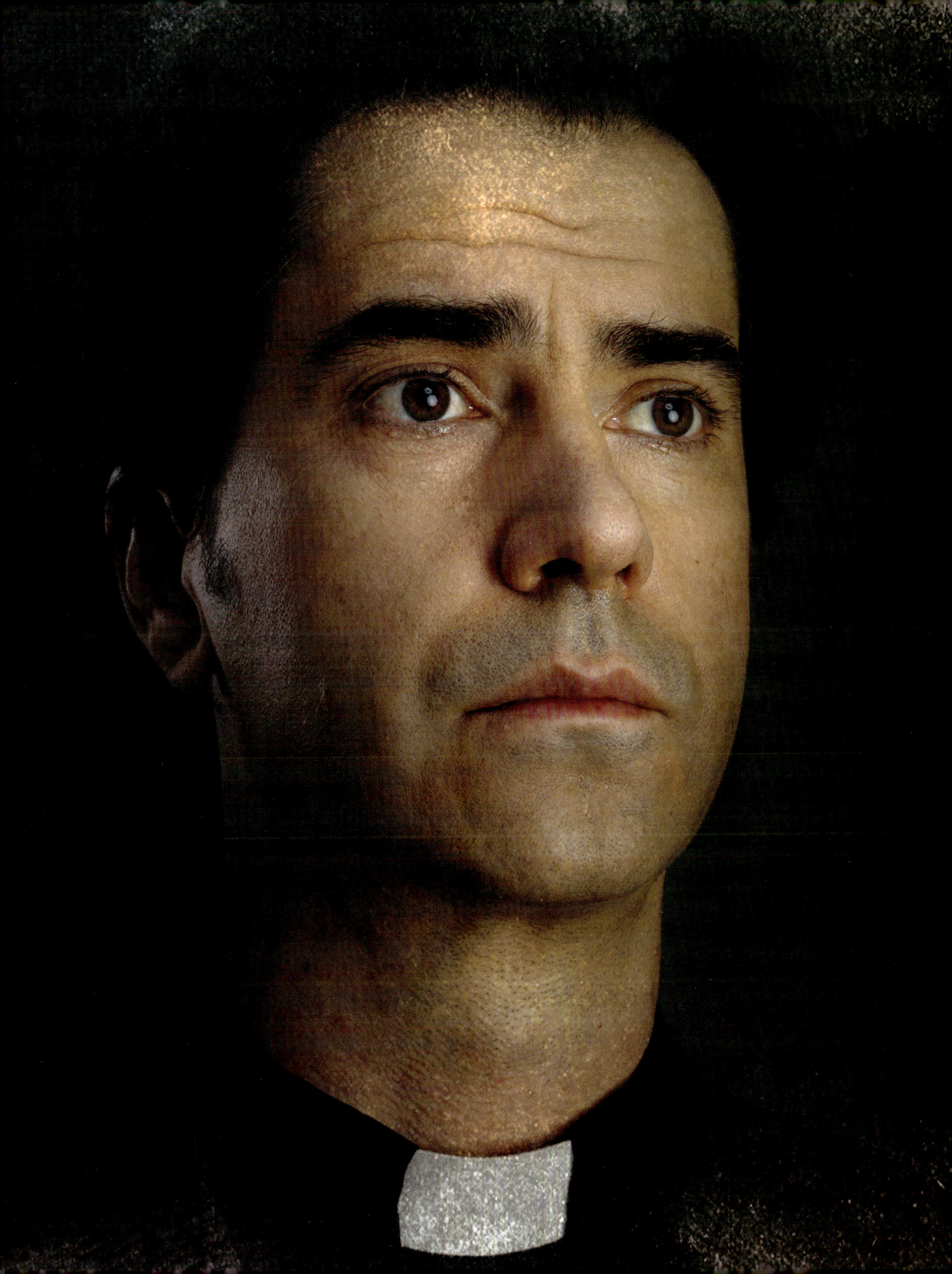

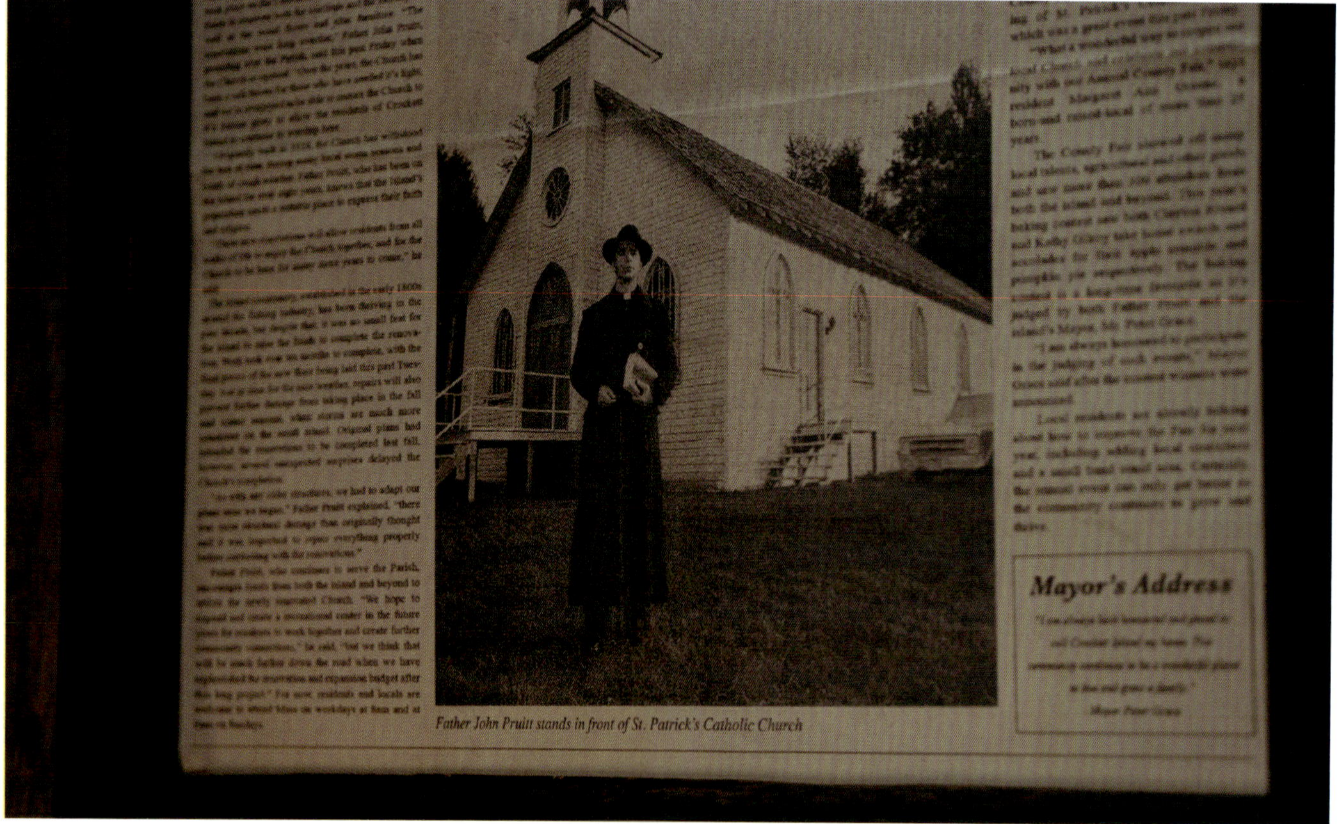

"CAN YOU IMAGE HAVING A FLOCK, RECEIVING CONFESSION FROM ALL THESE PEOPLE, FOR ALL THIS TIME, AND THEN GETTING TO LOOK AT THEM AGAIN AS A YOUNGER PERSON?"

HAMISH LINKLATER

Linklater grew up with his mother's Shakespeare company, so he is familiar with the mindset of classical antagonists. "In playing the character, you create a moral universe of one. How that bangs up against the moral universe of the audience, or other characters, that's what makes a good show. In my first conversations with Mike, I was relieved that he never was like, 'Oh, the character's crazy.' It was, 'He believes'."

To perform priestly functions, Linklater says, he got instruction at a West Vancouver church from a consulting Catholic priest, "who then was on set to make sure that the administering of the sacrament was done correctly." The priest observed that the liturgy is written down, so memorization wasn't necessary. Linklater, however, felt that Father Paul should know it by heart. "I'm an old guy who's been doing this for a long time. But, man, it made my head explode. It's wonderful literature, but there is repetition between God's passion, God's peace, God's glory, and they're all different."

Linklater views the sermons as "a conversation Father Paul is having with himself at the same time as he's having it with everybody in the room, particularly Riley. He has to evangelize, but he's giving the right argument. He is aware that the Scripture is telling them what is going to happen is good, and he is making that argument beautifully, all the way up to the end. I don't think ever does it occur to him that there are a lot of parallels with vampirism."

Linklater also had to learn how to bite people. "The bloodlust, I lean on the 'lust' side. You get close, and you pretend like that [blood] smell is a crazy aphrodisiac."

TOP/ The newspaper article and photo that alerts some characters to Father Paul's true identity.

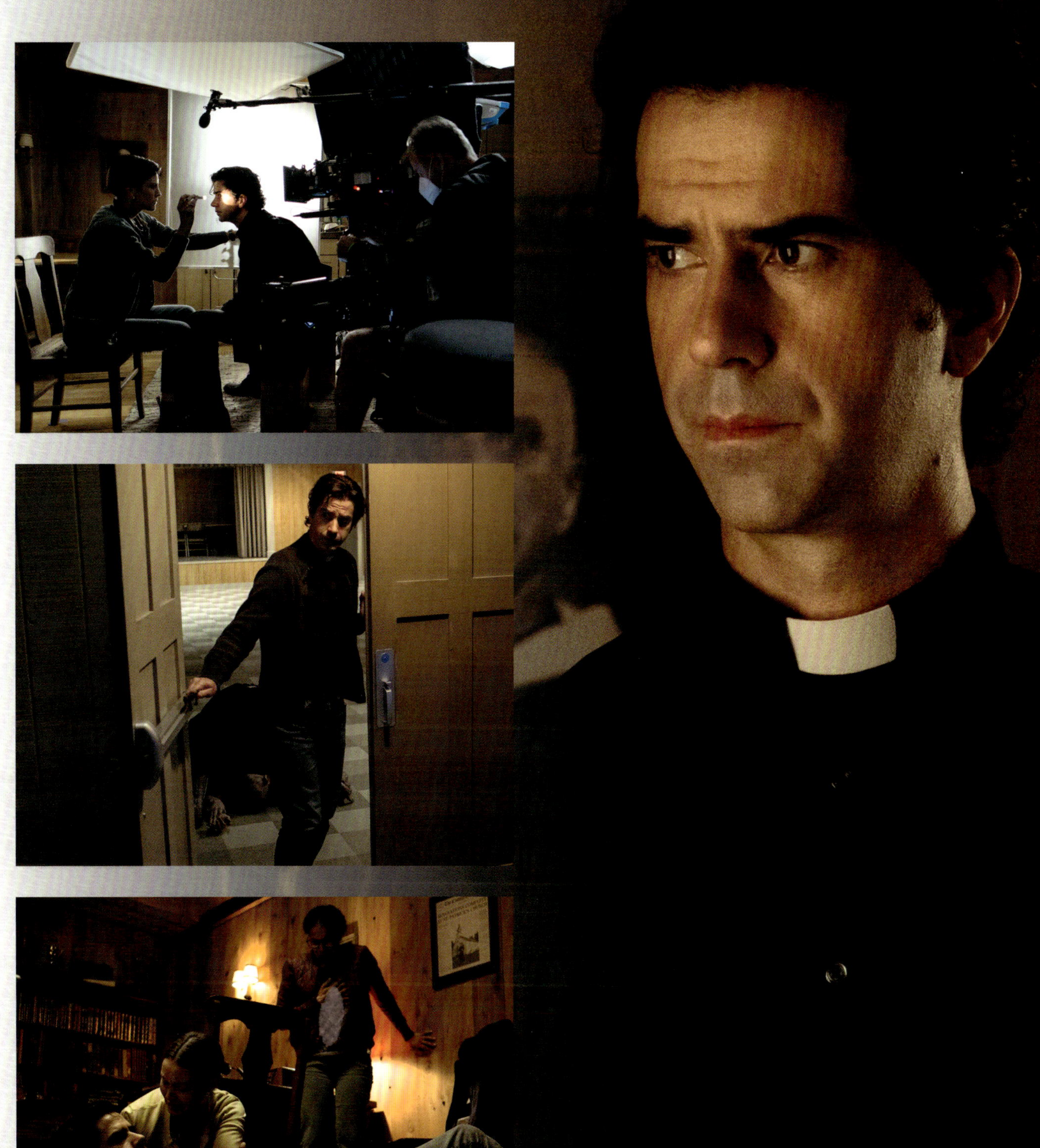

THIS PAGE/ (TOP) Filming Sarah examining Father Paul. (MIDDLE) Father Paul keeping lookout as the Angel feeds on Riley. (BOTTOM) Bev cradling Father Paul after he collapses.

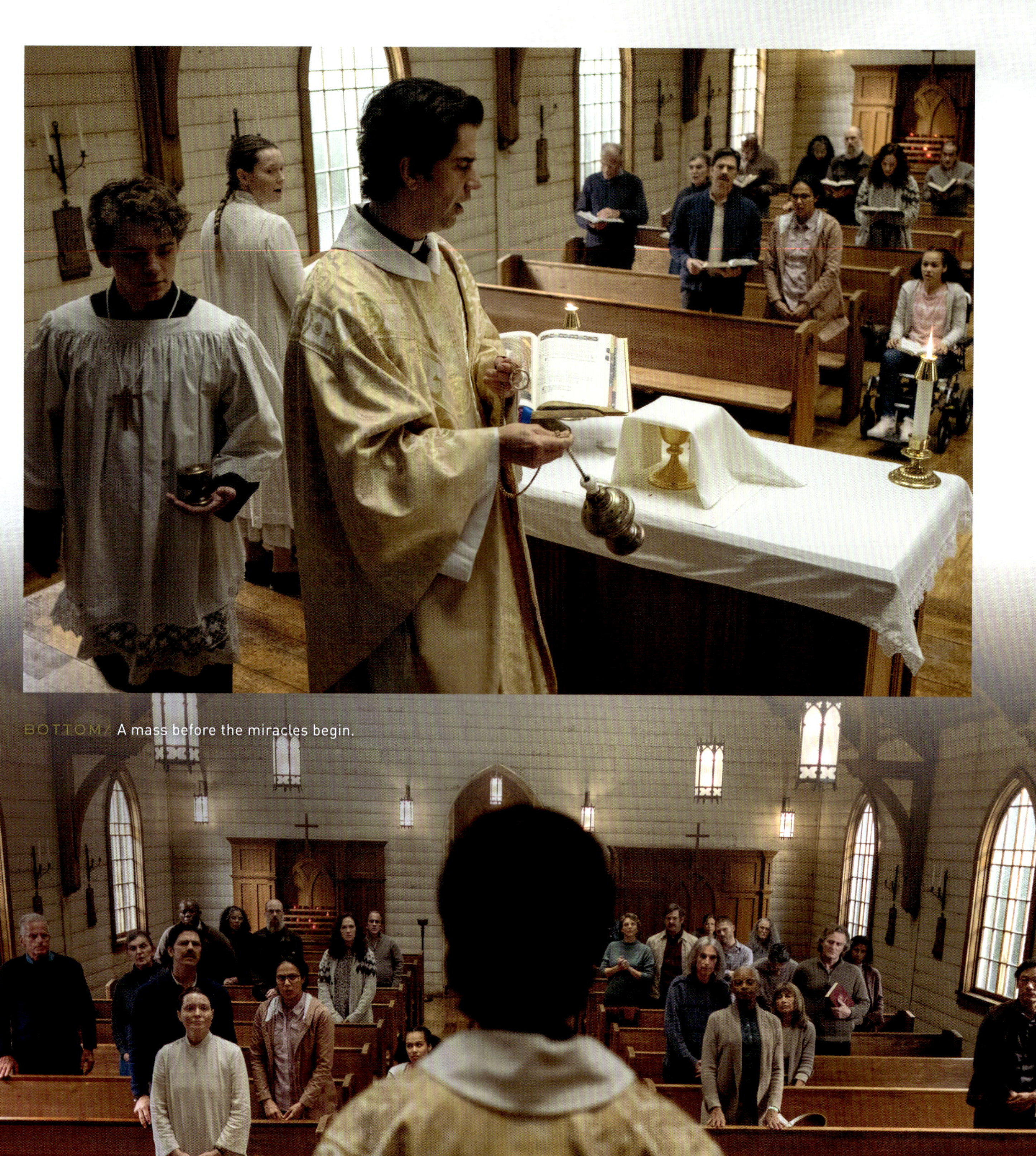

BOTTOM/ A mass before the miracles begin.

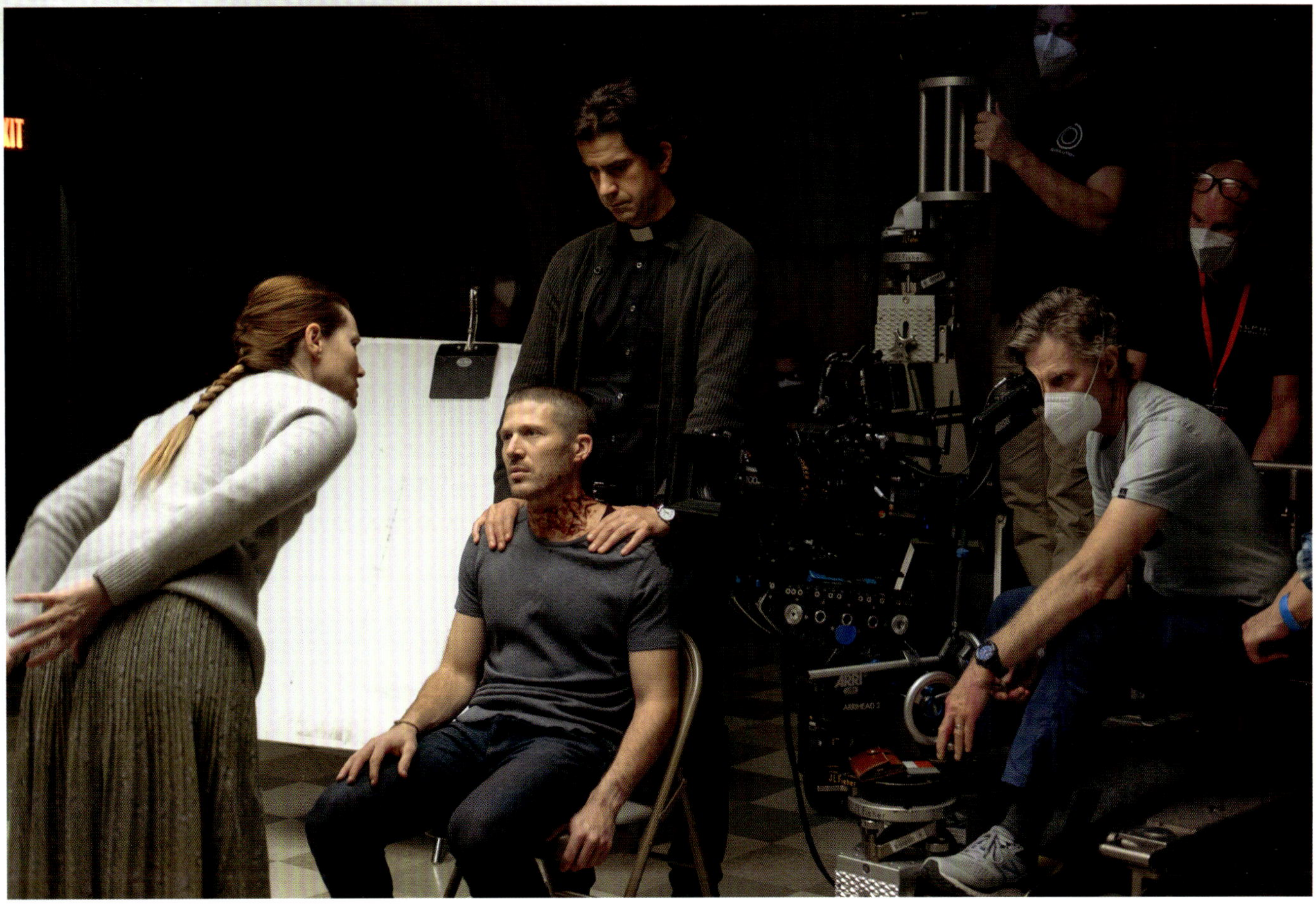

TOP/ Sloyan, Gilford, Linklater, Reid and Cruikshank.

Father Paul feels different kinds of love for a variety of people. "That's Mike's beautiful casting," says Linklater. "Being in love with Mildred, being [parentally] in love with Sarah, but also with Joe, and with Riley, they're like love scenes. It's looking into that person's eyes. It was also nice that those scenes came in the schedule before the sermon scenes, so that I had this time to make this personal connection with the people who would then be out there."

Asked about his most memorable scenes, Linklater replies, "I was terrified of the big AA meeting scene. In the script, although it's broken into four sections, it's twenty-five pages, with me using the Serenity Prayer as means for showing Riley that this is going to be good."

Linklater says that when he asked Flanagan questions, "like, 'Is that too much?' He'd be like, 'Try it and let's see.' He'd send amazing page-long notes on the scenes we were going to shoot, like, 'This is why he does this.' It was remarkable to receive those, and be in dialogue with him about it. And always, he'd be like, 'If it doesn't work for you, let's go your way'."

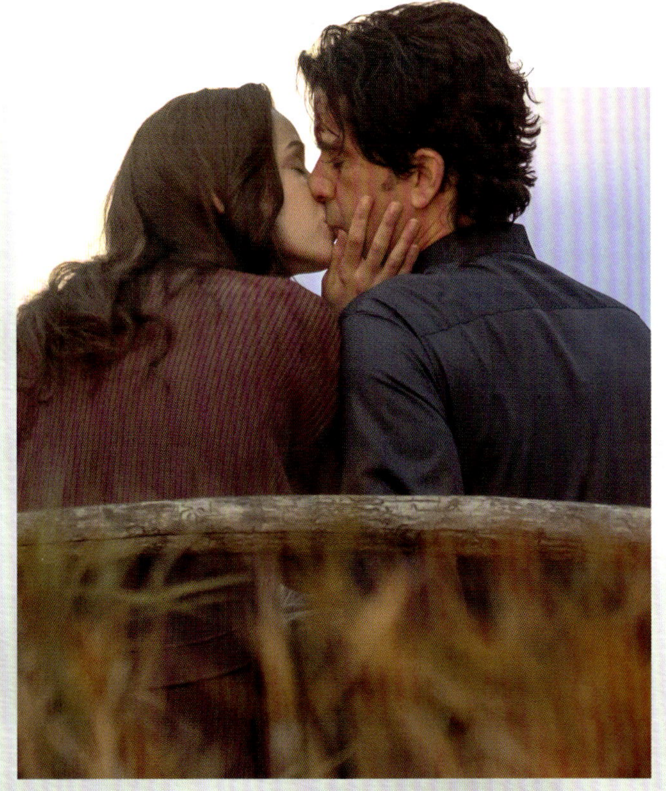

RISE OF THE ANGEL

QUINTON BOISCLAIR

Flanagan explains that it is Father Paul's idea, not the Angel's, to use the Angel's blood with the congregation. "There's a selfish motive for the Angel to get out of the desert, to have someone move it from Point A to Point B, and give it more food. After it had been locked away for so long, it would have latched onto anyone. Father Paul misread the youth that it gave him as a miracle. The Angel is communicating with Father Paul, and it's interested in the plan that he has for it."

But, Flanagan says, the Angel isn't strategic. "The Angel's this very old, gluttonous hunger. The tragedy of Father Paul is, he realizes at the end that the Angel is like any other radicalizing force, it's simple and it's stupid. [Father Paul] has unleashed it with, I would argue, good intentions at first. But that is very much just him. The Angel just does what it does – it eats."

Justin Raleigh of Fractured FX says that Flanagan had a specific vision of how he wanted the Angel to look. "We pulled in reference of emaciated-looking people and reference for low-light situations to figure out the translucency and luminescence that he wanted to achieve with the skin quality. Then we sat down and went into conceptual design, which [included] a 3D model that we created within a combination of rendering software."

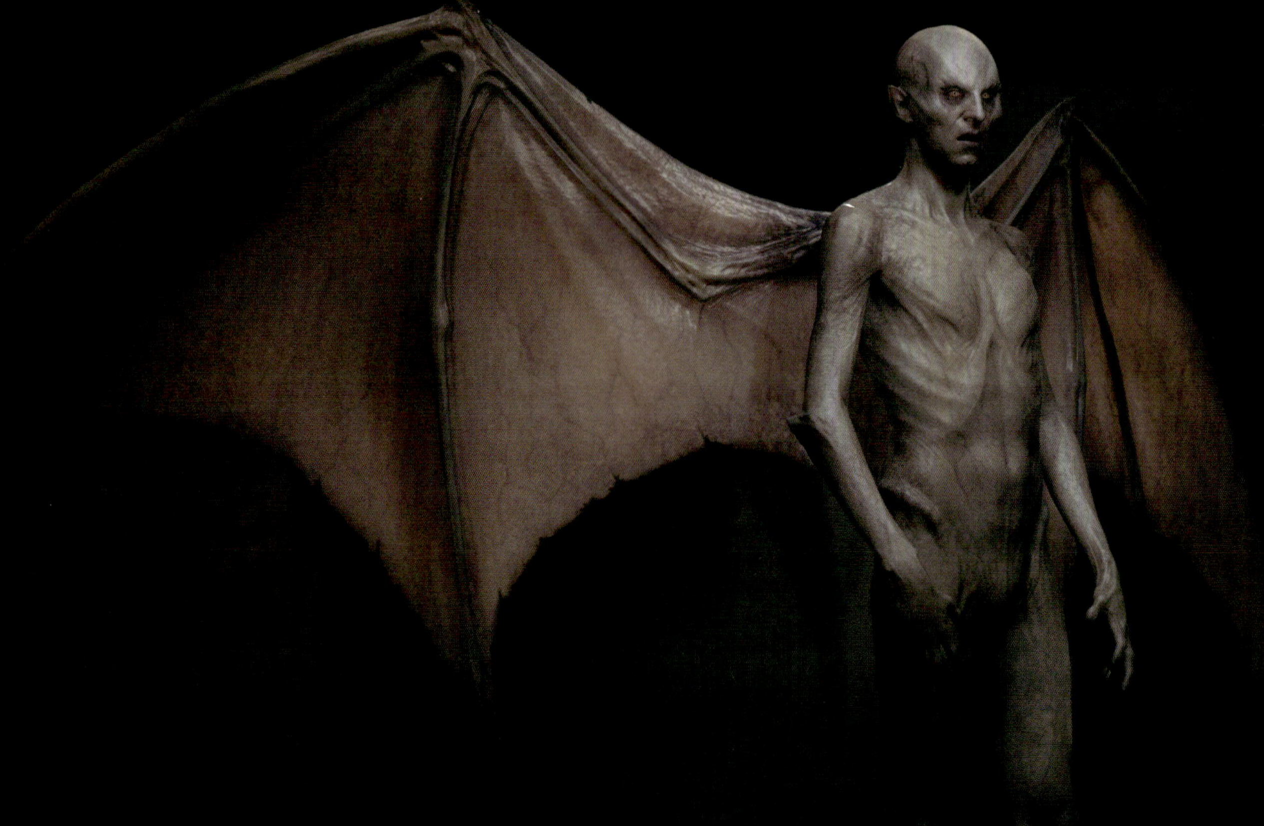

TOP/ Concept art of the Angel.

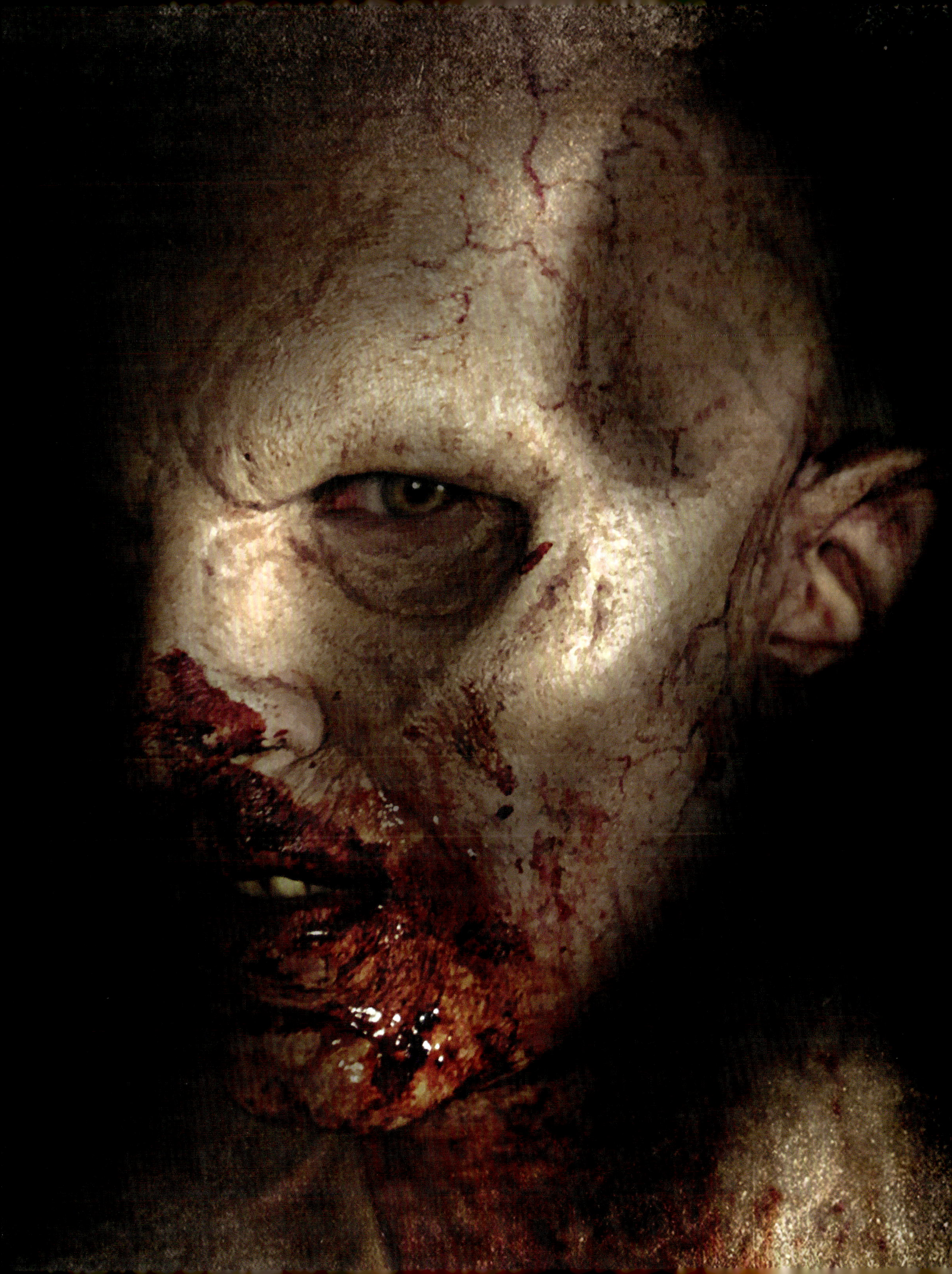

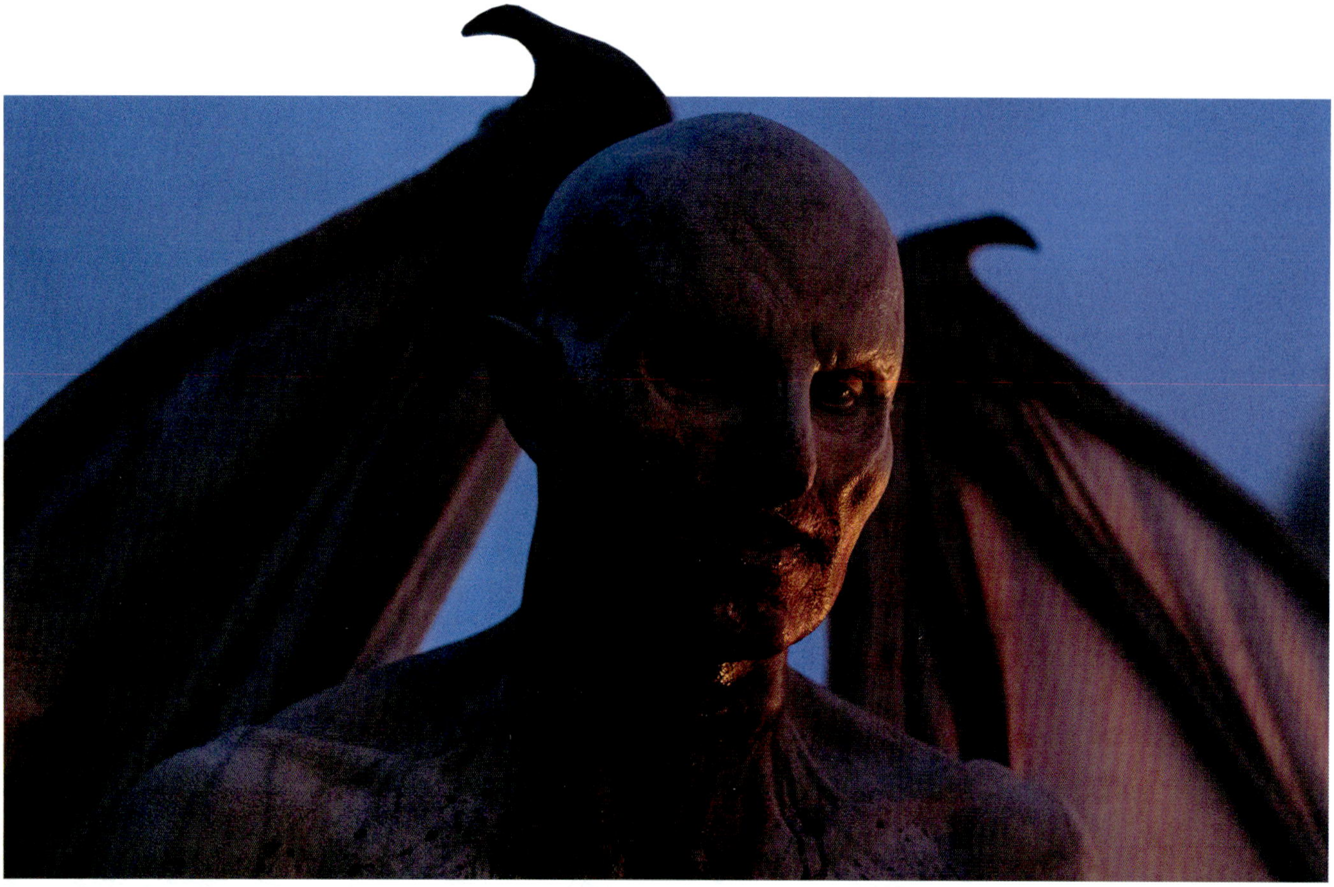

THIS PAGE/ (TOP) The Angel, with wingtip details. (BOTTOM) Boisclair in full Angel prosthetics with wings.

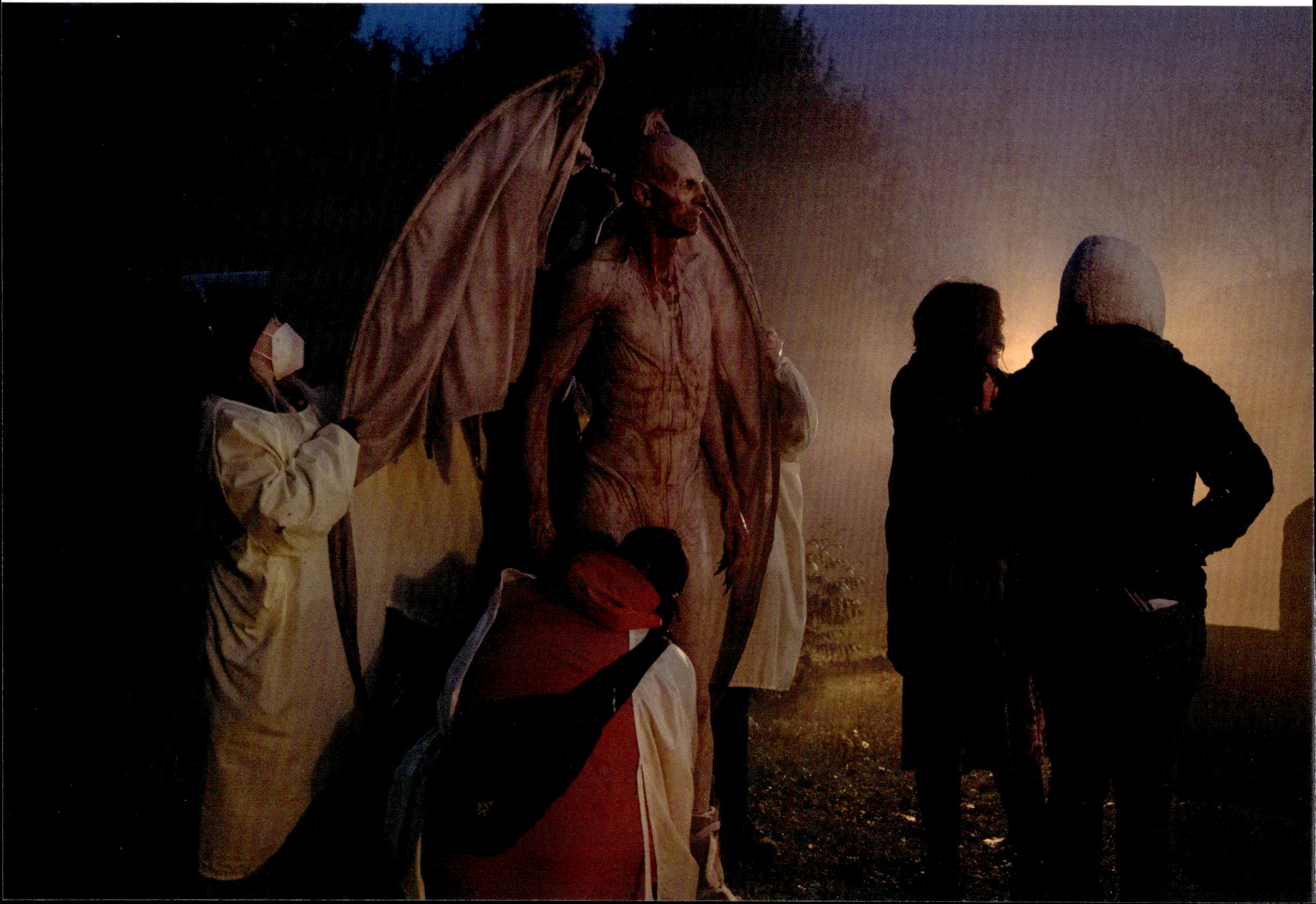

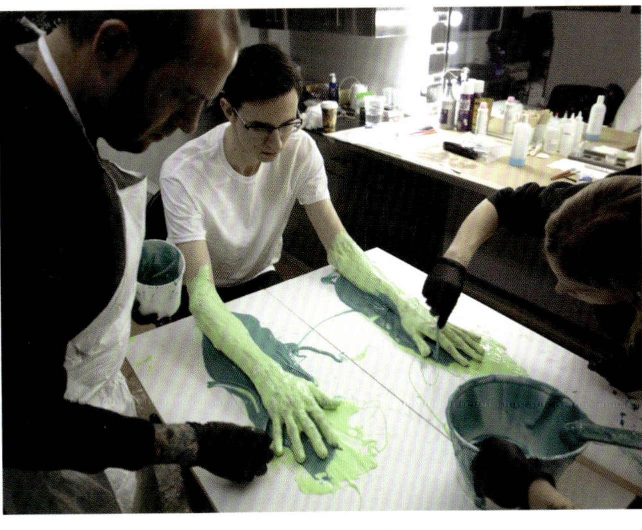

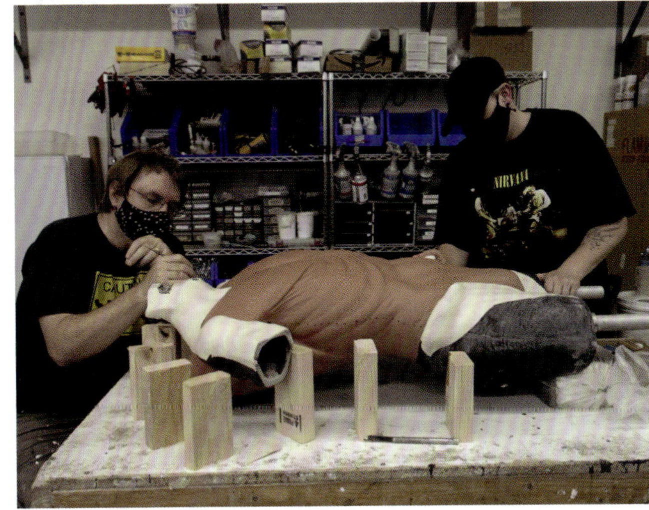

TOP/ Boisclair having molds taken of his arms; the SPFX makeup department working on the Angel's torso piece.

This meant making sketches within Photoshop, and then 3D-printing a maquette sculpture based on actor Quinton Boisclair, who plays the Angel. "Overall," Raleigh explains, "it looks like a human with a nod toward some bat-type elements. We kept it emaciated, but fleshy. It's androgynous, so there's no genitalia." The Angel suit was built with a flap for restroom use, and the ability to open up the back if Boisclair got too hot. "We want to make sure that it can move as full-range as possible, but we design everything for comfort, first and foremost."

The Angel, Raleigh continues, is "a hybrid between a creature suit and a prosthetic makeup. [Boisclair] gets into foam rubber bicycle-style shorts. Then he gets a full upper chest torso piece. The shorts get blended down onto the thighs. He has little blender pieces that help feather it into his own legs, with prosthetic augmentation, and separate feet pieces. The torso piece blends into a full cowl piece, and prosthetic head pieces. He has separate hand pieces, bicep/tricep prosthetics that wrap around, contact lenses, teeth, nail extensions, and elbow prosthetics."

The appliances are all hand-sculpted. "Where you're playing with thicknesses for a prosthetic, you need a tactile understanding of what that skin thickness on that person's body is going to look like."

The Angel's eyes are hand-painted contact lenses from Christina Patterson of Eye Ink FX. Raleigh notes that the irises are "a muted, hazel-greenish-yellow. The white of the eye is relatively human, with a little bloodshotting."

BOTTOM/ Angel torso piece; side and front views of the Angel, post-feeding.

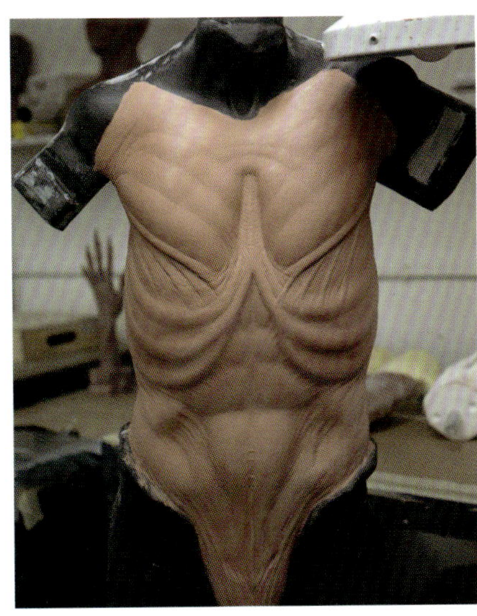

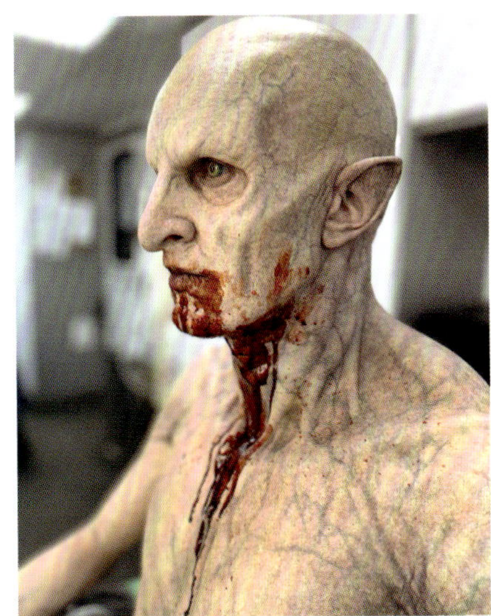

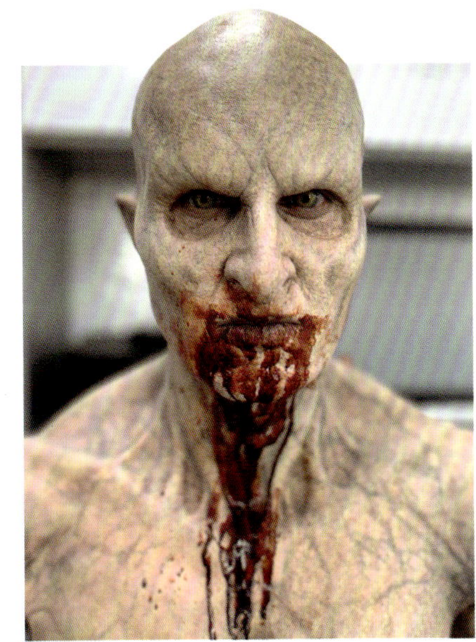

The mouth is also humanlike. "A key component in my conversations with Mike was, he did not want the standard vampire. He wanted it more grounded, and to get rid of the big canine fangs. So, there's a slight nod toward the teeth being sharp and serrated, but at first glance, they look like human teeth, until you get close on them." A full set of fitted Angel dentures went over Boisclair's real teeth.

The Angel's wings are practical when earthbound; in flight, the whole creature is entirely CGI. The wings are based on fruit bats, Raleigh says, "with our own skew, to give it a translucency and depth. The interior of the wing panels have a fleshy, translucent, milky-looking material, with a lot of veins."

There are two different versions of the wings, one folded and one extended. The latter requires puppeteers; both are attached by a harness concealed in the upper body piece.

On-set makeup FX department head Tony "Ozzy" Alvarez says that, to get Boisclair into suit and makeup, it took four makeup artists working simultaneously on different parts, "and the fastest we ever got it done was three-and-a-half hours." Besides the body pieces, "It's a full neck piece, and a head piece that goes from his forehead all the way back to the back of his neck. There's a butterfly piece, which goes over the cheek, the bridge of the nose, onto the other cheek. There's a nose tip, an upper lip, a lower lip, ear-tip pieces, and eyebags."

The facial appliances are attached with Pros-Aide, the same substance used to age up the older parishioners. "Our makeup removal time was over an hour every night."

As to the Angel's impact on the cast, Siegel offers, "It's like standing near an impossibly tall redwood. It just has a weight in the universe."

Kohli agrees. "It looked absolutely terrifying. If it scared the shit out of us on set, it's going to play well on-screen."

BOTTOM/ The Angel feeds on an unlucky victim.

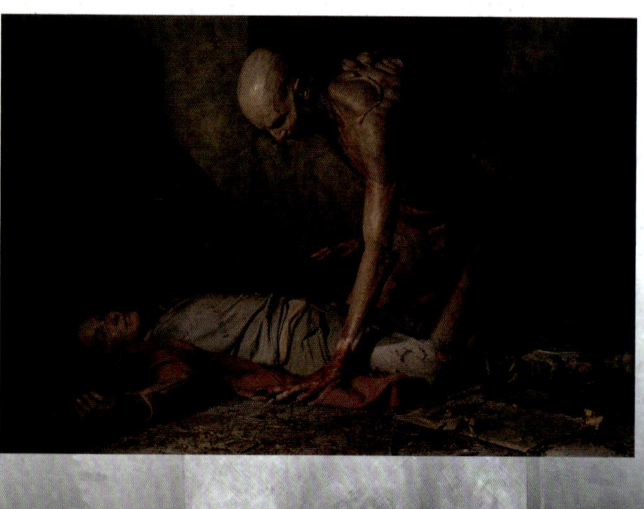

BOTTOM/ Bowl is held captive by the Angel.

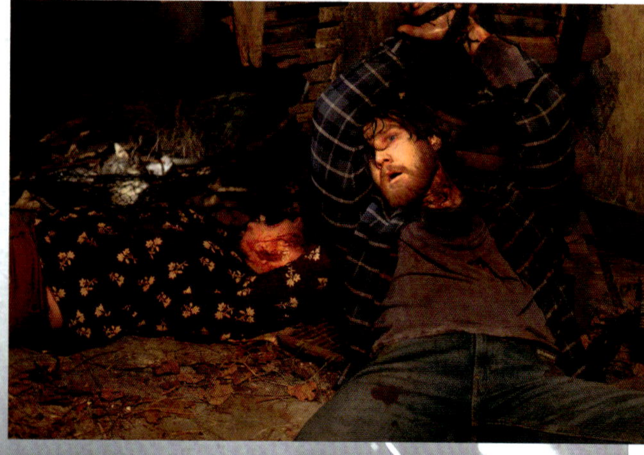

ANGEL'S HOUSE

Of the abandoned houses on Crockett Island, production designer Steven Arnold says that the Angel inhabits the one that looks most haunted. "That was very carefully dressed inside. There were a lot of dead animals," including some leftover cats from the beach, "and remnants of past life [of occupants] long gone."

Cinematographer Michael Fimognari says, "The abandoned house, and the area of town associated with it, represents that decay of the town that once thrived, that people were prosperous fishing, and now all that's gone, and the homes and the people are starting to crumble, and it's offering this safety for the Angel. When we lit that, it was about broken light coming in through the slats of the fallen rooftop, through another level of age and decay. It's one of those spaces where you can't see in-between the shadows."

There are also the corpses of the Angel's human victims. It was easier to hire actors to play dead than manufacture fake corpses, especially because, except for Bowl, no one had to match previously-seen characters.

Alvarez says, "A couple of them were in different stages of decay, so we adjusted the makeup accordingly, but they would have multiple prosthetics on. So, we would lighten the skin, or make the skin look rotted, depending on how long they were supposed to have been in the lair. Mike wanted it to look like the Angel's been feeding on them for a while. So, we overlapped different bite-looking prosthetics. Some might come up onto the cheek a little bit, further down onto the neck, some on the wrist. And then we would age it. So, we'd make the skin look dead, and rotting [by] layering different colors of paint on top of each other."

Father Paul brings the Angel from the Middle East to Crockett Island in an enormous trunk. Arnold says, "It started out as a prop. We looked at a bunch of different ones. Trevor and Mike decided that what was out there [commercially] wasn't big enough. We couldn't believe that this Angel, with these big wings, was going to come out of any of the trunks that props had come up with. So, we auditioned several different trunk sizes for them, just plywood boxes. Finally, we designed and built one that was not super-big, but big enough."

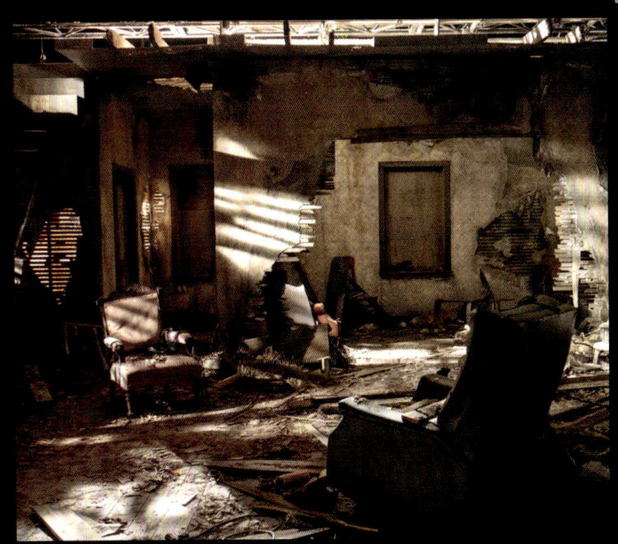

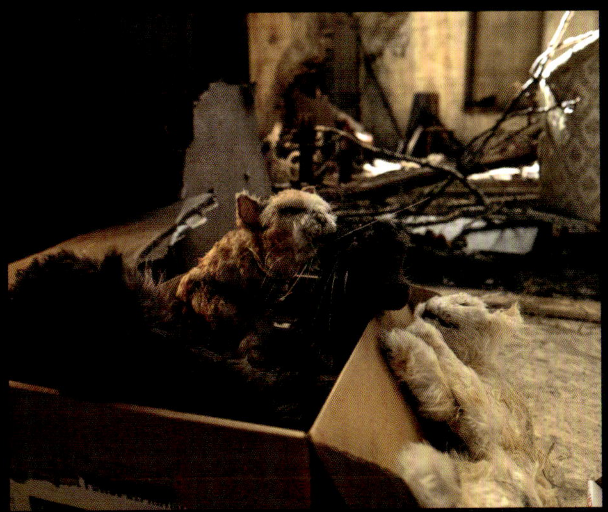

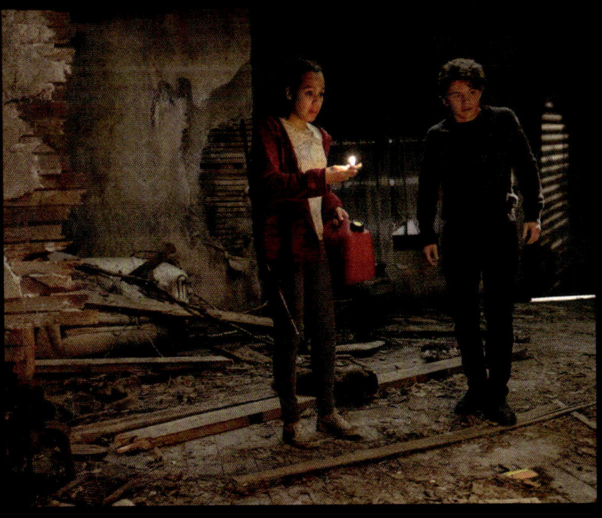

ABOVE/ (TOP) The Angel's lair. (MIDDLE) A box of prop dead cats. (BOTTOM) Leeza and Warren investigate.

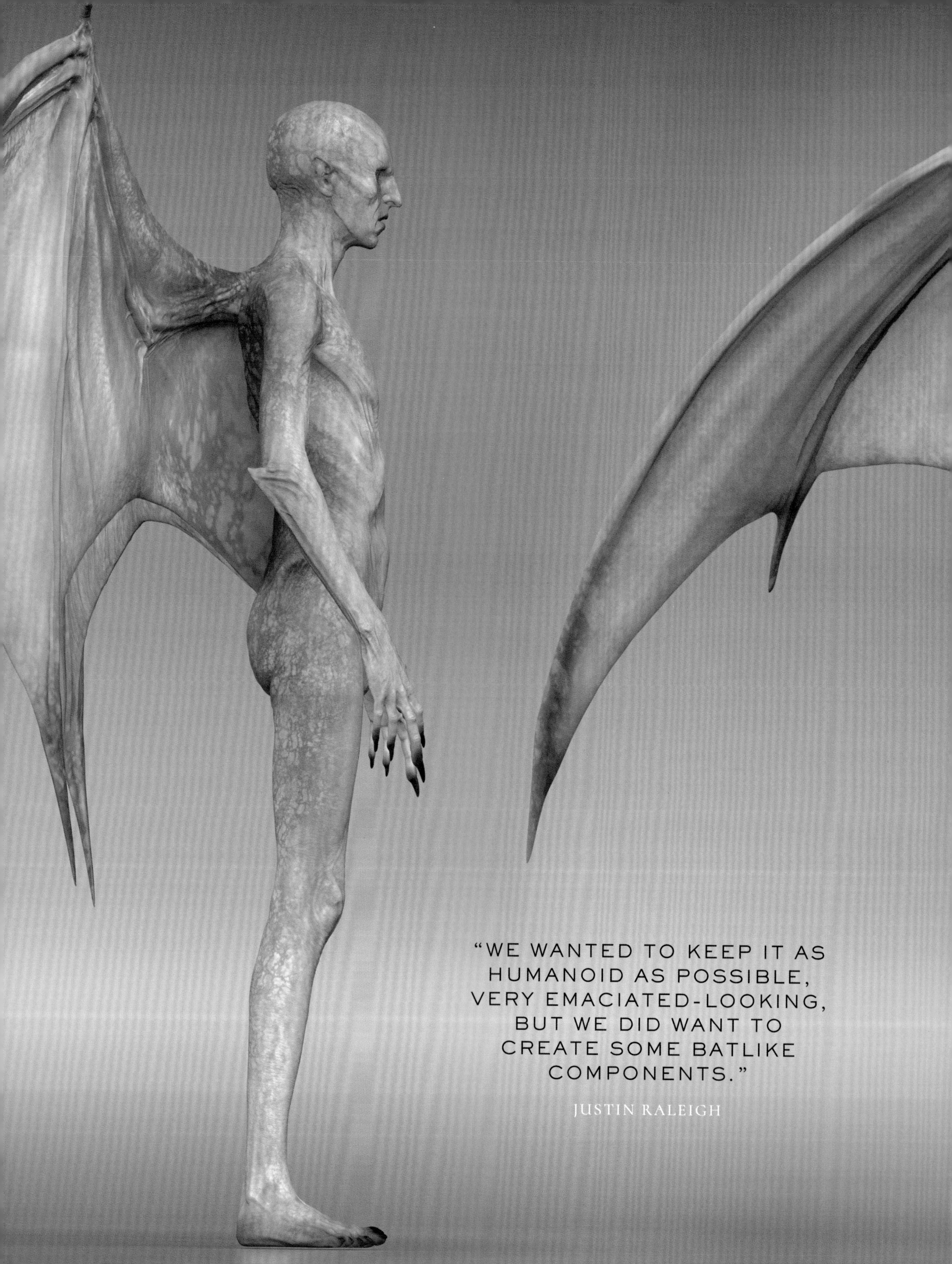

"WE WANTED TO KEEP IT AS HUMANOID AS POSSIBLE, VERY EMACIATED-LOOKING, BUT WE DID WANT TO CREATE SOME BATLIKE COMPONENTS."

JUSTIN RALEIGH

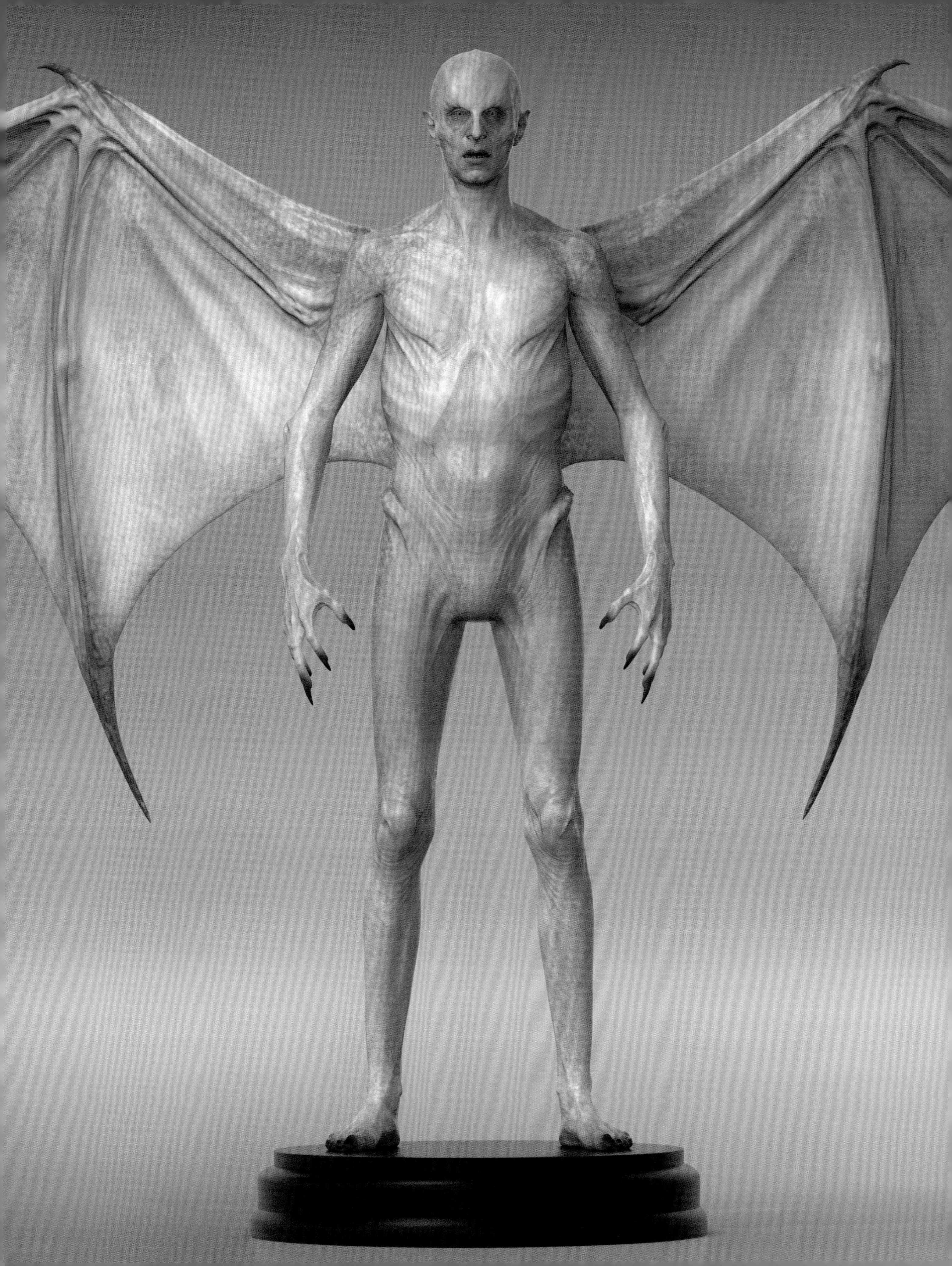

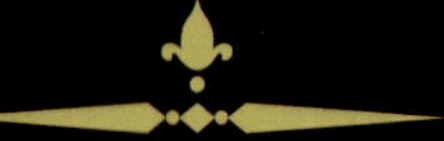

ERIN GREENE

KATE SIEGEL

Erin Greene is played by Kate Siegel, who has acted in the Flanagan and Macy projects *Hush* (which she and Flanagan wrote together), *Oculus, Ouija: Origin of Evil, Gerald's Game, The Haunting of Hill House*, and *The Haunting of Bly Manor*.

Siegel and Flanagan have been married to one another since 2016. He created the character of Erin a year before they met, but once Flanagan began the miniseries re-write, he tailored the character to Siegel. Flanagan explains, "[Originally], Erin got turned, and burned up in the sunrise, and Riley continued doing battle. It wasn't until the most recent pass at the story that that seemed wrong to me. It seemed that Father Paul, representing belief that is corruptible, and Riley, representing atheism that has closed itself off, meant that Erin, as the moderate, needed to be the hero of the story. That version of Erin was written with Kate's voice in my head."

Siegel says that she created a backstory for Erin with Flanagan "that I tried to lean on whenever Erin would retreat to her silences." This included the abuses by both Erin's alcoholic mother and her battering ex-spouse. Part of the reason Erin doesn't speak up more "is because she's afraid of drawing any attention that would bring her husband to where she is."

When we meet Erin, she is twenty weeks pregnant. Siegel has two children (with Flanagan), so she drew on her own experiences, "although my pregnancy had a lot more morning sickness than Erin's, and a lot less professional hair and make-up," she laughs. "I wanted to represent a body that looked twenty weeks pregnant. I gained about ten pounds, just cutting out some of my dietary restrictions. Terry, the costume designer, made sure a lot of my clothing was oversized and looked a little baggy. If Erin ran away from her husband, she had a backpack's worth of clothes. Everything [else] she wears, she found in her mom's closet, or the church donation box."

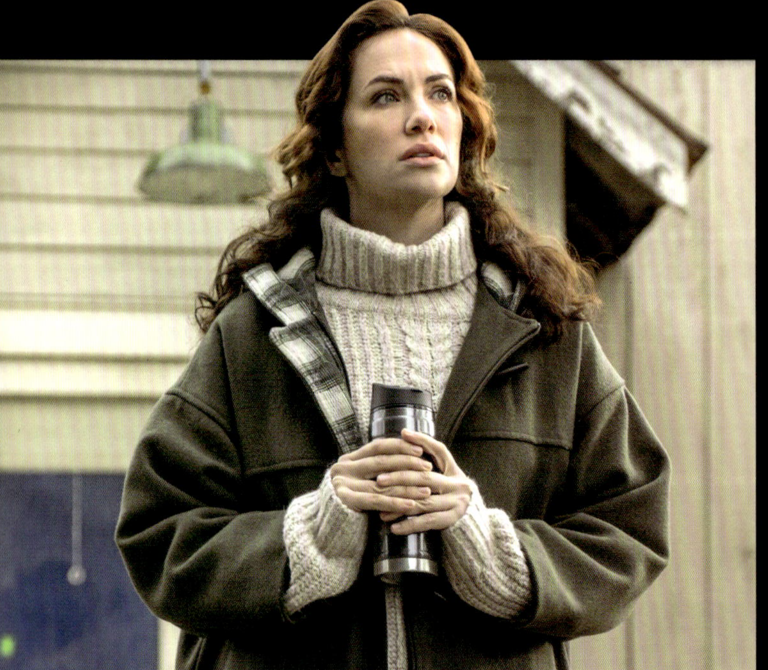

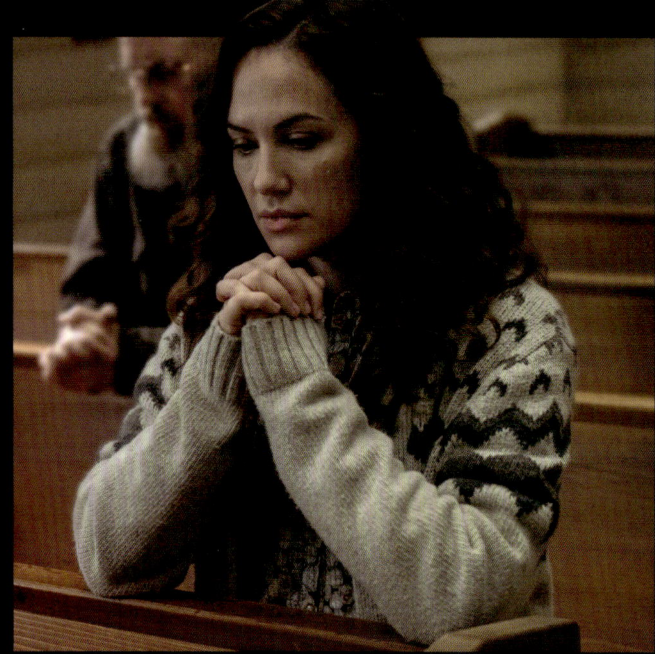

TOP/ (LEFT) Erin prepares for the day with her coffee thermos. (RIGHT) Erin at prayer.

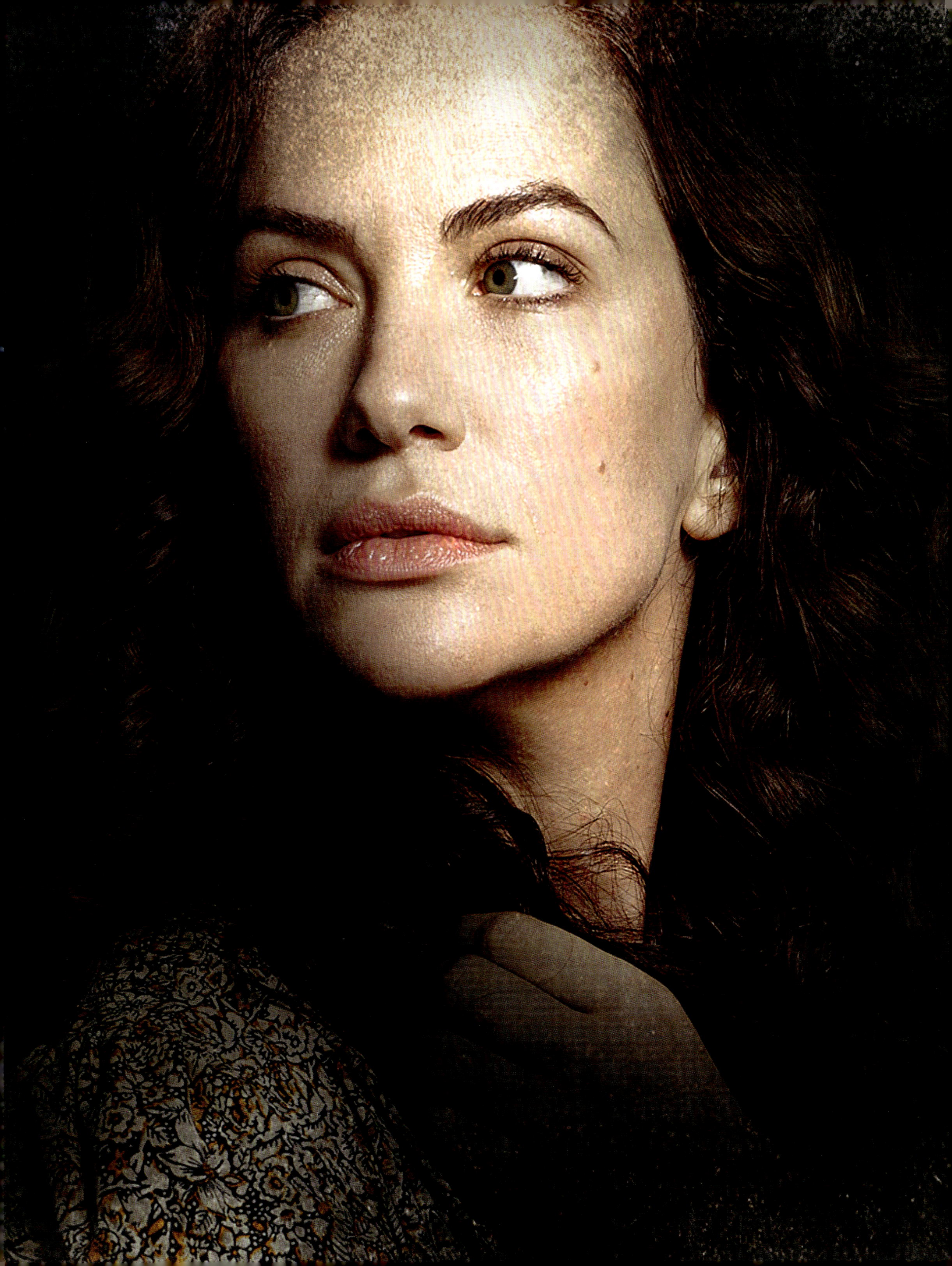

"AT A VERY YOUNG AGE, ERIN WAS A RUNNER. OVER THE COURSE [OF THE SHOW], ERIN DECIDES WHAT'S IMPORTANT TO HER, AND LEARNS TO STAND UP AND FIGHT FOR IT."

KATE SIEGEL

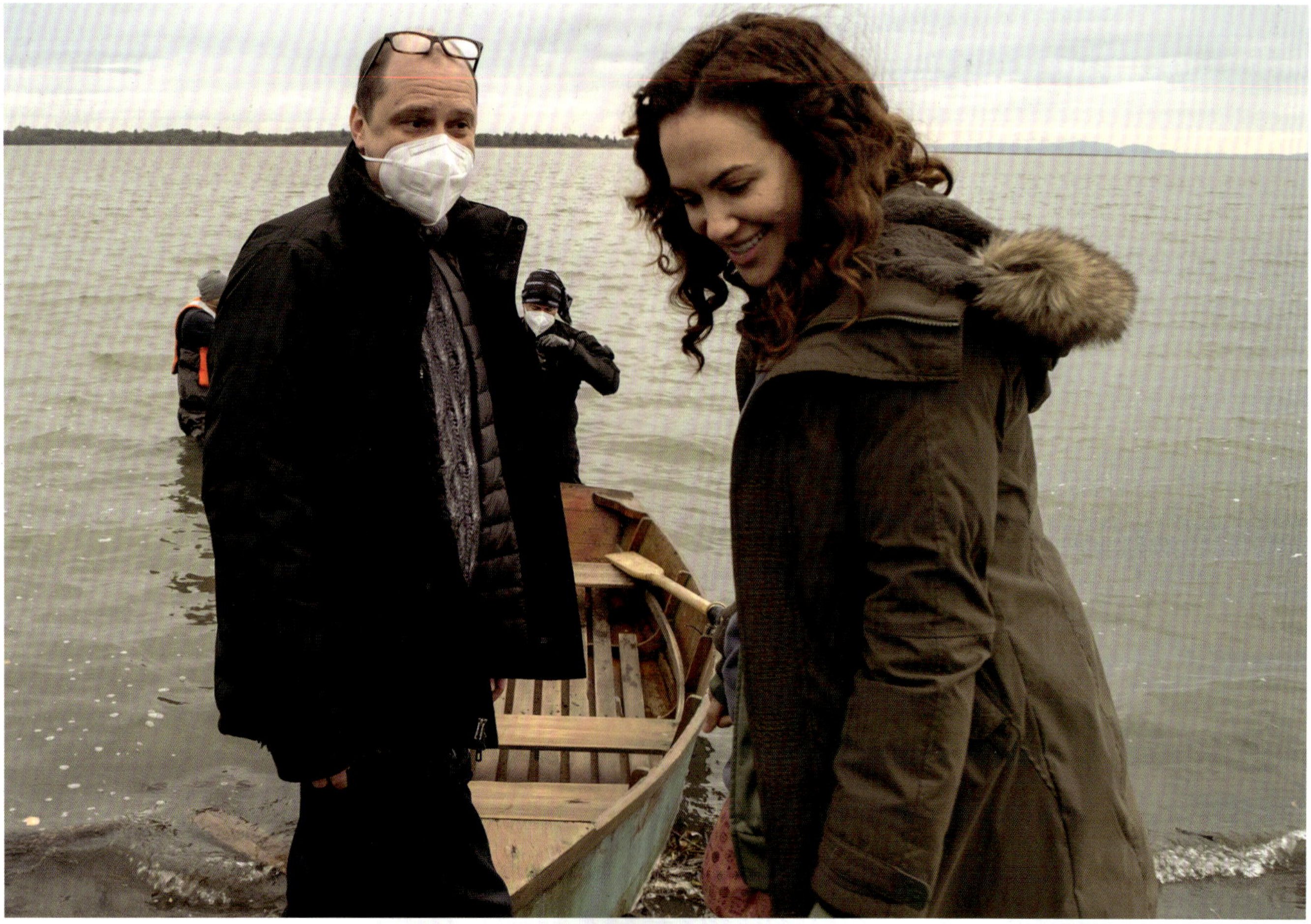

THIS PAGE/ (TOP) Working marriage: Flanagan and Siegel. (BOTTOM) Erin rows back to the island, alone.

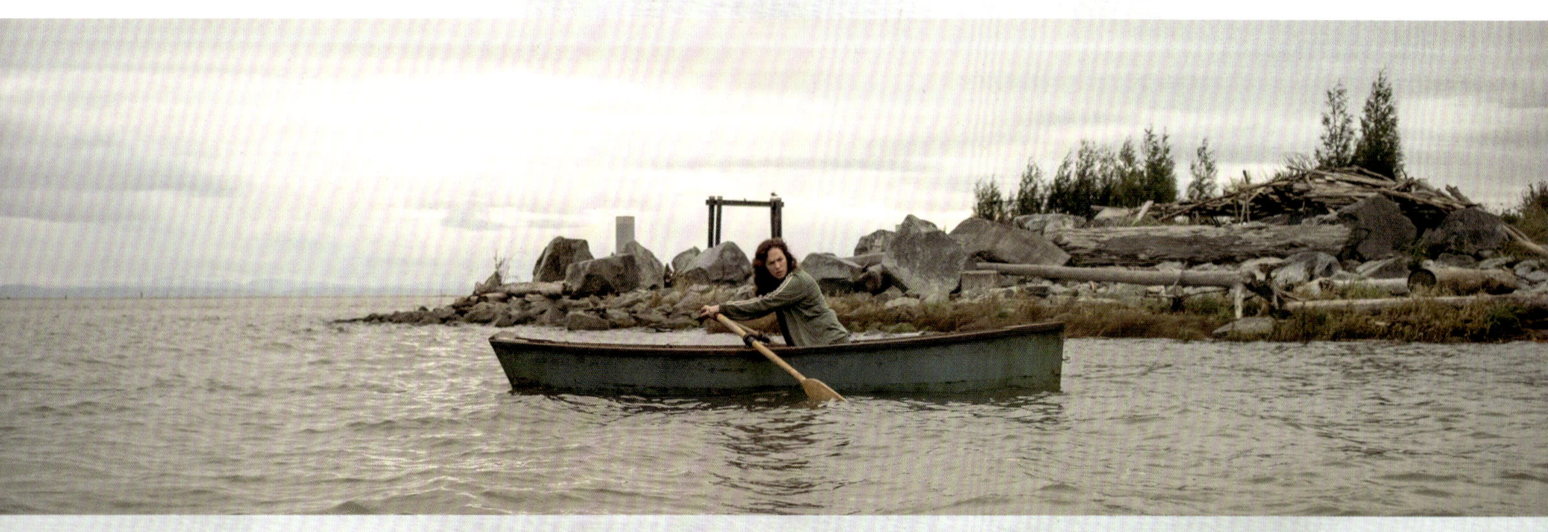

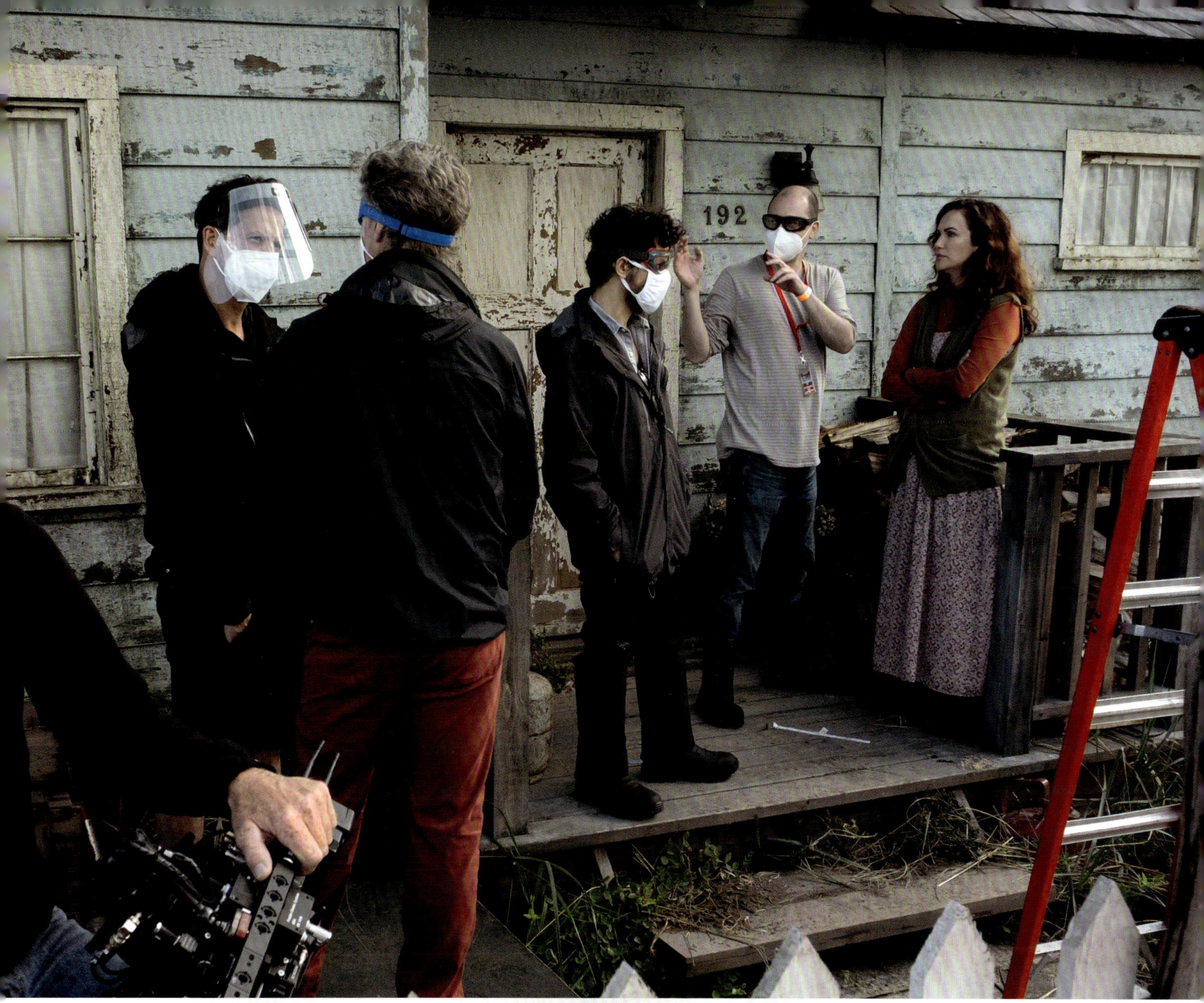

TOP/ Preparing for a scene on the porch.

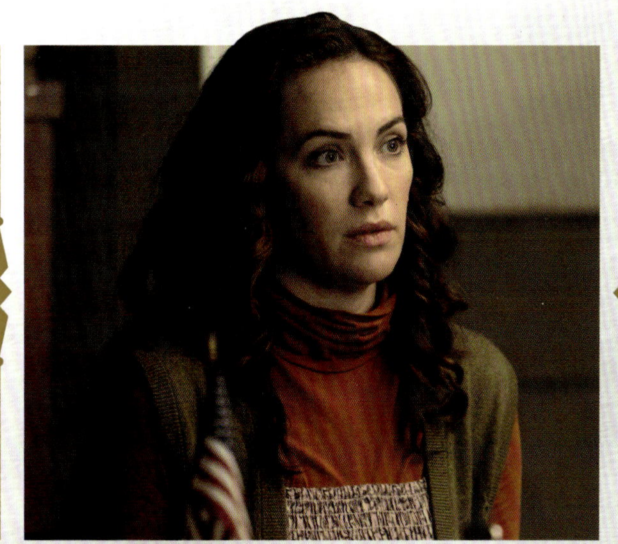

One of Erin's big moments is a monologue in which she discusses both her deceased mother and her unborn child. "That hit me right in the heart," Siegel relates, "because when you [become a] parent, you start to both forgive and blame your parents some more. As Erin was looking at becoming a mother, she was confronted with what she believes a mother is, and what kind of mother she wants to be. I thought it was important to express that that through-line is linked in most women, from our mothers to our children. We understand our mothers in a way maybe we never have, or never wanted to, before."

LEFT/ Erin prepares to talk to the sheriff.

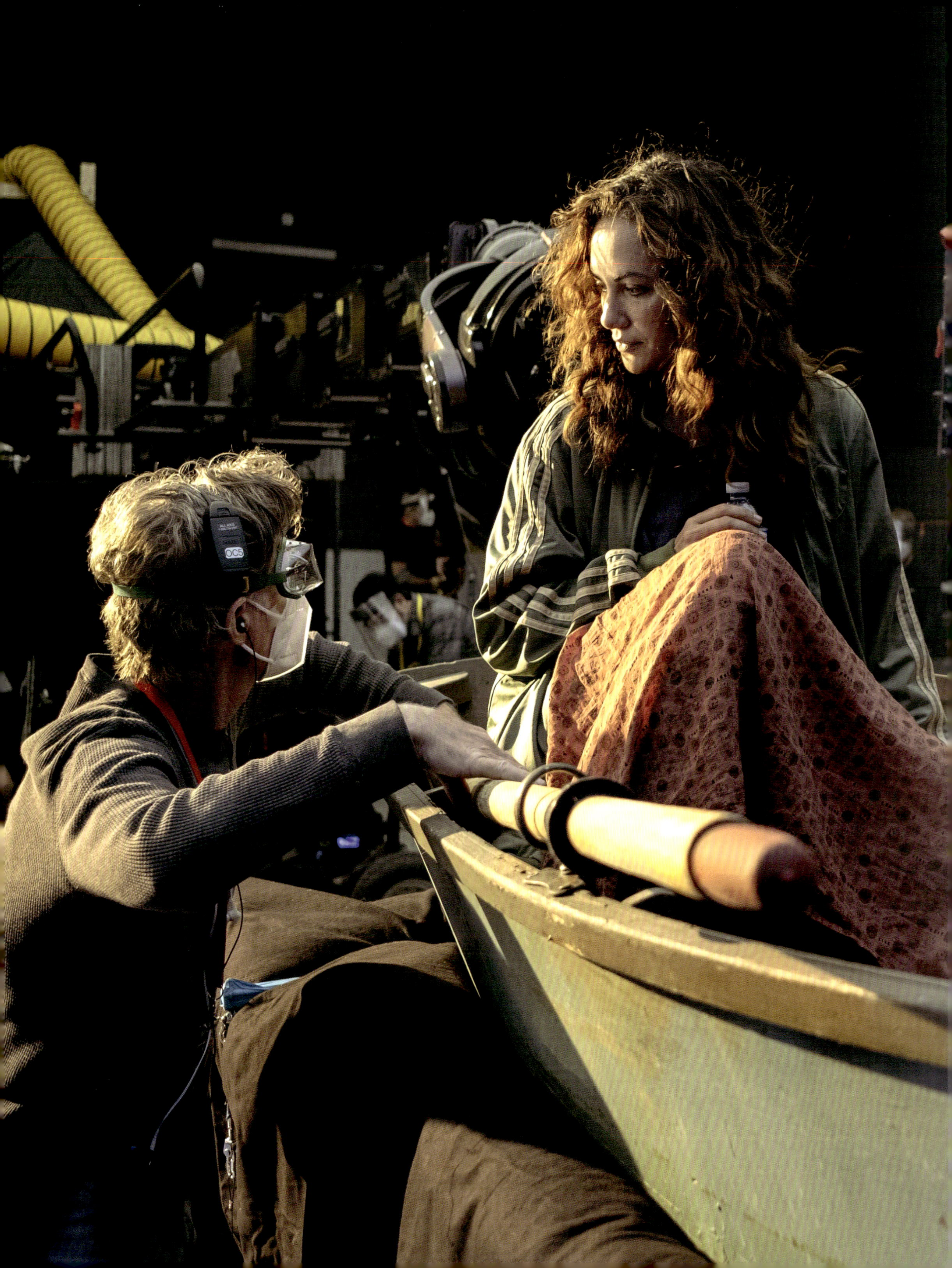
OC5

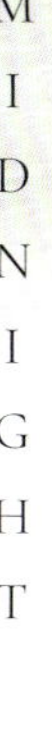

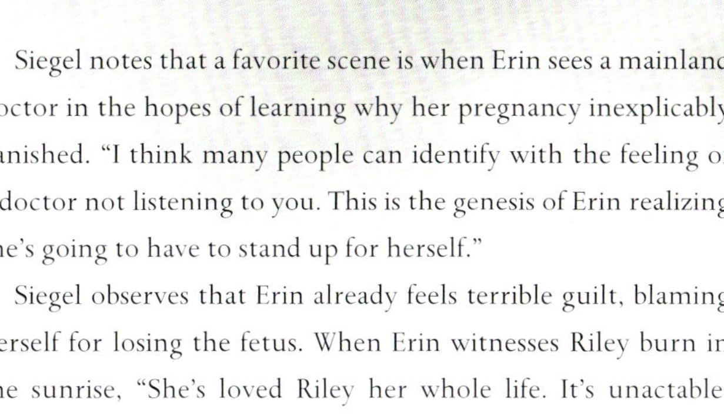

Siegel notes that a favorite scene is when Erin sees a mainland doctor in the hopes of learning why her pregnancy inexplicably vanished. "I think many people can identify with the feeling of a doctor not listening to you. This is the genesis of Erin realizing she's going to have to stand up for herself."

Siegel observes that Erin already feels terrible guilt, blaming herself for losing the fetus. When Erin witnesses Riley burn in the sunrise, "She's loved Riley her whole life. It's unactable. There is nothing that anybody could tell me what it would feel like to see your true love incinerate in front of you. I remember thinking about what it smelled like, and how long it must have taken, and what part of Erin is still in that boat forever, at that moment. It's that moment where she knows she's going to save [the people on Crockett] or die trying. In performing that, I just touched on some things in my life that just seemed so unfair, so cruel, and so unnecessary, and thought about what it would be like to be stuck in that moment for eternity."

As to how Erin views her faith, Siegel says, "Erin was raised Catholic. She rebelled against the Church in her teenage years, but believes in a Higher Power, she just doesn't know what it looks like. By the end, Erin conquers her cowardice of spirit. She is against organized religion, but has more faith in God than she ever knew possible. She just thinks God is something different than what Catholicism taught her. God is everything. God is love."

Besides Erin, were there any other characters Siegel would have liked to portray? "I would have loved to play any role in *Midnight Mass*. One of my favorites is Joe Collie, but I wasn't considered for that," she laughs.

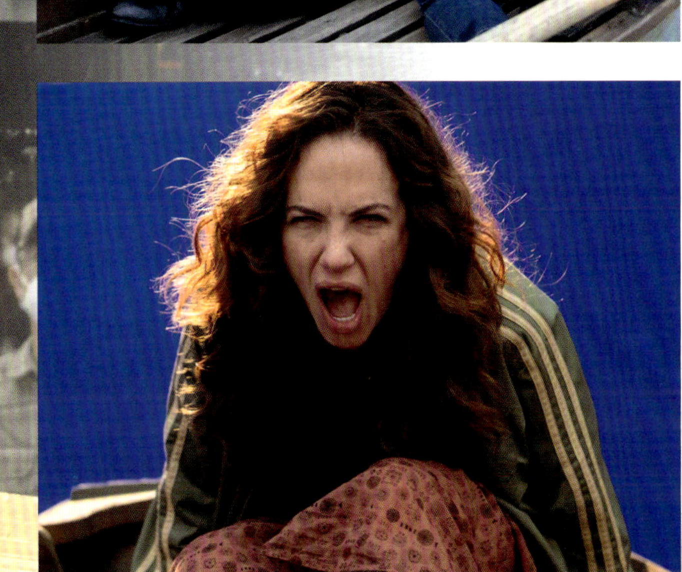

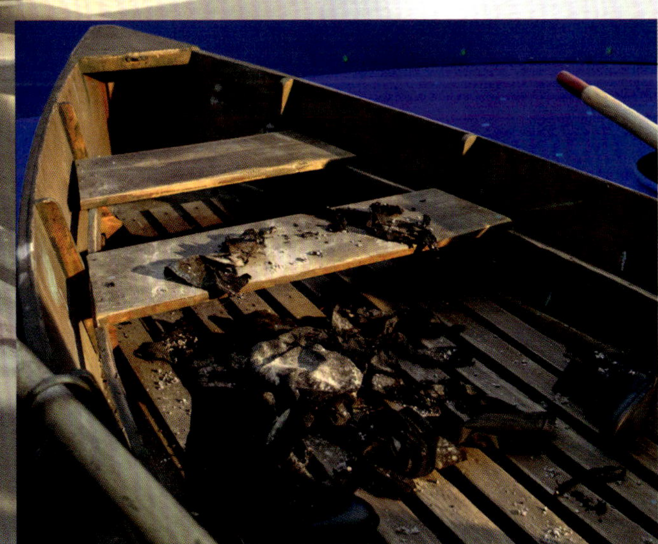

THIS PAGE/ [TOP] SPFX body for Riley disintegrating. [MIDDLE] Erin reacting. [BOTTOM] All that's left.

"ERIN FEELS LIKE THE UNLIKELY HERO. ALL THE OTHER HEROES ARE DEAD. AND THEN... SHE REALIZES 'THERE'S NO ONE ELSE BUT ME'."

KATE SIEGEL

GREENE HOUSE

AN INHERITED REFUGE

As with most *Midnight Mass* dwellings, the exterior for Erin's house was on the beach, and the interior was on a soundstage. However, Arnold says, "We did have a little bit of an interior of her house finished out at the park location. She has a front porch, like many of these little houses have. It's got a porch swing, where she can look out on the water. It had a bit of a nicer interior than maybe some of the other ones, just because of her character. But it was similarly aged on the outside to the rest of the houses."

For the interior, Arnold added little pops of yellow. "I wanted her house to be more hopeful, and sunnier. The Flynn house I made cooler, so I wanted to contrast that. Her outlook is a little more positive."

Siegel says, "I love the set for Erin's home. I felt a lot of ownership, especially when the crew would come in and start

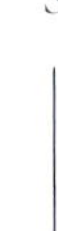
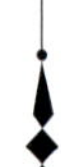
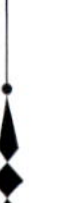
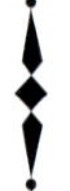
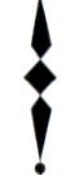

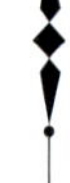

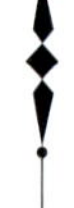

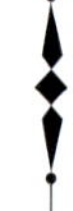

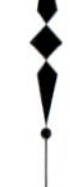
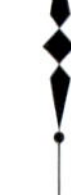

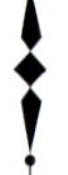
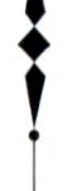

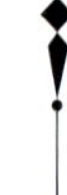

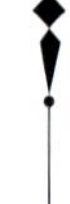

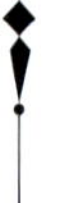

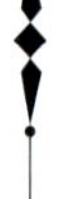

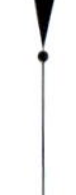
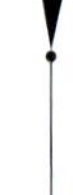
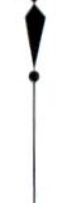
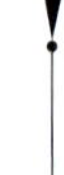
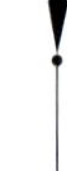
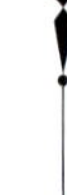
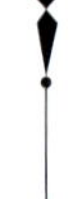

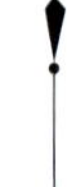
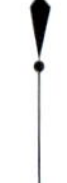
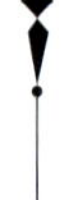
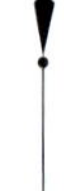
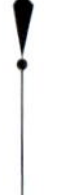
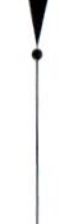
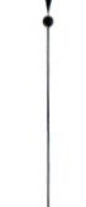
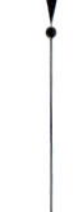
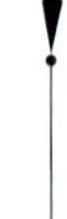
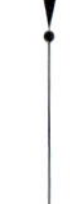
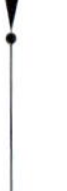
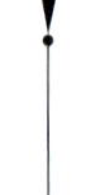
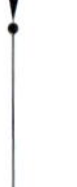
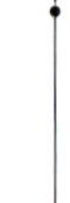
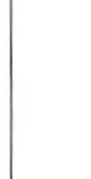
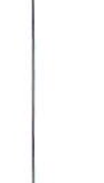
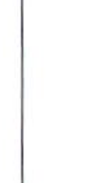

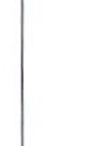
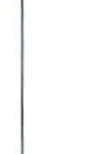
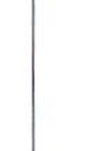
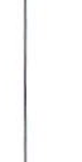
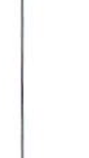
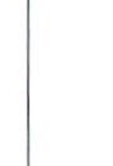

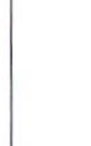
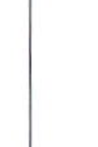
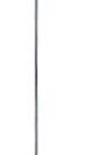
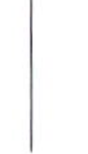
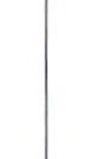
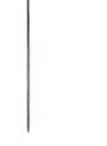
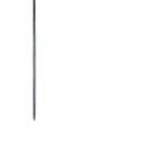
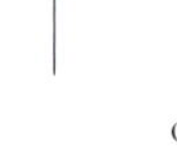

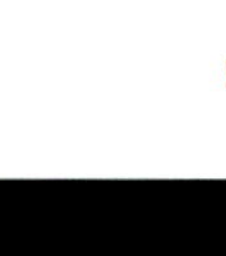
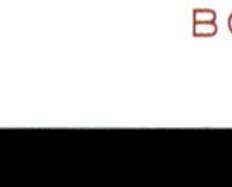
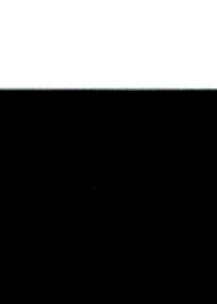
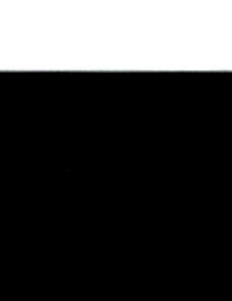
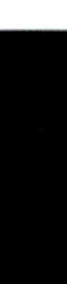
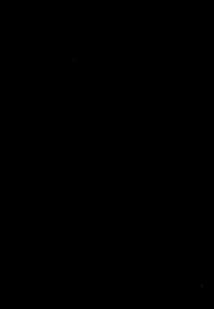
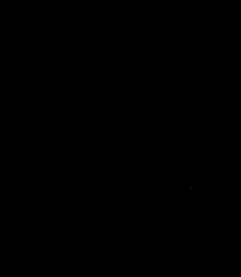
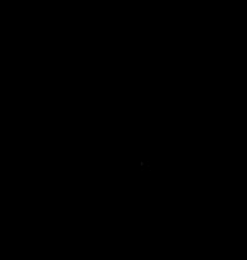
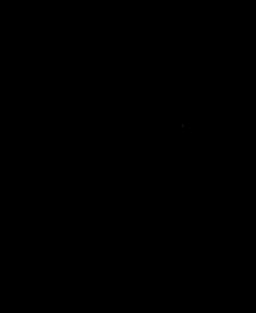
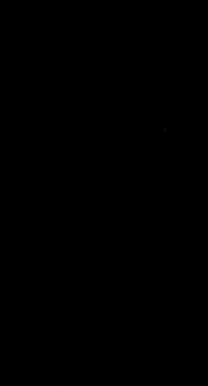
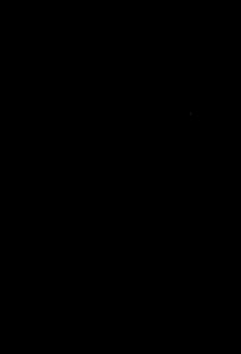
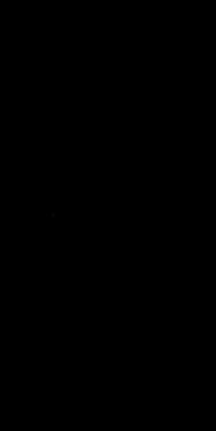
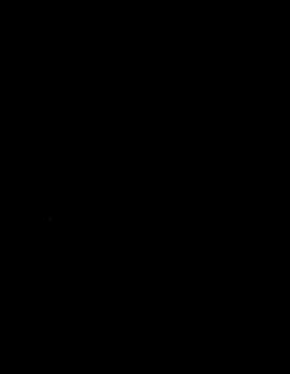
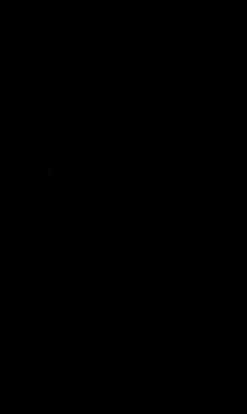
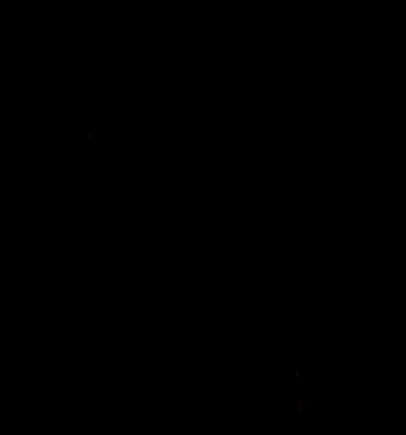
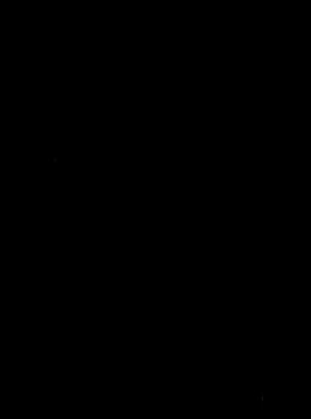
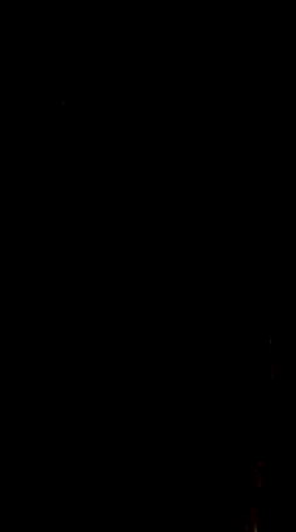
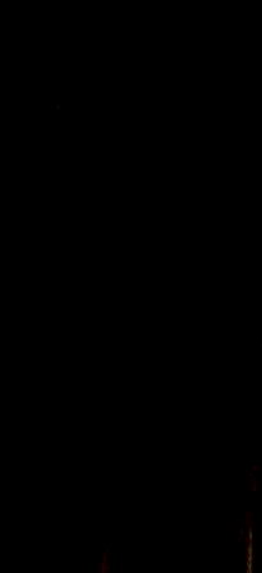

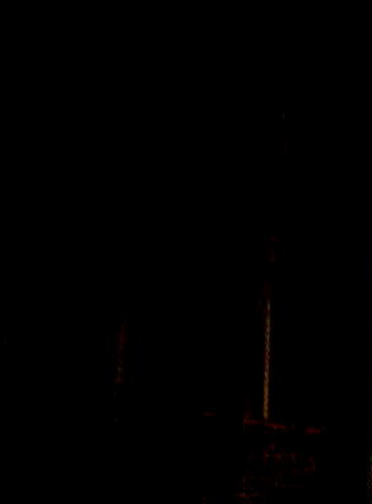
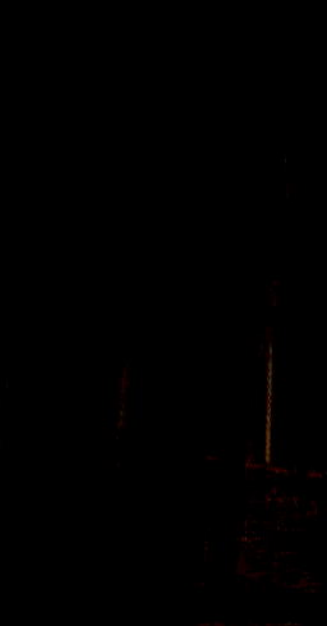
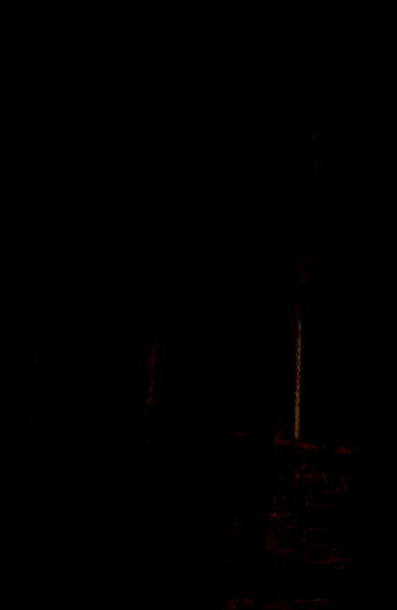
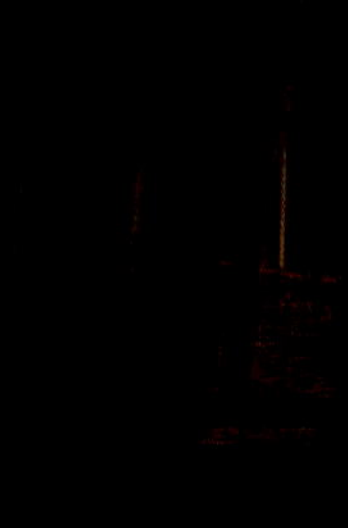
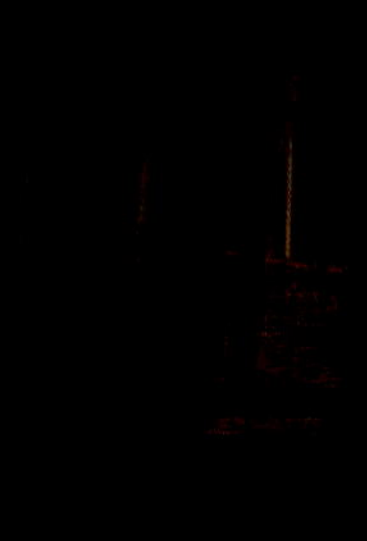
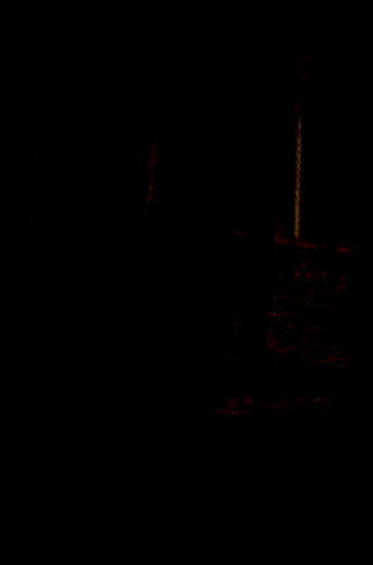
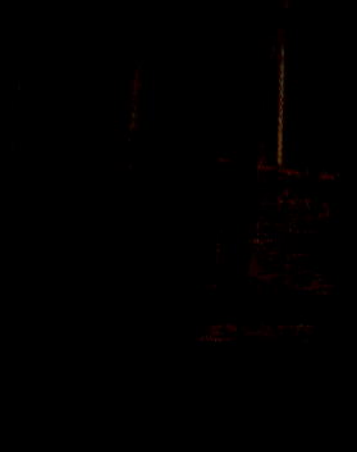

BOTTOM/ Riley comes to Erin's door at night.

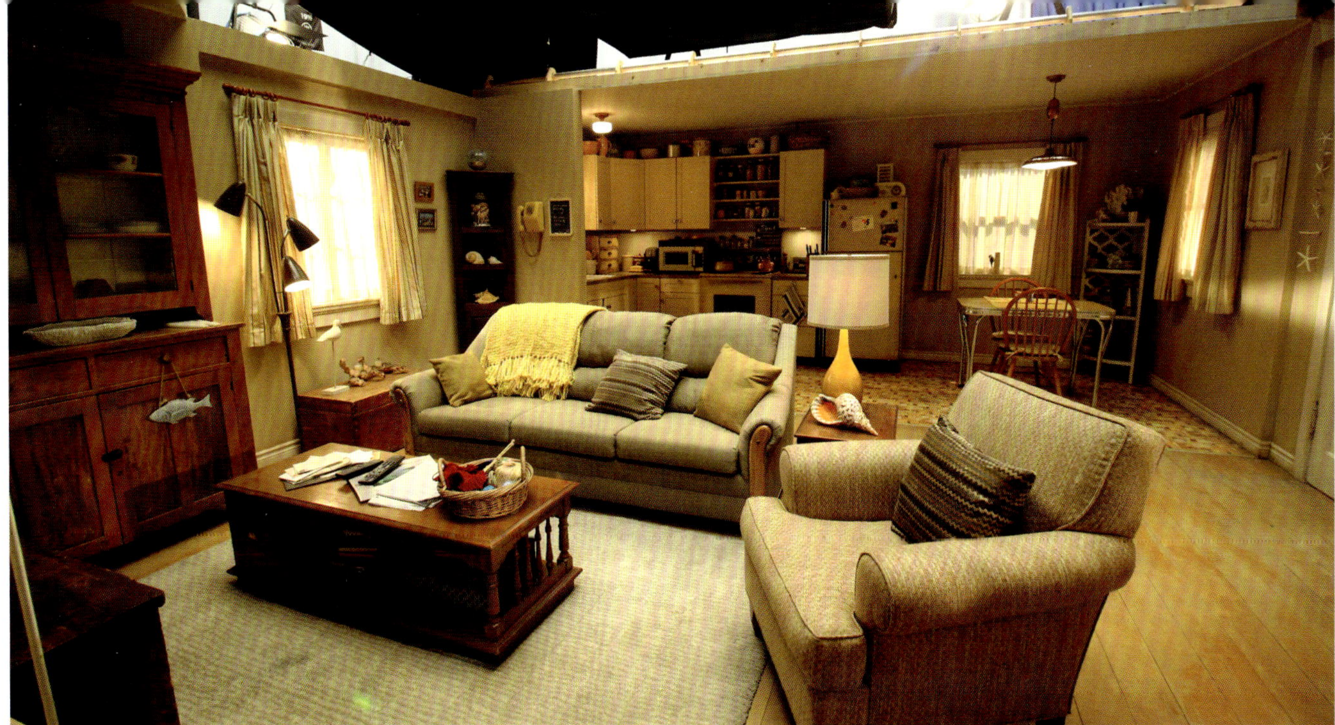

TOP/ Light colors indicate Erin's hope for better days to come.

moving things, I almost wanted to stop them. I had a running joke with Rahul Kohli. One of the first scenes we shot was where Bev throws the Molotov cocktail through the window. I would say, 'I have a backstory for every object in this house.' And Rahul would pick something up, and I'd go, 'Oh, that was my mom's.' And he'd pick something else up, and I'd go, 'That was my mom's, too'," she laughs.

Siegel acknowledges that she created more backstory with some set pieces. "If you're an actor, it's fun to build a life around you. There's a chalkboard next to the phone, [with] written little notes on it. And one of them says, 'Call John back.' And I'm constantly asking people on the set, 'Who's John? Why did he call?' I would go through all the books in Erin's house, and make sure there were things [she'd read]."

There were also some removals. "The first day I showed up on set," Siegel explains, "I walked into Erin's bathroom, and there was makeup and nail polish, and I asked the art department to take it away, because I didn't think Erin would have any of that."

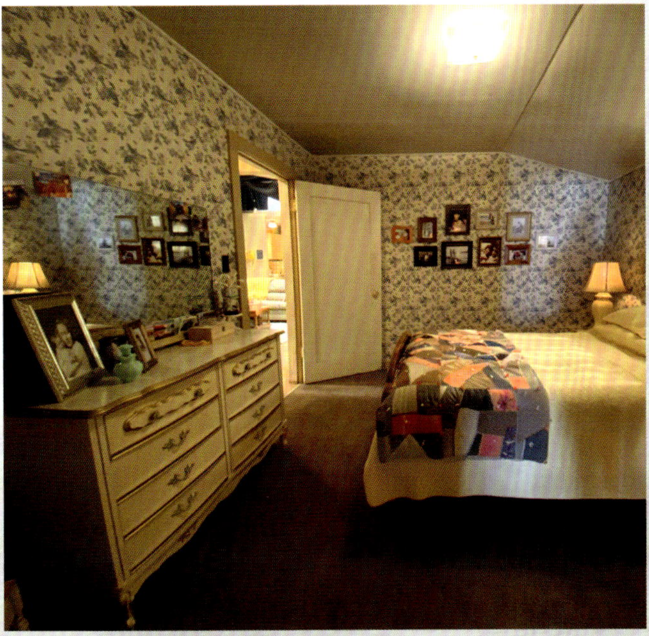

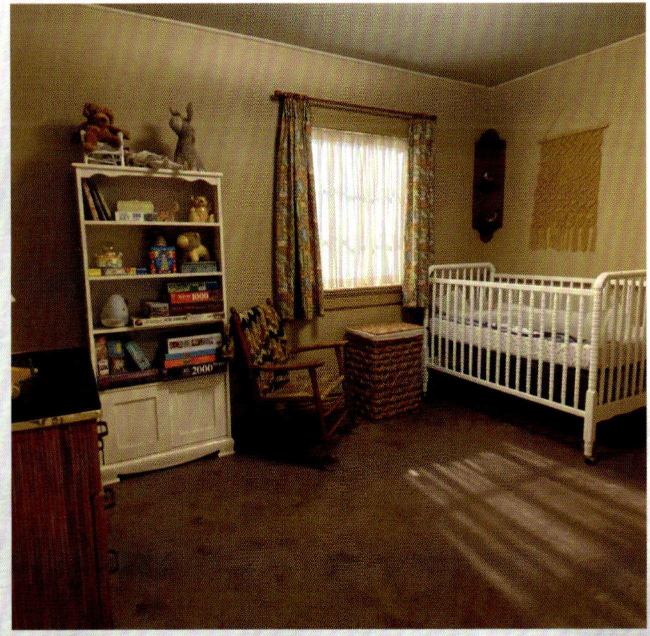

TOP/ (LEFT) Erin's bedroom, with the wallpaper from her mother's era. (RIGHT) Erin's nursery.

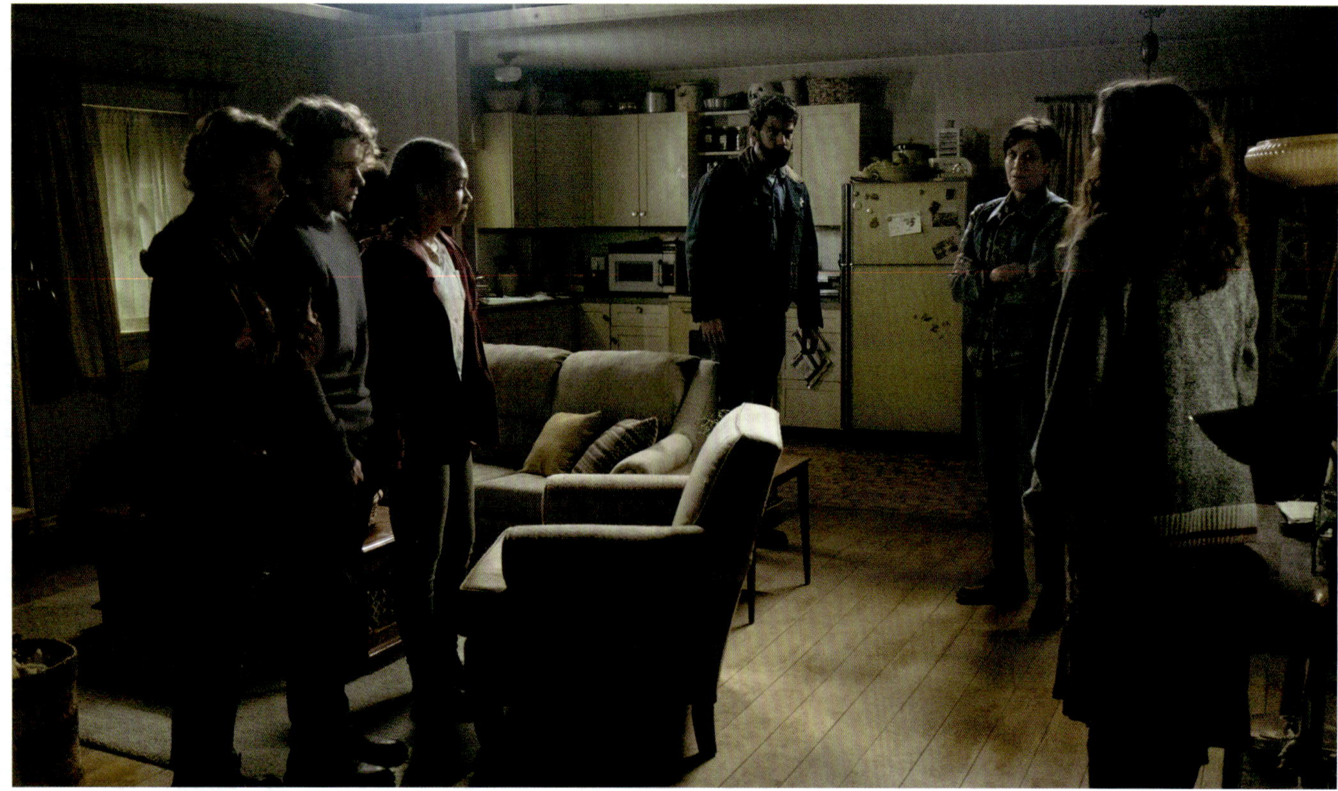

THIS PAGE/ Our heroes converge in Erin's living room to try to make a plan.

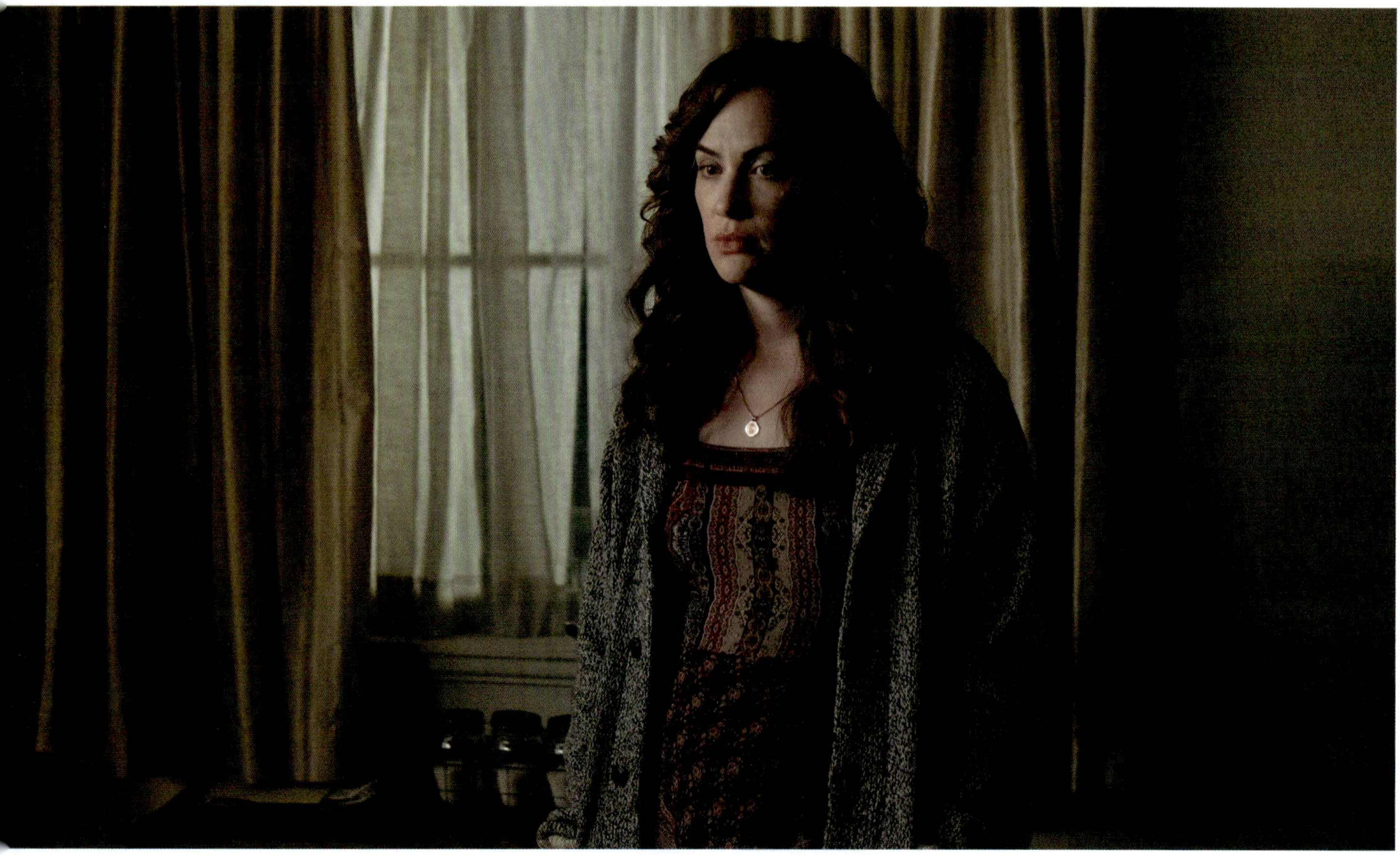

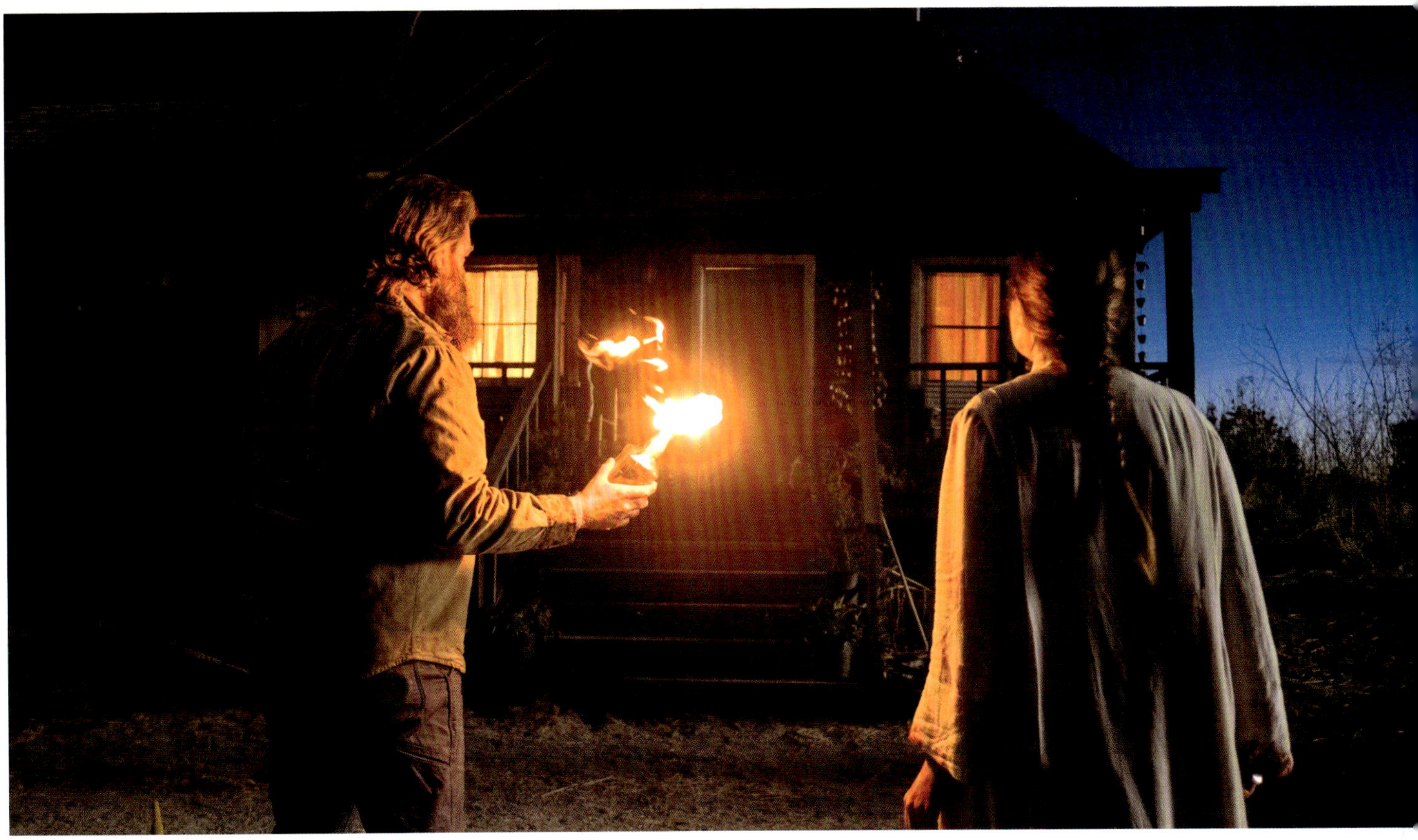

TOP/ Sturge and Bev firebomb Erin's house.

When Bev firebombs Erin's house, Siegel remembers, "There were specific places where they had pipes with a propane fire that they could flare up or turn down as needed." In reality, "They weren't going to spread, because they were surrounded by fire-resistant materials. But it was very unique to have the actual fire to look at. I imagine it being very poetic for Erin, like, 'Burn this town down.' But in the actual performance, I think there's a lot of in-the-moment panic. Fire is dangerous. Humans react to that in a very organic way of being terrified, because it's an unpredictable and dangerous thing. Which I think is some of the fun of performing in genre films, is there's not a lot of time to be in your head. You get to drop into a lot of these basic human instincts."

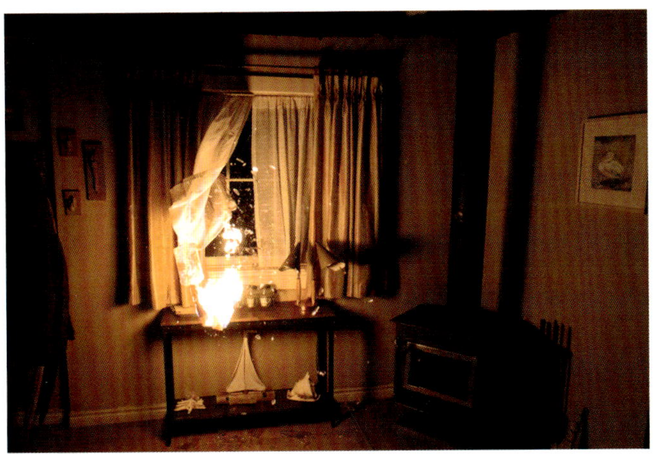

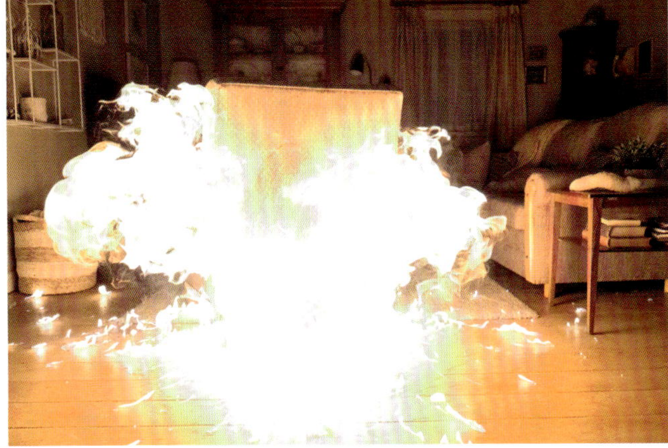

TOP/ The fire in Erin's living room catches and spreads.

THAT'S A WRAP!

INTERVIEW WITH THE TEAM

Virtually everyone interviewed for this book says Midnight Mass is a highlight of their careers; some cite it as their single best professional experience.

Gilford feels lucky to have done it. "I would work with any of these actors again. I am jumping through hoops to work with Mike any chance I get." Gilford's second child was born during production. "Everyone there was part of my son's birth story, and forever will be a part of my life."

Siegel says, "It was one of the great joys and privileges of my life. I think I will spend the rest of my life trying to find an experience that satisfying."

Linklater enthuses, "I'll never have a job like that again. Most people who work with [Flanagan] will say the same thing: 'I'd walk through fire to work with him again.' To get to have that much gorgeous stuff to say, knowing your director knows how the scenes are going to cut together, and he's going to put you in a place to succeed, it felt like flying."

Rigney at first jokes, "Mike is super-mean – I'm kidding. It's going to be a hard experience to beat. Mike gives his actors a lot of freedom, but he has this way of just saying maybe two words, and being able to shift your performance."

Lehman opines, "When you're in the hands of a director as skilled as Mike is, it evokes an immediate feeling of trust, which is necessary to bring something to life. It was incredibly gratifying [to work with] a great group of actors, who are also excellent human beings."

Thomas observes, "Mike is very gifted in being able to bring things to fruition in a way that is satisfying to him as an artist, and fulfilling as an audience member. It's great to work with someone who can tell you exactly what they want. And I like being surrounded by the people he likes to work with. I feel like I got invited to the best party I've ever been to."

> "YOU CAN CLOAK CONTEMPT, HATE AND FEAR IN ANYTHING. WE WERE LOOKING TO DELVE INTO THAT, RATHER THAN RENDER JUDGMENT."
>
> TREVOR MACY

Sloyan says, "It was one of my most, if not the most, enjoyable times I've ever had on a set. I don't know if I've worked with a finer group of actors, and better people."

Kohli states, "I love working with Mike. He's one of the most wonderful collaborators around."

Cymone feels, "Working with Mike is a team effort. I was able to come out of it with such a good group of people who I can call family now, making something we all love."

Gish relates, "I treasure working with Mike. His precision and preparation are unlike anything I've ever seen. The folks brought together by Mike and Trevor and Engine Casting, we're friends for life now. We're the Crocketteer Clan."

RIGHT/ Flanagan in the midst of the Midnight Mass.

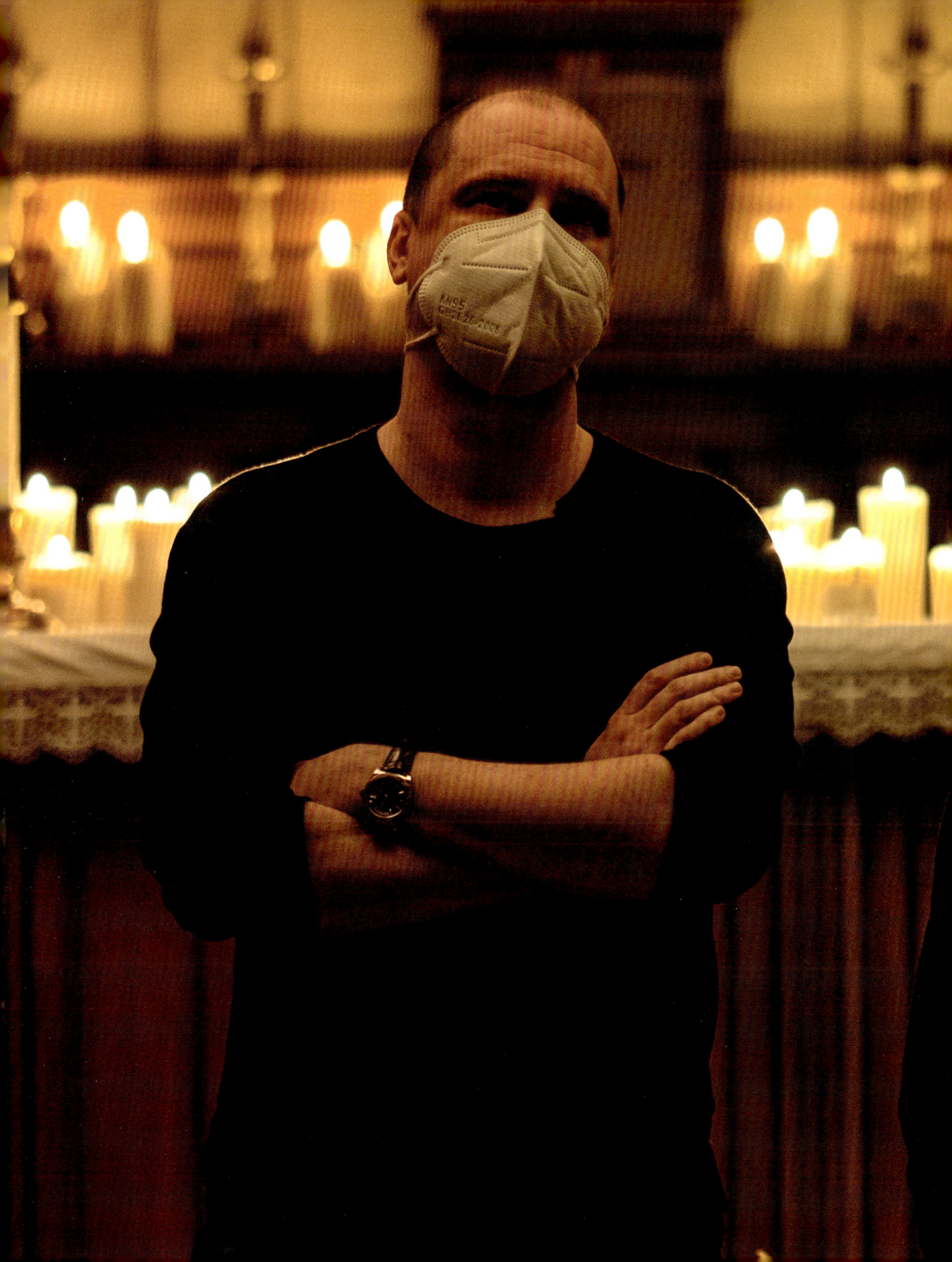
KN95

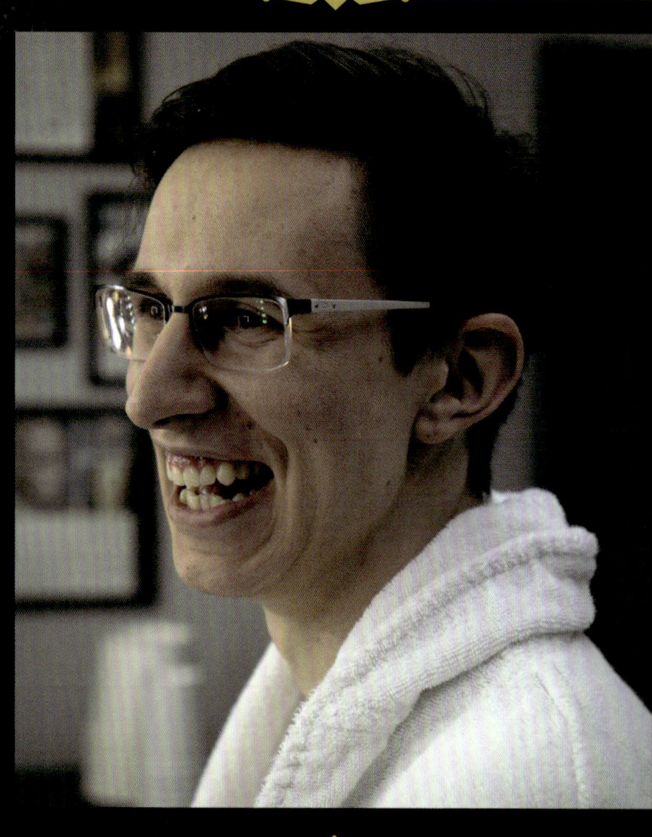

Essoe says, "Mike is my favorite. He is so devoted to the integrity of the story, and he is such a fan of actors."

Longstreet feels, "It's the best thing I've ever done. Mike is so enthusiastic, and so prepared, and he's thought [about] every single second of what he's about to make six ways to Sunday."

Aburri agrees. "It's the greatest experience I've ever had. We formed this crazy family."

Biedel concurs. "It's one of the best creative experiences I've ever had in my life."

Moffat observes, "[Flanagan] makes you want to work harder. I've never seen someone with a work ethic like his."

Trucco relates, "Mike is making a powerful piece here, and I could not be more thrilled to be part of it."

Balint says, "Mike and Trevor took immaculate care of everyone, so we knew that we were going to a safe place of work. This holds a special place in a lot of our hearts."

MacDonald observes of the vampirism and Catholicism themes, "I've never heard of anything like this being done before."

Fimognari relates, "Many things are exceptional about Mike. He has an incredible ability to then take what he's written, communicate its essence to each department that needs to know

TOP/ Quinton Boisclair, out of the Angel makeup.

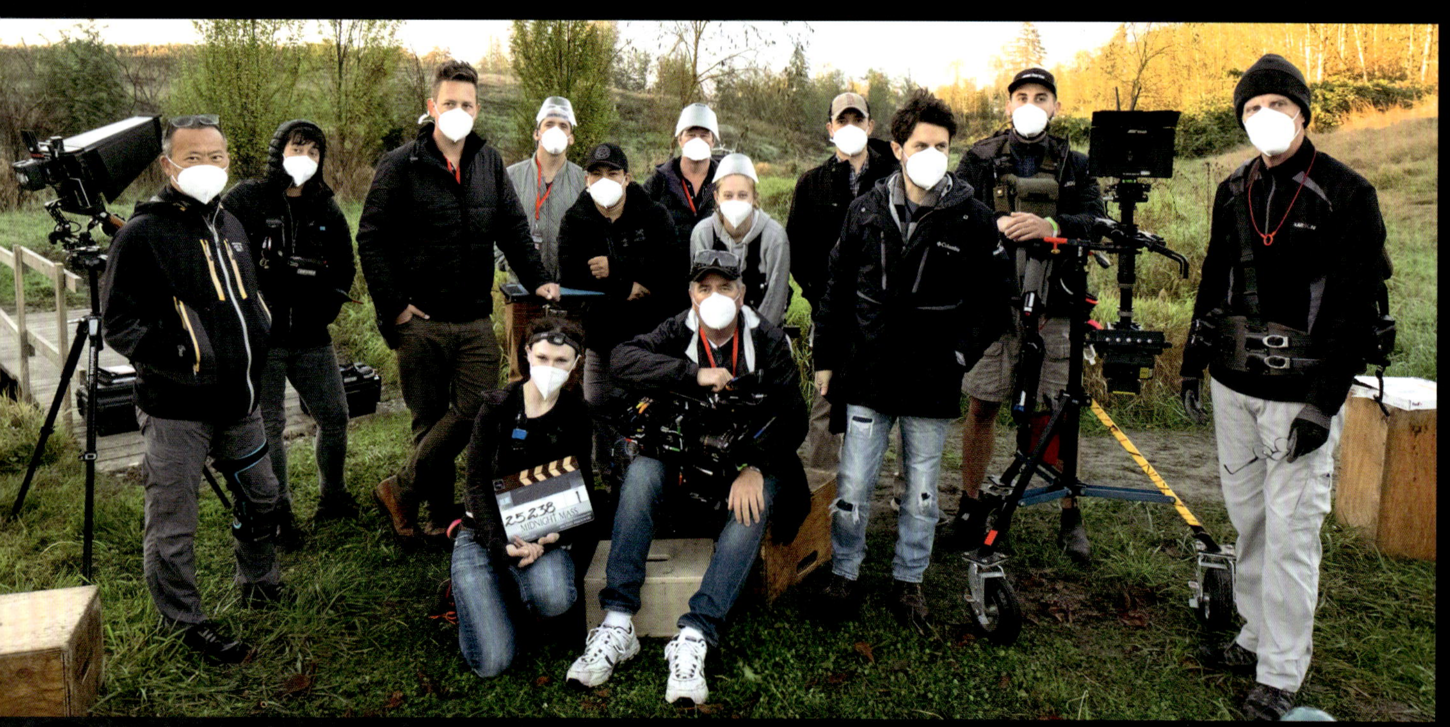

TOP/ From left to right, the camera department: Junichi Hosoi, Nadia Baptista, Aaron Haesler, Bran Caisse, Cheryl Siliekis, Jose Manzano, Paul Sheridan, Ally Lydnuik, Kevin Hall, Troy Wagner, Michael Fimognari, Lukas Fournier and James Reid.

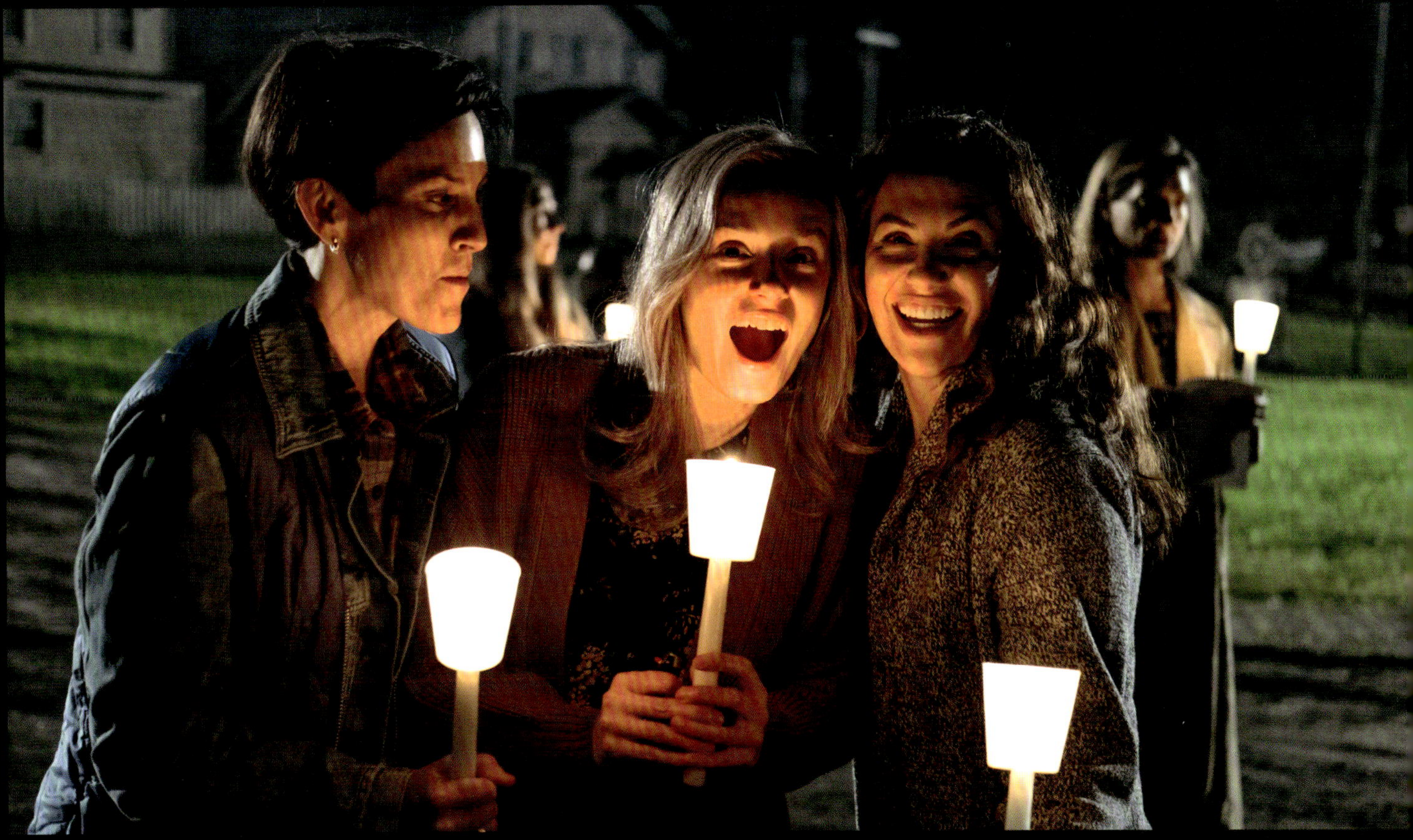

TOP/ Gish, Essoe, and Siegel have fun between takes for the Mass procession.

that, and, like a conductor of a symphony, to know when each note is going to take center stage. I appreciate our collaborations and our friendship."

Arnold appreciates that Flanagan could always give precise answers when asked, "'What are this character's interests, what is he into?'"

Anderson says, "All of these jobs with Mike Flanagan have ended up being a labor of love."

Grush feels, "It made for a wonderful experience."

Stewart relates, "We've worked with lots of directors, and the way Mike processes a project, it's unreal. He's so involved in the fabric of it."

Raleigh asserts, "The script was wonderful. I liked Mike Flanagan's approach with everything."

Alvarez says of Flanagan, "It was a pleasure to have somebody who was creative, and made sure we were on top of our game."

For Irvine, "The scariest part was prep, because I didn't know what it would look like filming [during COVID-19]. But as we go into [Intrepid's] next show, I feel like I know how we accomplish things while we're being safe."

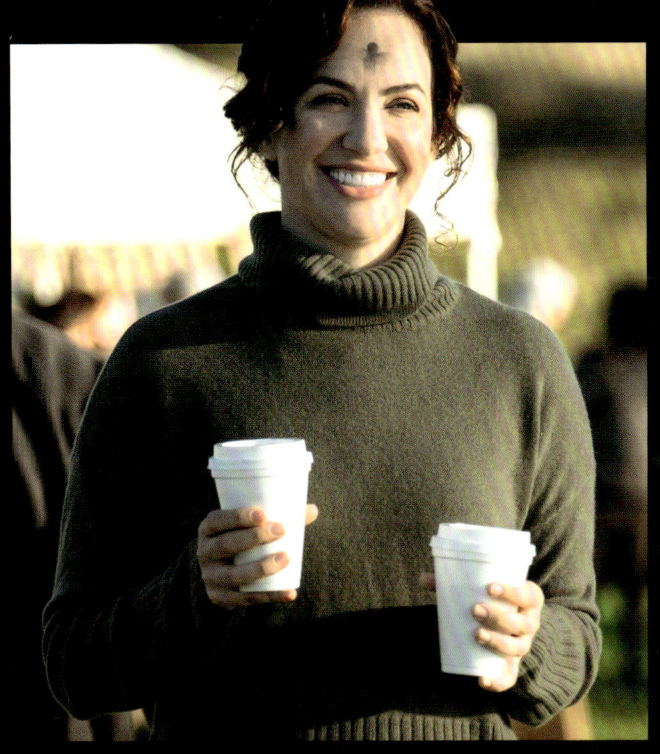

TOP/ Siegel, with Ash Wednesday marks, carrying coffee for two.

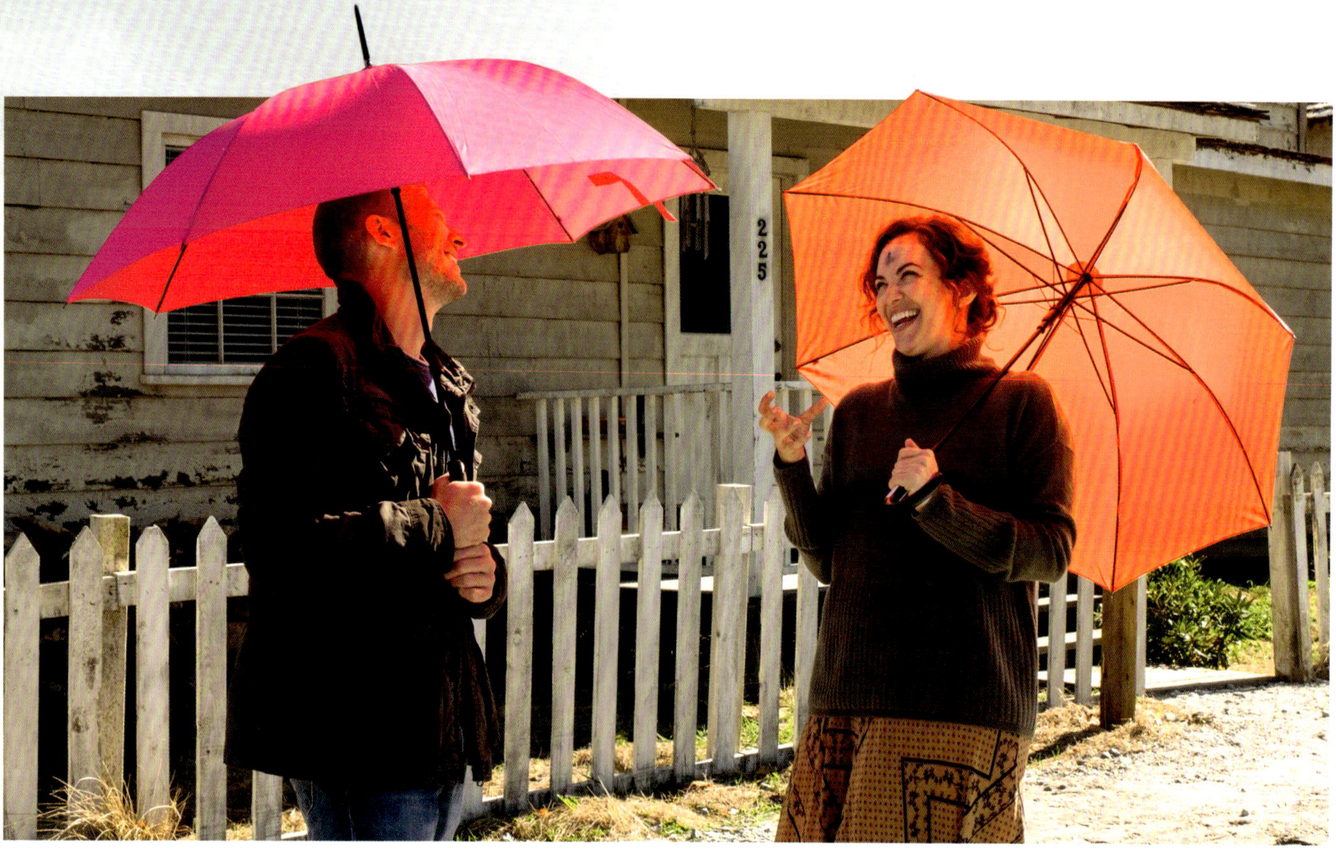

THIS PAGE/ (TOP) Gilford and Siegel, with parasols for shade, share a laugh. (BOTTOM) The actors playing the Flynn family chat between takes.

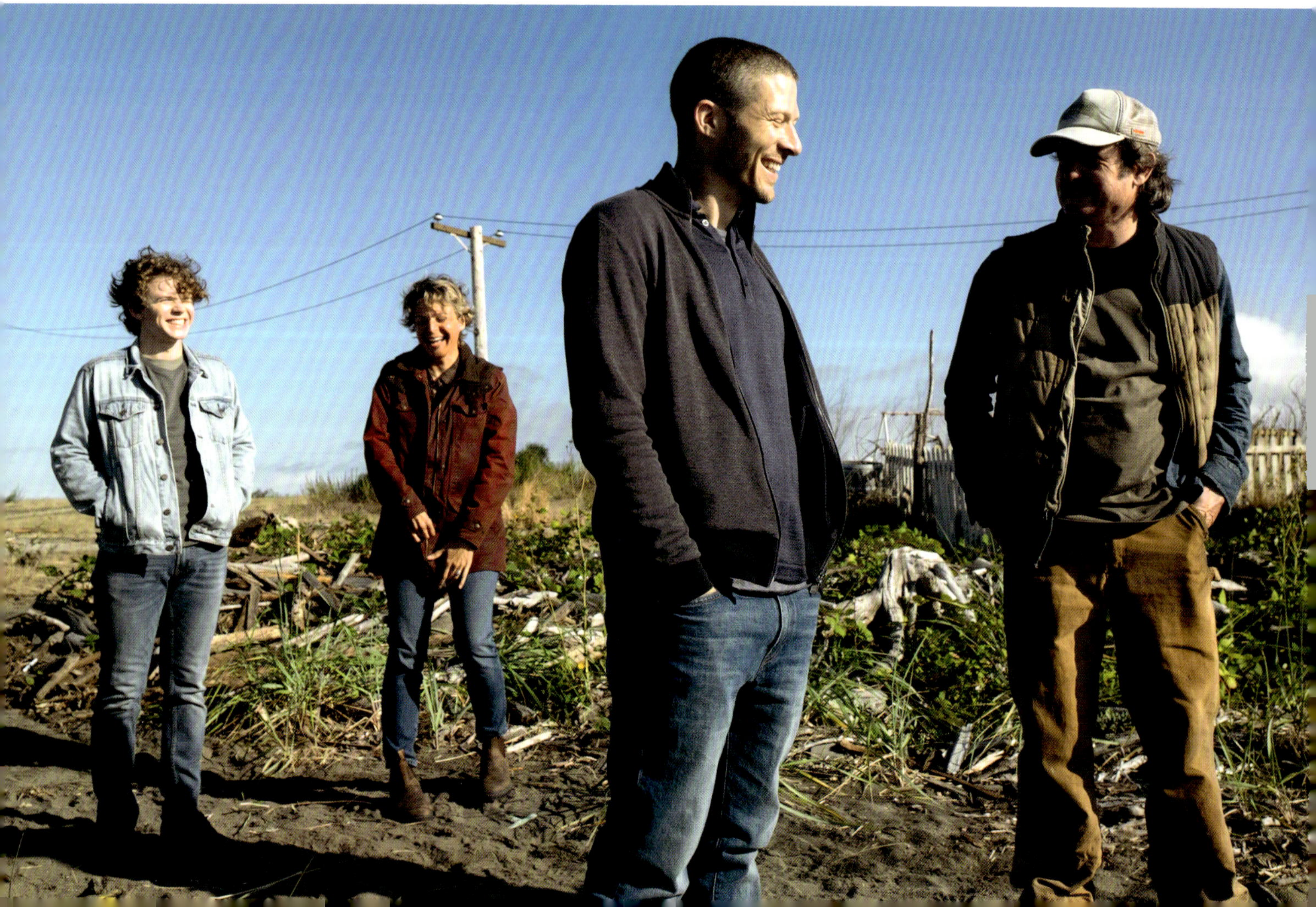

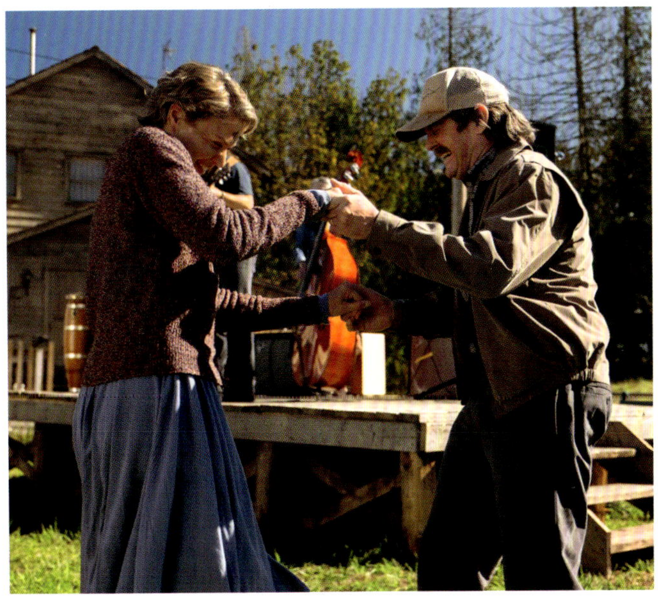

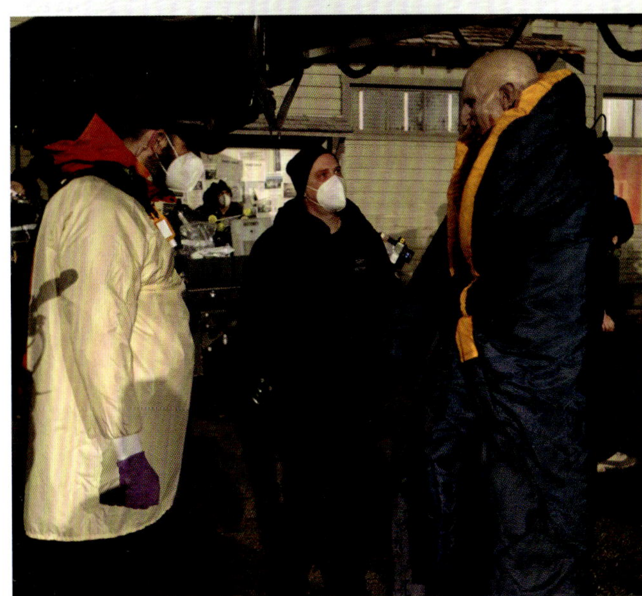

TOP/ (LEFT) Annie and Ed dance at the Crock-Pot-Luck. (RIGHT) SPFX makeup assistant and Mike Flanagan with Boisclair, wearing a coat over his Angel body appliances.

Macy says, "I've never worked with a filmmaker who has a movie or a TV show so completely in his head as Mike. We have a collaboration that you hope for once in a career."

Flanagan remembers, "When we called 'Cut' on the last scene, and realized that we just shot eighty-three days, and COVID-19 did not shut us down, that was a stunning revelation. I couldn't believe we got to the end."

As for what he hopes people will get out of *Midnight Mass*, Macy says, "One of my favorite things is how genre feeds its thematic resonance. We're not trying to send a message, but if you can scare people, and smuggle in a little thinking, that's fun."

Flanagan hopes that "it encourages conversation about faith, about fanaticism. I hope people of faith feel properly represented. I hope faith itself is represented well. I hope it encourages a little more kindness. I hope people have a great time, and they're scared, and that they think a little bit about belief, whatever they believe in."

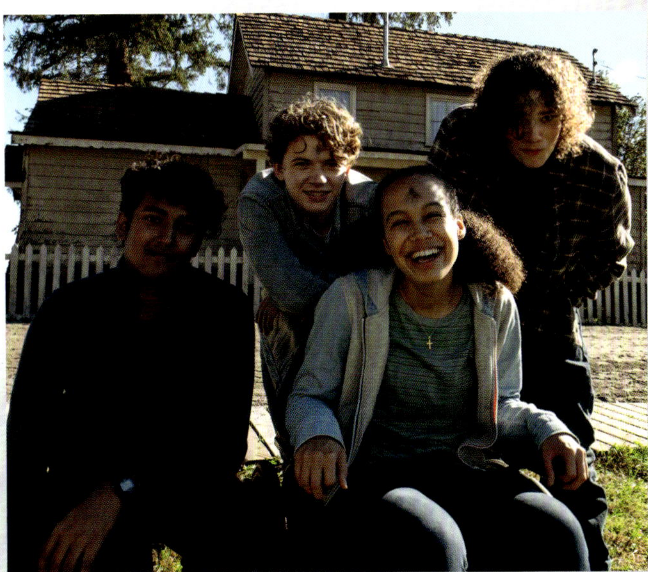

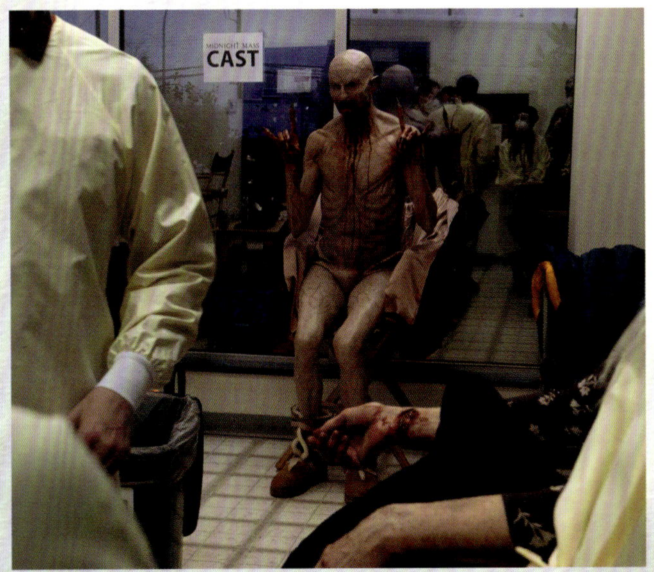

TOP/ (LEFT) Aburri, Rigney, Cymone and Moffat. (RIGHT) Boisclair in full Angel makeup sans wings, waiting to be called to set.

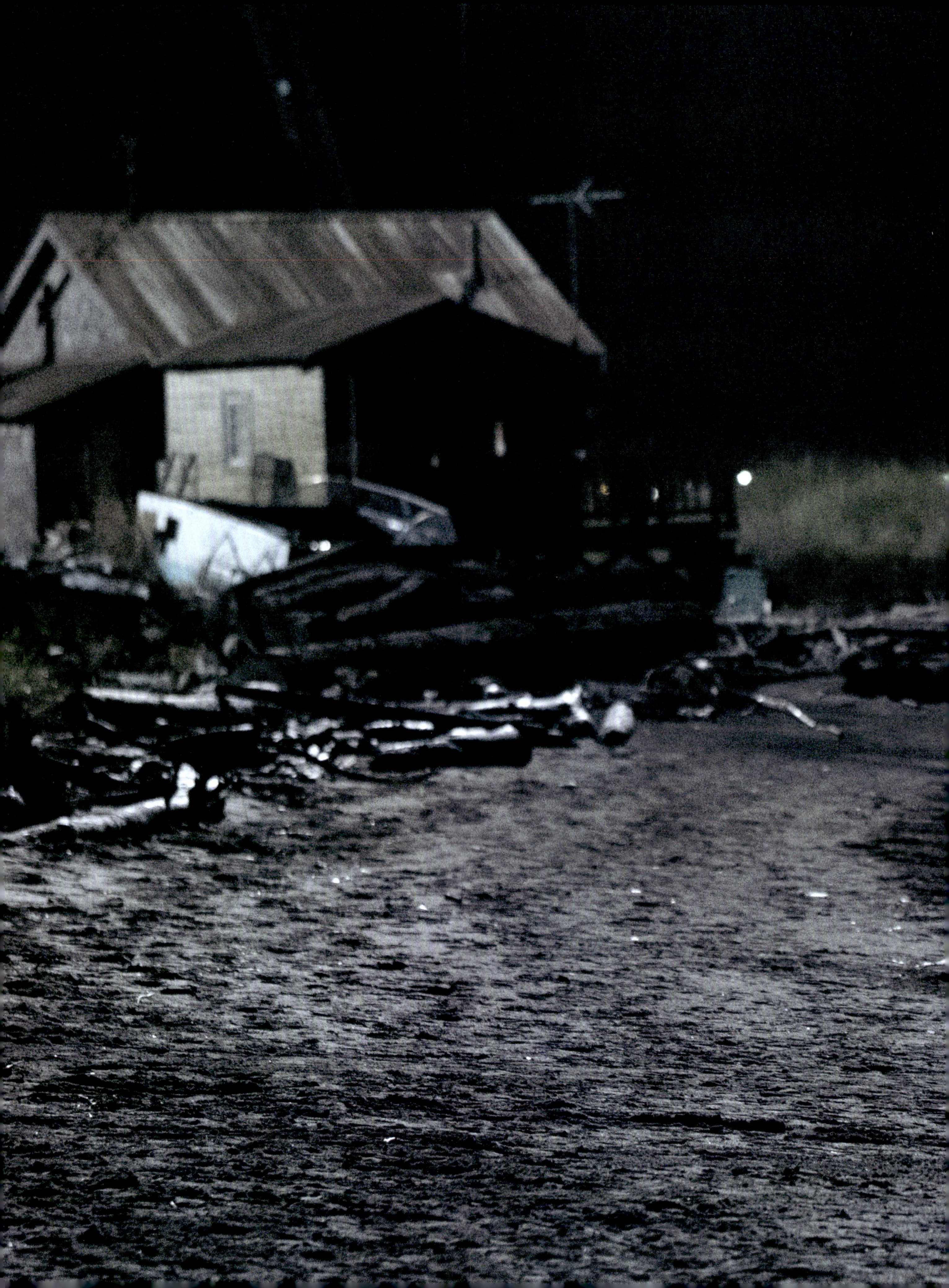

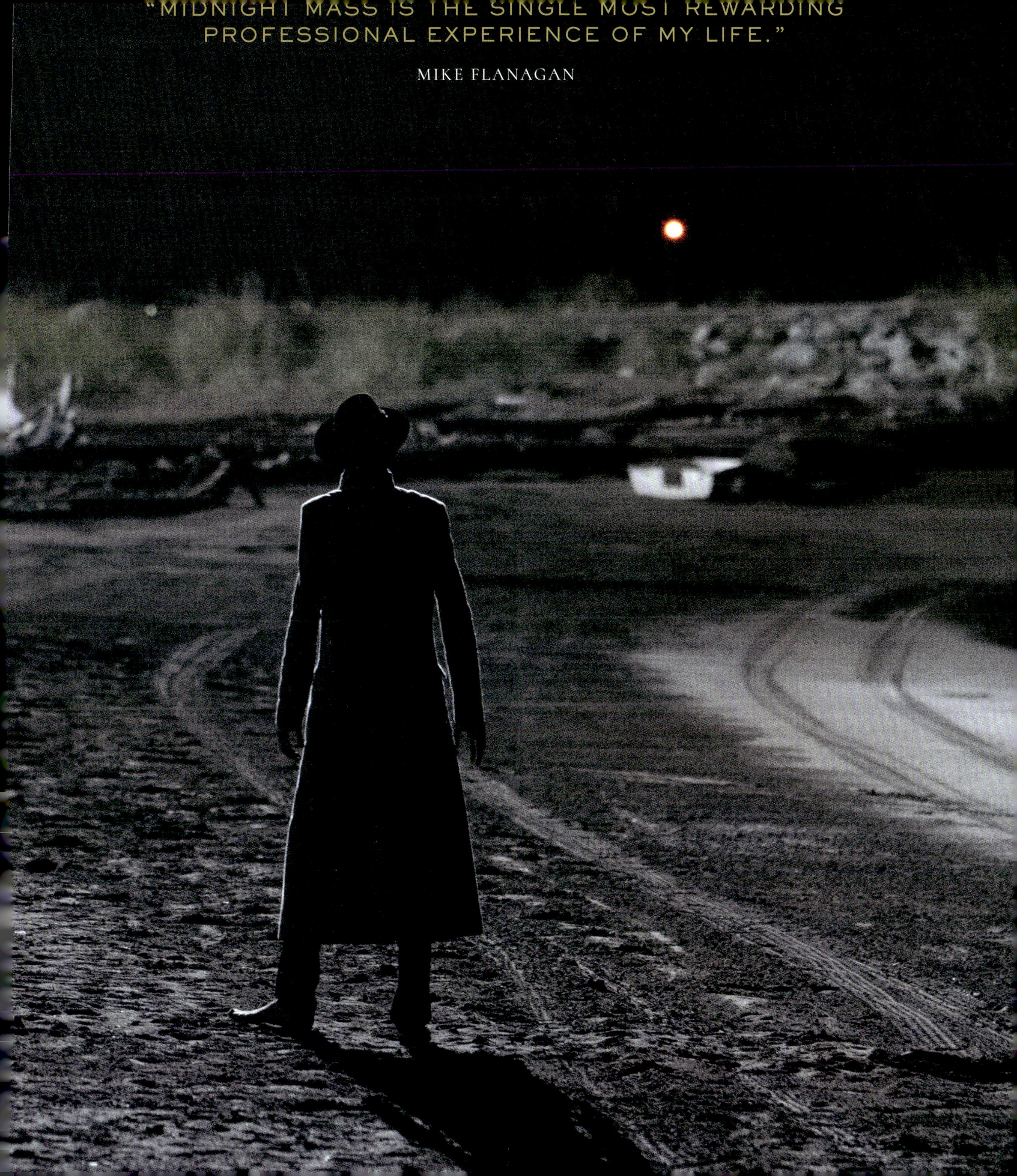
"MIDNIGHT MASS IS THE SINGLE MOST REWARDING
PROFESSIONAL EXPERIENCE OF MY LIFE."
MIKE FLANAGAN

ACKNOWLEDGMENTS

At Titan Books, I am very grateful to my splendid editor Frankie Piscitelli, extraordinary designer Natasha MacKenzie, wonderful non-fiction managing editor Jo Boylett, and everyone else at the company. I am also grateful for the talented Jhona Almeida for allowing us to use their artwork for the front cover.

At Netflix, thank you to the invaluable George Tew. With *Midnight Mass*, thank you to everyone who so articulately and generously gave of their time to be interviewed (in alphabetical order by surname): Rahul Aburri, Tony "Ozzy" Alvarez, Terry Anderson, Steven Arnold, Crystal Balint, Annarah Cymone, Matt Biedel, Alex Essoe, Michael Fimognari, Zach Gilford, Annabeth Gish, Jenna Irvine, Rahul Kohli, Kristin Lehman, Hamish Linklater, Robert Longstreet, John C. MacDonald, Louis Moffat, The Newton Brothers (Andy Grush & Taylor Stewart), Justin Raleigh, Igby Rigney, Kate Siegel, Samatha Sloyan, Henry Thomas, and Michael Trucco.

Special thanks to producer Trevor Macy, and thanks most of all to creator and director Mike Flanagan (who shares my joy about eavesdropping sharks).

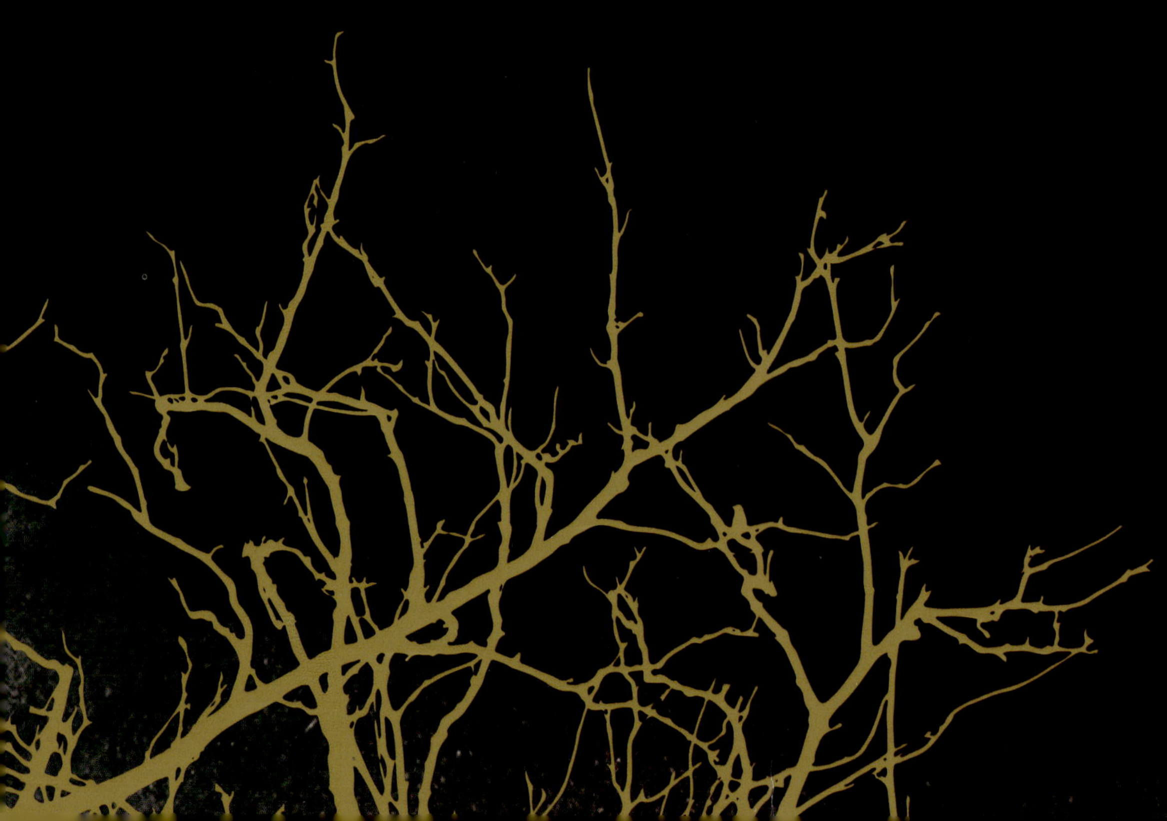